Contents

Acknowledgements   v

Introduction   *Jennifer Frances, Rosalind Levačić,*
Jeremy Mitchell, Grahame Thompson   1

Markets

Introduction   *Rosalind Levačić*   21

1 On markets   *Alfred Marshall*   24

2 Markets and government: an overview   *Rosalind Levačić*   35

3 Socialism, planning, and the market   *Hans Breitenbach,*
   Tom Burden and David Coates   48

4 Market process versus market equilibrium   *Israel M. Krizner* 53

5 Markets and managerial hierarchies   *Tony McGuinness*   66

6 Creating the Single European Market   *Dennis Swann*   82

7 Which internal market? The NHS White Paper and internal
   markets   *Penelope M. Mullen*   96

Hierarchies

Introduction   *Jeremy Mitchell*   105

8 In praise of hierarchy   *Elliott Jaques*   108

9 Legal authority in a bureaucracy   *Max Weber*   119

10 Models of bureaucracy   *David Beetham*   128

11 Survival inside bureaucracy   *Guy Benveniste*   141

12 Market, capitalism, planning and technocracy
   Giovanni Sartori   154

13 New directions for industrial policy in the area of regulatory
   reform   *John Vickers*   163

Networks

Introduction   *Grahame Thompson*   171

14 Network analysis: basic concepts   *David Knoke and James H. Kuklinski*   173

15 Neither friends nor strangers: informal networks of subcontracting in French industry   *Edward H. Lorenz*   183

16 Beyond vertical integration – the rise of the value-adding partnership   *Russell Johnston and Paul R. Lawrence*   193

17 Policy networks and sub-central government   *R.A.W. Rhodes*   203

18 Taking and giving: working women and female bonds in a Pakistani immigrant neighbourhood   *Pnina Werbner*   215

19 Community, market, state – and associations? The prospective contribution of interest governance to social order *Wolfgang Streeck and Philippe C. Schmitter*   227

Comparison between models

Introduction   *Grahame Thompson*   243

20 Markets, bureaucracies and clans   *William G. Ouchi*   246

21 Interorganizational relations in industrial systems: a network approach compared with the transactions-cost approach *Jan Johanson and Lars-Gunnar Mattsson*   256

22 Neither market nor hierarchy: network forms of organization *Walter W. Powell*   265

23 Price, authority and trust: from ideal types to plural forms   *Jeffrey L. Bradach and Robert G. Eccles*   277

24 Spontaneous ('grown') order and organized ('made') order *Frederick von Hayek*   293

Index   302

MARKETS, HIERARCHIES AND NETWORKS

The Coordination of Social Life

edited by
Grahame Thompson
Jennifer Frances
Rosalind Levačić
Jeremy Mitchell

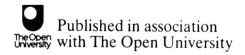

Published in association
with The Open University

SAGE Publications
London • Thousand Oaks • New Delhi

First published 1991
Reprinted 1993, 1994, 1996

 SAGE Publications Ltd
6 Bonhill Street
London EC2A 4PU

SAGE Publications Inc
2455 Teller Road
Thousand Oaks, California 91320

SAGE Publications India Pvt Ltd
32, M-Block Market
Greater Kailash – I
New Delhi 110 048

British Library Cataloguing in Publication Data

Markets, hierarchies and networks.
 I. Frances, Jennifer   II. Levačić, Rosalind
 III. Mitchell, Jeremy
 302.5

 ISBN 0–8039–8589–4
 ISBN 0–8039–8590–8 pbk

Library of Congress catalog card number 91–050668

Typeset by Mayhew Typesetting, Rhayader, Powys
Printed and bound in Great Britain by
Biddles Ltd, Guildford and King's Lynn

Acknowledgements

The editors would like to thank the Open University D212 *Running the Country* Course Team for their advice and guidance during the preparation of this set of readings. In addition special mention must go to Betty Atkinson and Deborah Scotney for their secretarial help as the manuscript was produced and to David Wilson who ably assisted in the transformation of the manuscript from the Open University publications department to the eventual publishers.

The authors and publishers wish to thank the following for permission to use copyright material: Administrative Science Quarterly for material from William G. Ouchi, 'Markets, Bureaucracies, and Clans', *Administrative Science Quarterly* Vol. 25, No. 1 (March 1980); Anglo-German Foundation for material from John Vickers, 'New Directions for Industrial Policy in the Area of Regulatory Reform' in K. Cowling and H. Tomann, eds., *Industrial Policy After 1992*, 1990; Annual Review Inc., for material adapted from Jeffrey L. Bradach and Robert G. Eccles, 'Price, Authority, and Trust: From Ideal Types to Plural Forms', *Annual Review of Sociology*, Vol. 15. Copyright © 1989 by Annual Review Inc.; Basil Blackwell Ltd. for material from Penelope M. Mullen, 'Which Internal Market? The NHS White Paper and Internal Markets', *Financial Accountability and Management*, Vol. 6, No. 1 (Spring 1990); Edward H. Lorenz, 'Neither Friends nor Strangers: Informal Networks of Subcontracting in French Industry' in D. Gambetta, ed., *Trust: Making and Breaking of Cooperative Relations*, 1989; and Tony McGuinness, 'Markets and Managerial Hierarchies' from R. Clarke and T. McGuinness eds., *The Economics of the Firm*; Boyd and Fraser Publishing Company for material from Guy Benveniste, 'Survival Inside Bureaucracy' in *Bureaucracy*, 1977; Causeway Press Ltd. for material from Dennis Swann, 'Creating the Single European Market' in B. Atkinson, ed., *Developments in Economics*, 1990; Chatham House Publishers for material from Giovanni Sartori, 'Market, Capitalism, Planning, and Technocracy' in *The Theory of Democracy Revisted;* Part II, 1987; JAI Press Inc. and JAI Press Ltd. for material from Walter W. Powell, 'Neither Market nor Hierarchy: Network Forms of Organization', *Research in Organizational Behavior*, Vol. 12, 1990; Macmillan Ltd. for material from Alfred Marshall, *Principles of Economics*, 8th ed., 1936; Open University Press for material from David Beetham, 'Models of Bureaucracy' from *Bureaucracy*, 1987; Routledge for material from F. Von Hayek, 'Spontaneous ('Grown') Order and Organized ('Made') Order' from *Law, Legislation and Liberty*; and Pnina Werbner, 'Taking and Giving: Working Women and Female Bonds in a Pakistani Immigrant Neighbourhood' from Sallie Westwood and Parminder Bhachu eds., *Enterprising Women: Ethnicity, Economy, and Gender Relations*, 1988; Sage Publications Ltd. for material from W. Streeck and P.C. Schmitter, 'Community, Market, State and Associations?' in *Private Interest Government*, 1985; M.E. Sharpe, Inc. for material from Jan Johanson and Lars-Gunnar Mattsson, 'Interorganizational Relations in Industrial Systems: A Network Approach Compared with the Transaction–Cost Approach', *International Studies of Management & Organisation*, Vol. XVII, No. 1, 1987; Simon & Schuster International Group for material from H. Breitenbach, 'Socialism, Planning and the Market' from H. Breitenbach, T. Burden and D. Coates, *Features of a Viable Socialism*, Harvester, 1990; and with Barnes and Noble Books for material from R. Levačić, 'Markets and Government: An Overview' from *Economic Policy Making*, Wheatsheaf, 1987; The University of Chicago Press for material from Israel M. Kirzner, 'Market Process Versus Market Equilibrium' in *Competition and Entrepreneurship*, 1973.

Every effort has been made to trace all the copyright holders, but if any have been inadvertently overlooked the publishers will be pleased to make the necessary arrangement at the first opportunity.

Introduction

Jennifer Frances, Rosalind Levačić,
Jeremy Mitchell, Grahame Thompson

I

How is social life coordinated? Indeed, is it coordinated? And what do
we mean by coordination anyway? In the set of chapters included in this
reader we aim to answer these kinds of question. These questions arose
in the context of developing a second-level Open University course D212:
Running the Country as a wide-ranging introduction to the way a country
like the United Kingdom is run. The course uses three 'models of coordination' to analyse a range of case studies dealing with central aspects
of contemporary social life. These models are those of markets, hierarchies and networks – and it is these models that are focused upon in
this reader.

Such a threefold classification was found not just to be applicable to
the internal domestic arrangement of national social, political and
economic life but also of considerable use in analysing the external
international relationships between individual states. Thus the three
forms of social organization have a general applicability that transcends
any particular geographical space or temporal order. They exemplify
genuine 'models' of coordination that can be characterized abstractly
and then deployed in an analytical framework for understanding the
way social life in general is organized. Clearly, this raises one of the key
features in any social analysis: with what theoretical tools do we
approach the analysis of events and processes? In our case this means
asking what are the relationships between the three models we have
chosen to work with? One section is devoted to precisely this issue. In
addition it means asking the question: what is the relationship between
our models of coordination and that social life they are meant to represent?

Not all of these questions can be fully answered in this introduction.
They are posed in order to give an idea of the kinds of issue discussed
in the associated course. However, we should at least attempt a discussion
of some of these important problems here. This we do in the rest of the
introduction. We approach this by exploring what is meant by 'models of
coordination' in the next section and then go on to look at each of the

three models so defined in turn. Finally, we return to the comparison between the models.

II

Let us take the terms in the phrase 'models of coordination' by turn. First, what do we mean by models?

Clearly, a proper answer to this question could take us well into epistemology and the methodology of the social sciences. This we do not wish to do here. From the point of view of the readings included in this book we treat models simply as a kind of mapping device with the aid of which we hope to find our way through the organizational forms of contemporary social, political and economic life. We thus take a rather straightforward view of the term model. Further, we can accept that it represents an abstraction from the detail of empirical reality. A model presents only the bare bones or framework for the richness of those elements of social life it is aiming to elucidate. Using the analogy of a torch emitting a beam of light, by shining our model-torch on the complexity of social existence we only expect it to highlight *some* of that complexity.

In our case we clearly have three torches to work with – one labelled hierarchy, one labelled markets and the third labelled networks. If we were to shine each of them on to that aspect of running the country under examination, we would expect each torch to highlight just a part of the landscape. Perhaps one or other of the torches would highlight more than the others do. As a result we can say which of the models was most appropriate in analysing that particular aspect of social existence under scrutiny. So our models act as a kind of sifting device. The first three sections of this reader are devoted to exemplifying the features that characterize each of the different models. The readings in these parts of the book highlight not so much the social terrain itself but more the map used to organize our understanding of that terrain when we begin any social analysis.

In some quarters what we have said above might be taken as an example of the classical empiricist notion of models. Put simply, empiricism implies that empirical reality acts as the touchstone for the construction of models designed to analyse that reality. Thus reality acts as the privileged site from which we generate the maps, by which we organize our understanding of the world.

Against this notion could be contrasted a more overtly 'theoretical' idea of models, based upon the model-building activity of mathematics for instance. In this case it would be formal and abstract thought experiments that would be privileged as the place where model construction should be located. This approach emphasizes the role of theory in organizing our thoughts about the world and any analysis of it. Models in this sense are not so much detailed maps of an already existing reality but more like a set of tools and techniques with the aid of which we begin to build an image of the world. What is highlighted as 'reality' is a consequence of the theoretical tools (or models) we bring to bear in organizing our understanding of it. We do not uncover models, we impose an order of models on the world.

The continuing debate between these two conflicting images of models (and lots of variation in between) is the stuff of many a social science dispute. We are not about to solve this dispute here. For the purposes of this introduction it is sufficient just to register its nature. Our attitude is agnostic. We are quite prepared to take insights from both approaches if called upon to justify the use of the three models deployed in the course and as exemplified by the readings included below. Models for us are a convenient device for organizing an analysis of social life that at least has some pretence to intellectual rigour.

What about the term *coordination*? This is perhaps easier to define and defend. Coordination implies the bringing into a relationship otherwise disparate activities or events. Tasks and efforts can be made compatible by coordinating them. Bottlenecks and disjunctures can be eliminated, so coordination is usually discussed under a sign of *efficiency*. By coordinating a set of items something can be achieved which otherwise would not be. It is the positive performative consequence of coordination that makes it such an attractive social practice and objective. Various agents and agencies can be 'ordered', 'balanced', 'brought into equilibrium', and the like, by the act of coordination. Without coordination these agents and agencies might all have different and potentially conflicting objectives resulting in chaos and inefficiency.

So much is relatively uncontroversial. But disputes arise when we turn to the best *way* in which coordination is to be achieved. This is where our three models appear again, since each embodies its own distinctive approach to how social coordination is achieved.

One suggestion is that it is best left to the market. The market coordinates 'automatically', so to speak. The pursuit of self-interest by individually motivated and welfare-maximizing individuals leads to the best outcome not just for them but also for society as a whole. Coordination takes place in an 'unseen' manner – via the 'guiding hand' of market exchange and the price system it supports.

But in some cases such coordination cannot be left to these 'unconscious' mechanisms. By contrast, it needs to be consciously organized in the form of a hierarchy. Administrative means need to be brought to bear if coordination is to be effectively achieved. Control must be overtly exercised.

Finally, it may be that neither the market nor hierarchy will lead to proper coordination because both neglect the informal mechanisms that typify a network of relatively independent social elements. It is only by emphasizing the cross-cutting chains of social, political and economic relationships that constitute networks that coordination will be, and is, achieved.

Notice how in this preliminary discussion of the way the three models go about approaching the problem of coordination we have presented the issue in terms of a conflict or dispute between them. In fact this is more or less the way the issue is set up in popular debate, so we are mirroring it here. It might be more productively discussed, however, in terms of complementary insights rather than as antagonistic or mutually exclusive ones. This is the approach pursued below.

As we shall see, each of these three approaches to coordination is typified by a range of different *forms*. These are illustrated in the readings and we discuss them more fully below. The point is that there is no single and totally accepted view of how the market works, of how hierarchy works, or of how networks work to 'produce' coordination. Each of these approaches represents a contested territory where different and often competing claims are made as to the proper understanding of their respective coordinative effects. There are different forms of the market, of hierarchy and of networks, each of which leads to a different understanding of the manner in which coordination might be secured.

But here we reach another important point. All these models claim to show how coordination operates. They assume it is possible. They do not in themselves suggest that coordination might not be achievable. Why should we think that social, political and economic life is *necessarily* coordinated or coordinatable? Supposing it exists as a mess which we just have to learn to cope or live with?

By raising this issue we do not mean to challenge all the positive aspects the previous discussion of models and coordination involved or, indeed, to undermine the very reasons for reading the rest of the chapters in this book. What it usefully raises is the possible *limits to coordination*.

Clearly we might be prepared to accept that there will be resistance to conscious attempts at introducing coordination in an otherwise disorganized social milieu. But are there limits to coordination of any kind, limits built into the very social structure itself? In other words, are there limits that exceed the capacity of any of our models to overcome?

Here it is the issue of the *boundaries* around social agents and agencies that needs to be addressed. The fact that the world is made up of different social agents, operating with different purposes and objectives, forming overlapping systems of existence but with definite (though often porous) boundaries between them, implies that a total *reconciliation* of the calculations such agents might make is impossible. It might be argued that to think otherwise is a delusion and thus to think that any 'total coordination' is possible is also a mistake. Organizational differences between social agents and agencies, implying their necessary semi-autonomous operation, puts one set of powerful limits on total coordination. Secondly, the different agents and agencies will deploy different and perhaps even competing conceptual apparatuses of calculation in establishing their objectives, sorting out their priorities, undertaking their activities, and so on which again powerfully limits a total coordination of everything (for example agents may attempt to 'maximize' or they may attempt only to 'satisfy' their objectives). So it is these organizational and conceptual constraints that provide a final limit to the operation of coordination. It is precisely the objective of coordination to overcome these organizational and conceptual constraints but such a 'rationalistic' conception is bound to 'fail' if the analysis outlined above is acceptable. What is more, even from the rationalist perspective coordination mechanisms involve costs. Therefore 'total' coordination may be undesirable when the costs of achieving this outweigh its positive benefits.

This just goes to raise another problem. What has been argued above is controversial, to say the least. There are some social theories that do indeed argue that all of social life is ultimately capable of being coordinated (see Chapter 24 by von Hayek in this reader). In principle, this is the case with all those theories that conceive of the social as a *totality*. If the social is a totality, where everything is linked together in some way, then in principle it is either already coordinated 'automatically' without our noticing it or at least has the potential for that total coordination to be imposed. Clearly this is also true of religious approaches that argue there is one single ultimate principle, or reason for existence.

This section defined and discussed the terms 'models' and 'coordination' as used in the expression 'models of coordination'. In the following section we consider the characteristics of the models themselves. But since we have raised the question of general theories it might be useful to end this section with some comments about the relationships between the models we use – market, hierarchy and network – and the more general theories that are pervasive within the social sciences.

Our use of the term *models of coordination* in driving the analysis of how Britain is run represents an attempt to provide a middle-level theory which is not totally subsumed under either the grand general theories that typify much of social science nor a blind empiricism that could equally pervade it. This might be termed a kind of 'meso-theory'.

Markets, hierarchies and networks are intermediate theoretical categories. They are not in any way *necessarily* connected to the 'big-isms' of social, political or economic analysis. These traditional 'big-isms' – liberal-pluralism, Marxism, structuralism, classicism, Fordism and others, and their 'neo-' equivalents – are all very well and clearly have their place. But there is room for another level of analysis that perhaps makes for a less ambitious and more modest claim on how the social is organized. Whilst its purview might be limited, this may be one of its strengths rather than a weakness. It is always tempting to try to explain everything with one general, all-embracing theory. In our intellectual culture *generalization* is the driving motive. But is there any necessary virtue in such a search for generalization? Perhaps particularization and difference should be promoted more forcefully. The models elaborated here are particular models. They do not attempt to explain everything in one grand intellectual sweep. Their differences and limits are recognized, or should be. We view the models of coordination as partial in that each of them is only likely to highlight a part of the overall coordinative effort and outcome. In the final section of this introduction we illustrate this point in greater detail.

III

Markets

The term *market* seems obvious enough. But there are many forms of market and a number of ways the market might work. In addition, the market *system* (as an idea or abstraction) can be distinguished from the operation of any one particular market. The readings in the section dealing with markets broach these issues.

For instance, the neo-classical conception of the market and the neo-Austrian one are two somewhat different ideas of how the market might operate. In the neo-classical conception the dominant idea is of a series of separate firms maximizing their profits via adapting their outputs to the given ruling price. This is sometimes called the 'perfect competition' approach. Decision-makers, already in possession of the required information about market conditions and the ruling price, adjust their behaviour to reach a 'static' equilibrium position where no one can be made better off without at least one person being made worse off (a Pareto equilibrium position). Here prices act as the crucial equilibrating mechanism. This position is exemplified by the reading from Marshall (Chapter 1) and is further discussed in the reading from Levačić (Chapter 2).

With the neo-Austrian position, however – often termed the 'competitive process' approach – the market is seen as a *process* of selection, turmoil and change where *dis*equilibrium conditions prevail. This is an overtly dynamic theory of the market. Less emphasis is placed upon price and more on the (beneficial) effects of the competitive process that markets engender. The reading from Krizner (Chapter 4) reflects this position.

The differences between the two approaches can be drawn out by comparing their attitude towards monopoly. Monopoly is a situation where there is only one supplier of a good or service in question. For the neo-classical school this is a highly undesirable state of affairs that undermines all the advantages of the competitive market. It can lead to the exploitation of the monopolist's power in the market so that prices are fixed above their economically efficient level and excess profits are earned by the monopolist. Monopolists thus need to be closely monitored by the public authorities and dismantled by government action as and when they abuse their dominant market position. For the neo-Austrian, on the other hand, there is nothing necessarily wrong with monopoly. Monopoly may simply be the result of past successful entrepreneurial initiative and dynamic competitive activity. Firms need to be allowed to capture the monopoly rents that research and development investment and advertising capital produce if society is to reap the full benefits that dynamic competition fosters. So the 'social costs' of monopoly profits and disequilibrium prices may be exaggerated and anyway these will be transitory and short-run as they are bid away by the long-term operation of the market process's 'creative destruction'. As long as the market process is given free reign monopolists will not last. The long-term benefits of new products, processes and information will undermine existing monopolies and outweigh any static, partial equilibrium calculation of their cost to society.

This discussion of the role of monopoly in the two approaches to the operation of the market included in this set of readings points to the different forms of market condition that economists have identified. Perfect competition is one where there are a large number of buyers and sellers, none of whom is large enough relative to the market overall to have any direct control over the market price. The market price is set here by the interaction of the decisions these market agents make in the light of the prevailing price but over which they individually have no direct control. It is set by the market system working overall – by an 'unseen hand' (a kind of social auctioneer). Here, then, price is set *by* or in the market.

With monopoly, on the other hand, it is the single monopolist that sets the market price. This is because the monopoly *is* the market in this case. Here it is decisions internal to the organizational unit that determine price, and goods or services have a price attached to them when they enter the market.

In between the strict monopolist case and the perfect competition case lies a range of market conditions that economists call monopolistic or oligopolistic competition. Here there are a number of competitive enterprises operating large enough to have at least some control over the market price, though not total control. Under these conditions competitors have the option of either setting their price and taking the output that is demanded by consumers in the light of that decision, or of setting their output targets and letting the price fluctuate accordingly, or of some combination of these two options.

The importance of these different market forms is obvious from the point of view of the issue of coordination through the market. It operates quite differently depending upon the conditions and conceptions underlying any analysis. The considerations we have been discussing in the above paragraphs help to organize the 'beam' we might shine on that part of the country under consideration. But there are further considerations we need to bear in mind when discussing the market model.

From the point of view of the competitive process approach outlined above the problem for the firm is how it is financially (and legally) to reproduce itself – how it is to continue in existence and even prosper in the face of the continual threat posed by new entrants to the market. So far we have discussed the importance of price and its formation in this process. Price provides the basis for the income of the firm, which, relative to its costs, is what determines the firm's profits. But this is not the only way a company can reproduce itself financially. As well as a pricing/marketing strategy, firms must have investment strategies. Real investment is a crucial mechanism for the survival of the firm in a competitive market. But in addition to this, firms can promote their survival and growth via takeover and merger strategies. These are sometimes recognized as financial investment in contrast to real investment. A lot of British companies rely almost exclusively on this kind of financial investment in their efforts to reproduce themselves, neglecting their real investment strategies. The final element in this discussion of the response of the firm within the competitive processes is to emphasize the importance of the relationship between firms and governmental agencies. Firms can help reproduce themselves by accepting government grants and subsidies, for instance. Or they might have privileged access to government procurement contracts, defence production and so on.

The discussion so far about markets has mainly indicated their role in coordinating economic activity *between* units. Traditionally it has been hierarchical methods that have coordinated activity *within* organizations, something we outline in the next section of this introduction. But recently a novel and interesting development designed to better coordinate the internal activity of organizations has involved the establishment of 'quasi-' or 'internal markets'. These have been introduced into several areas of publicly provided services, like the health and education services in the United Kingdom. The intention here is to provide the conditions for a more 'productively efficient' provision of the services offered in these areas by making sure they are produced at the lowest price (or perhaps at a *lower* price than they are at present supplied). With this type of approach the attempt is to mirror some of the features of the 'external' market in the internal functioning of the organization. In the reading by Mullen (Chapter 7) the experience of the NHS in this respect is discussed. In some ways this kind of strategy on the part of the government could be seen as a combination of market *and* hierarchy.

The establishment of the quasi-markets in health and education has been further justified under the heading of an increase in *choice* for consumers of these services. With all the discussion of firms and market forms above we must not forget the prime reason that markets are thought to be the best way of coordinating things by those who support this approach. Markets guarantee 'consumer sovereignty'. It is consumer sovereignty that is celebrated as the foundation of the market system. Such a commitment and objective is shared by all those who promote market competition, under whatever banner they might operate. The supreme advantage of a price system, it is suggested, is that it allows consumers to choose independently how they will deploy their spending power and in turn this will lead to the correct allocation of resources to meet those consumer needs. Prices embody a crucial information system, that suits a decentralized decision-making environment. It is claimed by the supporters of the market system that prices produce a signalling device that contributes spontaneously and voluntarily to an efficient and prosperous coexistence of all the elements in the social process. This potentially perfectly functioning system can reconcile economic conflicts and establish an apparent harmony amongst diverse interests from which *all* will ultimately benefit.

No wonder that this most powerful of images has been attractive to those designing *new* markets, like the internal quasi forms now taking shape in the United Kingdom's public sector. But it is not just here that this image strikes a bell. We do not discuss the experience of what used to be called Eastern Europe, with its rapid and headlong move towards a price and market system. But we do discuss the obverse of this: the creation of the 'internal market' around the 1992 Single Market programme of the European Community (see Chapter 6). This new market for Western Europe is being celebrated and constructed in precisely that image of a barrierless, open, consumer-dominated and decentralized system of beneficial market exchange.

Hierarchy

Many of the virtues of the market outlined above are seen as in opposition to the supposed detrimental consequences of hierarchy, at least at first sight and in popular discussion. But as with the market itself, we should not necessarily take popular discussion as the appropriate starting point. Even firms working in a highly competitive market framework have to organize their production internally and this is likely to be done in a manner that evokes the attributes of a hierarchy in one way or another. So in practice we can hardly escape the notion of hierarchy as an organizational technique.

It is convenient to discuss the concept of hierarchy in two different respects. The first of these involves the one just invoked: the 'internal' organizational configuration of institutions. The second concerns the 'external' relationship between different institutional or organizational units. Both dimensions might be organized hierarchically. Let us take the internal dimension first.

The term hierarchy immediately conjures up the idea of bureaucracy. Bureaucracy, according to Weber (Chapter 9) represents one of the defining 'rationalities' of the modern era. In an attempt to define an order in the world and to control social existence, bureaucratic rationality emerges – most widely under capitalism in the first instance – whose defining characteristics are systematic administration involving the specialization of functions, objective qualifications and qualities of office, acting only according to a fixed set of rules and a hierarchy of authority. The process of bureaucratic operation involves the progressive breaking down of complex tasks into a discrete number of sub-tasks, which are then carefully reordered so that coordination between them can take place. Hierarchy involves the overt operation of relations of superordination and subordination in the process of coordination.

The administration of a hierarchy, according to the above definition, is by the operationalizing of a set of rules. Such practices can appear in the form of edicts, orders, statutes and the like, which are invoked in a definite procedural configuration. These techniques of administration are designed to 'govern' the organization in question, which can be either a public or a private one. In turn, to govern means to exercise power and authority over some subordinate function or functionary.

These very general attributes of hierarchies do not of themselves tell us everything about the manner in which institutions will be internally governed. A number of forms of this have appeared historically, probably the most celebrated of which are the 'U-form' and the 'M-form' business organizational units. The term *U-form* refers to a unitary organizational entity, broken up along functional lines, where there is a single unit of authority and direction at the top of a narrowly pinnacled hierarchy. By contrast, the *M-form* refers to a much looser departmentalized, compartmentalized and 'multi-divisional' (but still hierarchical) organizational configuration, divided up on an operational rather than a functional basis, where a good deal of autonomy might be given to the multiplicity of divisions existing within the overall umbrella of the company. This particular form of the production unit, first discussed in a systematic way by Alfred Chandler in the 1960s (and described in Chapter 5 by McGuinness), was seen as a response to the development of the horizontally and vertically integrated firm midway through the nineteenth century.

Horizontal integration refers to the way a number of complementary economic activities existing 'alongside' each other, so to speak, can become internalized into the single firm and become part of its own business. Companies operating in the travel business, for instance, might acquire, develop or be absorbed into a sequence of activities paralleling their own main business. These might include other leisure-type activities like the operation of casinos or the brewing business and public houses, or the development of tourist-type financial services such as travellers' cheques and insurance provision.

Vertical integration, by contrast, refers to the way such travel firms – originating in the provision of inclusive tour holidays only – may begin to organize all the separate features of a holiday under one single company umbrella. This could involve the establishment of a chain of high street travel agencies to market the holidays, the setting up or absorption of an airline division to transport holiday customers to their destinations, the development of resorts and hotel chains to provide accommodation at holiday sites when customers get there.

Each of these tendencies – horizontal and vertical integration – represents real attempts to coordinate more effectively (and profitably) some part of social existence and process. Such tendencies are widespread in industry and commerce and they pose the issue of exactly how the multifarious activities included within the company are to be hierarchically controlled: via the U-form or the M-form.

The above example was drawn from economics. But when we think of bureaucracy we most often think of the public sphere and problems of public administration. It is here that the derogatory meaning of bureaucratic is more often encountered. Bureaucrats – civil servants of all kinds – are derided for their inefficiencies and lack of initiative. Bureaucratic in this sense, besides invoking the notion of lack of initiative, implies the constant striving for more power and authority, the lack of flexibility in decision-taking and the continual reference upward in the hierarchy for any decision to be made or authority for action to be taken. Once inside bureaucracies, the sensitivity to public opinion or a response to sensible pressure by functionaries can quickly become abandoned. Survival inside a bureaucracy means self-adaptation to the norms and ethic of the bureau and a conformity to its aspirations (see Chapter 11 by Benveniste). However, while usually directed at public institutions, these negative features of bureaucracy can also haunt private sector organizations, as anyone familiar with large private firms can testify.

Yet there are some clear advantages of bureaucratic hierarchy (Jaques, Chapter 8). In the first place, it can reduce the amount of arbitrariness in decision-making. Formally all people or decisions are treated the same, according to a set of clear rules. In turn this can cut down on the discretion given to decision-takers, which might otherwise lead to abuse. Secondly, clear lines of authority and competence are demarcated, which should help with the consistency of decision-taking. It also enables accountability to be generated. Thirdly, it means that a great many complex and large-scale tasks can be undertaken and coordinated so that actual actions are forthcoming.

If we now turn to the relationships *between* organizational units as discussed under the heading of hierarchical coordination, here a number of different types of relationship can occur. An extreme and thoroughly unfashionable form of this is central (economic) planning. As practised in the Soviet Union and the Eastern Bloc this kind of hierarchical planning was crucial to the way these economies were run, from the 1930s in the Soviet case and during the postwar period in the case of Eastern Europe, up until the events of the late 1980s and early 1990s. This form of economic organization is now in full-scale retreat as these countries begin their rapid embrace of various forms of market system.

But central economic planning was (indeed, still is) just one type of the general category of 'planning', which can embrace private sector activity as well as that organized by the state. Central economic planning involves a rigidly centralized coordinating mechanism that allocates economic resources, ostensibly at least, according to a predetermined assessment of consumer demands and wants. The ownership of productive resources is collectively organized so there is no competition between different economic agents, there being no necessity for this. Efficiency and cost-effectiveness is secured by technical means and social commitment. Democratic political bargaining between the planners – operating on behalf of the consumers – and the producers is the mechanism providing the necessary information to enable production priorities and objectives to be set and met. The whole process is 'consciously' managed. (Sartori outlines further general characteristics of planning in Chapter 12). Needless to say perhaps, the actual experience of central planning has been far from this picture.

A more familiar type of planning in the mixed economies of the West over the postwar period was 'indicative planning'. This involved the state trying to reconcile the disparate investment, output and pricing plans of private sector organizations by laying down or negotiating with them indicative goals for the growth of various macroeconomic aggregates of the economy as a whole. In this case the attempt was made to coordinate the private and the public sectors of the economy without altering the ownership mix of those sectors.

Such an indicative planning in many ways resembles Keynesian demand management, which represents another form of macroeconomic planning. The distinctive feature of this kind of 'semi-hierarchical planning' (as it might be termed) is the way it leaves the private sector to its own devices as far as decision-making is concerned but alters the government's own economic stance with respect to that sector by trying either to stimulate aggregate demand or to dampen it down. This the government is able to do by varying its fiscal policy (involving taxation and government expenditure decisions) and by monetary policy (involving variation of interest rates and credit restrictions and exchange rate adjustments at times). During a downturn in the business cycle the government's objective becomes the stimulation of demand, while at a time of inflation and overheating of the economy the objective becomes to deflate the economy by restricting the growth of aggregate demand.

What has just been outlined represents attempts at the 'hierarchical' planning or control of aggregate output in an economy. But governments also maintain a battery of interventionary techniques to try to 'plan' more micro aspects of the economic mechanism. A traditional, though increasingly discredited, form of this is *nationalization*. In recent years this technique has given way to *regulation* (Chapter 13 by Vickers). As the previously nationalized industries in the United Kingdom have been dismantled and privatized, turning them into private monopolies or duopolies in the main, a new set of regulatory devices has emerged to try to control their pricing and investment decisions. Such a new regulatory assault has also been extended to other areas of the private sector in recent years (for example the financial system). Traditionally regulation has been used to protect the consumer from some of the potentially undesirable consequences of the market structure that have been created. Finally, we should point to the continued use of the technique of *subsidization* by governments in their attempts to direct the economic mechanism on a micro basis into areas of activity where the government thinks there are benefits to be gained for society, but the operation of which the private sector would not otherwise undertake.

We have termed Keynesian demand management a form of 'quasi-hierarchical planning' since it does not involve planning in the usual sense of the word. Rather it 'regulates' the market system overall. Similarly the other interventionary mechanisms are only quasi-hierarchically organized and they also regulate the market mechanism. These are instances of a mixed mode of coordination, further illustration of which we reserve until a later section of this introduction.

Clearly, planning can go on within various types of organization, both public and private. A public education system can be planned as well as a private marketing campaign to sell soap powder. Both involve decisions to be made about resource allocation. Both depend upon bureaucratic and hierarchical means of implementation.

Running in parallel to these techniques deployed to try to coordinate public and private aspects of the economic mechanism more effectively are a set of political administrative apparatuses – a crucial element in any attempt to coordinate and run the country. The whole machinery of government and the state is implicated here, organized as it is in a hierarchical fashion. Various levels of local and central government defer to higher bodies for finance and decision-making. Administrative competences and capacities are highly ordered – though not always well demarcated or functioning in practice – so that the pinnacle of power resides in the sovereignty of Parliament in our system, at least in theory.

How are we to understand where the appropriate boundaries around the organizations that make up a hierarchical order are located? In the case of the economic organizations involving vertical and horizontal integration discussed above one important theory claiming to explain this is that of 'transactions cost'. In principle this claims a general explanation of the boundary conditions affecting institutions, so it could be applied (in a modified form) to non-economic organizations as well.

The idea is that there are transactions costs associated with market-type exchanges between contracting partners. There are costs of information collection, legal costs, service costs themselves, uncertainties and the like. These are 'externalities' to the firm in its dealings with other economic organizations. When firms find these transactions costs are high they will have an incentive to 'internalize' them within the boundaries of their firm by performing the operation 'inhouse' which was otherwise contracted with an outside supplier. Strictly speaking, firms should conduct a cost-benefit analysis of the operation performed either internally or externally and only if the net benefit of internal supply is positive should they give up an external market exchange for an internal bureaucratic one. Continual calculations of this kind will lead to the boundaries of firms changing as conditions change (transactions costs change) and firms react to them. This approach appears in a number of the chapters (5, 15, 16 and 20–3) and while developed in relation to hierarchy here, has a broader applicability in organizational theory. It can be used to compare where market, hierarchy and networks might be the most appropriate form of inter-unit organization.

Networks

It might be tempting to think that market and hierarchy exhaust the possible mechanisms of social coordination but that would be to leave a very important additional mechanism – networks – out of the account. Indeed, it is possible to think of market and hierarchy as just two examples of the more general category of networks (see Chapter 14 by Knoke and Kuklinksi, and below). But in this section we want to distinguish networks from the other two models so far discussed.

A network is often thought of as a 'flat' organizational form in contrast to the vertically organized hierarchical forms just discussed (contrast Jaques, Chapter 8, with Johnston and Lawrence, Chapter 16). It conjures up the idea of informal relationships between essentially equal social agents and agencies. The collegiate organization is a classic example of a network. These kinds of organizational units are often cooperatively run. They can be informal, operating on the basis of friendship, gender or kin relationships (Werbner, Chapter 18). In the business world the idea of partnership sums up the central notion for a network (Johnston and Lawrence. Chapter 16). In the political world elite and professional groups often form a network; they share a common ethic and outlook and can discuss and decide policy informally between themselves (Rhodes, Chapter 17).

In fact, it is the very informality of networks that gives rise to a certain hesitancy and concern about how they work and their impact. Coordination in this case may be settled in a less than open manner and not subject to any obvious accountability. A lot of networks are highly exclusive of outsiders. In one sense the Mafia is a perfect network structure. It relies upon informality, clan and kin loyalty; it is far from open; and has its own secret system of rewards and punishments which is quite clearly corrupt in many respects. Interestingly, corruption can be one of the most potent and successful coordinating mechanisms in many societies, if a rather debilitating one.

However, we do not want to give the impression that all networks are necessarily corrupt or devious. Networks can be highly positive in the way that they lubricate social relations and help coordinate political and economic life. In some areas of life they can be all pervasive. They tend to exist within the interstices of social relations, sometimes hidden (because informal), usually operating on a small scale, modest in their purview and range but nonetheless important and central to a good deal of the real coordination that contributes to running a country. For those people close to networks operating at this level, they may constitute a more important contribution to the richness of their social existence than the rather anonymous operation of the market or hierarchy. A possible disadvantage for networks is that very large-scale coordination via informal means becomes extremely difficult as the range of social actors expands.

The real problem with networks is not to justify them as an object of study but to analyse how they work. We have already mentioned some of the mechanisms involved, amongst the most important of which are cooperation and loyalty. These in turn implicate the most important attribute of network operation – the formation and sustaining of *trust* within and between networks.

If it is price competition that is the central coordinating mechanism of the market and administrative orders that of hierarchy, then it is trust and cooperation that centrally articulates networks. Exactly how such trust and cooperation might be generated and sustained remains the prime analytical problem in understanding networks (an important way of discussing this can be found in Chapter 15 by Lorenz).

Just as in the case of our other two models, networks appear in various forms and at various levels. We can discuss networks *within* organizations and we can discuss them as *between* organizational units. One important area in which the idea of networks has surfaced in recent years concerns the contemporary restructuring and reorganization of manufacturing activity in advanced industrial countries. Above we discussed the development of the M-form organization in the light of the tendency towards vertical and horizontal integration. However, under contemporary conditions there may be a trend working in the opposite direction. Because of the increased uncertainty associated with the rapidity of technological advance and changes in the demand and market characteristics of modern economic activity, hastened by the break-up of traditional aggregate economic regulatory mechanisms (the demise of Keynesianism and indicative planning, broadly speaking), the modern corporation's reaction has been to begin divesting peripheral activities, concentrating once again on core activities only and thus beginning to 'dis-integrate'. Alongside this, new networks of essentially small and medium scale, localized enterprises have emerged that form robust subcontracting supply networks for the main businesses with which they are linked (see Lorenz, Chapter 15; Johnston and Lawrence, Chapter 16). The outcome is twofold: on the one hand an internal reorganization of the big corporation to allow a renewed flexibility and less bureaucratic style of operation, with semi-autonomous departments and divisions contracting amongst themselves in a network framework; on the other hand a re-emphasis on external flexibility with respect to supply contracting associated again with network-type structures.

The point about these new (and one must add contentious) developments is that they do not spell a return to straightforward market contracting between units – based upon price competition. Nor do they imply renewed bureaucratic administrative relations – involving planned orders and deliveries within the boundary of the firm. Rather they rely upon the operation of cooperation and trust between the new semi-autonomous units and subcontracting firms that make up the networks on both counts.

Another manifestation of networks, this time straddling the political and economic spheres, involves 'interlocking directorships'. The relationships between the directors of companies – how particular directors appear to sit on the boards of a number of different companies – can be traced and the links between companies' decision-takers established. Elite groups of business people can be formed in this manner who decide on important financial and output matters for the big corporations they control, thereby 'governing the economy'. And inasmuch as these groups share a common outlook with political elites, both can combine to create a formidable 'politico-financial oligarchy' with considerable power and influence.

In addition, and as something of an antidote to these kinds of elite network, it has been suggested that a wide range of political associations forming a kind of pluralist political network might be argued for as a way of increasing the democratic accountability of the increasingly centralized representative state. Streeck and Schmitter in Chapter 19, for instance, point to the way 'private interest group governance' is organized semi-independently of the state, the market and the community via the mechanism of a wide variety of neo-corporatist political associations. All these are examples of the way the idea of networks has been rendered into a usable analytical technique for social analysis.

IV

In this final section we say something about the possible relationship between the three models illustrated in this reader. Clearly this has already been broached on a number of occasions in the discussion above; it is difficult to discuss any of the models separately without at the same time comparing them with each other. The issues raised explicitly in the final selection of chapters concern a more systematic comparison between the three models to highlight the differences between each, and their respective strengths and weaknesses.

Many of the chapters in the previous sections demonstrate that, although formally focused on one or other of the models, any analysis of a particular model usually involves elements of another model as well.

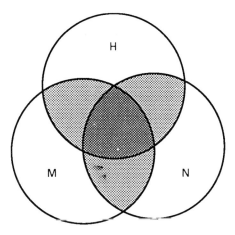

Figure 1

This is particularly the case in readings that introduce concrete examples of an area of analysis to illustrate the model under consideration. In these cases it is the differences and relationships *between* the models that tend to be highlighted or that come to the fore (for example Chapters 3, 5, 7, 12, 15, 16 and 19). In the final section the chapter by Powell (Chapter 22) explicitly brings the three models into a comparative framework and assesses them together.

Any actual social analysis of coordination will usually involve the employment of the models in combination or in a comparative framework.

Of course, this may be no bad thing. It enables the insights from each of the models to be mobilized together, thereby enriching the analytical investigation. If these are initially pitched against each other, so that the question is asked as to which one best exemplifies the way coordination works, all the better perhaps. In these circumstances the strengths and weaknesses of the different approaches to coordination can be debated and argued. This way of looking at model assessment is indicated by Johanson and Mattsson's discussion of the differences between a trans-actions-cost approach and a network approach in Chapter 21.

One way of developing this point is to extend our analogy of the three torches with their beams of 'analytical light'. These are illustrated in Figure 1. For whatever aspect of running the country is under investigation the three beams of light can be focused on it and the 'footprints' of the three models outlined. They will tend to highlight different aspects of the coordinative activity under scrutiny. While a certain aspect of this activity may well be best explained by one or other of the models separately, it is also likely that two in combination will highlight more, or a different aspect, and that there will be some of the activity for which all three beams overlap and produce the most accurate picture. The

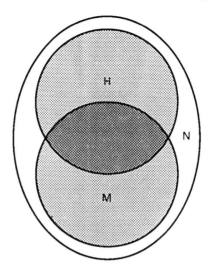

Figure 2

intensity of the picture developed along these lines is illustrated by the
shading in Figure 1. The greater the degree of overlap, the darker the
shading, and the more it is the two or three models *in combination* that
best illustrate the workings of the country.

Another way of thinking about the relationship between the models that
is broached by the readings in the final section is the production of hybrid
cases rather than simply the coexistence of the models in combination.
Bradach and Eccles in Chapter 23, for instance, argue for the existence
of a plurality of interdependent forms of coordinative exchange rather
than the continued mutually exclusive existence of the models in combination.

Earlier it was pointed out that some have argued the idea of 'networks'
might be used to encompass both markets and hierarchy. Thus networks
could be considered as the most general category of coordination; the
market is a network of competing price- and information-emitting firms
and their customers; while hierarchy is also a network of bureaucratically
administered, order-giving and receiving departments. This can be
illustrated by Figure 2, where this new idea of a network entirely encompasses the market and hierarchy. In these circumstances there could still
be room for a differentiated category of the network model as we have
described it above, but now it would be just a sub-category of the more
general notion of network deployed in the context of Figure 2.

The comparative discussion organized around Figures 1 and 2 could be
further supplemented by a rather more 'normative' assessment of the
models against a common set of criteria. This would involve an evaluation
of model X as being better than or worse than model Y for a given
purpose or coordination problem. The chapters in the final section also

conduct this kind of assessment, though it tends to be more implicit. The subtext of the evaluations is often to provide a justification for the network model since this is the one that has been least discussed in the literature. But in the final chapter von Hayek broaches a slightly different problem and one pitched at a different level to the other four assessment articles. In characteristic polemical style von Hayek argues for the appropriateness of the spontaneous coordination of the market process against the debilitating effects, as he sees it, of all other 'designed' attempts to impose a coordinative order where it was not spontaneously present before. For von Hayek there is no other proper coordination than the market process. A theme of our times perhaps, but, it must be said, not one that all the editors of this volume would necessarily share.

Markets

Introduction

Rosalind Levačić

The crucial feature of the market as a coordination device is that it involves voluntary exchange of goods and services between two parties at a known price. Through a complex set of such exchanges the economic activities of people who are widely dispersed and who are entirely unaware of each other's existence can be coordinated. Price serves as the key signal in this coordination. A high price relative to the costs of production of a good means large profits, which entice producers to raise output and so satisfy consumers' wants. Similarly, a fall in demand by consumers is signalled by price falling relative to production costs and gives rise to losses for producers which may well lead to factory closures and job losses.

The evolution of increasingly complex forms of market coordination has been fundamental to the economic development of capitalist economies and, through international trade, to sufficient economic integration to create the notion of a world economy. Conceptualizing the nature and significance of markets has been a key element in economic and political thought since Adam Smith's *Wealth of Nations*, published in 1776. By the end of the nineteenth century, neo-classical theory of how price is determined through the interaction of demand and supply was formulated by Alfred Marshall in his *Principles of Economics*. The section on markets opens with extracts from this classic work (Chapter 1).

The characteristic feature of neo-classical theory is its analytical device of equilibrium – a state of affairs in which all participants in the market cannot make themselves better off by changing the quantities of goods and services they wish to trade at the prevailing prices. The equilibrium price is the price at which demand and supply are the same and so there is perfect coordination of the wishes of purchasers and sellers. Neo-classical economists have been much preoccupied with exploring the conditions under which market coordination leads to the 'best' or 'socially optimal' allocation of resources. By the allocation of resources is meant the kinds and quantities of goods produced, the production methods used and the distribution of income to individuals to enable them to consume output. Perfect competition, a market structure in which there are so many buyers and sellers that no one of them individually can affect price, provides the theoretical conditions under which the market will allocate resources optimally.

Since perfect competition does not exist in practice – at best it is approximated in some markets – the stringent conditions for efficient resource allocation by the market are not met. In this event there is said to be market failure. Markets fail to allocate or coordinate efficiently when competition is not perfect because there are few enough sellers or buyers, or both, to affect price by the amount they trade. An additional source of market failure is externalities. These are costs or benefits which are not reflected in market prices, such as pollution costs. Keynes' work was directed at yet another source of market failure – inadequate information available to market traders, in particular firms and workers, so that the market cannot achieve the equilibrium wage rate at which there would be full employment. Quite apart from market failure, another reason for rejecting unregulated market coordination is the inequality of social outcomes it produces. Levačić (Chapter 2) provides an overview and summary of the market failure and equity issues in the evaluation of market coordination. While Levačić deals with criticisms of market coordination mainly from a neo-classical perspective, Breitenbach *et al.* (Chapter 3) provide a succinct radical critique of markets together with advocating socialist planning as an alternative.

The neo-classical view of how markets work has been increasingly challenged by the Austrian school, whose approach is explained by Krizner (Chapter 4). Austrians are highly critical of neo-classical theory for its static treatment of markets and its assumption of perfect information; these assume away the very factors that explain how markets work and why market coordination is more efficient than the alternative of regulation and planning. Austrians emphasize that market coordination is a dynamic process in which entrepreneurship, or the ability to seek out and act upon opportunities for beneficial exchange, plays a crucial role. Because they reject static analysis and consider the market structure of perfect competition irrelevant, Austrians strongly favour market coordination and are highly critical of government regulation of markets. Austrians view markets as a spontaneous social order that arises naturally to provide for beneficial exchanges.

A key issue is what factors determine which mode of coordination is the most appropriate for particular economic arrangements. The question of why markets are used to coordinate some activities while others are coordinated within firms, often hierarchically, has now become of central interest in much of the work on the economics of firms and public sector agencies. A survey of this important development in our understanding or the interrelationships of market and hierarchical coordination is provided in Chapter 5 by McGuinness.

As a broad generalization, the half-century since the end of the Second World War, has witnessed the gradual retreat of state hierarchical coordination in favour of greater elements of market coordination. The closer integration of countries' economies through increasing trade, fostered by the gradual removal of trade barriers, has been one of the most significant developments of the postwar period. The creation and expansion of the European Community is a major element of this economic integration. The EC is currently attempting to achieve greater economic integration with the creation of the Single European market. This development is discussed by Swann in Chapter 6.

Another area where there has been an advance of market coordination in the 1980s is the public sector. Again these changes have been in response to legislation and have taken a number of forms. One is contracting out to private sector firms the production of goods and services which the state provides free or at subsidized prices to consumers. Another development is the creation of what is known as an internal market for the production and delivery of certain collectively provided services such as health, education and community care. An internal market is created by splitting up the service agency into buyers and sellers, who then trade on a highly regulated market. Provision to the ultimate client remains largely free. In the late 1980s the Conservative government legislated for the introduction of internal markets in the public sector, notably in community care, health and education. Mullen (Chapter 7) analyses the concept of the internal market and its application to the NHS.

The internal market is also used in the private sector as an alternative to hierarchy as a mode of internal coordination within the firm. It is suited to large multi-divisional firms producing a wide range of products and/or operating across several countries.

Taken together, the chapters in this section show how different explanations of how markets work lead to different evaluations of the relative advantages and disadvantages of markets. But whichever approach one adopts, market coordination has characteristics which differentiate it from hierarchies and networks. It is a decentralized coordinating device, in contrast to hierarchy. Its defining relationship is exchange motivated by individual self-interest, with prices crucial in signalling information, to which participants respond. However, it is important to appreciate that market coordination could not function in the absence of the other modes of coordination. It requires collective agreement in the form of government to define the property rights that are the objects of exchange and to enforce contract through the legal system. But trust is also an important ingredient of market relationships. If exchange relationships were based totally on unscrupulous self-interested behaviour, the resulting distrust and the cost of legal action to enforce contracts would render market coordination much less efficient than it is in the presence of trust built up through networks and embedded social expectations that contracts will be honoured.

1

On markets

Alfred Marshall

[. . .]

When demand and supply are spoken of in relation to one another, it is of course necessary that the markets to which they refer should be the same. As Cournot says, 'Economists understand by the term *Market*, not any particular market place in which things are bought and sold, but the whole of any region in which buyers and sellers are in such free intercourse with one another that the prices of the same goods tend to equality easily and quickly.' Or again as Jevons says 'Originally a market was a public place in a town where provisions and other objects were exposed for sale; but the word has been generalized, so as to mean any body of persons who are in intimate business relations and carry on extensive transactions in any commodity. A great city may contain as many markets as there are important branches of trade, and these markets may or may not be localized. The central point of a market is the public exchange, mart or auction rooms, where the traders agree to meet and transact business. In London the Stock Market, the Corn Market, the Coal Market, the Sugar Market, and many others are distinctly localized; in Manchester the Cotton Market, the Cotton Waste Market, and others. But this distinction of locality is not necessary. The traders may be spread over a whole town, or region of country, and yet make a market, if they are, by means of fairs, meetings, published price lists, the post-office or otherwise, in close communication with each other.'

Thus the more nearly perfect a market is, the stronger is the tendency for the same price to be paid for the same thing at the same time in all parts of the market: but of course if the market is large, allowance must be made for the expense of delivering the goods to different purchasers; each of whom must be supposed to pay in addition to the market price a special charge on account of delivery.

Temporary equilibrium of demand and supply

Let us then turn to the ordinary dealings of modern life; and take an illustration from a corn-market in a country town, and let us assume for

Adapted from A. Marshall, *Principles of Economics* (London: Macmillan, 1936), pp. 270–1, 277–89, 304–10.

the sake of simplicity that all the corn in the market is of the same quality. The amount which each farmer or other seller offers for sale at any price is governed by his own need for money in hand, and by his calculation of the present and future conditions of the market with which he is connected. There are some prices which no seller would accept, some which no one would refuse. There are other intermediate prices which would be accepted for larger or smaller amounts by many or all of the sellers. Everyone will try to guess the state of the market and to govern his actions accordingly. Let us suppose that in fact there are not more than 600 quarters, the holders of which are willing to accept as low a price as 35s.; but that holders of another hundred would be tempted by 36s.; and holders of yet another three hundred by 37s. Let us suppose also that a price of 37s. would tempt buyers for only 600 quarters; while another hundred could be sold at 36s., and yet another two hundred at 35s. These facts may be put out in a table thus:

At the price	Holders will be willing to sell	Buyers will be willing to buy
37s.	1000 quarters	600 quarters
36s.	700 quarters	700 quarters
35s.	600 quarters	900 quarters

Of course some of those who are really willing to take 36s. rather than leave the market without selling, will not show at once that they are ready to accept that price. And in like manner buyers will fence, and pretend to be less eager than they really are. So the price may be tossed hither and thither like a shuttlecock, as one side or the other gets the better in the 'higgling and bargaining' of the market. But unless they are unequally matched; unless, for instance, one side is very simple or unfortunate in failing to gauge the strength of the other side, the price is likely to be never very far from 36s.; and it is nearly sure to be pretty close to 36s. at the end of market. For if a holder thinks that the buyers will really be able to get at 36s. all that they care to take at that price, he will be unwilling to let slip past him any offer that is well above that price.

Buyers on their part will make similar calculations; and if at any time the price should rise considerably above 36s. they will argue that the supply will be much greater than the demand at that price: therefore even those of them who would rather pay that price than go unserved, wait; and by waiting they help to bring the price down. On the other hand, when the price is much below 36s., even those sellers who would rather take the price than leave the market with their corn unsold, will argue that at that price the demand will be in excess of the supply: so they will wait, and by waiting help to bring the price up.

The price of 36s. has thus some claim to be called the true equilibrium price: because if it were fixed on at the beginning, and adhered to throughout, it would exactly equate demand and supply (i.e. the amount which buyers were willing to purchase at that price would be just equal to that for which sellers were willing to take that price); and because every dealer who has a perfect knowledge of the circumstances of the market expects that price to be established. If he sees the price differing much from 36*s.* he expects that a change will come before long, and by anticipating it he helps it to come quickly. [. . .]

Equilibrium of normal demand and supply

We have next to inquire what causes govern supply prices, that is prices which dealers are willing to accept for different amounts. Above we looked at the affairs of only a single day; and supposed the stocks offered for sale to be already in existence. But of course these stocks are dependent on the amount of wheat sown in the preceding year; and that, in its turn was largely influenced by the farmers' guesses as to the price which they would get for it in this year. This is the point at which we have to work [here].

Even in the corn-exchange of a country town on a market-day the equilibrium price is affected by calculations of the future relations of production and consumption; while in the leading corn-markets of America and Europe dealings for future delivery already predominate and are rapidly weaving into one web all the leading threads of trade in corn throughout the whole world. Some of these dealings in 'futures' are but incidents in speculative manoeuvres; but in the main they are governed by calculations of the world's consumption on the one hand, and of the existing stocks and coming harvests in the Northern and Southern hemispheres on the other. Dealers take account of the areas sown with each kind of grain, of the forwardness and weight of the crops, of the supply of things which can be used as substitutes for grain, and of the things for which grain can be used as a substitute. Thus, when buying or selling barley, they take account of the supplies of such things as sugar, which can be used as substitutes for it in brewing, and again of all the various feeding stuffs, a scarcity of which might raise the value of barley for consumption on the farm. If it is thought that the growers of any kind of grain in any part of the world have been losing money, and are likely to sow a smaller area for a future harvest; it is argued that prices are likely to rise as soon as that harvest comes into sight, and its shortness is manifest to all. Anticipations of that rise exercise an influence on present sales for future delivery, and that in its turn influences cash prices; so that these prices are indirectly affected by estimates of the expense of producing further supplies.

But in this . . . chapter we are specially concerned with movements of prices ranging over still longer periods than those for which the most far-sighted dealers in futures generally make their reckoning: we have to consider the volume of production adjusting itself to the conditions of the market, and the normal price being thus determined at the position of stable equilibrium of normal demand and normal supply.

In this discussion we shall have to make frequent use of the terms *cost* and *expenses* of production; and some provisional account of them must be given before proceeding further.

We may revert to the analogy between the supply price and the demand price of a commodity. Assuming for the moment that the efficiency of production depends solely upon the exertions of the workers, we saw that 'the price required to call forth the exertion necessary for producing any given amount of a commodity may be called the supply price for that amount, with reference of course to a given unit of time'. But now we have to take account of the fact that the production of a commodity generally requires many different kinds of labour and the use of capital in many forms. The exertions of all the different kinds of labour that are directly or indirectly involved in making it; together with the abstinences or rather the waitings required for saving the capital used in making it: all these efforts and sacrifices together will be called the *real cost of production* of the commodity. The sums of money that have to be paid for these efforts and sacrifices will be called either its *money cost of production*, or, for shortness, its *expenses of production*; they are the prices which have to be paid in order to call forth an adequate supply of the efforts and waitings that are required for making it; or, in other words, they are its supply price.

The analysis of the expenses of production of a commodity might be carried backward to any length; but it is seldom worth while to go back very far. It is for instance often sufficient to take the supply price of the different kinds of raw materials used in any manufacture as ultimate facts, without analysing these supply prices into the several elements of which they are composed; otherwise indeed the analysis would never end. We may then arrange the things that are required for making a commodity into whatever groups are convenient, and call them its *factors of production*. Its expenses of production when any given amount of it is produced are thus the supply prices of the corresponding quantities of its factors of production. And the sum of these is the supply price of that amount of the commodity. [. . .]

In calculating the expenses of production of a commodity we must take account of the fact that changes in the amounts produced are likely, even when there is no new invention, to be accompanied by changes in the relative quantities of its several factors of production. For instance, when the scale of production increases, horse or steam power is likely to be substituted for manual labour; materials are likely to be brought from a greater distance and in greater quantities, thus increasing those expenses of production which correspond to the work of carriers, middlemen and traders of all kinds.

As far as the knowledge and business enterprise of the producers reach, they in each case choose those factors of production which are best for their purpose, the sum of the supply prices of those factors which are used is, as a rule, less than the sum of the supply prices of any other set of

factors which could be substituted for them; and whenever it appears to
the producers that this is not the case, they will, as a rule, set to work
to substitute the less expensive method. And further on we shall see how
in a somewhat similar way society substitutes one undertaker for another
who is less efficient in proportion to his charges. We may call this, for
convenience of reference, *the principle of substitution.*

The applications of this principle extend over almost every field of
economic inquiry.

The position then is this: we are investigating the equilibrium of normal
demand and normal supply in their most general form; we are neglecting
those features which are special to particular parts of economic science,
and are confining our attention to those broad relations which are
common to nearly the whole of it. Thus we assume that the forces of
demand and supply have free play; that there is no close combination
among dealers on either side, but each acts for himself, and there is much
free competition; that is, buyers generally compete freely with buyers, and
sellers compete freely with sellers. But though everyone acts for himself,
his knowledge of what others are doing is supposed to be generally sufficient to prevent him from taking a lower or paying a higher price than
others are doing. This is assumed provisionally to be true both of finished
goods and of their factors of production, of the hire of labour and of the
borrowing of capital. We have already inquired to some extent, and we
shall have to inquire further, how far these assumptions are in accordance
with the actual facts of life. But meanwhile this is the supposition on
which we proceed; we assume that there is only one price in the market
at one and the same time; it being understood that separate allowance is
made, when necessary, for differences in the expense of delivering goods
to dealers in different parts of the market; including allowance for the
special expenses of retailing, if it is a retail market.

In such a market there is a demand price for each amount of the
commodity, that is, a price at which each particular amount of the
commodity can find purchasers in a day or week or year. The circumstances which govern this price for any given amount of the commodity
vary in character from one problem to another; but in every case the more
of a thing is offered for sale in a market the lower is the price at which
it will find purchasers; or in other words, the demand price for each
bushel or yard diminishes with every increase in the amount offered.

The unit of time may be chosen according to the circumstances of each
particular problem: it may be a day, a month, a year, or even a generation: but in every case it must be short relative to the period of the market
under discussion. It is to be assumed that the general circumstances of the
market remain unchanged throughout this period; that there is, for
instance, no change in fashion or taste, no new substitute which might
affect the demand, no new invention to disturb the supply.

The conditions of normal supply are less definite. [. . .] They will be
found to vary in detail with the length of the period of time to which the

investigation·refers; chiefly because both the material capital of machinery and other business plant, and the immaterial capital of business skill and ability and organization, are of slow growth and slow decay

Let us call to mind the 'representative firm', whose economies of production, internal and external, are dependent on the aggregate volume of production of the commodity that it makes; and, postponing all further study of the nature of this dependence, let us assume that the normal supply price of any amount of that commodity may be taken to be its normal expenses of production (including *gross* earnings of managements) by that firm. That is, let us assume that this is the price the expectation of which will just suffice to maintain the existing aggregate amount of production; some firms meanwhile rising and increasing their output, and others falling and diminishing theirs; but the aggregate production remaining unchanged. A price higher than this would increase the growth of the rising firms; and slacken, though it might not arrest, the decay of the falling firms; with the net result of an increase in the aggregate production. On the other hand, a price lower than this would hasten the decay of the falling firms, and slacken the growth of the rising firms; and on the whole diminish production: and a rise or fall of price would affect in like manner though perhaps not in an equal degree those great joint-stock companies which often stagnate, but seldom die.

To give definiteness to our ideas let us take an illustration from the woollen trade. Let us suppose that a person well acquainted with the woollen trade sets himself to inquire what would be the normal supply price of a certain number of millions of yards annually of a particular kind of cloth. He would have to reckon (i) the price of the wool, coal, and other materials which would be used up in making it, (ii) wear-and-tear and depreciation of the buildings, machinery and other fixed capital, (iii) interest and insurance on all the capital (iv) the wages of those who work in the factories, and (v) the gross earnings of management (including insurance against loss), of those who undertake the risks, who engineer and superintend the working. He would of course estimate the supply prices of all these different factors of production of the cloth with reference to the amounts of each of them that would be wanted, and on the supposition that the conditions of supply would be normal; and he would add them all together to find the supply price of the cloth.

Let us suppose a list of supply prices (or a supply schedule) made on a similar plan to that of our list of demand prices: the supply price of each amount of the commodity in a year, or any other unit of time, being written against that amount. As the flow, or (annual) amount of the commodity increases, the supply price may either increase or diminish; or it may even alternately increase and diminish. For if nature is offering a sturdy resistance to man's efforts to wring from her a larger supply of raw material, while at that particular stage there is no great room for introducing important new economies into the manufacture, the supply price will rise; but if the volume of production were greater, it would perhaps be profitable to substitute largely machine work for hand work and steam power for muscular force; and the increase in the volume of production would have diminished the expenses of production of the commodity of our representative firm. [. . .]

When therefore the amount produced (in a unit of time) is such that the demand price is greater than the supply price, then sellers receive more than is sufficient to make it worth their while to bring goods to market to that amount; and there is at work an active force tending to increase the amount brought forward for sale. On the other hand, when the amount produced is such that the demand price is less than the supply price, sellers receive less than is sufficient to make it worth their while to bring goods to market on that scale; so that those who were just on the margin of doubt as to whether to go on producing are decided not to do so, and there is an active force at work tending to diminish the amount brought forward for sale. When the demand price is equal to the supply price, the amount produced has no tendency either to be increased or to be diminished; it is in equilibrium.

When demand and supply are in equilibrium, the amount of the commodity which is being produced in a unit of time may be called the *equilibrium-amount*, and the price at which it is being sold may be called the *equilibrium-price*.

Such an equilibrium is *stable*; that is, the price, if displaced a little from it, will tend to return, as a pendulum oscillates about its lowest point; and it will be found to be a characteristic of stable equilibria that in them the demand price is greater than the supply price for amounts just less than the equilibrium amount, and vice versa. For when the demand price is greater than the supply price, the amount produced tends to increase. Therefore, if the demand price is greater than the supply price for amounts just less than an equilibrium amount; then, if the scale of production is temporarily diminished somewhat below that equilibrium amount, it will tend to return; thus the equilibrium is stable for displacements in that direction. If the demand price is greater than the supply price for amounts just less than the equilibrium amount, it is sure to be less than the supply price for amounts just greater: and therefore, if the scale of production is somewhat increased beyond the equilibrium position, it will tend to return; and the equilibrium will be stable for displacements in that direction also.

When demand and supply are in stable equilibrium, if any accident should move the scale of production from its equilibrium position, there will be instantly brought into play forces tending to push it back to that position; just as, if a stone hanging by a string is displaced from its equilibrium position, the force of gravity will at once tend to bring it back to its equilibrium position. The movements of the scale of production about its position of equilibrium will be of a somewhat similar kind. [. . .]

But in real life such oscillations are seldom as rhythmical as those of a stone hanging freely from a string; the comparison would be more exact if the string were supposed to hang in the troubled waters of a mill-race, whose stream was at one time allowed to flow freely, and at another partially cut off. Nor are these complexities sufficient to illustrate all the disturbances with which the economist and the merchant alike are forced to concern themselves. If the person holding the string swings his hand with movements partly rhythmical and partly arbitrary, the illustration will not outrun the difficulties of some very real and practical problems of value. For indeed the demand and supply schedules do not in practice remain unchanged for a long time together, but are constantly being changed; and every change in them alters the equilibrium amount and the equilibrium price, and thus gives new positions to the centres about which the amount and the price tend to oscillate. [. . .]

Equilibrium of normal supply and demand [. . .]

[. . .] The element of time is a chief cause of those difficulties in economic investigations which make it necessary for man with his limited powers to go step by step; breaking up a complex question, studying one bit at a time, and at last combining his partial solutions into a more or less complete solution of the whole riddle. In breaking it up, he segregates those disturbing causes, whose wanderings happen to be inconvenient, for the time in a pound called *Ceteris Paribus*. The study of some group of tendencies is isolated by the assumption *other things being equal*: the existence of other tendencies is not denied, but their disturbing effect is neglected for a time. The more the issue is thus narrowed, the more exactly can it be handled: but also the less closely does it correspond to real life. Each exact and firm handling of a narrow issue, however, helps towards treating broader issues, in which that narrow issue is contained, more exactly than would otherwise have been possible. With each step more things can be let out of the pound; exact discussions can be made less abstract, realistic discussions can be made less inexact than was possible at an earlier stage.

Our step towards studying the influences exerted by the element of time on the relations between cost of production and value may well be to consider the famous fiction of the 'Stationary state' in which those influences would be but little felt; and to contrast the results which would be found there with those in the modern world.

This state obtains its name from the fact that in it the general conditions of production and consumption, of distribution and exchange remain motionless; but yet it is full of movement; for it is a mode of life. The average age of the population may be stationary; though each individual is growing up from youth towards his prime, or downwards to old age. And the same amount of things per head of the population will have been produced in the same ways by the same classes of people for many generations together; and therefore this supply of the appliances for production will have had full time to be adjusted to the steady demand.

Of course we might assume that in our stationary state every business remained always of the same size, and with the same trade connection. But we need not go so far as that; it will suffice to suppose that firms rise and 'fall, but that the 'representative' firm remains always of about the same size, as does the representative tree of a virgin forest. [. . .]

But nothing of this is true in the world in which we live. Here every economic force is constantly changing its action, under the influence of other forces which are acting around it. Here changes in the volume of production, in its methods, and in its cost are ever mutually modifying one another; they are always affecting and being affected by the character and the extent of demand. [. . .]

The stationary state has just been taken to be one in which population is stationary. But nearly all its distinctive features may be exhibited in a place where population and wealth are both growing, provided they are growing at about the same rate, and there is no scarcity of land: and provided also the methods of production and the conditions of trade change but little; and above all, where the character of man himself is a constant quantity. For in such a state by far the most important conditions of production and consumption, of exchange and distribution will remain of the same quality, and in the same general relations to one another, though they are all increasing in volume.

This relaxation of the rigid bonds of a purely stationary state brings us one step nearer to the actual conditions of life: and by relaxing them still further we get nearer still. We thus approach by gradual steps towards the difficult problem of the interaction of countless economic causes. In the stationary state all the conditions of production and consumption are reduced to rest: but less violent assumptions are made by what is, not quite accurately, called the *statical* method. By that method we fix our minds on some central point: we suppose it for the time to be reduced to a *stationary* state; and we then study in relation to it the forces that affect the things by which it is surrounded, and any tendency there may be to equilibrium of these forces. A number of these partial studies may lead the way towards a solution of problems too difficult to be grasped at one effort.

We may roughly classify problems connected with fishing industries as those which are affected by very quick changes, such as uncertainties of the weather; or by changes of moderate length, such as the increased demand for fish caused by the scarcity of meat during the year or two following a cattle plague. [. . .]

Let us then [. . .] suppose a great increase in the general demand for fish, such for instance as might arise from a disease affecting farm stock, by which meat was made a dear and dangerous food for several years together. We now impound fluctuations due to the weather in *ceteris paribus*, and neglect them provisionally: they are so quick that they speedily obliterate one another, and are therefore not important for problems of this class. And for the opposite reason we neglect variations in the numbers of those who are brought up as seafaring men for these variations are too slow to produce much effect in the year or two during which the scarcity of meat lasts. Having impounded these two sets for the time, we give our full attention to such influences as the inducements which good fishing wages will offer to sailors to stay in their fishing homes for a year or two, instead of applying for work on a ship. We consider what old fishing boats, and even vessels that were not specially made for fishing, can be adapted and sent to fish for a year or two. The normal price for any given daily supply of fish, which we are now seeking, is the price which will *quickly* call into the fishing trade capital and labour enough to obtain that supply in a day's fishing of average good fortune; the influence which the price of fish will have upon capital and labour available in the fishing trade being governed by rather narrow causes such as these. This new level about which the price oscillates during these years of exceptionally great demand, will obviously be higher than before. Here we see an illustration of the almost universal law that the term Normal being taken to refer to a short period of time *an increase in the amount demanded raises the normal supply* price. [. . .]

But if we turn to consider the [. . .] supply price with reference to a *long period* of time, we shall find that it is governed by a different set of causes, and with different results. For suppose that the disuse of meat causes a permanent distaste for it, and that an increased demand for fish continues long enough to enable the forces by which its supply is governed to work out their action fully (of course oscillation from day to day and from year to year would continue: but we may leave them on the side). The source of supply in the sea might perhaps shown signs of exhaustion, and the fishermen might have to resort to more distant coasts and to deeper waters, Nature giving a diminishing return to the increased application of capital and labour of a given order of efficiency. On the other hand, those might turn out to be right who think that man is responsible for but a very small part of the destruction of fish that is constantly going on; and in that case a boat starting with equally good appliances and an equally efficient crew would be likely to get nearly as good a haul after the increase in the total volume of the fishing trade as before. In any case the normal cost of equipping a good boat with an efficient crew would certainly not be higher, and probably be a little lower after the trade had settled down to its now increased dimensions than before. For since fishermen require only trained aptitudes, and not any exceptional natural qualities, their number could be increased in less than a generation to almost any extent that was necessary to meet the demand; while the industries connected with building boats, making nets, etc. being now on a larger scale would be organized more thoroughly and economically. If therefore the waters of the sea showed no signs of depletion of fish, an increased supply could be produced at a lower price after a time sufficiently long to enable the normal action of economic causes to work itself out. [. . .]

Whether the new production for which there appears to be a market be large or small, the general rule will be that unless the price is expected to be very low that portion of the supply which can be most easily produced, with but small prime costs, will be produced: that portion is not likely to be on the margin of production. As the expectations of price improve, an increased part of the production will yield a considerable surplus above prime costs, and the margin of production will be pushed outwards. Every increase in the price expected will, as a rule, induce some people who would not otherwise have produced anything, to produce a little; and those, who have produced something for the lower price, will produce more for the higher price.

2

Markets and government: an overview

Rosalind Levačić

[. . .]

Markets and government provide different ways in which voluntary exchange takes place. In the market individuals exchange goods and services at a mutually agreed price, normally using the medium of money. The political basis of society is also held to rest on voluntary agreement, in the sense that citizens are conceived of entering into an implicit social contract whereby each surrenders the liberty to do whatever he wants and agrees to pay taxes and abide by laws in exchange for the advantages of living in a governed society, which provides him with law and order and, nowadays, a whole range of goods and services. In a liberal democracy government is held accountable to citizens by means of regular free elections, in which citizens choose between competing parties of politicians. As a government has to win majority support, the electorate have recurrent opportunities to change the nature of the contract between themselves and the state. Markets are the arena where the choices of individual economic agents determine allocation and distribution; government is the prime embodiment of *collective choice*.

How the market allocates

The market serves to bring together buyers and sellers to enable them to engage in mutually advantageous exchanges. Given that individuals undertake exchange voluntarily, it is presumed that they must thereby be no worse off and that at least one party to the exchange is better off as a result. This, of course, assumes that individuals have enough information to assess accurately the net advantages of the exchange, and this would include an assessment of the risks associated with the contract. It is also based on the value judgement that individuals are the best judge of their own welfare. The efficiency of market allocation is in question if either of these assumptions is judged not to hold. [. . .].

Adapted from R. Levačić, *Economic Policy Making* (Brighton: Wheatsheaf, 1987), pp. 112–13, 118–28, 133–8.

The *competitive market* is advocated because it is held to promote efficiency in resource allocation and the liberty of the individual citizen. Certain individuals also do well out of market distribution. [. . .]

Efficiency provides one important criterion against which to assess how well markets or government perform their allocative function with respect to different types of goods and services. If the market does not achieve an efficient allocation of resources there is said to be *market failure*. Three main sources of *market failure* are generally distinguished. These are *externalities*, *imperfect competition* and *inadequate information*.

Market failure due to externalities

[. . .] An *externality* occurs when the actions of one economic agent affect the welfare of others in a way that is not reflected in market prices. An *external cost* arises from coal burning for example because the emission of sulphur dioxide causes air pollution, for which the sufferers receive no compensation. Coal mining imposes costs on others because of subsidence, but this is not an external cost as British Coal is liable to pay compensation. The subsidence costs are incurred by British Coal and so are said to be internalized. Example of *external benefits* attributed to keeping open existing pits are the preservation of mining communities and the benefits to future generations of having cheaply worked coal seams left to them. (The problem with the concept of external costs and benefits is that while they undoubtedly exist, almost anything can, with a bit of imagination, be classified as a cost or benefit.)

The *social costs* of an activity are its *private costs* – those costs incurred directly by the agent undertaking the activity – plus any *external costs* associated with it. Similarly the *social benefits* of an activity are the *private benefits* accruing to the agent engaged in the activity plus any *external benefits*. Private benefits and costs are reflected in market prices. For instance, the private costs of providing air travel are indicated by the price of air tickets. Consumers indicate the extent to which they value air travel by the price they are willing to pay. But the external costs of air traffic noise to those living and working around airports are not included in the price of air tickets. If social costs and benefits differ from private costs and benefits, then the market will fail to transmit the correct information about the costs and values attached to goods and services. The market will undervalue goods that yield social benefits in excess of private benefits and will consequently produce too few of these goods. Similarly the market overvalues goods which have social costs in excess of private costs. The price of such goods is less than it would be if producers had to take account of the external costs associated with the production of the good. Consequently, consumers demand more of the good than if its price reflected all social costs and so too much of the good is produced. Thus *discrepancies between social costs and benefits and private costs and benefits mean, that market allocation is socially inefficient.*

The existence of externalities gives government a role in trying to correct for market failure. There are three main sets of instruments government can use: taxes and subsidies to private firms, regulation and public sector production. Goods with external costs, such as cigarettes, can be taxed in order to induce consumers to buy less. Additional output of goods which yield external benefits can be obtained by giving subsidies to private sector firms for producing them. Or those suffering external costs can be compensated: grants towards double glazing near airports is an example. Alternatively the government can try to produce the goods in the public sector in socially efficient quantities. [. . .] Legal prohibition is an important way of either preventing individuals and firms from creating external costs, or forcing the perpetrators to internalize the cost and so reflect them in market prices. Planning regulations, pollution controls, speed and weight restrictions on roads, are all methods of reducing external costs. For example, the proposed EC limits on car exhaust emissions will require more expensive car engines or catalytic converters, so internalizing the cost of air pollution by making motorists pay for preventive action.

But government intervention is not the only way to cope with the problem of socially inefficient resource allocation due to externalities. Private collective action is possible and does occur. For instance volunteer groups create external benefits by improving the appearance of the environment, through best-kept village competitions or reclaiming old canals. Local residents could band together and pay a local firm to reduce air or water pollution. The justification for government action on efficiency grounds is that the costs of organizing private sector collective action are too great for this to occur in many cases.

Collective goods

A further dimension to the externality problem concerns goods which yield external benefits from which people enjoying them cannot be excluded. Common examples are national defence, and law and order. Everybody living in a country obtains the benefits (or disbenefits in the case of pacifists) of national defence and cannot be excluded from them. Street lighting and roads are another example, for although it is physically possible to exclude users unless they pay a charge, it is prohibitively expensive to do so, except for roads in great demand like motorways and major bridges. There are other goods which are held in common ownership, such as the air, the sea and common land, which it is difficult to prevent people from using because *property rights* in them are not assigned to individual owners. However the benefits of these goods held in common ownership are largely private, like using air to discharge smoke, taking fish from the sea, or grazing animals on common land. Goods that yield benefits, either external or private, from which it is difficult or costly to exclude consumers are termed *non-excludable*, in contrast to goods like food, clothing or housing from which people can be easily excluded unless they pay for them. So goods which yield either private or external benefits, or some combination of both, are further characterized by whether they are *excludable* or *non-excludable*.

Some goods with external benefits, from which it is difficult to exclude people, possess a further characteristic: the consumption of their benefits by one person does not reduce the amount available for others. This characteristic is known as non-rivalry in consumption. Defence again has this characteristic since the consumption of the benefits of a national deterrent by one individual does not in general reduce the amount available for others. The same is true of TV and radio channels. One person's reception of them does not reduce the ability of others to receive them. There are many goods which are partly *non-rivalrous* in consumption. Roads are one example. An additional vehicle on a quiet road does not reduce the amount of road space available for others. On a busy road, though, an extra car adds to congestion and so reduces the benefits other motorists are enjoying. Parks, golf courses, and concerts can all, up to a point, be consumed by additional users without detracting from the enjoyment of other users. In contrast, other goods, like food, electricity, the use of a personal computer, are *rivalrous* in consumption. Their consumption by one individual reduces the amount available for others. Goods which are completely *rivalrous*, by definition, cannot yield external benefits. Some goods can give private and external benefits. Education, for example, benefits those who receive it because it enhances their employment prospects or because they enjoy studying, but it is also held to yield external benefits in producing a socialized, literate and informed citizenry. These external benefits are enjoyed by all and so are non-rivalrous.

So there are two characteristics, *excludability* and *rivalry in consumption*, that we can use to classify goods. This gives the fourfold classification set out in Table 1. Goods which are *rivalrous* in consumption and *excludable*, are called *private goods*. Goods which are *non-excludable* and *rivalrous* in consumption are termed *common goods*. Those which are *non-rivalrous* in consumption – at least until congestion occurs – and *excludable*, such as road tunnels, motorways or parks, are called *toll goods* in Table 1, since it is feasible to charge for them. Finally, goods which are both *non-excludable* and *non-rivalrous* are known as *public goods*. It is important to appreciate that goods do not fall neatly into one of the four cells in Table 1. Rather, *excludability/non-excludability* and *rivalry/non-rivalry* in consumption vary along a spectrum.

In fact there are very few goods that are *pure public goods*; that is, goods that yield benefits from which nobody can be excluded and for which the amount the individual can consume does not diminish as the number of consumers increases. Take defence, for example: the dispatch of the Task Force to the Falkland Islands in 1982 diminished the Navy's capacity to defend mainland Britain. Given the few nuclear shelters that

Table 1 *Private, common, public and toll goods*

	Rivalry in consumption	Non-rivalry in consumption
Excludable	Private goods e.g. 1ood, houses	Toll goods e.g. golf courses, motorways
Non-excludable	Common goods e.g. fisheries, wild animals	Public goods e.g. defence, public health

exist in the UK, most people would be excluded from them. So this aspect of defence is quite close to being a private good as it is excludable and rivalrous, hence some households build their own shelters. While pure public goods are hard to find, there are many goods with a considerable *public goods element*: they yield external benefits from which it is costly to exclude people and are, to a degree, non-rivalrous in consumption.

The importance of this taxonomy of goods as *private*, or having a *collective* element (this embraces common, public and toll goods) is to determine whether markets will provide an *allocatively efficient* quantity of each type of good. In the case of private goods there are no significant external costs or benefits associated with their production and use and hence the market system can be efficient. In a *competitive market* the good's price will reflect both the cost of producing it, in terms of foregone alternatives, and its value to consumers. Hence a *competitive market* will produce a *socially efficient* quantity of *private goods*.

However the market will not provide a sufficient quantity of *public goods*. This is because people can obtain the non-excludable benefits of public goods without paying for them. [. . .]

Because its benefits are non-excludable, anybody providing a public good will find it difficult to get the other beneficiaries to pay for it. This is known as the *free-rider* problem. The social benefits of a public good are the sum total of the benefits enjoyed by all individuals, but because there are many beneficiaries, the benefit to each individual will be quite small. An individual cannot enlarge his benefit by producing the good and charging others for using it, because of the *free-rider* problem. So a private sector agent will only provide a public good if his private benefits exceed the costs of producing the good. Consequently too little of a public good will be produced by the market. Collective provision by government can solve the problem as the government has the power to tax everybody in order to finance the provision of public goods. The nature of public goods explains why defence and law and order were the first areas where government provision became dominant. It also explains why the bulk of basic research, which provides technical knowledge that is non-rivalrous in use and largely non-excludable, is funded by governments. However, because of the problems of discovering how much people value public goods, it is virtually impossible for government to determine the most socially efficient quantity of public goods.

Because *toll goods* can be made excludable, they may be provided by a variety of private sector organizations, such as profit-maximizing firms or clubs and associations. Toll bridges, roads and canals were privately provided in the eighteenth century. Collective provision of services can be organized privately as in the case of golf clubs and motoring associations. However, collective provision is also provided by government which may charge a zero toll and finance the good out of tax revenues. This is how roads are funded and charged for in Britain, while in France and in parts of the USA tolls are charged for motorways. State provision of toll goods is justified on efficiency grounds if exclusion is relatively costly to enforce or too little of the good is consumed because people are excluded from using a good which is non-rivalrous in consumption.

The opposite problem arises with *common goods*: too much is consumed if there is no collective agreement to desist. Seas are overfished, pastures overgrazed, wild animals hunted to near extinction, or smoke-released into the atmosphere, because it is not in the interests of one individual to reduce his consumption if others do not. The benefits of a single individual's restraint are experienced by all users and become negligible private benefits. The allocative outcome is inefficient because the social costs of depletion and usage exceed the social benefits from the extra consumption. One solution is to allocate *property rights* over the resources, so that the cost of the individual's use of them falls only on the individual. This is possible with land, but not feasible for seas and even less so for the atmosphere. Users can reach their own collective agreements on usage, but these may be costly to organize and enforce. Hence there is a role for government collective action to improve the efficiency of resource allocation by negotiating and enforcing regulations regarding the use of common goods. Examples are controls over the release of pollutants into rivers, seas and the atmosphere and international agreements between governments, as in the case of fishing limits and quotas or nuclear test ban treaties.

Providing collective goods

Government *allocation* with respect to public and toll goods need not involve public sector *production* of the goods in question. There is a considerable variety of ways in which such goods are financed and provided by a combination of private and public sector activity and different practices can be observed around the world. Government can perform any one of three functions with respect to public and toll goods: arranging for their provision, financing their provision, and undertaking the actual production.

Take broadcasting for example. Radio and TV waves are public goods in that the reception of signals is non-rivalrous and it is difficult to exclude consumers once they have reception equipment. However the use of radio and TV wave frequencies for transmitting programmes from the earth is rivalrous. So at a minimum government needs to arrange for broadcasting to be undertaken by allocating and enforcing private sector property rights in these frequencies. In Britain these are allocated administratively to the BBC while independent broadcasters compete for franchises to operate programme channels and pay a levy for their use. The state also produces broadcasting services via the BBC but does not finance them. The private sector finances broadcasting either through the BBC TV licence or via advertising on independent TV and radio. The government tackles the free-rider problem with respect to the financing of BBC services by legal means. The alternative would be for the government to finance the state provision of broadcasting through general taxation. Another alternative would be for the state to pay private sector firms to produce TV and radio programmes.

The point is that various combinations of government and private sector organization, finance and production are possible. From a social efficiency point of view, the methods chosen in any specific instance should be determined by efficiency considerations. This would mean a bias to methods which give consumers a way of registering their preferences and those which encourage competition amongst suppliers. Privatization need not mean that the government no longer affects how a good is produced and distributed. Government can hand over the production of a good to the private sector while still financing it, as with refuse collection or cleaning and maintaining public sector buildings.

Market failure due to imperfect competition

[. . .] Markets need to be competitive if they are to allocate resources efficiently. The *degree of competition* in a market is an imprecise concept, as it depends on those factors which force firms to take account of the possibility that their business will be lost to rivals if they do not satisfy their customers. The larger the number of firms already supplying a market and the more difficult it is for them to collude, the more competition there is likely to be. Competition is also related to the likelihood that new suppliers will enter the market if they perceive profit opportunities because the existing suppliers charge high prices or are *x-inefficient* and have high costs.

In order for markets to be *allocatively efficient*, prices must correctly reflect the *opportunity costs* of goods. This will not occur if lack of competition enables firms to keep their prices above the lowest attainable costs of production. There are two ways in which this can occur. [. . .] One is that firms with *market power* will maximize their profits by charging prices in excess of *marginal costs*. As a consequence not enough of the good is produced. As price is in excess of marginal cost, consumers would value additional units of the product more highly than goods being currently produced with the resources that could be reallocated to the monopolized product. But rather than extract monopoly profits, firms can enjoy their market power by operating with higher costs so being *x-inefficient*. This also leads to higher prices for consumers.

Firms producing and selling output are not the only sources of market or monopoly power. It can be possessed by other types of seller, or by buyers if a few of them dominate the market. Trade unions exist in order to increase the market power of labour as otherwise most workers would face competition from other workers offering to work for lower wages or worse conditions. Many labour markets are now characterized by counter-vailing market power; there is bilateral bargaining between unions and large firms or employers' organizations.

Nationalization and regulation of natural monopolies

The kinds of measure governments can adopt to combat the problem of allocative inefficiency due to imperfect competition depend for their efficacy on the reasons for the lack of competition. Some markets are inherently monopolistic because of the nature of the production process. Industries like gas, electricity, telephone and water supplies are regarded as *natural monopolies* because duplicating their supply networks is extremely costly. One solution to the allocative efficiency problem posed by natural monopolies is public ownership, as in Britain in the postwar period. The main problem with this solution is that a public sector monopoly can be as x-inefficient as a private sector one, and may be more so, as the market sanction of bankruptcy has been removed.

An alternative solution, practised in the USA, is to keep the industries in the private sector but to *regulate* their performance in terms of such variables as profits, prices and quality of service, via special agencies. For instance, when the government sold British Telecom to private shareholders in 1984, it set up the Office of Telecommunications as the *regulatory agency* and limited the permitted rise in telephone charges to 3 per cent below the rate of inflation. There is another regulatory agency [. . .] for British Gas. [. . .] However the problem with regulation, as US experience testifies, is that the regulatory agency can become captured by the political interests of the industry it is regulating and fail to act as the guardian of consumers' interests. Furthermore, limits on profit rates dull the firm's incentive to reduce costs, as it gets no advantage in the form of higher profits, and so does little to combat x-inefficiency.

Competition policy

If the industry is not a natural monopoly then in order to promote allocative efficiency the appropriate policy for government is to remove *barriers to competition* in the marketplace. Left to their own devices, sellers have an incentive to reduce competition in order to increase prices and profits and diminish uncertainty about the actions of rivals. Firms can collude to fix prices, to restrict sales outlets, to enforce tie-in sales or refrain from advertising, to mention just some of the *restrictive practices* by which firms and labour organizations reduce competition between existing sellers and erect *barriers to entry* from new competition. Buyers can also collude to strengthen their position *vis-à-vis* sellers. Under British and EC law various types of restrictive practice are illegal and firms are kept under surveillance by the Office of Fair Trading and the Competition Directorate of the European Commission. The Office of Fair Trading can investigate uncompetitive practices, both by individual firms and associations of firms, and put pressure on them to desist, or recommend government to outlaw specific practices. The [. . .] abandonment of the opticians' monopoly of spectacles is one such instance. Another form of competition policy is to remove obstacles to competition from foreign firms, by reducing or eliminating import tariffs and quotas, or technical standards and government purchasing contracts which favour domestic firms.

Competition policy is generally restricted to measures applying to firms and the professions, such as solicitors, architects and doctors, and not to measures directed at trade unions. However legislation regarding the rights and duties of employers and the powers, responsibilities and liabilities of trade unions, greatly affects the degree of competition in labour markets. For instance [. . .] minimum wages laws prevent wages from falling due to competition from unemployed workers. The Thatcher government [. . .] reduced trade union power by limiting closed-shop agreements and making unions liable to civil court actions in specified circumstances, such as secondary picketing. Widely interpreted, competition policy embraces a great variety of methods by which governments influence the operations of buyers and sellers on all forms of markets. Nor is government policy in general biased towards increasing competition: it often has the reverse effect because policies are brought in for other reasons than promoting allocative efficiency, as discussed later in the chapter.

Market failure due to inadequate information

The final type of *market failure* to be considered is that due to the market producing and transmitting insufficient *information*. The market participants are unable to undertake all the mutually advantageous exchanges that would be entered into if buyers and sellers possessed the requisite information. The market therefore does not produce a *socially efficient* allocation of resources. Many types of informational failure have been suggested, as this form of market failure has proved a fruitful source for critics of market allocation.

If market allocation is to be efficient, then the buyers and sellers must have enough information to be able to undertake voluntary exchanges that improve their welfare. Given that the outcome of market transactions is inevitably uncertain, though some transactions are more uncertain than others, the amount of information required for exchange to be efficient cannot be precisely established, leaving plenty of scope for argument. Consumer protection laws are justified on efficiency grounds, in order to prevent consumers making unwise decisions because of insufficient knowledge of firms' products. Products are obliged to meet specified safety standards and firms are required to inform consumers of the conditions attached to the sale of goods. Similarly, health and safety legislation can be designed to protect workers from agreeing to work in conditions which they do not realize are unsafe. Some of these regulations may not promote efficiency but be justified on paternalistic grounds: workers are held not to be the best judges of their own interests and so are prevented by law from taking risks they would voluntarily undertake for money.

Market failure due to informational inadequacies provides the underlying theoretical rationale for *Keynesian macroeconomic policy* as a cure for unemployment. In Keynesian analysis the labour market fails to clear: the supply of labour remains in excess of the demand for labour because market forces cannot bring about equilibrium. Because workers are unemployed, their incomes are low and so *aggregate demand* for goods is depressed. The market mechanism fails to provide a means whereby workers can signal to firms that they would demand more goods and services if only they could get jobs and so have more money to spend. Firms decline to take on more labour because the effective demand for their goods is deficient. So the government can correct for this type of market failure by increasing aggregate demand, either by spending more itself or by getting the private sector to increase its spending, through tax cuts or an expansion in the money supply and lower interest rates. However critics of Keynesian economics consider that labour markets would clear if government and institutional impediments to greater flexibility were removed.

Another source of informational inadequacy concerns uncertainty about the future. It is argued that private sector firms are too risk-averse and too concerned with short-term profits. Consequently they underinvest in long-term projects which take many years before they yield a positive return. It is further argued that financial markets fail to reflect the collective rate at which society wants to save and invest. Thus interest rates may be too high and so discourage investment, while what finance there is for investment is channelled into socially inefficient uses. According to these critics the government should put into effect society's desire to invest more so as to promote growth. Because of the scale of its command over resources, the government can spread its risks over many projects and so is justified in undertaking more investment in research and development than would occur if left to the private sector. These arguments have been used to buttress a wide range of government investments, such as

Concorde, nuclear reactors, BL vehicles, microelectronics and computers. This rationalization for state intervention on efficiency grounds presupposes that government can determine the socially desirable rate of investment and innovation, and that it can take a dispassionate, long-term view of these investment possibilities, rather than make short-run responses to the demands of political interests.

[. . .]

Government failure

Although markets fail to achieve the most *socially efficient* allocation of resources or to distribute welfare according to subjective principles of *social justice*, there is no automatic guarantee that government action will improve matters, especially when the net effect of uncoordinated policies is taken into account. Much of this lack of coordination is inevitable, given the problems of acquiring information on the effects of policy measures and the impossibility, in a pluralist democracy, of taking highly centralized decisions over the whole range of state responsibilities. The concept of *government failure* mirrors that of *market failure* and encompasses a number of reasons why government is also unlikely to allocate resources with maximum social efficiency or sometimes to achieve the objective of equitable distribution sought from specific policies.

Information problems

If markets fail to allocate resources efficiently because of the existence of *externalities*, then the first prerequisite for efficient government intervention is making good the market's informational failures. To apply the social efficiency criterion the government needs information on *social costs* and *benefits*. Given that the market has failed to produce the information, government decision-makers are faced with the problem of valuing social costs and benefits from evidence other than direct market prices. [. . .] The social efficiency decision rule, that the optimal quantity of a good is produced when the amount it adds to social benefits (its marginal social benefit) equals the amount it adds to social costs (its marginal social cost) is difficult to apply. The best that can be hoped for is that government intervention improves the social efficiency of resource allocation, rather than achieving optimality.

Imperfect competition

It is in the interests of particular groups of buyers and sellers to restrict *competition* between themselves. Their ability to do this is highly dependent on specific regulations affecting their markets and on the attitude of government to their uncompetitive practices. These interests try to persuade government and the general public that the restrictions on competition in their markets is in the public interest and is worthy of state support. Many professional associations, for example, ban advertising by their members and impose other restrictions on competition, arguing that this is in the interests of their customers. Some of these practices are protected by legal sanctions, as was, until recently, the reservation of house conveyancing for solicitors. [. . .]

There is no general consensus on the beneficial effects of competition on resource allocation in all circumstances. The legal limitations placed on trade unions and the extent to which particular markets should be protected from foreign competition are two particularly contentious areas. [. . .] Government-sanctioned restrictions on competition permeate the economy. The extent to which they actually promote social efficiency (because of externalities or informational failures of markets) or other social goals is hotly contested. Certainly for advocates of market allocation, government is a major source of imperfect competition which unjustifiably impedes voluntary exchanges between individuals and contributes to social inefficiency.

Bureaucratic self-interest

How well public sector employees perform in providing the goods and services their customers and clients want depends on the system of incentives and sanctions within which they operate. An important factor that affects this is the degree of *competition* from rival suppliers. As already noted, the absence of strong market pressures on public corporations with monopoly power weakens the incentives to keep costs at their feasible minimum. *X-inefficiency* can be even more of a problem in organizations producing *non-marketed goods*, like health and education, where it is extremely difficult to measure efficiency and where alternative sources of supply are not readily available, except to the affluent.

X-inefficiency can result if bureaucrats pursue their own self-interest, rather than the objectives of the electorate or the politicians, or of the clients being directly served by the organization. In the absence of markets, the problem is to devise a means whereby state bureaucrats will respond to the preferences of those they are supposed to serve. A whole range of behaviour is subsumed under the umbrella of bureaucratic self-interest. Laziness, self-aggrandizement or status-seeking will all lead to the inefficient production of public sector output. Even more laudable behaviour, such as the pursuit of specific professional goals, can operate against the interests of the clients for whom the service is provided and the taxpayers who finance it. Doctors' desires to advance specialisms that they find intellectually exciting, university lecturers pursuing research at the expense of their teaching commitments, engineers wishing to develop technologically advanced products such as Concorde, are just a few examples of the kind of professional aspirations that lead to the misallocation of resources from the clients' or taxpayers' point of view.

As public sector managers often benefit in terms of status, pay and conditions from the size of their bureaucracy, they will attempt to produce more of a non-marketed good than its customers would buy if they had to pay a price which reflected the cost of the good. The pursuit of self-interest by government employees results in allocative inefficiency and the subversion of the social goals that are sought via state collective action. [. . .]

However, human motivation is complex: people are not entirely driven by the desire for money or to do as little in the job as they can get away with. Many are attracted to public sector work by the desire to help others. The adherence to professional standards and the desire to do a job well are motives that induce workers to serve their employers and customers well. The problem of devising systems of incentives and sanctions that promote good performance from workers and managers is by no means unique to the public sector. Competitive markets provide one such system and their absence necessitates other institutional devices.

Political interests

Yet another problem in securing efficient resource allocation by means of government, is the influence of political interests on allocative decisions. [. . .] In a *pluralist* system [. . .] a wide range of political interests influence decision-making. Political decisions emerge from the interaction of groups who have conflicting objectives as well as mutually advantageous bargains to make with each other. [. . .] The decision-makers have no agreed set of objectives or common definition of social welfare. Pluralist political decision-making also contrasts with decisions taken by non-political units, such as households or firms, where the decision-makers are much more likely to have a common set of objectives and so are able to follow *rational* decision-making procedures. Because decision-makers in the political arena have conflicting objectives, policy measures are not chosen with a view to maximizing some conception of social welfare, but emerge as the result of implicit and explicit *bargaining* between the political interests. The resulting allocative decisions depend on the relative strengths of the political interests involved, the tactics they employ and on the chance influence of time and place. So although the pluralist decision-making system is widely supported as a process in which diverse political interests can wield influence, the outcomes of the political bargaining process are frequently allocatively inefficient or fail to promote social justice. [. . .]

3

Socialism, planning, and the market

Hans Breitenbach, Tom Burden and David Coates

In attempting to specify the features of a viable socialist economy we are
not embarking on entirely uncharted water, though there are surprisingly
few texts on which to draw, given the size and long history of the Western
socialist movements. [. . .] The Revolutionary Left since Marx's time has
normally been reluctant to specify in any great detail the nature of the
society it seeks to create. It has preferred instead to concentrate the bulk
of its intellectual energies on developing a critique of capitalism and the
bulk of its political energies on the devising of strategies for its removal.
With these preoccupations, the Left's vision of socialism has often been
negative in form: socialism is a society without the private ownership of
the means of production because private ownership is a key feature of
capitalism; socialism is a society free of private profit, because of the
centrality of private profit to a capitalist way of motivating economic life;
socialism is a society free of inequalities of class, because capitalism
systematically produces just those inequalities; socialism is a society
without politics of a class kind because this is the normal form taken by
politics under capitalism. Put this way, the socialist alternative is to be
understood as the antithesis of capitalism, but such an understanding is
hardly prescriptive of a specific form of social and economic organization.

Socialism in its Eastern European sense has come to be understood as
a society whose economy is centrally planned, whose major industrial
plant and equipment is state-owned, and where state power is monopolized by a single party. On that model, the use of the market for the
allocation of investment goods, the toleration of any private ownership of
the means of production, and the persistence of liberal democratic
political institutions and conventions are all seen as features of capitalist
societies, not of socialist ones. Yet it is precisely those features of the
capitalist West which social-democratic forms of socialism have been
determined to retain as central to their specification of an ideal socialist
society. For socialists of this persuasion, their model society has required
little more than the superimposition of a substantial state sector on to
societies characterized by markets, private ownership and liberal

Adapted from H. Breitenbach et al., *Features of a Viable Socialism* (Brighton: Harvester
Wheatsheaf, 1990), pp. 13–19.

democracy. That state sector has been made up of nationalized industries, and of extensive welfare services provided on the basis of need, and not on the basis of the ability to pay. This model of socialism has involved some limited changes in economic ownership, but in practice has invariably amounted to little more than state direction of predominantly privately owned economic activity, and the maintenance of some minimum standards of social provision for all.

As both those particular models of socialism have lost credibility, a debate has opened on the possibility of an alternative definition of the socialist goal – one that occupies a space somewhere between regulated capitalism and centrally planned state socialism, and one that finds a new balance of the strengths and weaknesses of planning and the market. That debate has already generated a number of very sophisticated position-statements, each of which contains a different interplay of the plan and the market. [. . .] What we have chosen to do here is to use a report on the general character of the current debate to clarify certain of the key issues that have to be resolved in the design of a socialist economy.

Socialism and markets

The case against markets

The standard Marxist critique of market relationships under capitalism has long been that what Marx called 'the noisy sphere of exchange' constitutes an illusory area of equality and freedom, one that helps to stabilize capitalism by obscuring the uneven distribution of power between social classes in the more basic sphere of social production. Under capitalism the market serves to 'fetishize commodities'. When in market exchange under capitalism something is treated as a commodity, whether it is labour or goods, the fact that it appears simply as 'a thing with a price' obscures the exploitative social relationships within which it has been produced. From a Marxist viewpoint, market exchange under capitalism may appear as an area of individual freedom and choice; but in reality the commodities exchanged there constitute an alienated and uncontrolled social force whose existence dominates rather than liberates the lives of those who produce them.

To this rather philosophical critique have then been added arguments about the economic inadequacies of markets. The use of markets for economic allocation in a capitalist system has been seen to possess the following drawbacks:

1. Markets only work at the cost of perennial insecurity for producers. They allow the economically strong to drive out the economically weak, and so generate monopoly power which robs workers and consumers of any effective economic control.

2. Markets intensify economic inequality and add to the numbers of the poor.
3. Markets produce unavoidable economic cycles of expansion and contraction.
4. Markets do not ensure that producers respond to human needs, only to the needs of those who have the necessary purchasing power.

It is argued that markets necessarily coordinate demand and supply *ex post* rather than *ex ante*. In an economic system coordinated solely by markets there is no guarantee that what is produced can be sold. Individuals act within markets unaware of the cumulative consequences of their individually rational responses to the information at their disposal; and neither historical experience nor theoretical modelling has yet found a way of integrating those individually rational decisions through markets without creating cycles of boom and slump, unemployment and inflation.

Markets are also insensitive to what economists call 'externalities'. The only costs that figure automatically in capitalist market exchanges are those private costs of the immediate producers, their costs of raw material, labour and capital. The real costs of production (which include such things as the environmental damage characteristically associated with the desperate pursuit of profit, the stress to workers of their immersion in the capitalist labour process, and the social deprivation associated with poverty) do not figure in the cost systems to which market exchanges are responsive.

Finally, the case against markets often goes even further, to assert the basic incompatibility of markets and socialism. The claim here is not just that market coordination is necessarily anarchic. It is also that, even were it not, the reliance on competition between economic units inevitably generates individual/sectional self-interest, and so reproduces in a socialist economy the individualist attitudes and self-seeking practices characteristic of capitalism. In this argument, the use of competition to stimulate efficiency, innovation and consumer sensitivity in a socialist economy runs the risk of the effective reappearance of the private ownership of property, and the consequent draining of the socialist content from a market socialist system.

The case for markets

However, not all socialists take a negative view of the market. The idea of market socialism has appealed to economic reformers in Eastern Europe as a possible way of overcoming glaring problems of bureaucratic inefficiency and worker alienation evident in centrally planned economies. Many reformers in these states have become concerned with the role of plans and markets in socialist economies, with the way the state and political life should be organized, and with the kinds of property relationships compatible with socialism. Market socialism has also looked attractive to some socialists in the West, as a possible respecification of socialism worth struggling for in capitalist countries whose proletariats are now long used to high living standards and extensive consumer choice. In recent years Western socialists have formulated wide-ranging proposals for socialist economic organization in which markets play a key role.

The general case for markets is a long-established one, built around the following propositions:

1. Markets necessarily act as a powerful incentive to producers to operate as efficiently as possible in order to survive.
2. Markets force firms perpetually to develop new products and production processes.
3. Markets coordinate, without conscious human intervention, the literally millions of individual decisions made in a complex economy by a multiplicity of producers and consumers.
4. Markets allow individuals greater freedom of choice as producers and consumers than they can experience in any system of central planning.

Many non-socialist supporters of markets argue too that the pursuit of *ex ante* planning as a substitute for the *ex post* coordination of economic activity through the market cannot be achieved in a complex society and that its pursuit is actually destructive of very basic individual freedoms. They insist that planners do not and cannot have the scale and quality of knowledge and foresight to regulate prices and output effectively. They also argue that the waste of resources associated with the *ex post* coordination of supply and demand through markets is as nothing when set against the loss of production associated with the weak incentives of a planned economy and when compared to the inefficiency, bungling and corruption of every economic planning bureaucracy yet devised.

Socialist proponents of the use of markets do not suggest that markets can simply be retained, so long as private ownership of the means of production is abolished. Instead, they generally suggest some restrictions on their scope and some modifications of their operation. Pro-marketeers of a social democratic type have been prepared to manage markets: restricting the area of their use (keeping them out of such things as health care); moderating their tendency to generate inequality (by policies of income redistribution); and preserving some of the market's industrial casualties by nationalizing bankrupt firms and industries. More radical socialists have been prepared to go even further: either insisting that markets operate within a framework of planning, or even proposing that markets themselves be 'socialized', by inserting into them new institutions and procedures which will rob them of their tendencies to inequality and producer dominance.

Planning

Very few people on the Left these days advocate centralized and bureaucratized models of economic allocation. It is generally recognized now that a totally planned economy is no longer a desirable or viable option for socialists, in either the East or the West. A centralized planning system in which the centre communicates its requirements directly to the producing units can operate effectively only in brief moments of national emergency (with its associated national consensus on priorities). When centralized planning is used as the normal mode of economic control, a number of deficiencies loom into view:

1. It cannot cope with the vast complexity of modern economic systems without seriously blunting industrial efficiency and individual freedom of choice.
2. It creates a concentration of power in the hands of central state agencies, which jeopardizes individual freedom.
3. It is inherently vulnerable to bureaucratic stagnation and corruption.
4. It leads to the stimulation of a privately run black economy as its crucial lubricant.
5. It is prone to generate new social divisions of a hierarchical kind based on political or bureaucratic position.

These difficulties reinforce the view of many non-socialists that there is no alternative to purely market forms of economic allocation in a complex society. But many socialists, though increasingly aware of the difficulties associated with highly centralized and bureaucratized modes of planning, have tended to interpret these difficulties differently. They have seen them as evidence of the need for different kinds and structures of planning, rather than as evidence of the impossibility or undesirability of planning as such. Decentralization and democracy, local participation and negotiation, are all very much in vogue in models of contemporary socialist planning . . . and they remain in vogue because of a continuing recognition of the strengths, as well as the weaknesses of economic planning. There are a number of reasons why many socialists have argued strongly for the replacement of market mechanisms by state planning.

1. Planning can include social and environmental costs.
2. Planning can ensure high levels of income equality.
3. Planning can balance demand and supply *ex ante* rather than *ex post*, so avoiding substantial waste of resources.
4. Planning can remove the economic insecurity to which capitalism is prone.

These are the reasons why many socialists continue to insist that planning is still superior to the market. They remain certain that planning, when in the proper hands and organized in a proper way, can bring a degree of social responsibility, security of conditions, and avoidance of waste and duplication, that no market system of atomized competitive production units can ever hope to achieve.

4

Market process versus market equilibrium

Israel M. Krizner

[. . .] The focus of attention, in neo-classical price theory, is [. . .] on the *values of the price and quantity variables*, and in particular on the set of values consistent with *equilibrium* conditions. In investigating the consequences of a particular market structure, this approach examines the associated pattern of equilibrium prices, costs and outputs. In investigating the consequences of a particular change in taste, or technology and the like, it examines the equilibrium conditions after the change, comparing them with those before the change. The very efficiency of the market system as an allocator of society's resources is appraised by examining the allocation of resources at equilibrium. In investigating the desirability of particular government policies, this approach appraises the effects of the changes these policies will bring about in the equilibrium situation. In all this the emphasis is on the *prices* and *quantities* and, in particular, on these prices and quantities as they would emerge under *equilibrium* conditions.

By contrast, the Austrian approach to the theory of price [. . .] perceives its task in a significantly different way. The market is still, of course, seen as made up of the activities of the market participants – the consumers, producers, and factor owners. Their activities result from decisions to produce, to buy, and to sell commodities and resources. And once again there exists a pattern of decisions which are mutually consistent, so that all planned activities can be carried out without disappointment. Furthermore, this pattern of decisions is recognized as of very special interest because it makes up the state of equilibrium. *But it is not this equilibrium situation which is the focus of attention.* The task of price theory is not seen as primarily concerned with the configuration of prices and quantities that 'satisfies the conditions for equilibrium. [. . .]

Rather, in the Austrian approach [. . .] we look to price theory to help us understand how the decisions of individual participants in the market interact to generate the market forces which compel *changes* in prices, in outputs, and in methods of production and the allocation of resources.

Adapted from I.M. Krizner, *Competition and Entrepreneurship* (Chicago and London: University of Chicago Press, 1973), pp. 5–29.

We look to price theory to elucidate the nature of the mutual influence exercised by decisions so that we may understand how changes in these decisions, or in the data which underlie them, systematically set in motion further alterations elsewhere in the market. The object of our scientific interest is these alterations themselves, not (except as a matter of subsidiary, intermediate or even incidental interest) the relationships governing prices and quantities in the equilibrium situation.

From the normative point of view, too, the approach to price theory adopted here sees its function in a way that is not related in any essential manner to the state of affairs at equilibrium. The efficiency of the price system, in this approach, does not depend upon the optimality (or absence of it) of the resource allocation pattern at equilibrium; rather, it depends on the degree of success with which market forces can be relied upon to generate spontaneous corrections in the allocation patterns prevailing at times of disequilibrium.

As we will discover, this difference in the conceptions of the task and purpose of price theory has far-reaching implications for the methods and the substantive content of the alternative approaches. [. . .] The many important differences in analysis that separate the dominant approach from that of the Austrians are most neatly summed up as reflecting disagreement (possibly only implicit disagreement) concerning the aim of price theory in general. [. . .] With these basic considerations concerning the purpose of price theory in mind, let us survey the major theoretical issues. [. . .] Thereafter, we will return to further development of the contrast between a theory of equilibrium prices and a theory of the market process.

Competition and entrepreneurship

Much of our discussion will revolve around two notions crucial to an understanding of the market and central to its theory – *competition* and *entrepreneurship*. Both terms are widely used in the everyday speech of laymen concerning economic and business affairs. [. . .]

Competition, as many writers have told us, is a term that has been used in innumerable senses. Economists have worked with many different models, each marked with one form or another of the competitive label. Still central to much of contemporary price theory is the model of perfect competition. Despite all the criticisms showered on this model during the past forty years, it still occupies the center of the stage, both in positive and in normative discussions. The dissatisfaction with perfectly competitive theory produced new models dealing with various imperfectly competitive market structures, but these have not succeeded in dislodging the perfectly competitive model from its preeminent position. Much of the discussion here will have to do with all of these models. My position will be not only that the model of perfect competition fails to help us understand the market process, but that the models of imperfect competition developed to replace it are little more helpful. I will maintain that the theorists who developed these models of imperfectly competitive markets failed to recognize the really important shortcomings of the perfect competition theory. As a result they were unable to perceive the direction in which a genuine rehabilitation of price theory must be developed and proceeded instead to construct models which suffer from the very defects that invalidate the perfectly competitive model.

[. . .] A feature common to all these competitive models to which I am taking exception is their exclusion of the entrepreneurial element from the analysis. We will find that a useful understanding of the market process requires a notion of competition that is analytically inseparable from the exercise of entrepreneurship. [. . .] Our notions of competition and entrepreneurship will lead us to a quite unorthodox view of the nature of monopoly in a market. The fact that entrepreneurship may be a step toward monopoly power will call for a new evaluation of both the allegedly harmful effects of monopoly and the reputedly beneficial effects of entrepreneurship. It will be useful at this point to outline the picture of the market process which incorporates our views on competition and entrepreneurship, contrasting it briefly with the dominant concept of the market. [. . .]

The market process

We see the market as made up, during any period of time, of the interacting decisions of consumers, entrepreneur-producers, and resource owners. Not all the decisions in a given period can be carried out, since many of them may erroneously anticipate and depend upon other decisions which are in fact not being made. Again, many decisions which are successfully carried out in a given period may not turn out to have been the best possible courses of action. Had the decision-makers been aware of the choices others were making during the same period, they would have perceived opportunities for more attractive courses of market action than those actually adopted. In short, ignorance of the decisions which others are in fact about to make may cause decision-makers to make unfortunate plans – either plans that are doomed to disappointment or plans which fail to exploit existing market opportunities.

During the given period of time, exposure to the decisions of others communicates some of the information these decision-makers originally lacked. If they find that their plans cannot be carried out, this teaches them that their anticipations concerning the decisions of others were overly optimistic. Or they may learn that their undue pessimism has caused them to pass up attractive market opportunities. This newly acquired information concerning the plans of others can be expected to generate, for the succeeding period of time, *a revised set of decisions*. The overambitious plans of one period will be replaced by more realistic ones; market opportunities overlooked in one period will be exploited in the next. In other words, even without changes in the basic data of the market (that is, in consumer tastes, technological possibilities and resource availabilities), the decisions made in one period of time generate systematic alterations in the corresponding decisions for the succeeding period. Taken over time, this series of systematic changes in the interconnected network of market decisions constitutes the market process.

The market process, then, is set in motion by the results of the initial market-ignorance of the participants. The process itself consists of the systematic plan changes generated by the flow of market information released by market participation – that is, by the testing of plans in the market. As a matter of considerable theoretical interest we may investigate the possibility of a state of affairs in which *no* market ignorance is present. We would then have a pattern of perfectly dovetailing decisions. No decision made will fail to be carried out, and no opportunity will fail to be exploited. Each market participant will have correctly forecast all the relevant decisions of others. [. . .] Clearly, with such a state of affairs the market *process* must immediately cease. Without autonomous change in tastes, or in technological possibilities, or in the availability of resources, no one can have any interest in altering his plans for the succeeding period. The market is in equilibrium; the pattern of market activity will continue without change period after period. [. . .]

Competition in the market process

We have seen the market during any period of time as made up of decisions of market participants. These decisions, I said, presupposed corresponding decisions on the part of others. Consumers' decisions to buy depend on the decisions of entrepreneur-producers to sell. Decisions by resource owners to sell depend on the decisions of entrepreneur-producers to buy – and vice versa. Each pair of dovetailing decisions (each market transaction completed) constitutes a case in which each party is being offered an opportunity which, to the best of his knowledge, is the best being offered to him in the market. Each market participant is therefore aware at all times that he can expect to carry out his plans only if these plans do in fact offer others the best opportunity available, as far as they know. This is simply saying that each market participant, in laying his buying or selling plans, must pay careful heed not only to the prospective decisions of those to whom he hopes to sell or from whom he hopes to buy – as an implication of the latter – also to the prospective decisions of others whose decisions to sell or to buy may compete with his own.

And as the market process unfolds, with one period of market ignorance followed by another in which ignorance has been somewhat reduced, each buyer or seller revises his bids and offers in the light of his newly acquired knowledge of the alternative opportunities which those to whom he may wish to sell, or from whom he may wish to buy, can expect to find available elsewhere in the market. In this sense the market process is inherently *competitive*. The systematic alteration in decisions between each period and the succeeding one renders each opportunity offered to the market more competitive than that offered in the preceding period – that is, it is offered with fuller awareness of the other opportunities being made available, against which it is necessary to compete.

[. . .] In the course of the market process the participants are continually testing their competitors. Each inches ahead by offering opportunities a little more attractive than theirs. His competitors, in turn, once they become aware of what *they* are competing against, are forced to sweeten still further the opportunities they make available to the market; and so on. In this struggle to keep ahead of one's competitors (but at the same time to avoid creating opportunities more attractive than necessary), market participants are thus forced by the competitive market process to gravitate closer and closer to the limits of their ability to participate gainfully in the market. Competition between consumers for a given commodity may, for example, tend to force its price upward; each consumer is careful not to consume beyond the point where the marginal purchase is just worthwhile; during the process, those who are less eager consumers of marginal units drop out of the race earlier. Competition among the owners of a particular resource may tend to force its price downwards; those owners for whom its sale involves the greater sacrifices will tend to drop out of the race as the falling price makes it worthwhile for them to sell only fewer and fewer units of the resource.

Were this competitive process to run its course to completion – in other words, were all decisions to become fully dovetailed – each participant would no longer be under pressure to improve the opportunities he is currently offering to the market, since no one else is offering more attractive opportunities [. . .] It is unnecessary, under these circumstances, for any participant to inch ahead of his competitors (in the attractiveness of opportunities offered), since all current plans can be carried out in the market without disappointment. This situation of market equilibrium is surely one in which competition is no longer an active force. The cessation of the market process which we have already seen as characteristic of the equilibrium state is the cessation of a *competitive* process. [. . .]

Entrepreneurship in the market process

Essential to the notion of the market process as I have described it is the acquisition of market information through the experience of market participation. The systematic pattern of adjustments in market plans which makes up the market process arises, as we have seen, from the market participants' discovery that their anticipations were overly

optimistic or unduly pessimistic. It can be shown that our confidence in
the market's ability to learn and to harness the continuous flow of market
information to generate the market process depends crucially on our belief
in the benign presence of the entrepreneurial element.

To see this, let us imagine a market in which all those currently
participating are in fact *unable* to learn from their market experience.
Would-be buyers who have been returning home empty-handed (because
they have not been offering sufficiently high prices) have *not* learned that
it is necessary to outbid other buyers; would-be sellers who return home
with unsold goods or resources (because they have been asking prices that
are too high) have *not* learned that they must, if they wish to sell, be
satisfied with lower prices. Buyers who have paid high prices do not
discover that they could have obtained the same goods at lower prices;
sellers who have sold for low prices do not discover that they could have
obtained higher prices. Into this imaginary world of people unable to
learn from their market experience let us now introduce a group of
outsiders who are themselves neither would-by sellers nor would-be
buyers, but who *are* able to perceive opportunities for entrepreneurial
profits; that is, they are able to see where a good can be sold at a price
higher than that for which it can be bought. This group of entrepreneurs
would, in our imaginary world, immediately notice profit opportunities
*that exist because of the initial ignorance of the original market
participants* and that have persisted because of their inability to learn
from experience. They would move to buy at low prices from those sellers
who have not discovered that some buyers are paying high prices. And
they would then sell these goods at high prices to those buyers who have
not discovered that some sellers have been selling for low prices.

It is easy to perceive that so long as this group of entrepreneurs is active
in the market, and so long as they are alert to the changing prices their
own activity brings about, the market process can proceed in an entirely
normal fashion. These entrepreneurs will communicate to the other
market participants the market information which these other participants
are themselves unable to obtain. The competition between the various
entrepreneurs will move them to offer to buy from the low-price sellers,
at prices higher than these sellers had thought possible; entrepreneurs in
competition with one another will also sell to high-price buyers at prices
lower than these buyers had thought possible. Gradually, competition
between the entrepreneurs as buyers, and again as sellers, will succeed in
communicating to market participants a correct estimate of the other
market participants' eagerness to buy and to sell. Prices will move in
exactly the same way as they would move in a world in which buyers and
sellers *were* able to learn from their market experience.

Clearly then, it is not *necessary* for us, in constructing the analytical
model of a market in process, to postulate such a rigid compartmentaliza-
tion of roles. Instead of one group of market participants who do not
learn from experience and another (entrepreneurial) group who do, we

can work with market participants who *are* alert to changing buying and selling possibilities. The *process* will still remain an essentially entrepreneurial one, but instead of working with a group of 'pure' entrepreneurs, we could simply recognize an entrepreneurial aspect to the activities of each market participant.

The outcome is always the same: the competitive market process is essentially entrepreneurial. The pattern of decisions in any period differs from the pattern in the preceding period as market participants become aware of new opportunities. As they exploit these opportunities, their competition pushes prices in directions which gradually squeeze out opportunities for further profit-making. The entrepreneurial element in the economic behavior of market participants consists [. . .] in their alertness to previously unnoticed changes in circumstances which may make it possible to get far more in exchange for whatever they have to offer than was hitherto possible.

Our insights into the competitive nature of the market process and its entrepreneurial character teach us that the two notions of competition and entrepreneurship are, at least in the sense used here, analytically inseparable. [. . .] The key point is that *pure* entrepreneurship is exercised only in the *absence* of an initially owned asset. Other market roles invariably involve a search for the best exchange opportunities for translating an initially owned asset into something more eagerly desired. The 'pure' entrepreneur observes the opportunity to sell something at a price higher than that at which he can buy it. It follows that *anyone* is a potential entrepreneur, since the purely entrepreneurial role presupposes no special initial good fortune in the form of valuable assets. Therefore, whereas the market participation of asset owners is always to *some* extent protected (by the peculiar qualities of the assets possessed), the market activity of the entrepreneur is *never* protected in any way. The opportunity offered in the market by an asset owner cannot be freely duplicated or surpassed by just anyone; it can be duplicated only by another owner of a similar asset. In a world in which no two assets are exactly the same, no opportunity offered by an asset owner can be exactly duplicated. But if an entrepreneur perceives the possibility of gaining profit by offering to buy at a price attractive to sellers and by offering to sell at a price attractive to buyers, the opportunities he thus offers to the market can in principle be made available by anyone. The entrepreneur's activity is essentially competitive. And thus competition is inherent in the nature of the entrepreneurial market process. Or, to put it the other way around, entrepreneurship is inherent in the competitive market process.

The producer and the market process

The considerations outlined above are rather general. They would apply to a world in which no production is possible at all – a pure exchange economy – and they apply with equal validity to a world in which nature-given raw materials and labor are converted through production into consumer goods. [. . .] But it will be useful, especially in respect to future discussions on monopoly and on selling costs, to explain a little more specifically how the market process operates in a world of production.

Production involves converting resources into commodities. Therefore the market in a world of production is most simply seen as a network of decisions in which resource owners make plans to sell resources to producers, producers make plans to buy resources from resource owners in order to sell them (in the form of produced commodities) to consumers, and consumers make plans to buy commodities from producers. The producer, it turns out, need not initially be an asset owner. He may simply be an entrepreneur who perceives the opportunity to buy resources at a total cost lower than the revenue he can obtain from the sale of output. Even if the producer happens to be a resource owner, he is to be considered an entrepreneur with respect to the other resources he needs for production. And it is convenient to consider him as an entrepreneur even with respect to the resource he owns (in the sense that, in using it for his own production process, rather than selling it at its market price to other producers, he is 'buying' it at an implicit cost).

An interesting observation is relevant to this way of seeing the market in a world of production. I said in the preceding section that the market process is essentially entrepreneurial. [. . .] It turns out now that in the world of production we find ourselves endowed, as it were, with a built-in group of entrepreneurs – the producers. We have just seen that production involves a necessarily entrepreneurial type of market activity. It thus becomes highly convenient to view the market, in a world of production, *as if all* entrepreneurial activity were in fact carried on by producers; in other words, it now becomes convenient to think of resource owners and consumers as passive price-takers, exercising no entrepreneurial judgement of their own and simply reacting passively to the opportunities to sell and buy which the producer-entrepreneurs hold out to them directly. Of course this is only an analytical convenience, but it will simplify much of the discussion and will help lay bare the inner workings of the market in the complex world of production.

We see the producer, then, as one who perceives profit opportunities in the market, consisting in the availability of sellers who ask less than what buyers are willing to pay somewhere else in the market. In the production context, of course, what can be bought are resources, and what can be sold are products. [. . .]

In searching out these opportunities and exploiting them the producer is thus performing the entrepreneurial role in the market process. In this process the plans of consumers and of resource owners are gradually brought into greater and greater consistency with one another. Consumers' initial ignorance of the kinds of commodities technologically possible with currently available resources and of the relative prices at which these commodities can in principle be produced gradually diminishes. Resource owners' initial ignorance of the kinds of commodities consumers will buy and of the relative prices which can in principle be obtained for these commodities gradually diminishes. The new knowledge is acquired through changes in the prices of resources and of products, brought about by the bids and offers of the entrepreneur-producers who are eagerly competing for the profits to be won by discovering where resource owners and consumers have (in effect) underestimated each other's eagerness to buy or to sell. This process of bringing the plans of market participants into dovetailing patterns is, as we have seen, competitive. No one producer – in his role of entrepreneur – can ignore the possibility that a profit opportunity may be grabbed by another entrepreneur. After all, an entrepreneur needs no assets to engage in profitable market participation. A producer need not own any resources in order to engage in production; he merely has to know where to buy resources at a price that will make it worthwhile to produce and sell the product at its attainable price. Since, then, anyone can, at least in principle, be a producer (since no special natural or other endowment is necessary), the market process, which is channeled through the activities of the producers, is competitive. The question then arises, What are economists referring to when they talk of 'monopolistic markets'? And, in particular, What is to be understood by the term 'monopolistic producer'? Have we not seen that producers are entrepreneurs who can *never* be immune from the forces of competition?

Monopoly and the market process

[. . .]

A competitive process, I have said, proceeds because participants are engaged in an incessant race to get or to keep ahead of one another (where, as always, 'to be ahead' means 'to be offering the most attractive opportunities to other market participants'). Clearly, then, any circumstances which render a market participant immune from the necessity to keep ahead would not merely hamper competition, but also impede the course of the market process. But (and here was the apparent cause of difficulty) we have seen that entrepreneurship can *never* be immune from the competitive pressure. It thus *seems* that competition can never be absent from the market, and so the market process can never be impeded by its absence. Is there no possibility of an absence of competition? Is there no possibility of monopoly?

The answer must be that, in the sense in which we have used the term 'competition' (a sense which, although sharply divergent from the terminology of the dominant theory of price, is entirely consistent with everyday business usage), the market process is indeed always competitive, so long as there is freedom to buy and sell in the market. Nonetheless, there remains a definite place for monopoly within the framework of analysis we have developed. Entrepreneurship is necessarily open to all who wish to deal in the market; hence production, involving the purchase of resources and the sale of products, is necessarily competitive. But *resource ownership* may well be monopolistic in character, and where a resource is owned by a monopolist, this may have important implications for the course of production. It is as a result of resource monopoly that those important cases arise which in the language of the layman, the economist and the antitrust lawyer are called monopolistic production. Our own position will be to insist on the crucial distinction between the possibility of a monopolist producer *qua* producer (which, in our terminology, is ruled out almost by definition) and the possibility of a monopolist producer *qua* resource owner (which is very real and significant).

If nature has endowed a particular market participant with *all* the current endowment of a certain resource, he is in the fortunate position of being a monopolist resource owner. This may sharply affect the price of this resource and, as a further result, may affect the prices of other resources and products, as well as the entire pattern of production. But it is important to observe that the competitive character of the market process *has not been affected in the slightest*. The final equilibrium position toward which the market is tending may be drastically affected by monopoly resource ownership, but the process of bringing the decisions of market participants into more closely dovetailing patterns remains unchanged. All this does not at all mean that monopoly, within our framework of discussion has become less potentially dangerous or less important. But it does mean that in analysing the effects of what appear to be clear cases of monopoly, we know where to look for the source of the problem. Most important, this way of looking at things teaches us that if a producer controls the production of a given commodity he is a monopolist – if he is such – not by virtue of any entrepreneurial role, but as a result of a resource monopoly. As an immediate implication of this we distinguish very sharply between a producer who is the sole source of supply for a particular commodity because he has unique access to a necessary resource and one who is the sole source of supply as a result of his entrepreneurial activities (which can easily be duplicated by his competitors, if they choose). During the course of the market process the competitive efforts of a particular producer-entrepreneur may lead him to offer something to the market which no one else is currently producing. In our theory this is simply an example of the *competitive* process at work. It has nothing in common with cases in which a particular producer, by acquiring monopoly control over a resource, is able to maintain his position as sole source of supply indefinitely. The one case is an example of competitive entrepreneurship; the other is one of monopolistic resource ownership. Nonetheless, a very important possibility must be considered in which a monopolist producer has acquired monopoly control over one of his factors of production *by means of his entrepreneurial activities*.

The entrepreneur as monopolist

This possibility may arise very simply. A market participant with no initial assets perceives the possibility of making large profits by buying up all the available supply of a given resource, and then establishing himself as the monopolist producer of a particular commodity. His role, taking the long-range perspective, is clearly entrepreneurial (he had no initial assets), and thus competitive. (Since he had no initial asset endowment, anyone else could have done what he did; again, he was able to do what he did only because in so doing he was offering both to those from whom he bought and to those to whom he sells opportunities more attractive than those offered by others.) And yet, once his entrepreneurial resource purchase has been made, he is in the position of a producer who is a monopolist by virtue of being a resource owner. It seems, then, that not only may an entrepreneur-producer be a monopolist because he *happens* at the same time to be a monopolist resource owner, he may be a monopolist because he has made himself a monopolist resource owner *in the course of his entrepreneurial activities*.

If we recognize this possibility we may gain much valuable insight into the complex forces acting in the real world. Many real-world cases of what appears to be monopoly in production can be disentangled and understood in the light of the theoretical possibilities being examined here. [. . .] When one looks merely at the situation *after* the resource has been monopolized by the entrepreneurial skill of the producer, one sees only a monopolist producer – exempt from competition to the extent his resource monopoly permits. When one takes a longer-run view of the monopoly situation, one sees that it was won *by* competition, and that it represents, as such (and as far as it goes) a step forward in the entrepreneurial process of the market. This entrepreneur's capture of his monopoly position was a step toward eliminating the inconsistencies between the decisions of consumers and those of the earlier resource owners. The profits won by the producer, which in the short-run view seem clearly a monopoly rent attributable to the monopolized resource, turn out to be, in the long-run view, the profits of competitive entrepreneurship. This insight will be of great value in the normative analysis of monopoly situations.
[. . .]
Our discussion has shown that so long as the resources used by producers are accessible to all, all their activities are entrepreneurial-competitive. That one producer has expended resources in order to educate or manipulate consumer tastes may perhaps offend the ethical values of some observers of the market, and it is not a simple matter, on strictly scientific terms, to evaluate the effect of this kind of activity. But

so long as no resources used in 'selling' or in producing are owned
monopolistically, we are forced to conclude that this activity is essentially
competitive and cannot result in any kind of monopolistic control over
production or any impairment of the competitive process.

The fact that at any given moment only one producer is making a
particular product is not by itself an impairment of the competitive
process. It may simply mean that at this moment only one entrepreneur
has taken the step of presenting this particular opportunity to the market.
If the step is a wise one, it will tend to attract others to do even better
in this regard. If it proves to have been a mistake this entrepreneur
himself will be under market pressure to abandon this line of production.
Insofar as our interest is in the market process and its competitive
character, we should no more be surprised that only one producer is
making a product at a particular time than that of many producers of a
particular product one is charging a price which no other producer is
asking. Both possibilities may simply be evidence that the market process
has not yet run its course. [. . .]

Equilibrium economics, entrepreneurship and competition

We have already noticed earlier in this chapter that our disagreement with
the neo-classical theory of price centers in particular on its unsatisfactory
treatment of entrepreneurship and competition. [. . .]

In equilibrium there is no room for the entrepreneur. When the decisions of all market participants dovetail completely, so that each plan
correctly assumes the corresponding plans of the other participants and no
possibility exists for any altered plans that would be simultaneously
preferred by the relevant participants, there is nothing left for the
entrepreneur to do. He will be unable to discover possibilities of buying
from those who underestimated the eagerness of potential buyers and of
then selling to these eager buyers (who might in turn have underestimated
the eagerness of the sellers). Thus he cannot contribute to a reallocation
of resources or products that will overcome inefficiencies and lack of
coordination generated by market ignorance, since no such ignorance and
lack of coordination exist in equilibrium. [. . .]

Instead of the entrepreneur, the dominant theory of price has dealt with
the firm, placing the emphasis heavily on its profit-maximizing aspects. In
fact, this emphasis has misled many students of price theory to understand the notion of the entrepreneur as nothing more than the locus of
profit-maximizing decision-making within the firm. They have completely
overlooked the role of the entrepreneur in exploiting superior awareness
of price discrepancies within the economic system.

Emphasis on the firm (which in our view is to be seen as a combination
of entrepreneur and resource owner) also led to a failure to recognize the

significance of pure resource ownership in securing monopoly positions in production. Monopoly came to be associated with the firm and thus, most unfortunately, with the entrepreneur.

At the same, the emphasis on equilibrium hampered any possible appreciation of the notion of competition which we have seen to be the outstanding characteristic of the market process. By definition, a state of equilibrium does not permit activity designed *to outstrip* the efforts of others in catering to the wishes of the market. Thus, whatever the layman might mean by the term 'competition', the equilibrium theorist came to use it to connote a market in which each participant is too weak to effect any change in price. This is entirely understandable. If the attention of the theorist is focused upon a particular state of affairs – equilibrium – rather than upon the market process, the adjective 'competitive' cannot be used in the sense of the characteristic of a process. [. . .] Competition, to the equilibrium price theorist, turned out to refer to a state of affairs into which so many competing participants have already entered that no room remains for *additional* entry (or other modification of existing market conditions). The most unfortunate aspect of this use of the term 'competition' is of course that, by referring to the situation in which no room remains for further steps in the competitive market process, the word has come to be understood as the *very opposite* of the kind of activity of which that process consists. Thus [. . .] any real-world departure from equilibrium conditions came to be stamped as the opposite of 'competitive' and hence, by simple extension, as actually 'monopolistic.'

[. . .] Neo-classical theories failed to perceive that the characteristic features of the real world (to which nothing in the perfectly competitive model corresponds) are simply the manifestations of entrepreneurial competition, a process in which would-be buyers and sellers gropingly seek to discover each other's supply and demand curves. [. . .] In the course of attempting to account for such market phenomena as quality differentiation, advertising, or markets in which few producers are to be found [. . .] neo-classical theories were led to conclusions which grossly misinterpret the significance of these phenomena.

5

Markets and managerial hierarchies

Tony McGuinness

The aim of this chapter is to present and evaluate Oliver Williamson's theory of the firm. Before launching into the details of his explanation, however, it will be useful to state clearly what it is that is to be explained. This will help also to put Williamson's work in perspective in relation to past and contemporary ideas about the firm.

[. . .] Though firms in the real world, like markets involve a subtle mixture of control mechanisms, this chapter assumes that the essence of firm-type organization is the use made of authority to direct and coordinate resources. The object of the analysis is then to identify and explain in what circumstances the authoritarian direction of resources has advantage over market-type alternatives.

This definition of the essential nature of firm-type organization must not be confused with the idea that only authority is used to direct resources within firms that exist in the real world. The internal operations of real-world firms are controlled by a blend of authority and market-like mechanisms. This fact of life is reflected in recent economic analysis of the firm, which addresses the limits of authority and the options available *within* firms when direct supervision of a subordinate by a superior is difficult, perhaps because of information asymmetry. [. . .] In passing, it should be noted that the conceptual framework developed by Williamson claims to provide an explanation of organizational forms in general, in that it seeks to explain the circumstances in which a variety of institutional forms – including classical market contracts, non-standard market contracts, government regulatory agencies, and trades unions – have, in turn, a comparative advantage in the organization of resources.

Despite recognizing the need for theory to explain market-type control mechanisms within real-world firms, this chapter accepts that some use of direct, non-delegated authority is the necessary, defining feature of a firm, and turns to Williamson's work for an explanation of the circumstances in which it has a comparative advantage over other control mechanisms. Section 1 presents the general concepts used by him. Section 2 uses these concepts to explain when and why a market is replaced by an authority-based form of organization; why authority might be

Adapted from R. Clarke and T. McGuinness (eds) *The Economics of the Firm* (Oxford: Basil Blackwell, 1900), 42–59.

distributed and used in a hierarchical way; and when the authority to make certain kinds of decisions might be delegated within a hierarchy. [. . .]

Before proceeding with the details, it is worth pointing out that at least one influential modern article on the theory of the firm denies that authority is the essence of the firm. Alchian and Demsetz (1972: 777) state unequivocally: 'It is common to see the firm characterized by fiat, by authority, or by disciplinary action superior to that available in the conventional market. This is a delusion.'

From what has been said, this is not the view of this chapter. Nor is it consistent with Coase's (1937) attempt to define the abstract nature of the firm (author's emphasis):

> owing to the difficulty of forecasting [. . .] the less possible, and indeed, the less desirable it is for the person purchasing to specify what the other contracting party is expected to do [. . .] Therefore, the service which is being provided is expressed in general terms, the exact details being left until a later date [. . .] The details of what the supplier is expected to do is not stated in the contract but is decided later *by the purchaser*. When the direction of resources (within the limits of the contract) becomes dependent *on the buyer* in this way, the relationship which I term a 'firm' may be obtained.

The interpretation of this statement here is that the contractual arrangements that define the firm are left open-minded, with the details of resource direction to be decided later by a member (or members) of the firm in whom authority is voluntarily vested. [. . .] It is perhaps no coincidence that only when one is prepared to recognize that the firm is based on authority do issues of power come to the fore in the theory of the firm.

1 Concepts

This section discusses the concepts used by Williamson in his analysis of the firm. The problems and costs of organizing transactions depend on both their nature and the assumed characteristics of decision-makers in the model. In addition, the way in which they are organized is determined, at least in a competitive environment, by the principle of economizing on transaction costs. The aim of the analysis is to explain, and possibly to predict, the institutional arrangements by which transactions are negotiated, enforced and adjusted. To serve this purpose, Williamson uses a model of human nature based on three behavioural attributes: bounded rationality, opportunism and dignity. (See, for example, Williamson, 1984: 196–202).

Bounded rationality is a weak form of rationality. People are assumed to try to make rational decisions but their ability to do so is constrained by limits on their capacity to receive, process, store and retrieve information. The importance of bounded rationality is stressed in the work of Herbert Simon (1957, 1978). One implication is that people are unable to take full account of, or possibly even imagine, all future situations that might require changes in the terms of a transaction. Transactions that are more than just once-only exchanges cannot be organized, therefore, by a long-term market contract, agreed at the outset, specifying terms appropriate to any future state of the world. Complete, contingent-claims contracts of the type discussed by Radner (1968) are just not feasible, and some other institutional arrangement must be used.

Opportunism is a devious kind of self-interested behaviour. Williamson assumes that at least some people might behave in strategic, guileful ways, if they can do so undetected and thereby promote their own interest. This might involve representing their position (abilities, preferences, intentions) in a way that is less than completely honest, or even, perhaps, downright dishonest. An example inspired by Akerlof (1970) is the seller of a second-hand car who is much more knowledgeable about its true quality than any potential buyer. It is in the seller's interest to be selective in the information he gives the buyer, emphasizing the car's good points and downplaying its defects, since this would raise the price he will receive. The opportunistic seller will selectively reveal and distort information, even provide false information, if he can do so without later penalty. The implication is that, even though gains from trade are potentially available, the transaction might not take place unless some means can be found to protect one party from the opportunistic representations of the other. The kind of institution that can best provide the protection depends on the nature of the transaction, an issue discussed later. If the assumption of opportunism is something you regard as an unnecessarily cynical view of human nature, note that its importance requires only that some, not all, people behave in this way and that it is difficult to tell who is opportunistic and who is not.

The third human attribute in Williamson's model is dignity, though it is one of the least-developed concepts. It captures the idea that humanity should be respected for its own sake, so that people should not be treated in organizations solely as the means in an economizing process. However, taking account of dignity requires the acceptance of any necessary tradeoffs between it and other valued objectives. For example, if society believes workers should be democratically represented on firms' boards of directors, it also should be recognized that additional costs of democracy are to be borne by someone: shareholders who get lower profits, workers who get lower wages, customers who pay higher prices, or taxpayers. The need for tradeoffs should be recognized clearly, so as to avoid the implicit assumption that dignity is to be pursued at all costs. [. . .]

Nature of transactions

Transactions differ in the strains they place on decision-making ability, the scope they give for opportunism, and the degree to which they involve human dignity. Consequently, the best institutional arrangement to use depends on the nature of the transaction. There are three relevant dimensions along which transactions can differ: asset specificity; uncertainty and frequency (Williamson, 1984: 202–7).

Asset specificity refers to the extent to which the resources used in a transaction have a value therein that is higher than in any other use or to any other user. Highly specific assets are ones whose values elsewhere are comparatively low and, consequently, whose owners have a strong interest in continuing the transaction because of the high quasi-rents they receive. One expects durability to be a hallmark of highly specific assets. [. . .] However, this does not imply that transaction specificity is confined to physical durable assets: human investment in individual or team knowledge that is not fully transferrable is also transaction specific. Physical examples include equipment designed to make components that will fit into the product of only one buyer (for example, exhausts for Rolls-Royce cars) or dispensing machines that can handle packsizes peculiar to one supplier. Human capital examples include a manager's knowledge of the idiosyncrasies of his firm's administrative system, or a team's knowledge of the comparative advantages of its members and thus of how tasks can be allocated most efficiently within the team. Site specificity occurs where, for example, separable stages of production are placed in close proximity to economize on transport costs, and their relocation costs are high. Finally, 'dedicated' asset specificity refers to resources which, in principle, are usable elsewhere but for which no effective demand exists outside the present transaction; their installation was conditional on continuing demand from a particular buyer (see Williamson, 1983: 526).

[. . .]

Asset specificity has implications for organization because of the reluctance of parties to terminate transactions to which they have committed specific assets. Owners are aware of the capital losses they must incur if they redeploy their assets, and people with whom they are transacting know that nowhere else can they find assets as suitable to their needs as those already committed. In other words, both parties are to some extent 'locked into' a transaction to which highly specific assets have been assigned. Such a situation offers great scope for opportunism when occasion arises for changing the original terms of the contract. Bargaining is then confined within a small group, and there are no pressures from a large number of competing sources or bidders to oblige people to present their positions in a fully honest way. Some institutional arrangement other than large-numbers competition needs to be found to safeguard the transaction from excessive opportunistic wrangling, which could siphon off the available gains from trade. The importance of these considerations is underlined by what Williamson (1984: 207–8) calls the 'fundamental transformation', by which a transaction whose original terms were negotiated in an environment of large-numbers competition is transformed during its implementation to one where small-numbers bargaining is inevitable at the stage of contract renewal. This would occur if the winner of the initial contract benefited from learning-by-doing during its execution and was able to appropriate those benefits, enabling him to compete advantageously when terms are renegotiated.

The second relevant attribute of a transaction is uncertainty about the environment in which it is to be executed. Where there are very many known alternatives, or there are known to be currently unimaginable possibilities, the ability of people to make detailed plans for the future is limited, given bounded rationality. Under these circumstances the future details of a transaction can be settled only when uncertainty is resolved by the passage of time. If time also gives advantages to the initial winners of a contract, arrangements for the final settlement of terms must not only be flexible, but also able to deal with opportunistic behaviour at the final settlement date. Here, coping with greater uncertainty requires a form of organization that is both adaptive and able to control opportunism in small groups.

Frequency is the third relevant attribute. If the original parties to a transaction effectively have no other outlet or source once the original contract has been awarded, and they are highly uncertain about the contemporary environment at the time when terms must be renegotiated, an organizational form (for example a monitoring and control system) that is tailor-made for that transaction might substantially reduce bargaining costs on each occasion when renegotiation takes place. However, governance structures differ in terms of their set-up and running costs. Whether or not it is sensible to invest in a tailor-made structure depends on the capitalized value of the savings derived from it in relation to the present value of its costs. The greater the frequency of a transaction, the more justifiable is a (relatively) expensive governance structure that brings about (relatively) large savings in transaction costs.

Economizing

The hallmark of economic analysis is how to make best ('efficient') use of resources that are in scarce supply. In situations that involve uncertainty, bounded rationality and opportunism it is important to economize on resources used in negotiating, implementing and adapting contracts as well as on those used for more narrowly defined productive tasks. The efficient objective is to minimize the sum of production and transaction costs for the tasks required.

Williamson's advice to the organizational designer is to operate in a discriminating way, that is only after making a comparative assessment of the costs of using one organizational form rather than another. This advice is offered to designers in any field where resources are scarce: government departments, non-profit bureaucracies and families, in addition to profit-oriented businesses. But beyond this normative use of the analysis, Williamson claims that the economizing principle actually operates in the commercial world; that here, transactions do get organized, sooner or later, in efficient ways. This proposition amounts to an efficiency explanation of both the variety of organizational forms that exists at any one time and the way in which the pattern of organizations in the commercial world evolves over time.

The efficiency explanation contrasts sharply with attempts to explain organizational forms in terms of power, drawing on political and sociological concepts. A comparative evaluation of the alternative approaches should be based not on ideological issues, but on their ability to make sense of empirical observations. Williamson and Ouchi (1983: 29–30) admit the relevance of power to the analysis of organization but submit that

> power considerations will usually give way to efficiency – at least in profit-making enterprises, if observations are taken at sufficiently long intervals [. . .] This does not imply that power has no role to play, but we think it invites confusion to explain organisational results that are predicted by the efficiency hypothesis in terms of power. Rather power explains results when the organisation sacrifices efficiency to serve special interests. We concede that this occurs. But we do not believe that major organisational changes in the commercial sector are explained in these terms. The evidence is all to the contrary.

The efficiency thesis should also be contrasted with the 'inhospitality tradition' of attempting to explain non-conventional institutions in the commercial world in terms of efforts to enhance monopoly power. The 'efficiency' versus 'monopoly' debate has dominated theoretical and applied work in the field of industrial economics. Williamson argues that giving due recognition to the importance of transaction costs serves to redress the balance towards efficiency explanations, particularly if one accepts that rather stringent structural preconditions must be satisfied before anti-competitive behaviour is plausibly successful (1983: 537, n. 38).

A critical evaluation of Williamson's analysis is given later in the chapter. At this stage, two points are worth making. Firstly, a purely 'efficiency' view of how organizations develop ignores the possibility that the nature of transactions is not completely exogenous: the development of technology and the kinds of production techniques used might depend on whose interests they promote. It is possible that efficiency considerations dominate once the nature of transactions is given, but that power is important in explaining their nature. Secondly, one might accept the view that efficiency should not be ignored in analysing the firm, without believing that monopoly issues are relevant in only a few situations. Some organizational developments might occur because they are more efficient ways of extracting consumer surplus.

2 Internal organization

The concepts outlined in Section 1 are relevant to the design of markets, the replacement of markets by some internal form of governance (the 'internalization' issue) and the design of internal forms of organization. [. . .] The rest of this section deals with internalization, and with two aspects of the design of internal forms of organization: hierarchy and hierarchical decomposition.

Internalization

A transaction is said to be internalized when its administration involves the use of authority rather than voluntary bargaining between people in a market. Coase (1937) argued that familiar tools of economic analysis could be used to explain why one system of organizing transactions would prevail over another. Williamson (1971) pursued Coase's line of inquiry by using the concepts of Section 1 to explain the 'failure' of markets to organize transactions between vertically related, technologically separable stages of production. Later, the internalization of financial and international transactions within conglomerate and multinational firms were also analysed within the same framework. [. . .]

Markets and internal organization are two alternative types of 'governance structure' analysed by Williamson. The type of transaction to which each is most suited can be explained after describing their characteristics.

In a market, bargaining is constrained by threats of imminent termination of any existing or proposed contracts; opportunism is controlled by the readiness of people to sever their dealings with other resource owners; and continuity of an agreement between people is not valued for its own sake: transactions are administered in an impersonal way, typified by the 'faceless' bargaining of competitive market models. The costs of using a market to organize transactions will be lowest when the threat to terminate a contract is an effective control mechanism.

Such a threat is credible only if carrying it out would impose little loss on the person terminating the contract. This requires the availability of other potential contractors, prepared to offer terms no worse than those available from the original parties to the contract. But these conditions do not exist where the original parties have invested in transaction-specific assets. As discussed in Section 1, any later renegotiation of terms would then be confined to parties to the initial contract. If this small group tried to draw up a new market contract, bargaining would be protracted because of the known absence of alternative partners. The costs of using a market, therefore, will be high for the organization of transactions that involve highly specific assets.

In comparison, internal organization is a more attractive way of administering such transactions. Bounds on rationality are eased by adjusting terms within the small group of people in an adaptive way, as time reveals new circumstances. Protracted bargaining, Williamson argues, is less likely for three reasons: people feel part of a unified organization, and so are less inclined to argue; management has the right to demand information from workers in the organization, and therefore can restrict opportunism; and, ultimately, management can use its authority to guillotine any dispute that threatens to be prolonged.

In Williamson's framework, therefore, an internal form of organization is an effective way of economizing on bounded rationality and controlling opportunism in the context of recurring transactions that involve specific assets. A market would be a relatively costly way of adjusting the uses made of specific assets in response to unforeseen changes revealed over time.

Two general aspects of Williamson's analysis of organizational forms are seen in this explanation of internalization. Firstly, the question of the best form to use hinges on efficiency in the use of decision-making resources. Secondly, the advantage that internal organization possesses in certain circumstances turns on its recourse to authority as a means of eliminating information asymmetry or terminating any prolonged wrangling between employees. There can be little doubt that this explanation of internal organization is an explanation of those authoritative aspects of management in real-world firms that, earlier in this chapter, were taken to be the *sine qua non* of Coase's (1937) definition of a firm. [. . .]

Hierarchy

Issues of institutional design don't disappear once a decision has been made to adopt internal organization. The details of its form influence organizational behaviour and performance just as structure influences conduct and performance within a market system. An important feature to explain is why a hierarchical system is invariably found in organizations such as firms.

The debate on the rationale of hierarchy has been a heated one. It is an important focus of the conflict between 'efficiency' (economic) and 'power' (political/sociological) explanations of organizational forms. Williamson's views are hardly equivocal:

> it is no accident that hierarchy is ubiquitous within all organisations of any size. This holds not merely within the private-for-profit sector but among non-profits and government bureaus as well. It likewise holds across national boundaries and is independent of political systems. In short, inveighing against hierarchy is rhetoric: both the logic of efficiency and the historical evidence disclose that non-hierarchical modes are mainly of ephemeral duration. (1980: 35).

His efficiency arguments for hierarchy are connected with both bounded rationality and opportunism. First, let us define what we mean by hierarchy. Internal organization is a class of governance whose distinguishing feature is that a resource owner accepts restrictions on his sole rights to use his resources in whatever way he might choose. Within the bounds of some agreed domain, he allows his resources to be controlled by an authorized decision-making unit to which he might or might not belong. How might one define an increase in hierarchy across governance structures within the class? Williamson (1980) discusses both contractual and decision-making bases for defining hierarchy, and chooses the latter as the most relevant to organizational performance. On this basis the degree of hierarchy could be said to increase, *ceteris paribus*, with increases in the domain delegated to authorized control, and with reductions in the extent to which resource owners are involved in making decisions about the deployment of their resources. In other words, holding constant the controlled domain, hierarchy increases as authorized decision-making becomes more concentrated amongst people in an organization.

In assessing the comparative efficiency of non-hierarchical and hierarchical forms of internal organization, it is instructive to contrast the peer group with a simple hierarchy (see Williamson, 1975: Chapter 3). The peer group makes decisions in a democratic way, with all owners having a say in the final decision. This might be achieved either by having all owners involved in all decisions, or having people take turns to make the decisions. A simple hierarchy puts decision-making authority permanently in the hands of a few people. Williamson argues that, compared to simple hierarchy, the peer group is inefficient in both making and implementing decisions.

If all input owners have a say in all decisions, decision-making is a costly process: the greater the number of decision-makers, the more resources are used up in sending out the information needed to make the decision; and the more time is needed, in total, to give each person the opportunity to argue his preferred solution to any problem. One way round this, that remains consistent with the democratic spirit of the peer group, is to have a central decision-making unit comprising, at any one time, only a few people, but to rotate membership of this unit, each person taking a turn. However, this solution prevents the group achieving any gains from assigning people to tasks according to their comparative advantage. People can be expected to differ in their abilities and this inevitably gives some people a comparative advantage in processing information, making decisions, and communicating them to others. Failure to exploit this involves efficiency losses. But making permanent appointments to a group that has the authority to make decisions creates an elite, and effectively transforms the peer group into a hierarchy.

Opportunism is claimed to be particularly relevant to the implementation of decisions. If it were absent, all transactors could be relied on to keep a promise to implement any decision to the best of their ability. With opportunism, a central monitoring unit is a possible way of controlling shirking, by monitoring input performance and adjusting compensation accordingly over time. Again, the fundamental principles of the peer group would not be compromised if monitoring roles were rotated. But rotation involves efficiency losses if (as seems likely) some people have a comparative advantage in monitoring. In the case of both decision-making and monitoring, therefore, Williamson argues that realizing gains from comparative advantage requires forming an elite, and therefore a hierarchy.

One possible situation in which a peer group would not cause a loss of efficiency is where democracy acts as a spur to individual effort and productivity. Whether or not this is a common occurrence is a matter for empirical investigation. Ben-Ner (1984: 248), for example, cites, among explanations for the high incidence of liquidations of producer cooperatives, 'their inability to settle personal disputes, their lack of discipline in the absence of a central monitor [and] their low motivation caused by excessive egalitarianism'. This would seem to suggest that a high price, in terms of efficiency, is paid for democracy. However, more empirical evidence on this is needed.

Criticisms of Williamson's efficiency rationale of hierarchy have the same basis as criticisms of his approach in general, and are dealt with in Section 3 below. It should be noted at this stage, however, that democracy might be a 'desirable output' of an organization, in which case its production at the expense of other outputs would not necessarily involve inefficiency.

Hierarchical decomposition

Within hierarchical organizations of any size, more complex structures are observed than the simple (two-level) system discussed in the last section. In assessing the relative efficiency of alternative forms of hierarchy, the extent to which they economize on bounded rationality and control opportunism is of some importance. In this section, two forms of complex hierarchy are compared: the unitary form ('U-form') and the multi-divisional structure ('M-form'). Williamson argues that the M-form is a more efficient way of administering certain types of transaction. He claims, therefore, that one of this century's most important innovations in business organization is explained by his approach.

The U-form, illustrated in Figure 1, is a hierarchy organized on functional lines in which the chief executive office (CEO) has responsibility for both long-run ('strategic') planning of the organization as a whole and day-to-day ('operational') coordination of the functional departments (production, marketing, purchasing, personnel, finance). Each functional department is hierarchically organized, and is in the charge of a middle manager responsible for coordinating activities within his or her department. By 1917, vertical integration was a common feature of large US industrial firms, many of whom had adopted the U-form to administer their activities (see Chandler, 1976: 29). Some of these firms (typically, ones that possessed marketing or technological knowledge that could find application in new product lines: see Chandler, 1962) next tried to grow by diversifying, a strategy which revealed that the U-form had weaknesses

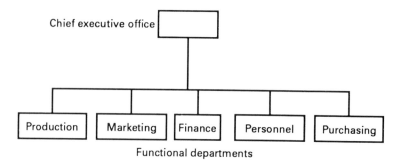

Functional departments

Figure 1 *U-form organization*

when used to administer activities in several different markets. If a firm operates in several different markets the occasion more frequently arises for adjustments to be made in coordinating operational activities between functional areas. With a U-form structure, in which the functional basis of decomposition is preserved all the way up the hierarchy, more of top management's time is devoted to these operational matters, whose pressing need for resolution gives them an urgency not usually attached to issues of a more long-run, strategic kind. Because of cognitive limits within top management (that is, bounded rationality), the effect that diversification has, therefore, in the U-form firm is for strategic planning to be 'crowded out' by operational decisions. As Simon (1960) pointed out, one of the main tasks in designing a hierarchy is to decide the appropriate level of authority for each class of decision that has to be made. To economize on top management's bounded rationality there is an obvious need within the diversified firm for operating decisions to be decentralized. This would not be possible in a U-form because middle management has only functional responsibility: no one below the CEO has responsibility for overall operating performance in a given market.

Strategic planning with a diversified U-form organization is difficult not only because top management's limited attention is more frequently diverted to operational matters. Problems are caused also by the absence of information on overall operating performance in each separate market. Firstly, this makes it difficult to decide where best to expand or contract the firm's resources. Secondly, without such information, the performance of each department within the U-form is assessed by the CEO on the basis of criteria specific to that department, rather than by aggregating its contributions to overall performance in the separate markets. This severely distorts the incentive system within the organization: since their efforts are judged and rewarded on the basis of functional criteria, middle managers have the incentive to pursue functional (sub-global) goals beyond levels that are optimal from the corporate (global) point of view. This is an example of opportunism by middle

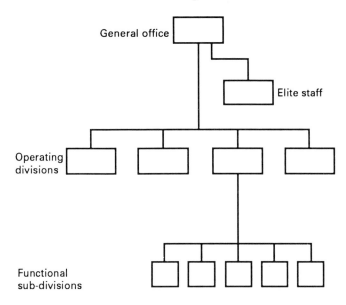

Figure 2   *M-form organization*

managers, due to their superiors' inability to check their claims about
what is actually in the best interests of the firm.

Williamson argues that the M-form, illustrated in Figure 2, avoids these
weaknesses in administering the diversified firm, by economizing on
bounded rationality and improving control of opportunism. In the M-
form, below the top level of management, the hierarchy is organized on
an operating rather than on a functional basis. Each division controls the
operations of a fairly self-contained part of the organization's activities
(for example, a particular product line, or a geographical area). The aim
is to place in one division activities which interact strongly, and put
weakly interacting parts in different divisions. The head of each division
is responsible for its operating performance, which is judged by indicators
of overall success in its markets (for example, by operating profits, sales
growth or market share). Divisional heads therefore have incentives that,
compared to the U-form, are aligned more closely with corporate (global)
goals and which discourage over-pursuit of functional (sub-global) goals.
Each division is itself organized on U-form lines.

The M-form economizes on the bounded rationality of top management
by decentralizing operational decisions to the divisional level. Strategic
planning for the organization as a whole is the responsibility of top
management in a 'General Office'. People here are not functional
specialists and, therefore, are less likely to advocate policies that promote
functional at the expense of corporate interests. The General Office
chooses organizational goals, monitors the performance of the separate
operating divisions, and allocates the organization's resources among these
divisions. In doing these things, it is supported by an 'elite staff', again

comprising people with no functional interests, whose roles are to audit the operating divisions and advise the General Office.

The M-form was independently developed by several US corporations (Du Pont, General Motors, Standard Oil of New Jersey, Sears) in the 1920s and 1930s, in response to management problems that emerged from their attempts to diversify. However, its efficiency advantages in these circumstances should not be used to infer that it is a panacea of organizational design. The general principle is that net gains can be made by identifying and giving effect to decomposability amongst the organization's activities. The M-form is not appropriate if divisions are formed between which there are strong links on either the supply or the demand side (see Williamson, 1970: Chapter 8). Steer and Cable (1978) found, among large UK companies, evidence that profitability was increased by having the form of internal organization appropriate to the firm's environment. The M-form is suitable only in some environments. As markets and technology evolve, one would expect the nature of transactions to change and present new configurations of administrative problems. [. . .]

3 Critique

Williamson's theory of the firm, presented in Section 2, is an explanation of why some resources are managed, rather than allocated by markets, and why managerial functions are divided into several different, specialized roles within the firm. This section briefly reviews the essential features of Williamson's theory, then presents two types of criticism: firstly, that the theory is a confusing mixture of static and dynamic elements, analysed in a loose way that does not make clear which things are endogenous and which are exogenous; secondly, that the approach is too sanguine about the desirability of the organizational forms that are explained.

That transaction-specific assets are organized by management rather than markets is explained by savings on the resources used to decide how to adjust to changes unanticipated at the start of the contract. Given that resources are managed, hierarchy is explained by gains from allowing people to specialize according to their comparative advantage: in particular, those with a comparative advantage in deciding how to coordinate the diverse resources used in the firm and how to adjust this coordination in response to unforeseen changes, are assigned specialist managerial roles. Finally, the decomposition of managerial hierarchies allows some managers to specialize in strategic decision-making and for this task to be performed by people who not only possess a relevant comparative advantage but also whose corporate loyalties are not compromised by undue devotion to narrow functional goals. In essence, therefore, Williamson's theory of the firm explains the existence, division and specialization of management in terms of economizing on resources used to make decisions. In addition, allocative efficiency may be improved if the shift to an M-form of internal organization leads to behaviour that is more profit-oriented.

It is a strength of Williamson's theory that attention is drawn to the need for decision-making resources and to the importance of economizing on these. A further attraction of the approach is its discussion of the role of such resources in deciding how to respond to changes unanticipated at the start of a contract: it is this feature that adds a fundamentally dynamic element to the theory. A major weakness, however, is that this element is fitted only roughly into the discussion, in a way that makes it difficult to integrate the dynamic with the static features of the analysis. In particular, given the importance attached by Williamson to efficiency, there is no clear treatment of the tradeoffs that might be necessary between short-term and long-term efficiency. One example of the inadequacies that arise from such informal presentation of the theory is the absence of a clear analysis of the interdependence of production technique and organizational form. Instead of focusing on this interdependence, as one would expect of a truly dynamic theory, Williamson discusses the efficient resolution of contractual problems that are associated with given techniques of production. The techniques themselves, it would seem, are regarded by him as exogenous to his analysis. If so, only limited claims, if any, should be made for the theory as an explanation of the historical evolution of the firm, and of industrial organization. [. . .]

The second type of criticism made of Williamson's analysis is its emphasis on efficiency at the expense of distribution. Malcolmson (1984: 126) argues that 'an essential feature of the world Williamson is interested in [. . .] is not one in which one can simply *assume* that economic efficiency will win out in the end'.

The reason is that the organizational changes discussed by Williamson influence the distribution of power both within and between firms, and one cannot presume that power is used to produce efficient outcomes. Within firms, the existence of a specialized managerial hierarchy inevitably sacrifices equality in the distribution of power, and raises the issue of whether workers are adequately compensated for their loss of autonomy in controlling the work process. Marglin (1975) argues that the development of the factory system was not in the interest of workers who, being left with no alternative but the freedom to starve, were forced to comply. Putterman (1984), whilst accepting the necessity for hierarchy in a complex organization, questions whether this needs to be associated with the domination of capital over labour.

There is also the possibility that organizational changes might alter the distribution of market power between firms. Williamson's expressed aim is to redress the balance, in industrial organization theory, between arguments that emphasize the consequences of organizational changes for monopoly power, and those that focus on their efficiency consequences. Nevertheless, [. . .] the monopoly power effects of decisions such as vertical integration and multinational production should not be ignored. If read in isolation, Williamson's analysis is far too sanguine about the efficiency effects of the organizational forms it explains.

4 Summary

Williamson's theory of the firm is an attempt, following Coase, to explain the existence and internal structure of firms rather than to take them for granted. In doing so, it rightly emphasizes the need for an economic analysis of decision-making resources. Despite introducing some dynamic elements into the discussion, these are not treated in a formal way. This lack of formal analysis leaves the dynamic features of the theory inadequately specified, and thereby limits the relevance of claims it makes to explain the historical evolution of the firm. In isolation, Williamson's discussion neglects the effects of organizational changes on distribution and monopoly power.

References

Akerlof, G. (1970) 'The market for "lemons": quality uncertainty and the market mechanism', *Quarterly Journal of Economics*, 84: 488-500.

Alchian, A.A. and Demsetz, H. (1972) 'Production, information costs and economic organization', *American Economic Review*, 62: 777-95.

Ben-Ner, A. (1984) 'On the stability of the cooperative type of organization', *Journal of Comparative Economics*, 8: 247-60.

Chandler, A.D.Jr (1962) *Strategy and Structure: Chapters in the History of Industrial Enterprise*. Cambridge, Mass.: MIT Press.

Chandler, A.D.Jr (1976) 'The development of modern management structure in the US and UK', in L. Hannah (ed.), *Management Strategy and Business Development*. London: Macmillan.

Coase, R.M. (1937) 'The nature of the firm', *Economica*, n.s., 4: 386-405.

Malcolmson, J. (1984) 'Efficient labour organization: incentives, power and the transactions cost approach', in F. Stephen (ed.), *Firms, Organisations and Labour: Approaches to the Economics of Work Organisations*. London: Macmillan.

Marglin, S. (1975) 'What do bosses do?', in A. Gorz (ed.), *The Division of Labour*. Hassocks: Harvester Press.

Putterman, L. (1984) 'On some recent explanations of why capital hires labour', *Economic Inquiry*, 22, 171-87.

Radner, R. (1968) 'Competitive equilibrium under uncertainty', *Econometrica*, 36: 31-58.

Simon, H. (1957) *Models of Man*. New York: John Wiley.

Simon, H. (1960) 'The new science of management decision', reprinted in D.S. Pugh (ed.) (1984), *Organisation Theory*, 2nd edition, Harmondsworth: Penguin Books.

Simon, H. (1978) 'Rationality as process and as product of thought', *American Economic Review*, 68: 1-16.

Steer, P. and Cable, J. (1978) 'Internal organisation and profit: an empirical analysis of large UK companies', *Journal of Industrial Economics*, 27: 13-30.

Williamson, O.E. (1970) *Corporate Control and Business Behaviour*. New Jersey: Prentice-Hall.

Williamson, O.E. (1971) 'The vertical integration of production: market failure considerations', *American Economic Review*, 61: 112-23.

Williamson, O.E. (1975) *Markets and Hierarchies: Analysis and Antitrust Implications*. New York: Free Press.

Williamson, O.E. (1980) 'The organisation of work: a comparative institutional assessment', *Journal of Economic Behaviour and Organization*, 1: 5–38.

Williamson, O.E. (1983) 'Credible commitments: using hostages to support exchange', *American Economic Review*, 73: 519–40.

Williamson, O.E. (1984) 'The economics of governance: framework and implications', *Zeitschrift für die gesamte Staatswissenschaft*, 40: 195–223.

Williamson, O.E. and Ouchi, W.G. (1983) 'The markets and hierarchies programme of research: origins, implications and prospects', in A. Francis, J. Turk and P. Willman (eds), *Power, Efficiency and Institutions: A Critical Appraisal of the 'Markets and Hierarchies' Paradigm*. London: Heinemann.

6

Creating the Single European Market

Dennis Swann

In 1986 the twelve member states of the European Community[1] signed the Single European Act (SEA). By doing so they amended the three basic treaties which respectively created the European Coal and Steel Community (which came into existence in 1951), the European Atomic Energy Community and the European Economic Community (Euratom and EEC – both of which came into operation in 1958). In respect of the latter, the SEA strengthened the decision-making powers under the founding Rome Treaty and a more firmly entrenched certain policy objectives, for example research and development cooperation and balanced regional development. It also accorded formal recognition to the European Political Cooperation Procedure. It should be explained that while the above three communities were primarily concerned with economic matters, it was always anticipated that the process of integrating economies would spill over into the political sphere. In other words the members would also begin to collaborate on foreign policy matters. This has in fact happened. The process was initiated in 1970 and is now referred to as the European Political Cooperation Procedure. This *foreign policy* coordinating mechanism, together with the machinery of *economic integration* within the three economic communities, now constitute the twin pillars of European unity. Most important, however, was the modification to the Rome Treaty which committed the 'twelve' to completing the internal market by the end of 1992.

The 1992 aspect has attracted an unprecedented amount of attention both within the Community and in the rest of the world. Within the Community, governments have been actively campaigning in order to explain to business people and to the general public what it implies and promises. As a result business restructuring is already well under way. [. . .] Third country competitors, notably Japan, have also drawn the conclusion that the 1992 commitment demands a fundamental review of business strategy, [. . .] What then is 1992 all about?

Adapted from B. Atkinson (ed.) *Developments in Economics* (Causeway Press, 1990), pp. 87–99.

The origins of 1992

The Rome Treaty envisaged the creation of the EEC (by the original 'Six')[2] within a transition period of twelve years, which would end in December 1969. Its objectives were diverse. Central was the requirement that internal tariff (customs duty), quota and non-tariff barriers to trade in goods should be abolished so as to create an enlarged European economic space. In other words, goods produced in one member state would be able to enter and compete in other member state markets, free of all obstacles and barriers. Around this there would be an economic fence in the shape of the common external tariff, that is a common level of import duty on any particular kind of good entering the Community from without. Complementing the *freedom to supply goods* within the EEC there would be a *freedom to supply services* such as insurance and banking across frontiers. The Rome Treaty also envisaged free and undistorted movement across frontiers of *factors of production*, that is labour, capital and enterprise. When all this was accomplished the Community would, in the language of economic integration theory, constitute a *Common Market*. The Treaty did not envisage carrying the process of economic integration to the stage of a monetary union – national currencies were to remain. Control over their supply and the exchange rates between them were, in the final analysis, to be left to national discretion.

In practice the requirement to create the Common Market was not achieved by the end of 1969. Indeed, even at the time of the negotiations which led up to the SEA the European Communities (EC) Commission (the Civil Service which administers the communities from Brussels) estimated that in excess of 300 measures remained to be adopted before the problem of what came to be called 'non-Europe' could be said to have been fully addressed. In some instances proposals for action had lain on the table of the Council of Ministers (the body which makes Community law) since the early 1970s!

Why the delay? Some of it could be ascribed to a basic weakness in the Council of Ministers' decision-making machinery. The need to harmonize national laws was bound to be frustrated by the Treaty's need for unanimity as between all twelve member states. When, as in the case of insurance, West Germany contemplated the competition from the City of London which would follow in the wake of measures to ensure freedom to supply insurance services, the unanimity rule provided ample scope for postponing the evil day. Even when the Treaty allowed for majority voting, thus hopefully preventing individual states from applying a veto, progress was frustrated in earlier days by French distaste for the principle and later the British were not averse to opposing majority voting when it suited them. But other factors also explain the lack of progress. Deepening the Common Market, that is pressing forward with existing policies, had to compete with the claims of policy widening, such as new initiatives in regional and monetary policy. Added to all this were wrangles over the Community Budget and the Common Agricultural Policy together with the protective responses which followed in the wake of the oil price recessions of the 1970s and growing foreign competition.

The renewed impetus which ultimately led to the SEA derived considerable support from the first directly elected European Parliament (EP). Originally the EP was indirectly elected, that is to say the members were selected by the members of the national parliaments. In 1979, however, the Community moved over to direct elections – the general public were allowed to vote for their own MEPs. On the basis of this greatly enhanced authority the EP decided to press ahead with the task of unifying Europe and to this end produced a draft treaty establishing a European Union. This was a visionary proposal which would have brought economic and foreign policy matters within the ambit of the Union decision-making process, would have strengthened the position of the EC Commission, would have phased out national vetoes to which I referred above and have given the EP an enhanced law-making (as opposed to its largely consultative) role. Whilst it is true that the summit meeting of heads of state and government (prime ministers and presidents) in Stuttgart in 1983 adopted a Solemn Declaration of European Union, it would be a mistake to assume that the prime ministers and presidents and the European Parliamentarians were on the same wavelength. Indeed, when an intergovernmental conference was finally convened in 1985 in order to negotiate a European Union treaty, some member states clearly had severe reservations. One was the UK whose position could be simplified, hopefully not too crudely, as follows. First things first. We have not yet completed the Common Market. What is the point of discussing visionary schemes when we have not even dealt with the basics. The EC Commission for its part threw into the discussion the now celebrated Cockfield Report[3] which detailed the host of measures which would have to be adopted before a single market could be said to exist. In the upshot the SEA, whilst it made some concessions to the *political* aspirations of the EP, was notable chiefly for its powerful commitment to the *economic* concept of completing the internal market.

1992 – the tasks

What does completing the internal market entail? Broadly speaking the EC Commission's original 300-plus measures were designed to create, in respect of economic activity across frontiers, a situation which would approximate, in terms of its freedom and lack of distortion and discrimination, to the situation which exists when goods, services and factors are supplied within a state. Putting it another way, movement of goods, services and so forth across the English Channel ought ideally to be no different to movement from England to Wales. This is a tall order. In the

Commission's eyes the following are the kinds of measure which must be introduced – they are, it should be emphasized, illustrative and by no means exhaustive.

Frontier controls

Frontier checks and controls would have to be rationalized and relaxed in the short term. In the longer term they should go so as to create a real 'Europe without frontiers'.

Standards relating to goods

National official and technical standards by virtue of their difference have in the past fragmented the European market. Somehow this extremely widespread problem needed to be swept away. All this requires further elaboration. The problem is quite simply as follows. The governments of member states interfere in the market on a very considerable scale by imposing standards upon the producers of goods and indeed services. These standards often have the force of law. They are introduced for a variety of reasons but often the aim is the laudable one of protecting the public against physical harm or deception. As an example of the first we can cite pharmaceuticals and foodstuffs. The need for government controls to prevent the marketing of dangerous medicines is obvious – the example of thalidomide indicates what can happen when inadvertently a dangerous drug gets through the net. In the case of foodstuffs a whole host of additives have been used to flavour, colour, emulsify and preserve the products in question. These can harm the consumer – the ban on the sweetening agent cyclamate on the grounds that it could cause cancer is a case in point. We have also noted that the problem may be one of preventing deception. Thus labelling rules may be necessary so that, for example, consumers know what 'pure wool' really means.

The desirability of such standards is not in question. However, to the extent that standards differ, either goods cannot be exported with a consequent loss of competition between countries, or if they are exported they have to be adapted to the rules of each national market. Either way the economies of large scale, in the form of longer production runs of a standardized product, are in some degree lost. There is also a reduction in choice. The idea that such standardization will lead to a lack of choice is not correct, rather it will increase it. Standardization only refers to certain aspects of a product's design – there is still scope for variation. Thus in Europe, automobiles have been subjected to a good deal of standardization in matters concerning safety and pollution, but that has not precluded the car industry from providing a vast range of choice in terms of styling and performance.

One obvious way round all this is to harmonize standards, that is to devise a European standard. All goods which conform to this standard would automatically have to be allowed into all other member state markets.

There are indeed provisions within the Rome Treaty – specifically Articles 100 to 102 – which provide for the approximation of national laws. This process involves the issuing by the Council of Ministers of harmonization directives. These lay down European standards and the member states are required to amend their own national laws so as to bring their own standards into line with the European harmonized standard.

All this sounds like the answer to the problem. In some degree it is and a considerable number of products have been so harmonized. Unfortunately it is an extremely time-consuming process and at the time of the SEA much yet remained to be done before all the products that needed to be dealt with had in fact been covered. The sheer size of the task in fact prompted the EC Commission to doubt whether the traditional approach to the standards problem, which had been adopted prior to the SEA, was any longer appropriate. More will be said on that point later.

Government purchasing

Public procurement is another area where the 1992 programme calls for further progress. The problem here is as follows. A substantial proportion of the goods and services which are purchased are bought not by private individuals and private businesses but by governments (central, regional and local) and by public enterprises, that is, nationalized industries. Such public procurement or purchasing has in the past not been carried out on the basis of buying the cheapest and/or the best. Rather governments have favoured a policy of buying home-produced goods. By so doing they have sought to protect domestic employment, the balance of payments and so forth. In fact such behaviour constitutes an act of discrimination and it should be noted that discrimination on the grounds of nationality, for example giving a preference to British goods as opposed to French goods rather than treating them on their merits, is an offence under Article 7 of the Rome Treaty. The Council of Ministers has indeed taken specific steps to root out such discrimination. In 1971 it did so in respect of public works contracts. Also from 1976 all public supply contracts above a specified limit awarded by local, regional and central governments had to be publicly advertised in advance. In considering tenders the contract-awarding body was obliged to treat all offers equally – there should be no discrimination between home and foreign bids. In spite of all this the EC Commission has, from time to time, had to instigate cases against member state governments who were flouting the non-discrimination rule.

The 1992 programme seeks to tighten up the public purchasing process so as to provide businesses with the prospect that in practice, rather than theory, the whole of the EC market is truly open to their competitive offers. To this end three further developments are envisaged. Firstly, the 1971 and 1976 directives need to be modified so as to deal with certain procedural weaknesses and to close the loopholes which member states have exploited. Secondly certain major areas of activity have been excluded from the directives – these are energy, transport, water and telecommunications. These now need to be specifically included. Thirdly, services, for example data processing, as well as goods need to be liberalized.

Free movement of capital

The original Rome Treaty required that factors of production such as labour, capital and enterprise should be free to move from one state to another. Such freedom of movement was far from complete at the time of the SEA. The 1992 programme therefore calls for the liberalization process to be carried to completion. A good example of this is provided by capital transactions. Whilst some progress had been made complete free movement of capital cannot be said to have been achieved by the time of the SEA. Rather, the internal market has been compartmentalized. Action was needed in respect of exchange controls. Here we are referring to the fact that capital movements require the exchange of currencies. A French company wishing to build a plant in West Germany needs to be able to turn its French francs into D-marks. Equally a Dutch investor wishing to buy shares on the London Stock Exchange needs to turn Dutch guilders into pounds sterling. But member states have sometimes refused to allow currency exchanges designed to facilitate certain kinds of transaction. Outward investment may be banned because it weakens the balance of payments and allows the life-blood capital to leak out of the system, whilst inflows of currency may be repulsed because they cause the exchange rate to rise to unacceptable levels or add to the domestic supply of money and thus threaten inflation.

In respect of the control of capital movements, the Community made a very significant breakthrough in 1988 when it was agreed that all restrictions on such movements between residents in different member states should be removed by July 1990. Spain, Greece, Ireland and Portugal were allowed to keep their controls until the end of 1992. An escape clause was, however, built in whereby in emergencies short-term capital movements could be controlled for periods of up to six months.

Free competition in services

The Rome Treaty aims to open up the Common Market to competition in respect of services as well as goods. Here too progress has been limited. Space does not permit us to review all the actions which needed to be taken so we will focus on two – banking services and air passenger transport.

Proposals concerning banking are part of a broader programme to create a common market in financial services. One of the main problems in banking is that banks have not been free to establish themselves in other member states – the technical phrase which applies here is the Right of Establishment. The Right of Establishment relates not merely to a situation where a parent bank in one member state sets up a subsidiary in another, but also to situations where a parent in one state sets up a branch in another state. Such activities have been inhibited by a variety of factors. I will outline just two.

Firstly, member states regulate their banks. This is often referred to as prudential regulation and it consists of setting down standards in respect of such matters as the capital reserves which have to be maintained by banks. These and other rules are designed (amongst other things) to guarantee bank solvency and therefore to protect depositors and indeed to maintain a stable monetary system. If the monetary system topples the economic system will also come crashing down. To the extent that these prudential rules vary the Right of Establishment tends to be inoperative. Thus country A may impose more onerous rules than country B and therefore a country B bank will not be admitted to country A. Secondly, some countries have required the branches of foreign banks to have their own endowment of reserve capital. This puts foreign banks at a disadvantage since the foreign parent has to hold capital reserves and its branch has to do likewise, whereas the home country bank does not have to bear this double burden.

The Community is now on the way to solving these problems on the following lines. Firstly, it has decided to adopt a system of home country supervision. In other words, a parent bank and its subsidiaries abroad will be supervised by the parent country regulatory authority. However, this will not solve the problem unless the supervisory rules in each parent country are brought substantially into line. Therefore it is proposed that national supervisory rules should be harmonized, not in every detail, but only in the key factors – other less crucial aspects of the rules can be allowed to vary from country to country and be subject to mutual recognition. In respect of the branch problem, this could probably be solved by building on the fact that a directive adopted in 1983 required that the supervision of credit institutions should be conducted on a consolidated basis. In other words the branch is part of the parent and therefore the requirement to hold two lots of reserves is really contrary to the spirit of the directive.

Prior to the SEA, scheduled (as opposed to charter)[4] air passenger transport was notable for the absence of any really significant Community impact. The spirit of the Rome Treaty would suggest that there ought to be competition between airlines in respect of air fares on scheduled services between member states. Equally the Rome Treaty principle of freedom to supply services suggests that airlines should be free to enter and compete on any inter-state route. In practice, matters have been quite the reverse. On particular routes the air fares were not competitive but were fixed by agreement between the national flag carriers, for example BA and Air France on the London/Paris route. These cartel prices were then rubber-stamped by the member state governments. Also routes were not open to competition. Rather, through the agency of bilateral (intergovernmental) air services agreements the traffic was divided up, usually on a fifty/fifty basis, between the two national flag carriers.

Under the inspiration of the 1992 programme all this is now in the process of changing. In 1987 the Community agreed to a package of measures which will create greater fare competition, will allow the airlines to increase market shares at each other's expense (rather than maintaining a rigid fifty/fifty split) and will allow other airlines (both from the bilateral partners and from other states) to ply for trade on particular routes.

Indirect tax harmonization

Another area where progress remained to be made was indirect taxation – specifically Value Added Tax (VAT) and excise duties. We will concentrate on the former. The Community long ago adopted VAT as its standard form of indirect tax. Whilst the *form* of indirect tax was thus harmonized on the VAT model, the *base* (the collection of goods upon which it is levied) still needs to be brought into line. In addition, the rate of the tax varies widely from state to state – the standard rate in Ireland is 23 per cent whilst in Spain it is only 12 per cent. The fact that rates vary does not distort competition since when goods are exported VAT is remitted and tax is applied in the country of destination. This means that imported goods are treated the same (in terms of the rate of tax levied) as home-produced goods. The Commission would, however, like to harmonize (in fact bring closer together – see below) national rates of VAT. Goods could then be exported bearing the tax.

Business cooperation across frontiers

The Commission has long wished to see greater industrial cooperation across frontiers. This would require companies to be able to merge across frontiers and be able to organize themselves on a Europe-wide basis without discrimination. Unfortunately fiscal and legal factors and differences have inhibited such arrangements. The Commission has therefore proposed that such inhibiting factors should be eliminated and that specific forms of cross-frontier business organization should be created. A European Economic Interest Grouping has already been approved, but the long awaited European Company Statute still lies on the table. This would provide a system of company law which would be adopted by each country side by side with its own national company law. The European company law, by existing in identical form in each member state, would provide a vehicle for cross-frontier business integration.

1992 – the techniques

How is all this to be accomplished? Clearly the task is considerable and calls for an efficient Community legislative system (which needs to be accompanied by a vigorous process of national compliance). The SEA focuses on the former and has made two contributions. Firstly, more harmonization activity has been brought within the scope of majority voting, thus getting rid of national vetoes. Secondly, institutional changes have also been introduced which hopefully will provide for a more cooperative relationship between the Council of Ministers and the EP. In addition, the EC Commission lays emphasis on a number of other changes which should contribute to the speeding up of the legislative process. Court of Justice rulings have stressed the general principle that goods which have been legally marketed in one member state should normally be freely admitted to others. This means that the ability of states to block imports is reduced. Thus just because beer is produced in a different way in one country as compared with another does not mean that either country can legitimately prevent imports from the other. The fact that the beer has been produced in a different way does not mean that it is therefore harmful, and so on. Thus there may be no grounds for refusing to import it. If, however, in some instances considerations such as danger to life and limb can legitimately be invoked to block imports then the need to harmonize cannot be avoided. But harmonization will now concentrate on the essentials – the peripherals will be left to a process of mutual recognition by states. Mutual recognition of national supervisory standards is also proposed in respect of banking. As we have seen, some prior harmonization of standards of authorization and supervision will be necessary but, those limited conditions having been met, banks will then be free to set up in other states. The EC Commission is also now arguing that *approximation* rather than total harmonization may well suffice. Thus national VAT rates will not have to be identical – it suffices that they will be sufficiently close to prevent significant distortions.

1992 – the expectations

What is the object of all this 1992 activity? The short answer is that the elimination of barriers to trade and the boost to competition will have an economic pay-off. Costs will fall due to the fuller exploitation of economies of scale in a truly European market. Efficiency will also improve as prices and costs move down under the pressure exerted by more competitive markets. More economic patterns of resource allocation will result as underlying comparative advantages are allowed to exert their full potential. Hopefully increased competition will stimulate a more rapid rate of innovation. By 1992 this could add 4.5 per cent to the EC GDP and create 1.8 million new jobs (Cecchini, 1988).

Internal problems

Inevitably achieving general agreement on market completion involved a delicate balancing of national interests. The relatively less developed southern members, e.g. Portugal, Spain and Greece, looked for some compensation if they were to face the rigours of a more competitive European marketplace. The result was a modification of the Rome Treaty which a ʼ.owledges the need to achieve social and economic cohesion. Under this heading the commitment to reduce disparities between the standards of living in the various countries and regions of the Community was given greater emphasis. This was achieved by transferring this commitment from the preamble to the original Treaty to the main text of the amended one. This was followed in 1988 by a reform of the Community Budget in which steps were taken to shift expenditure from agricultural to the structural funds, that is those concerned with regional and social matters, and the expenditure rules were recast so as to concentrate such structural spending on the poorest regions.

Having set the process of achieving an ever closer economic union once more in motion, almost inevitably concern arose in some quarters over the possibility that this could spill over into a closer political union. That after all has always been the federalist hope. Not surprisingly, those who are averse to surrendering their sovereignty have become increasingly restive of late. Mrs Thatcher, in her speech to the College of Europe at Bruges in 1988, articulated that concern by declaring that her first guiding principle was that 'willing and active cooperation between independent sovereign states' was the best way to build a successful European Community. Whilst federalism was not mentioned in her critique of Europe's future, she made her feelings plain when she expressed her opposition to the suppression of nationhood and to the fitting of British customs and traditions into an 'identikit European personality'.

British concerns do not of course merely consist of such generalities. They have manifested themselves in three specific areas. Firstly, there is the monetary issue. Most economists would agree that a single European currency, which would also imply a European Central Bank to control it, would encourage trade thanks to the absence of uncertainty in relation to exchange rates and to the elimination of transactions costs inherent in dealing in a multiple of currencies. Therefore, as part of the 1992 programme it was agreed at the Hanover summit meeting of heads of state and government in 1988 that the progressive realization of an economic and monetary union should be studied at the highest level. This ultimately emerged as the Delors Report. However, the prospects for a single currency, other than in the long run, seem remote. Against the benefits has to be set the loss of sovereignty. This manifests itself in various ways. One is the fear that, against a background of imperfectly working markets, whole regions and, indeed, whole countries could become uncompetitive as their labour costs failed to adjust to labour costs elsewhere. Such uncompetitiveness could be persistent and, with a single currency, the normal remedy of devaluation would not be available.

The UK is of course opposed to surrendering its monetary sovereignty and did not begin to participate in the relatively modest exchange rate mechanism of the European Monetary System until October 1990. Statements by the West German Bundesbank indicate that it views monetary union as a state which comes only at the end of a very long process of economic convergence.

Secondly, whilst Thatcherite thinking warmed to the free and open market aspect of the 1992 programme, EC Commission President Jacques Delors has quite correctly emphasized that the SEA also has a social dimension. It seeks to balance the greater play of market forces and a new-found freedom for business with an element of social protection and participation for labour. In practice the proposed social measures – the right of every worker to be covered by a collective agreement, the right of workers to lifelong educational opportunities, and so on – seem modest enough, but have provoked vigorous opposition in right-wing economic circles in the UK. Mrs Thatcher also pointed to the contrast between her domestic achievements in rolling back the frontiers of the state and the prospect that if the Delors of this world have their way, power over the economy would be re-centralized in Brussels. This, it must be said, is unfair to the EC Commission. If, for example, we survey the field of regulation in airline operation, financial services, and so on it is all too obvious that hitherto it is the member state governments that in the main have clung on to their controls and the EC Commission that has been in favour of deregulation and more competition.

The third area of UK concern, and one which has not yet been resolved, relates to frontier controls. The SEA declares that 'The internal market shall comprise an area without frontiers.' This, as noted earlier, is the EC Commission's long-run aim. The UK, however, is far from happy about the prospect and sees it as helping to create a paradise for criminals, terrorists and drug traffickers.

The external implications of the 1992 single market

When 1992 is finally accomplished, what will be the nature of the Community's relationship with the rest of the world? [. . .] Will the 'Twelve' have established a relatively open trading relationship with the rest of the world or will it, accepting that a common external tariff will remain, have gone the opposite way and created a protectionist Europe – what is often referred to as Fortress Europe?

[. . .] Third World countries have a choice. They could continue exporting to the Community, facing whatever tariff and other protection the 'Twelve' decide to impose. Alternatively they can seek to avoid the protective wall by setting up subsidiaries and branches within the Community.

These issues are nicely illustrated by the Community's relationship with Japan. Some member states, for example France and Italy, have already set quantitative limits to their imports of Japanese cars. To be effective these arrangements have to prevent indirect imports via other member states and such internal border controls fragment the European market. The completion of the internal market would therefore appear to imply the removal of such protective devices, but member states are not likely to comply until protective measures at the Community level are in place. This has yet to be agreed. The liberality or otherwise of such Community arrangements will help to answer our initial question.

Japanese producers of cars and many other products are in fact already behaving as if Fortress Europe is a reality – that is to say they are setting up full-scale manufacturing plants in Europe. In many cases they have done so because their goods, produced outside the Community, have been regarded as unfair competition and have attracted anti-dumping duties designed to make them more expensive and therefore less competitive. To avoid this they first of all transferred final assembly to Europe. That in turn provoked an attack on so-called screwdriver operations[5] – this was accomplished by the imposition of local content rules, that is rules which require a minimum amount of domestically produced content. The Commission's latest strategy now appears to be to devise origin rules which focus on the transfer of technology, since a local content ratio of 80 per cent can still allow Japanese producers to hang on to key technological processes.

In its 1992 programme for liberalizing financial services the Community is also exercising leverage by imposing reciprocity conditions. Third World country banks (Japanese are very much in mind) will be able to establish subsidiaries in the EC and enjoy the benefits of an enlarged market, but only if their home country reciprocates in respect of Community banks.

[. . .]

Democratic implications of 1992

Some time ago Jacques Delors let slip the speculation that in the mid-1990's perhaps 80 per cent of domestic economic legislation would derive from Brussels. Apart from sending a frisson of alarm down the spines of all those who cherish their national sovereignty, such a forecast, if only half true, does point to the emergence of a democratic gap. Since Community law is supreme, national parliaments would increasingly be consigned to the role of rubber-stamping the actions of the Council of Ministers. The EP, on the other hand, is largely consultative. It does not provide a substitute for national parliaments in that the Council of Ministers does not legislate through it and is not accountable to it in the way which is typical of representative democracies. It would therefore appear that if the Delors prediction is broadly correct there will, in the medium to long term, be a need to radically redefine the role of the EP in relation to the Council of Ministers. In other words, the EP would have to take on the role of approving Community legislation similarly to the way in which national parliaments currently make national laws.

Progress and prospects

The basic question is simple to state but more difficult to answer – will the 1992 programme succeed? This can be approached in a variety of ways:

(a) Will the Community achieve its legislative target?
(b) Are business people responding (wisely) in anticipation of the challenge?
(c) How big will the economic pay-off really be?
(d) Is an economic pay-off the only measure of success?

In respect of its legislative task, the EC Commission's report of November 1988 indicated that, whilst substantial progress had been made, only a third of the required measures had been adopted. The Community is therefore currently behind schedule. As members have to be given time to incorporate measures into national law, it follows that the Council of Ministers will have to complete most of its work by 1990. This is a formidable task. We may in fact anticipate some slippage in the timetable as a result of two factors. Firstly, there are clearly some issues where member states are beginning to dig in their heels. The proposal to harmonize VAT rates is one which cuts across the UK's wish to cling to its fiscal sovereignty. Whilst, as noted earlier, the SEA provides for harmonization measures to be dealt with on a majority voting basis, the British were able to insist that fiscal matters should be excluded from that rule. Slippage may also occur because of derogations from the 1992 deadline. Thus in the case of the non-life insurance directive, some states have been allowed until 1998 or 1999 to bring their laws into line with the Community standard.

The evidence, such as it is, suggests that business people are responding. We have already noted the Japanese inward investment reaction. Within Europe a major programme of corporate restructuring is under way. Corporate strategists point out that there is no single right answer. The correct strategy will be industry specific. This is what the evidence suggests since, while the tempo of mergers and acquisitions (both domestic and cross-border) has been rising rapidly, it is also apparent that some industries have been engaged in divesting themselves of activities which are peripheral or difficult to manage in order to concentrate on areas of strength.

It is clearly too soon to measure the actual as opposed to the estimated economic pay-off. It should be pointed out that even if the figures cited earlier are achieved, they are not overwhelming, since they constitute no more than about two years' growth. If, on the other hand, the single market has the dynamic property of shifting the Community on to a permanently higher growth path, a more favourable judgement would be called for. On the other hand an undue concentration on economic pay-offs is not what the SEA is all about. The fruits of European Union cannot be measured solely in terms of GDP.

Notes

1. West Germany, France, Italy, UK, Belgium, Netherlands, Luxembourg, Irish Republic, Denmark, Greece, Spain and Portugal.
2. West Germany, France, Italy, Belgium, Netherlands and Luxembourg.
3. Named after Lord Cockfield, a British member of the EC Commission, who was responsible for the internal market.
4. Scheduled flights are those which operate to a predetermined schedule, i.e. date and time, as in the case of rail passenger services. Charter flights are air passenger services which do not fly to any predetermined public schedule but are hired by, for example, tour operators as part of a package holiday deal. Charters are highly competitive.
5. Screwdriver operations are those where the parts are manufactured abroad. The parts are then imported, but most of the work has already been done and all that remains is the limited task of assembly.

Bibliography

Button, K.J. and Swann, D. (1989) 'European Community airlines – de-regulation and its problems', *Journal of Common Market Studies*, 27 (4).
Cecchini, P. (1988) *The European Challenge 1992*. Aldershot: Wildwood House, Gower.
Commission of the European Communities, (1985) *Cockfield Report, Completing the Internal Market*. Document COM(85) 310 final, 14 June.
Commission of the European Communities, June (1986) *Single European Act, Bulletin of the European Communities*, Supplement 2.86.
Delors, J. (1988) *Europe 1992: The Social Dimension, Address to the Trade Union Congress*. Bournemouth 1988, Commission of the European Communities.
Economist, (1988) 'Europe's Internal Market', 9 July.
Emerson, M. (1989) *The Economics of 1992*. Oxford: Oxford University Press.
Pelkmans, J. and Winters, A (1988) *Europe's Domestic Market*. London: Routledge.
Price, V.C. (1988) *1992: Europe's Last Chance*. London: Institute of Economic Affairs.
Office for Official Publications of the European Communities, *Europe Without Frontiers – Completing the Internal Market*. European documentation, 2.89.
Royal Bank of Scotland Review, 162, (June 1989) The whole issue is devoted to 1992.
Swann, D. (1988) *The Economics of the Common Market*. Harmondsworth: Penguin.
Thatcher, M. (1988) *Britain and Europe*, Text of the speech delivered in Bruges, 20 September. Conservative Political Centre.

7

Which internal market? The NHS White Paper and internal markets

Penelope M. Mullen

One of the fundamental proposals in the 1989 Health Service White Paper *Working for Patients* (DoH, 1989) is the separation of the funding of health care from the provision of health care, using what many commentators have termed an 'Internal Market'. However, although it is now widely used, the term 'Internal Market' would appear to embrace more than one concept. What, then is an 'Internal Market'?

The term 'Internal Market' is usually attributed to Enthoven, who put forward proposals for greater import and export of patients between health authorities. Enthoven explained his proposals thus:

> Each District would receive a RAWP (Regional Authority Working Party)-based per capita revenue and capital allowance. Each DHA (District Health Authority) would continue to be responsible to provide and pay for comprehensive care for its own resident population. [. . .] It would be paid for emergency services to outsiders at a standard cost. It would be paid for non-emergency services to outsiders at negotiated prices. It would control referrals to providers outside the District and it would pay for them at negotiated prices. [. . .] (Enthoven, 1985a)

He also stressed that: 'The theory behind such a scheme – which can better be called "market socialism" than "privatisation" – is that the managers could then buy services from producers who offered the best value' (Enthoven, 1985b).

This concept of the 'Internal Market' was adopted by most contributors during the debate prior to the publication of the White Paper 'Working for Patients'. [. . .]

However, statements from Ministers and interpretations in the press in the months leading up to the publication of the White Paper appear to describe a rather different concept of the 'Internal Market' – a patient-led system. For instance:

> moves to create an 'internal market' in the NHS where patients are encouraged to seek treatment where waiting lists are the lowest. (Hencke and Carvel, 1988)

Adapted from *Financial Accountability and Management* 6(1), Spring 1990: 33–50.

[. . .]

The Secretary of State strongly endorsed the idea of patients shopping around for treatment to cut waiting times [. . .] (Wood, 1988)

The front-runner for reform remains the adoption of the 'internal market', under which GPs could send patients to the health districts with the shortest waiting lists, with the money for their treatment travelling with them. (Brown, 1988)

This concept would appear rather different from that proposed by Enthoven.

Classification of 'Internal Markets'

Thus we find that two very different types of system are being described under the heading 'Internal Market'. These may be termed Type I and Type II systems or models. Whilst each of the two systems embraces a host of different proposals, the 'pure' forms of the two types of system can be characterized as follows [. . .]

Type I 'Internal Market' systems

With Type I systems the health authority receives funding for its population; has a specific responsibility for the health/health care of that population; and, in various combinations depending on how radical the proposal claims to be, provides and/or purchases services from other providers, public or private, to meet the health needs of the population. In the least 'radical' forms, the home authorities remain the main providers of services, but purchasing of services from other. health authorities is increased. In the most 'radical' forms, the home health authority does not provide any services at all directly, but puts out contracts (with or without competitive tendering) for the entire range of provision. With the Type I 'Internal Market' it is implied, although not always made explicit, that residents of the home health authority may be treated only by 'approved' or 'contracted' providers.

Type II 'Internal Market' systems

With Type II systems, the health authority receives funding for its population; may be a direct supplier of (some) services; but residents can seek treatment anywhere and their home authority is obliged to reimburse the providing authority. This reimbursement may be either at cost or according to some laid-down scale or negotiated scale of charges. Popularly when this type of 'Internal Market' is mentioned, it is in terms of 'patients being able to shop around to find the shortest waiting list, with their health authority being sent the bill'.

[. . .] The National Association of Health Authorities (NAHA, 1988) did in fact point to the two different concepts of the 'Internal Market'. Whilst it described an 'Internal Market' where '[. . .] the district health authority operates much like the Health Maintenance Organisation in America; here the patient and GP may have less choice concerning where treatment is obtained because the health authority will make its own assessment of value for money services from other authorities or the private sector', it also pointed out that there is another totally different model being advocated under the generic term 'Internal Market', that is 'Automatic and immediate cross-boundary flow reimbursement', which it states 'carries the internal market concept to its full fruition, involving transferring the initiative from the planners and treasurers, to the market customers (i.e. patients) and their advisers (i.e. GPs) with money following the patient'. Under this model residents can seek treatment anywhere and their home authority is obliged to reimburse the providing authority, either at cost or according to some laid-down scale of charges. [. . .]

Implications of the different models of the 'Internal Market'

[. . .] The Type I system has been likened to a Health Maintenance Organization (HMO), with the difference that the 'organization' is compulsorily responsible for all residents of a particular location, and thus has no choice over membership. The Type II system is basically a system of retrospective or prospective reimbursement, and is thus very similar to an insurance-based system or to systems such as the American Medicare payments system, where the insurance company, or the state, reimburses the hospital (provider) for care supplied. [. . .]

Insurance-based systems

Insurance-based health care systems raise questions in two directions. Firstly, by what mechanism do patients or consumers become insured and, secondly how is health care supplied and paid for? [. . .] under the pure Type II model described here, effectively all residents of a locality would be assumed to be 'insured' with their local health authority. The concern here is how health care is supplied and paid for.

Under most insurance systems, hospitals and health care providers supply services to insured patients and are then reimbursed for the services by the insurer either according to retrospective full cost reimbursement, or according to prospective reimbursement. In addition, in either case, the patient may have to make a payment at the point of receipt of service. [. . .]

Retrospective reimbursement

Under retrospective reimbursement schemes, the suppliers of health care receive payment in full from the insurer for all expenditure incurred. Under this system, suppliers have an incentive to maximize income by encouraging as much activity as possible. They thus have an incentive to maximize the number of patients treated, maximize the length of stay, maximize the number of surgical procedures performed, and maximize the number of diagnostic tests carried out and drugs supplied. Such a system is inherently inflationary as it encourages escalation of costs. Experience in the US, Canada and some European countries was that retrospective reimbursement led to enormous increases in health care costs.

There is no evidence that retrospective reimbursement gives any encouragement to the cost-effective use of different procedures since the health care suppliers know that, whatever the cost, they will be reimbursed. [. . .]

Prospective reimbursement

The escalation of costs under retrospective reimbursement was so great in the US that there were attempts to introduce regulations into the system to control costs. In a further attempt to control costs, the US Government and insurance companies turned to a prospective payment system, a form of prospective reimbursement. Under this system, health care providers are reimbursed at a predetermined price for each defined unit of workload, regardless of the actual cost involved in providing that unit of workload. The 'unit of workload' can be a day in hospital, a diagnostic test or a particular procedure, but more recently has been in the form of a case. This has led to the development of Diagnostic Related Groups (DRGs) – a method of 'classifying inpatients into a manageable number of groups, which are both clinically meaningful and homogeneous in resource use' (Culyer and Brazier, 1988). Providers are then reimbursed at a set price per case treated, according to the DRG into which the case falls.

Prospective payment systems have the advantage that health care suppliers are paid for the number of cases treated and are encouraged to be aware of the costs per case. Experience has shown that with the introduction of such systems the cost per case dropped, but there is little evidence of whether this resulted from greater efficiency or lower quality of care. Whilst this system controls the cost per case, the incentive to the supplier is still to treat as many cases as possible and experience suggests that overall expenditure does not necessarily fall, since more cases are treated. As mentioned above this system requires the classification of hospital activity by case complexity and difficulty. However, the prospective payment system produces incentives: (a) to treat the lowest-cost patients within any group, (b) to shift the cost of treatment to other agencies and (c) to classify patients in the highest cost group possible – known

as DRG creep. Thus, with a prospective payment system the funding agency still cannot control total expenditure, unless it can control the number of cases. Indeed, some insurance companies have tried to do this by requiring prior approval for treatment.
[. . .]

Type I v Type II 'Internal Markets'

Following on from the above arguments, the two types of 'Internal Market', Type I and Type II, will now be examined to determine their respective implications, according to the following criteria (see Table 1):

- Freedom of choice
    - for patients
    - for GPs

- Health care planning
    Ability to promote priorities
    Meeting the needs of the population
    Equality and equity

- Overall expenditure control

- Costing detail and information requirements

Freedom of choice for patients and general practitioners

Despite claims by some that 'Internal Markets' would increase the freedom of the patient to choose where to seek treatment, it is clear from the discussion above that such freedom is associated only with Type II systems. Indeed, almost all commentators stress that for Type I systems to work, the health authority must have control over the destination of referrals. Depending on the particular system used, patients would only be permitted to seek treatment from 'approved' or 'contracted' suppliers or would have to get prior agreement from their home authority to seek treatment elsewhere. Such restrictions would remove any rights GPs currently enjoy to choose where to refer their patients. [. . .]

However, if the GPs were to act as Health Maintenance Organizations (HMOs) and have a budget to cover the total care for their patients, a Type I system would give them considerable freedom of referral, but would not necessarily increase the patients' freedom.

Although theoretically the Type II system permits full GP (and consumer) choice and, indeed, this is seen by its advocates as one of its virtues, some commentators question how much choice would exist in reality. Firstly, the choice would be that of the GP rather than the consumer, and secondly, it is felt that the implied travelling to receive services would limit freedom. [. . .] However, this objection is raised in

Table 1   *Implications of the two types of 'Internal Market' model*

Criteria	Type I Model	Type II Model
Freedom of choice		
for patients	Very low	High (if able to travel)
for budget-holding		
GPs	Fairly high	Medium
non-budget holding GPs	Very low	High
Health care planning	Important for DHAs	Unimportant for DHAs
ability to promote		
priorities	High	Low
meet needs of		
population	Potentially high	Low
equality and equity	Medium (within group)	Fairly high (within group)
	High (between groups)	Low (between groups)
Overall expenditure control	High potential	Low potential
DHA information requirements and costing detail	Need, quality, outcome, financial	Financial, activity

respect of both types of system. Culyer *et al.* (1988) stress that 'care will have to be exercised to ensure that very sick and elderly patients are not treated or cared for long distances away from their homes and families' [. . .]

Planning, priorities, need and equity

Possibly one of the most dramatic implications is the effect of the two different systems on health (care) planning. Type I systems, because they allocate funds to a health authority, which is charged with responsibility for the health (care) of its (geographically defined) population, will not only ensure, but will require, an important planning role for the health authority [. . .] to ensure that local needs and priorities are pursued. However, the Type I system is not without problems. As discussed below, the problems of letting contracts, controlling payments and maintaining quality would be immense in the more radical proposals. In addition, individual health authorities would enter the 'Internal Markets' with different historical endowments of facilities and would be unlikely to be able to compete equally for contracts.

With extreme versions of the Type II systems, there would appear little health care planning role for the home health authority and little scope for ensuring that local needs and priorities are met, although, of course, business planning would be necessary for the providing authorities/ hospitals. This arises from the essence of this type of system which is that patients can go anywhere for treatment, and their home authority must pay for such treatment, whether or not it is considered necessary for that particular patient, whether or not that type of treatment figures in the

local priorities, and whether or not there are 'more deserving' cases within
the authority. Providing authorities/hospitals would be paid for cases
treated either on the basis of actual cost per case, or on some laid-down
or agreed cost per case, and there seems little to prevent them behaving
in the same manner as hospitals elsewhere where either 'Retrospective full
cost reimbursement' or 'Prospective reimbursement' systems are in operation. There would be no restraint on services provided or number of cases
treated, since the provider authority/hospital would be certain of
payment. The home authority, on the other hand, could find its funds
being compulsorily diverted to services and cases it considered low
priority.

However, it should not be thought that Type I systems are non-
problematic from the point of view of planning for the health (care) needs
of a population. With the more extreme proposals, problems arise from
the notion of 'packages' of services or care, which would be a corollary
of contracting and tendering for services. Essentially, the arguments
revolve around whether the health service should be considered as an
agent in the improvement of the health (status) of the population, and
thus concerned with promoting and restoring health and preventing ill-
health, or whether it is a provider of a commodity – health (care) services.
Much of the debate on the 'Internal Market' appears to relate to elective
surgery, which lends itself to 'packages' of care. It is easy to grasp the
concept of tendering for the oft-quoted '200 hip replacements' [. . .]
However, the 'most radical' proposals would put the entire health service
out to tender – in discrete parcels. How this could be done for, say,
general medicine, other than by letting a contract to provide all services
required by a defined population, is difficult to envisage. If the contract
has been given for, say, 100 pneumonia cases, or for 100 fractures (or 100
births!), what do you say to the 101st case that comes along? Thus, in its
most radical form, a Type I 'Internal Market' would have to involve a
mixture of contracts for numbers of cases, and contracts for particular
services for defined population. Other planning problems arise, of course,
from questions such as the interdependence of services. Is it really possible to 'contract-out' some specialities and still retain a comprehensive
service?

Considerations of equality and equity reveal somewhat contradictory
implications. Assuming that a health authority has incorporated equity
considerations into its planning and priority setting, Type I systems would
appear to safeguard equality and equity, especially between health care
groups. On the other hand, Type II systems would appear to allow little
scope for equity between groups since large amounts of a health
authority's budget would be compulsorily diverted to those areas where
patients are more mobile and where providers find it most profitable to
supply services, that is mainly elective surgery. However, Type I systems
do create their own form of inequality since, if different health authorities
differ in their priorities and make provision only for health care which

they consider to be a priority, residents of different health authorities will find, depending on their local HA's priorities, that access to some forms of health care may be even more unequal than at present. In contrast, Type II systems, by allowing patients to seek treatment anywhere, in theory avoid this form of inequality. However, it is argued that new inequalities would arise between patients with the resources and knowledge to seek care outside their district and patients without such resources and/or knowledge.

Overall expenditure control

It is virtually impossible to conceive of a Type II system operating with cash-limited health authorities. All discussion of retrospective and prospective reimbursement systems points to the difficulties of controlling overall expenditure. The NAHA proposals (NAHA, 1988) for workload funding, recognizing something of this point, do suggest that acute services should not be cash limited. They further suggest that regional planning would limit any unconstrained growth arising from operating what is essentially a reimbursement system. In practice, if a pure Type II system were operating, the effect would be that health authorities would find very large parts of their budgets being compulsorily removed to pay for a much higher consumption of acute (mainly elective surgery) health care, with a consequential diminution of money available for other services, especially the so-called priority services.

It can be argued that a fairly radical Type II 'Internal Market' has already developed in the care of the elderly, where much provision is private but much of the funding is public. It is however debatable how far this is a relevant model for the rest of the health service. Firstly, care of the elderly is essentially 'elective care' (cf. elective surgery). Secondly, the current pattern of provision grew up initially on the basis of 'full cost reimbursement' and latterly on 'prospective payment', in both cases from non-cash-limited public funds. How far would it have developed with cash-limited funds?

Costing detail and information requirements

It appears to be taken as axiomatic by many commentators that any system of 'Internal Markets' would require detailed case costing (Bevan *et al.*, 1989). However, Culyer *et al.* (1988) make the point that 'price mechanisms and contracting/franchising systems are not the product of the post-computer age! Markets have never depended on the existence of detailed information about costs and outcomes: [. . .] More cost and outcome data do, of course, help and are highly desirable; they are not, however, particularly more necessary in a provider market system than they are in the NHS as it is.'

However, both types of 'Internal Market' would generate a consider-able amount of activity in billing, payment and verification which, even in the computer age, would require vastly increased numbers of administrative and clerical staff. Type II systems are likely to require full paperwork for each case, whilst with Type I systems the scale of the clerical operations involved would depend on the type of contract. The proportion of health expenditure devoted to administration is likely to rise nearer to that found in most of Western Europe even if the excesses of the US system are avoided.

Conclusion

The debate on the 'Internal Market' has embraced two radically different types of system, both of which exist in minor forms at present and both of which feature in the proposals in the White Paper, *Working for Patients*. In their extreme forms, one type would preserve health authority responsibility for planning and meeting the needs of its population (but would have many other problems), the other would make planning and the pursuit of local priorities impossible and could probably not be operated with cash-limited budgets. However, in their less extreme forms, both types of system probably have a place, but both can be problematic. Type I systems could pose problems in the creation of 'packages' of care, quality, adverse selection, comprehensiveness and so on. Type II systems could exhibit the problems associated with fee-for-service and reimbursement systems elsewhere. Such problems would also, of course, be associated with workload funding.

References

Bevan, G., Holland, W. and Mays, N. (1989) 'Working for which patients and at what cost', *The Lancet*, 29 April: 947–9.

Brown, C. (1988) 'Internal Market "could lead to hospital closures"', *The Independent*, 9 July.

Culyer, A.J. and Brazier, J.E. (1988) 'Alternatives for organizing the provision of health services in the UK', IHSM Working Paper No. 4 on Alternative Delivery and Funding for Health Care.

Culyer, A.J., Brazier, J.E. and O'Donnel, O.O. (1988) 'Organizing health service provision. Drawing on experience', IHSM Working Paper No. 5 on Alternative Delivery and Funding for Health Care.

DoH (1989) *Working for Patients*, White Paper on the NHS, CM555. London: HMSO.

Enthoven, A.C. (1985a) *Reflections on the Management of the National Health Service*.: NPHT.

Enthoven, A.C. (1985b) 'National Health Service: some reforms that might by politically feasible', *The Economist*, 295 (7399): 19–22.

Hencke, D. and Carvel, J. (1988) 'Thatcher aims to wrap up NHS tax relief next week', *The Guardian*, 20 July.

Maynard, A. (1989) *Whither the National Health Service*, NHS White Paper, Occasional Paper 1, Centre for Health Economics, University of York.

NAHA (1988) *Funding the NHS: Which Way Forward?*, A NAHA consultation document.: National Association of Health Authorities.

Wood, N. (1988) 'Bigger health role for private sector', *The Times*, 5 July.

Hierarchies

Introduction

Jeremy Mitchell

In a market each element (individual, firm) pursues its own interest and the interaction between the elements produces a collective outcome – the market coordinates the separate activities. Coordination by hierarchy is different in that the actions of similar elements (individuals, firms) is to some extent constrained. Hierarchy presupposes an already determined outcome or purpose; the underlying idea of hierarchy is that such an outcome can be broken down into a set of sub-processes. So hierarchy depends upon ideas of organization, task specialization and rationality. In addition hierarchies involve a stratification of authority and the following of rules. Thus each level of a hierarchy directs the action of those 'lower down', ultimate authority resides with those at the 'top', and at each level those involved carry out more narrowly defined tasks with less and less autonomy. Jaques (Chapter 8) presents a general picture of hierarchy as a mechanism for 'running' or 'coordinating' large organizations. Indeed he suggests that despite its problems hierarchy remains the most efficient mechanism for integrating the activities of a large group of people, of making an organization work effectively. His examples are largely drawn from the world of business and the workings of private sector firms but the analysis of hierarchy is particularly associated with organizations acting on the authority of the state, that is with those in the public sector.

Much of these public sector organizations are concerned with administration, with the running of government and public agencies. Such organizations are usually referred to as bureaucracies and much contemporary analysis is derived from the work of the German sociologist Max Weber, who saw them as an essential element of contemporary capitalism. An extract from his work appears as Chapter 9. For Weber the growth of bureaucracy in the modern state was a consequence of the extension of rationality in the conduct of public affairs and the substitution of neutral administrative practice for previous modes of state activity. The growth of bureaucracy is associated with the growth of legality and the rule of law in contrast to previous administrative arbitrariness. The modern bureaucracy is a hierarchical organization which is staffed by individuals who have been recruited for a full-time career within such organizations. Weber draws out the defining function of the rules within such organizations, the nature of the bureaucratic career, the internal stratification of authority and other general characteristics. He also makes a distinction between the profit-making nature of a private organization such as a firm and the non-profit-making activity of public sector organizations like bureaucracies. This distinction is further elaborated by Beetham (Chapter 10), who discusses the important consequences that follow for the internal organization of bureaucratic hierarchies. It is important to recognize that there are general consequences of the use of hierarchy as a coordinating mechanism – the subdivision of tasks, the pyramidal structure of organization, the nature of individual activity within such large organizations, the mechanisms of control and communication, the gradation of autonomy and so on – that apply both to public bureaucracies and to similarly hierarchical organizations in the private sector. We can thus distinguish between the consequences of hierarchy in general and the particular problems facing public bureaucracies.

But what it is like to exist and survive within a bureaucracy? This is the issue taken up by Benveniste in Chapter 11. Here it is the behavioural responses of bureaucrats that is focused upon. How do they maximize their chances of career development? What are the strategies participants devise to avoid negative and critical evaluation of their activity? What risks are associated with innovative behaviour on their part and how are these coped with? All these issues are essential to the consequences and effectiveness of hierarchical coordination.

The distinction between government and the market is central to Sartori's discussion of planning in Chapter 12. He describes both market and government as mechanisms of coordination, but whereas bureaucracy/hierarchy is centralized, the market is decentralized. Hierarchies implement decisions that are made by those in authority; the market gives more autonomy to individual agents. In the period after 1945 planning was one mechanism used by governments as a substitute for market decision-making and Sartori analyses some of the problems associated with it. This choice between government (hierarchy, planning) and the market is important in understanding some of the recent changes in the overall process of coordination by central government in Britain, that is to understand how the country is run.

We can summarize a complex process by suggesting that since 1979 central government has tried to extend market provision and market coordination into areas in which non-market, governmental or hierarchical coordination had previously been the norm. This has been effected by changes such as privatization and liberalization. In privatization the ownership of an organization is transferred from the public to the private sector – and this theoretically changes one defining characteristic of the organization (see for example the discussion by Beetham). Liberalization, on the other hand, allows easier entry into particular markets. It is these changes that form the background to the discussion by Vickers (Chapter 13).

Some of the organizations that have been privatized – the telephone system for example – were public monopolies; now they have effectively become private monopolies. The problem of monopoly has been discussed elsewhere, in the general introduction and Chapter 4 by Krizner for example, and the solution adopted in most cases of privatization has been to place constraints upon the operation of these now private monopolies. Such constraints include the need to adhere to certain standards or a limitation upon their ability to make excessive profits. Vickers' analysis suggests that paradoxically this creation of new agencies to regulate such activities has actually increased the ability of government to intervene in certain areas of the economy.

In doing this it has also extended the role of hierarchical coordination in the overall process of running the country. However, this says nothing about coordination between agencies and it is here that one could point to the possible role of networks as well. It is these network forms of coordination that are considered in the third section of this book.

8

In praise of hierarchy

Elliott Jaques

At first glance, hierarchy may seem difficult to praise. Bureaucracy is a dirty word even among bureaucrats, and in business there is a widespread view that managerial hierarchy kills initiative, crushes creativity, and has therefore seen its day. Yet 35 years of research have convinced me that managerial hierarchy is the most efficient, the hardiest, and in fact the most natural structure ever devised for large organizations. Properly structured, hierarchy can release energy and creativity, rationalize productivity, and actually improve morale. Moreover, I think most managers know this intuitively and have only lacked a workable structure and a decent intellectual justification for what they have always known could work, and work well.

As presently practiced, hierarchy undeniably has its drawbacks. One of business's great contemporary problems is how to release and sustain among the people who work in corporate hierarchies the thrust, initiative and adaptability of the entrepreneur. This problem is so great that it has become fashionable to call for a new kind of organization to put in place of managerial hierarchy, an organization that will better meet the requirements of what is variously called the Information Age, the Services Age or the Post-Industrial Age.

As vague as the description of the age is the definition of the kind of new organization required to suit it. Theorists tell us it ought to look more like a symphony orchestra or a hospital or perhaps the British Raj. It ought to function by means of primus groups or semi-autonomous work teams or matrix overlap groups. It should be organic or entrepreneurial or tight-loose. It should hinge on management by walking around or perhaps on our old friend, management by objective.

All these approaches are efforts to overcome the perceived faults of hierarchy and find better ways to improve morale and harness human creativity. But the theorists' belief that our changing world requires an alternative to hierarchical organization is simply wrong, and all their proposals are based on an inadequate understanding of not only hierarchy but also human nature.

Hierarchy is not to blame for our problems. Encouraged by gimmicks and fads masquerading as insights, we have burdened our managerial

Reprinted from *Harvard Business Review*, January–February 1990: 127–33.

systems with a makeshift scaffolding of inept structures and attitudes. What we need is not simply a new, flatter organization but an understanding of how managerial hierarchy functions – how it relates to the complexity of work and how we can use it to achieve a more effective deployment of talent and energy.

The reason we have a hierarchical organization of work is not only that tasks occur in lower and higher degrees of complexity – which is obvious – but also that there are sharp discontinuities in complexity that separate tasks into a series of steps or categories – which is not so obvious. The same discontinuities occur with respect to mental work and to the breadth and duration of accountability. The hierarchical kind of organization we call bureaucracy did not emerge accidentally. It is the only form of organization that can enable a company to employ large numbers of people and yet preserve unambiguous accountability for the work they do. And that is why, despite its problems, it has so doggedly persisted.

Hierarchy has not had its day. Hierarchy never did have its day. As an organizational system, managerial hierarchy has never been adequately described and has just as certainly never been adequately used. The problem is not to find an alternative to a system that once worked well but no longer does; the problem is to make it work efficiently for the first time in its 3,000-year history.

What went wrong . . .

There is no denying that hierarchical structure has been the source of a great deal of trouble and inefficiency. Its misuse has hampered effective management and stifled leadership, while its track record as a support for entrepreneurial energy has not been exemplary. We might almost say that successful businesses have had to succeed despite hierarchical organization rather than because of it.

One common complaint is excessive layering – too many rungs on the ladder. Information passes through too many people, decisions through too many levels, and managers and subordinates are too close together in experience and ability, which smothers effective leadership, cramps accountability, and promotes buck passing. Relationships grow stressful when managers and subordinates bump elbows, so to speak, within the same frame of reference.

Another frequent complaint is that few managers seem to add real value to the work of their subordinates. The fact that the break-up value of many large corporations is greater than their share value shows pretty clearly how much value corporate managers can *subtract* from their subsidiary businesses, but in fact few of us know exactly what managerial added value would look like when it is occurring.

Many people also complain that our present hierarchies bring out the nastier aspects of human behavior, like greed, insensitivity, careerism and self-importance. These are the qualities that have sent many behavioral scientists in search of cooperative, group-oriented, non-hierarchical organizational forms. But are they the inevitable companions of hierarchy, or perhaps a product of the misuse of hierarchy that would disappear if hierarchy were properly understood and structured?

. . . And what continues to go wrong

The fact that so many of hierarchy's problems show up in the form of individual misbehavior has led to one of the most widespread illusions in business, namely that a company's managerial leadership can be significantly improved solely by doing psychotherapeutic work on the personalities and attitudes of its managers. Such methods can help individuals gain greater personal insight, but I doubt that individual insight, personality matching, or even exercises in group dynamics can produce much in the way of organizational change or an overall improvement in leadership effectiveness. The problem is that our managerial hierarchies are so badly designed as to defeat the best efforts even of psychologically insightful individuals.

Solutions that concentrate on groups, on the other hand, fail to take into account the real nature of employment systems. People are not employed in groups. They are employed individually, and their employment contracts – real or implied – are individual. Group members may insist in moments of great *esprit de corps* that the group as such is the author of some particular accomplishment, but once the work is completed, the members of the group look for individual recognition and individual progression in their careers. And it is not groups but individuals whom the company will hold accountable. The only true group is the board of directors, with its corporate liability.

None of the group-oriented panaceas face this issue of accountability. All the theorists refer to group authority, group decisions and group consensus, none of them to group accountability. Indeed, they avoid the issue of accountability altogether, for to hold a group accountable the employment contract would have to be with the group, not with the individuals, and companies simply do not employ groups as such.

To understand hierarchy, you must first understand employment. To be employed is to have an ongoing contract that holds you accountable for doing work of a given type for a specified number of hours per week in exchange for payment. Your specific tasks within that given work are assigned to you by a person called your manager (or boss or supervisor), who *ought to be held accountable* for the work you do.

If we are to make our hierarchies function properly, it is essential to place the emphasis on *accountability for getting work done*. This is what hierarchical systems ought to be about. Authority is a secondary issue and flows from accountability in the sense that there should be just that amount of authority needed to discharge the accountability. So if a group is to be given authority, its members must be held accountable as a group, and unless this is done, it is very hard to take so-called group decisions seriously. If the CEO or the manager of the group is held accountable for outcomes, then in the final analysis, he or she will have to agree with group decisions or have the authority to block them, which means that the group never really had decision-making power to begin with. Alternatively, if groups are allowed to make decisions without their manager's seal of approval, then accountability as such will suffer, for if a group does badly, the group is never fired (and it would be shocking if it were).

In the long run, therefore, group authority *without* group accountability is dysfunctional, and group authority *with* group accountability is unacceptable. So images of organizations that are more like symphony orchestras or hospitals or the British Raj are surely nothing more than metaphors to express a desired feeling of togetherness – the togetherness produced by a conductor's baton, the shared concern of doctors and nurses for their patients, or the apparent unity of the British civil service in India.

In employment systems, after all, people are not mustered to play together as their manager beats time. As for hospitals, they are the essence of everything bad about bureaucratic organization. They function in spite of the system, only because of the enormous professional devotion of their staffs. The Indian civil service was in many ways like a hospital, its people bound together by the struggle to survive in a hostile environment. Managers do need authority, but authority based appropriately on the accountabilities they must discharge.

Why hierarchy?

The bodies that govern companies, unions, clubs and nations all employ people to do work, and they all organize these employees in managerial hierarchies, systems that allow organizations to hold people accountable for getting assigned work done. Unfortunately, we often lose sight of this goal and set up the organizational layers in our managerial hierarchies to accommodate pay brackets and facilitate career development instead. If work happens to get done as well, we consider that a useful bonus.

But if our managerial hierarchical organizations tend to choke so readily on debilitating bureaucratic practices, how do we explain the persistence and continued spread of this form of organization for more than 3,000 years? And why has the determined search for alternatives proved so fruitless?

The answer is that managerial hierarchy is and will remain the *only* way to structure unified working systems with hundreds, thousands or tens of thousands of employees, for the very good reason that managerial hierarchy is the expression of two fundamental characteristics of real work.

First, the tasks we carry out are not only more or less complex but they also become more complex as they separate out into discrete categories or types of complexity. Second, the same is true of the mental work that people do on the job, for as this work grows more complex, it too separates out into distinct categories or types of mental activity. In turn, these two characteristics permit hierarchy to meet four of any organization's fundamental needs: to add real value to work as it moves through the organization, to identify and nail down accountability at each stage of the value-adding process, to place people with the necessary competence at each organizational layer, and to build a general consensus and acceptance of the managerial structure that achieves these ends.

Hierarchical layers

The complexity of the problems encountered in a particular task, project or strategy is a function of the variables involved – their number, their clarity or ambiguity, the rate at which they change, and, overall the extent to which they are distinct or tangled. Obviously, as you move higher in a managerial hierarchy, the most difficult problems you have to contend with become increasingly complex. The biggest problems faced by the CEO of a large corporation are vastly more complex than those encountered on the shop floor. The CEO must cope not only with a huge array of often amorphous and constantly changing data but also with variables so tightly interwoven that they must be disentangled before they will yield useful information. Such variables might include the cost of capital, the interplay of corporate cash flow, the structure of the international competitive market, the uncertainties of Europe after 1992, the future of Pacific Rim development, social developments with respect to labor, political developments in Eastern Europe, the Middle East, and the Third World, and technological research and change.

That the CEO's and the lathe operator's problems are different in quality as well as quantity will come as no surprise to anyone. The question is – and always has been – where does the change in quality occur? On a continuum of complexity from the bottom of the structure to the top, where are the discontinuities that will allow us to identify layers of hierarchy that are distinct and separable, as different as ice is from water and water from steam? I spent years looking for the answer, and what I found was somewhat unexpected.

My first step was to recognize the obvious, that the layers have to do with manager–subordinate relationships. The manager's position is in one layer and the subordinate's is in the next layer below. What then sets the necessary distance between? This question cannot be answered without knowing just what it is that a manager does.

The managerial role has three critical features. First, and *most* critical, every manager must be held accountable not only for the work of subordinates but also for adding value to their work. Second, every manager must be held accountable for sustaining a team of subordinates capable of doing this work. Third, every manager must be held accountable for setting direction and getting subordinates to follow willingly, indeed enthusiastically. In brief, every manager is accountable for work and leadership.

In order to make accountability possible, managers must have enough authority to ensure that their subordinates can do the work assigned to them. This authority must include at least these four elements: (1) the right to veto any applicant who, in the manager's opinion, falls below the minimum standards of ability; (2) the power to make work assignments; (3) the power to carry out performance appraisals and, within the limits of company policy, to make decisions – not recommendations – about raises and merit rewards; and (4) the authority to initiate removal – at least from the manager's own team – of anyone who seems incapable of doing the work.

But defining the basic nature of the managerial role reveals only part of what a managerial layer means. It cannot tell us how wide a managerial layer should be, what the difference in responsibility should be between a manager and a subordinate, or, most important, where the break should come between one managerial layer and another. Fortunately, the next step in the research process supplied the missing piece of the puzzle.

Responsibility and time

This second step was the unexpected and startling discovery that the level of responsibility in any organizational role – whether a manager's or an individual contributor's – can be objectively measured in terms of the target completion time of the *longest* task, project or program assigned to that role. The more distant the target completion date of the longest task or program, the heavier the weight of responsibility is felt to be. I call this measure the responsibility time span of the role. For example, a supervisor whose principal job is to plan tomorrow's production assignments and next week's work schedule but who also has ongoing responsibility for uninterrupted production supplies for the month ahead has a responsibility time span of one month. A foreman who spends most of his time riding herd on this week's production quotas but who must also develop a program to deal with the labor requirements of next year's retooling has a responsibility time span of a year or a little more. The advertising vice-president who stays late every night working on next week's layouts but who also has to begin making contingency plans for the expected launch of two new local advertising media campaigns three years hence has a responsibility time span of three years.

To my great surprise, I found that in all types of managerial organization in many different countries over 35 years, people in roles at the same

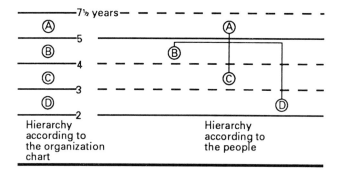

Figure 1 *Managerial hierarchy in fiction and in fact*

time span experience the same weight of responsibility and declare the same level of pay to be fair, regardless of their occupation or actual pay. The time-span range runs from a day at the bottom of a large corporation to more than 20 years at the top, while the felt-fair pay ranges from $15,000 to $1 million and more.

Armed with my definition of a manager and my time-span measuring instrument, I then bumped into the second surprising finding – repeatedly confirmed – about layering in managerial hierarchies: the boundaries between successive managerial layers occur at certain specific time-span increments, just as ice changes to water and water to steam at certain specific temperatures. And the fact that everyone in the hierarchy, regardless of status, seems to see these boundaries in the same places suggests that the boundaries reflect some universal truth about human nature.

Figure 1 'Managerial hierarchy in fiction and in fact' shows the hierarchical structure of part of a department at one company I studied, along with the approximate responsibility time span for each position. The longest task for manager A was more than five years, while for B, C and D, the longest tasks fell between two and five years. Note also that according to the organization chart, A is the designated manager of B, B of C, and C of D.

In reality, the situation was quite different. Despite the managerial roles specified by the company, B, C and D all described A as their 'real' boss. C complained that B was 'far too close' and 'breathing down my neck'. D had the same complaint about C. B and C also admitted to finding it very difficult to manage their immediate subordinates, C and D respectively, who seemed to do better if treated as colleagues and left alone.

In short, there appeared to be a cutoff at five years, such that those with responsibility time spans of less than five years felt they needed a manager with a responsibility time span of more than five years. Manager D, with a time span of two to three years, did not feel that C, with a time span of three to four, was distant enough hierarchically to take orders from. D felt the same way about B. Only A filled the bill for *any* of the other three.

As the responsibility time span increased in the example from two years to three to four and approached five, no one seemed to perceive a qualitative difference in the nature of the responsibility that a manager discharged. Then, suddenly, when a manager had responsibility for tasks and projects that exceeded five years in scope, everyone seemed to perceive a difference not only in the scope of responsibility but also in its quality and in the kind of work and worker required to discharge it.

I found several such discontinuities that appeared consistently in more than 100 studies. Real managerial and hierarchical boundaries occur at time spans of three months, one year, two years, five years, ten years, and twenty years.

These natural discontinuities in our perception of the responsibility time span create hierarchical strata that people in different companies, countries and circumstances all seem to regard as genuine and acceptable. The existence of such boundaries has important implications in nearly every sphere of organizational management. One of these is performance appraisal. Another is the capacity of managers to add value to the work of their subordinates.

The only person with the perspective and authority to judge and communicate personal effectiveness is an employee's accountable manager, who, in most cases, is also the only person from whom an employee will accept evaluation and coaching. This accountable manager must be the supervisor one real layer higher in the hierarchy, not merely the next-higher employee on the pay scale.

As I suggested earlier, part of the secret of making hierarchy work is to distinguish carefully between hierarchical layers and pay grades. The trouble is that companies need two to three times as many pay grades as they do working layers, and once they've established the pay grades, which are easy to describe and set up, they fail to take the next step and set up a different managerial hierarchy based on responsibility rather than salary. The result is too many layers.

My experience with organizations of all kinds in many different countries has convinced me that effective value-adding managerial leadership of subordinates can come only from an individual one category higher in cognitive capacity, working one category higher in problem complexity. By contrast, wherever managers and subordinates are in the same layer – separated only by pay grade – subordinates see the boss as too close, breathing down their necks, and they identify their 'real' boss as the next manager at a genuinely higher level of cognitive and task complexity. This kind of overlayering is what produces the typical symptoms of bureaucracy in its worst form – too much passing problems up and down the system, bypassing, poor task setting, frustrated subordinates, anxious managers, wholly inadequate performance appraisals, 'personality problems' everywhere, and so forth.

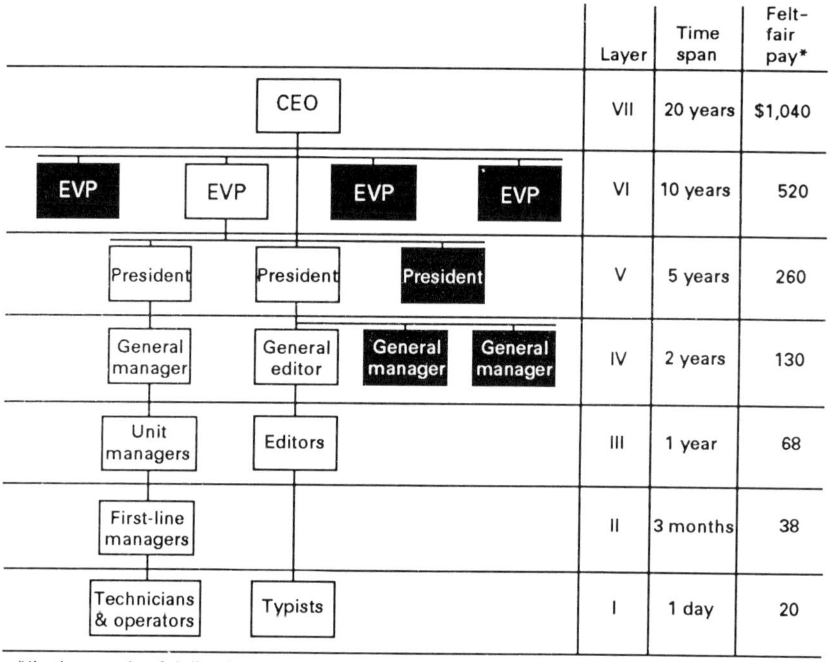

		Layer	Time span	Felt-fair pay*
CEO		VII	20 years	$1,040
EVP · EVP · EVP · EVP		VI	10 years	520
President · President · President		V	5 years	260
General manager · General editor · General manager · General manager		IV	2 years	130
Unit managers · Editors		III	1 year	68
First-line managers		II	3 months	38
Technicians & operators · Typists		I	1 day	20

*(in thousands of dollars)

Figure 2 *Two divisions of Corporation X*

Layering at Corporation X

Companies need more than seven pay grades – as a rule, many more. But seven hierarchical layers is enough or more than enough for all but the largest corporations.

Let me illustrate this pattern of hierarchical layering with the case of two divisions of Corporation X, which has 32,000 employees and annual sales of $7 billion. As shown in Figure 2, the CEO sets strategic goals that look ahead as far as 25 years and manages executive vice-presidents (EVPs) with responsibility for 12- to 15-year development programs. One vice-president is accountable for several strategic business units, each with a president who works with critical tasks of up to 7 years' duration.

One of these units (Y Products) employs 2,800 people, has annual sales of $250 million, and is engaged in the manufacture and sale of engineering products, with traditional semiskilled shop-floor production at Layer I. The other unit (Z Press) publishes books and employs only 88 people. Its funding and negotiations with authors are in the hands of a general editor at Layer IV, assisted by a small group of editors at Layer III, each working on projects that may take up to 18 months to complete.

So the president of Y Products manages more people, governs a greater share of corporate resources, and earns a lot more money for the parent company than does the president of Z Press. Yet the two presidents occupy the same hierarchical layer, have similar authority, and take home comparable salaries. This is neither coincidental nor unfair. It is natural, correct and efficient.

It is the level of responsibility, *measured in terms of time span*, that tells you how many layers you need in an enterprise – not the number of subordinates or the magnitude of sales or profits. These factors may have a marginal influence on salary; they have no bearing at all on hierarchical layers.

Changes in the quality of work

The widespread and striking consistency of this underlying pattern of true managerial layers leads naturally to the question of why it occurs. Why do people perceive a sudden leap in status from, say, four-and-a-half years to five and from nine to ten?

The answer goes back to the earlier discussion of complexity. As we go higher in a managerial hierarchy, the most difficult problems that arise grow increasingly complex, and, as the complexity of a task increases, so does the complexity of the mental work required to handle it. What I found when I looked at this problem over the course of ten years was that this complexity, like responsibility time span, also occurs in leaps or jumps. In other words, the most difficult tasks found within any given layer are all characterized by the same type or category of complexity, just as water remains in the same liquid state from 0° to 100° Celsius, even though it ranges from very cold to very hot. (A few degrees cooler or hotter and water changes in state, to ice or steam.)

It is this suddenly increased level of necessary mental capacity, experience, knowledge and mental stamina that allows managers to add value to the work of their subordinates. What they add is a new perspective, one that is broader, more experienced and, most important, one that extends further in time. If, at Z Press, the editors at Layer III find and develop manuscripts into books with market potential, it is their general editor at Layer IV who fits those books into the press's overall list, who thinks ahead to their position on next year's list and later allocates resources to their production and marketing, and who makes projections about the publishing and book-buying trends of the next two to five years.

It is also this sudden change in the quality, not just the quantity, of managerial work that subordinates accept as a natural and appropriate break in the continuum of hierarchy. It is why they accept the boss's authority and not just the boss's power.

So the whole picture comes together. Managerial hierarchy or layering is the only effective organizational form for deploying people and tasks at complementary levels, where people can do the tasks assigned to them, where the people in any given layer can add value to the work of those in the layer below them, and finally, where this stratification of management strikes everyone as necessary and welcome.

What we need is not some new kind of organization. What we need is managerial hierarchy that understands its own nature and purpose. Hierarchy is the best structure for getting work done in big organizations. Trying to raise efficiency and morale without first setting this structure to rights is like trying to lay bricks without mortar. No amount of exhortation, attitudinal engineering, incentive planning, or even leadership will have any permanent effect unless we understand what hierarchy is and why and how it works. We need to stop casting about fruitlessly for organizational Holy Grails and settle down to the hard work of putting our managerial hierarchies in order.

9

Legal authority in a bureaucracy

Max Weber

[. . .]

Legal authority: The pure type with employment of a bureaucratic administrative staff

The effectiveness of legal authority rests on the acceptance of the validity of the following mutually interdependent ideas:

1. That any given legal norm may be established by agreement or by imposition, on grounds of expediency or rational values or both, with a claim to obedience at least on the part of the members of the corporate group. This is, however, usually extended to include all persons within the sphere of authority or of power in question – which in the case of territorial bodies is the territorial area – who stand in certain social relationships or carry out forms of social action which in the order governing the corporate group have been declared to be relevant.
2. That every body of law consists essentially in a consistent system of abstract rules which have normally been intentionally established. Furthermore, administration of law is held to consist in the application of these rules to particular cases; the administrative process in the rational pursuit of the interests which are specified in the order governing the corporate group within the limits laid down by legal precepts and following principles which are capable of generalized formulation and are approved in the order governing the group, or at least not disapproved in it.
3. That thus the typical person in authority occupies an 'office'. In the action associated with his status, including the commands he issues to others, he is subject to an impersonal order to which his actions are oriented. This is true not only for persons exercising legal authority who are in the usual sense 'officials', but, for instance, for the elected president of a state.
4. That the person who obeys authority does so, as it is usually stated, only in his capacity as a 'member' of the corporate group and what

Adapted from *Economy and Society*, Vol. 1 (New York: Bedminster Press, 1968), pp. 217–26.

he obeys is only 'the law'. He may in this connection be the member of an association, of a territorial commune, of a church, or a citizen of a state.

5. In conformity with point 3, it is held that the members of the corporate group, in so far as they obey a person in authority, do not owe this obedience to him as an individual, but to the impersonal order. Hence, it follows that there is an obligation to obedience only within the sphere of the rationally delimited authority which, in terms of the order, has been conferred upon him.

The following may thus be said to be the fundamental categories of rational legal authority:

1. A continuous organization of official functions bound by rules.
2. A specified sphere of competence. This involves (a) a sphere of obligations to perform functions which has been marked off as part of a systematic division of labour; (b) the provision of the incumbent with the necessary authority to carry out these functions; and (c) that the necessary means of compulsion are clearly defined and their use is subject to definite conditions. A unit exercising authority which is organized in this way will be called an 'administrative organ'.

    There are administrative organs in this sense in large-scale private organizations, in parties and armies, as well as in the state and the church. An elected president, a cabinet of ministers, or a body of elected representatives also in this sense constitute administrative organs. This is not, however, the place to discuss these concepts. Not every administrative organ is provided with compulsory powers. But this distinction is not important for present purposes.
3. The organization of offices follows the principle of hierarchy; that is, each lower office is under the control and supervision of a higher one. There is a right of appeal and of statement of grievances from the lower to the higher. Hierarchies differ in respect to whether and in what cases complaints can lead to a ruling from an authority at various points higher in the scale, and as to whether changes are imposed from higher up or the responsibility for such changes is left to the lower office, the conduct of which was the subject of complaint.
4. The rules which regulate the conduct of an office may be technical rules or norms. In both cases, if their application is to be fully rational, specialized training is necessary. It is thus normally true that only a person who has demonstrated an adequate technical training is qualified to be a member of the administrative staff of such an organized group, and hence only such persons are eligible for appointment to official positions. The administrative staff of a rational corporate group thus typically consists of 'officials', whether the organization be devoted to political, religious, economic – in particular, capitalistic – or other ends.
5. In the rational type it is a matter of principle that the members of the

administrative staff should be completely separated from ownership of the means of production or administration. Officials, employees and workers attached to the administrative staff do not themselves own the non-human means of production and administration. These are rather provided for their use in kind or in money, and the official is obligated to render an accounting of their use. There exists, furthermore, in principle, complete separation of the property belonging to the organization, which is controlled within the sphere of office, and the personal property of the official, which is available for his own private uses. There is a corresponding separation of the place in which official functions are carried out, the 'office' in the sense of premises, from living quarters.

6. In the rational-type case, there is also a complete absence of appropriation of his official position by the incumbent. Where 'rights' to an office exist, as in the case of judges, and recently of an increasing proportion of officials and even of workers, they do not normally serve the purpose of appropriation by the official, but of securing the purely objective and independent character of the conduct of the office so that it is oriented only to the relevant norms.

7. Administrative acts, decisions and rules are formulated and recorded in writing, even in cases where oral discussion is the rule or is even mandatory. This applies at least to preliminary discussions and proposals, to final decisions, and to all sorts of orders and rules. The combination of written documents and a continuous organization of official functions constitutes the 'office' which is the central focus of all types of modern corporate action.

8. Legal authority can be exercised in a wide variety of different forms. The following analysis will be deliberately confined for the most part to the aspect of imperative coordination in the structure of the administrative staff. It will consist in an analysis in terms of ideal types of officialdom or 'bureaucracy'.

In the above outline no mention has been made of the kind of supreme head appropriate to a system of legal authority. This is a consequence of certain considerations which can only be made entirely understandable at a later stage in the analysis. There are very important types of rational imperative coordination which, with respect to the ultimate source of authority, belong to other categories. This is true of the hereditary charismatic type, as illustrated by hereditary monarchy, and of the pure charismatic type of a president chosen by plebiscite. Other cases involve rational elements at important points, but are made up of a combination of bureaucratic and charismatic components, as is true of the cabinet form of government. Still others are subject to the authority of the chief of other corporate groups, whether their character be charismatic or bureaucratic; thus the formal head of a government department under a parliamentary regime may be a minister who occupies his position because of his authority in a party. The type of rational, legal administrative staff is capable of application in all kinds of situations and contexts. It is the most important mechanism for the administration of everyday profane affairs. For in that sphere, the exercise of authority and, more broadly, imperative coordination consists precisely in administration.

The purest type of exercise of legal authority is that which employs a bureaucratic administrative staff. Only the supreme chief of the organization occupies his position of authority by virtue of appropriation, of election, or of having been designated for the succession. But even *his* authority consists in a sphere of legal *competence*. The whole administrative staff under the supreme authority then consists, in the purest type, of individual officials who are appointed and function according to the following criteria:

1. They are personally free and subject to authority only with respect to their impersonal official obligations.
2. They are organized in a clearly defined hierarchy of offices.
3. Each office has a clearly defined sphere of competence in the legal sense.
4. The office is filled by a free contractual relationship. Thus, in principle, there is free selection.
5. Candidates are selected on the basis of technical qualifications. In the most rational case, this is tested by examination or guaranteed by diplomas certifying technical training, or both. They are *appointed*, not elected.
6. They are remunerated by fixed salaries in money, for the most part with a right to pensions. Only under certain circumstances does the employing authority, especially in private organizations, have a right to terminate the appointment, but the official is always free to resign. The salary scale is primarily graded according to rank in the hierarchy; but in addition to this criterion, the responsibility of the position and the requirements of the incumbent's social status may be taken into account.
7. The office is treated as the sole, or at least the primary, occupation of the incumbent.
8. It constitutes a career. There is a system of 'promotion' according to seniority or to achievement, or both. Promotion is dependent on the judgement of superiors.
9. The official works entirely separated from ownership of the means of administration and without appropriation of his position.
10. He is subject to strict and systematic discipline and control in the conduct of the office.

This type of organization is in principle applicable with equal facility to a wide variety of different fields. It may be applied in profit-making business or in charitable organizations, or in any number of other types of private enterprises serving ideal or material ends. It is equally applicable to political and to religious organizations. With varying degrees of approximation to a pure type, its historical existence can be demonstrated in all these fields.

1. For example, this type of bureaucracy is found in private clinics, as well as in endowed hospitals or the hospitals maintained by religious orders. Bureaucratic organization has played a major role in the Catholic Church. It is well illustrated by the administrative role of the priesthood in the modern church, which has expropriated almost all of the old church benefices, which were in former days to a large extent subject to private appropriation. It is also illustrated by the conception of the universal Episcopate, which is thought of as formally constituting a universal legal competence in religious matters. Similarly, the doctrine of Papal infallibility is thought of as in fact involving a universal competence, but only one which functions *ex cathedra* in the sphere of the office, thus implying the typical distinction between the sphere of office and that of the private affairs of the incumbent. The same phenomena are found in the large-scale capitalistic enterprise; and the larger it is, the greater their role. And this is not less true of political parties. [. . .] Finally, the modern army is essentially a bureaucratic organization administered by that peculiar type of military functionary, the 'officer'.

2. Bureaucratic authority is carried out in its purest form where it is most clearly dominated by the principle of appointment. There is no such thing as a hierarchy of elected officials in the same sense as there is a hierarchical organization of appointed officials. In the first place, election makes it impossible to attain a stringency of discipline even approaching that in the appointed type. For it is open to a subordinate official to compete for elective honours on the same terms as his superiors, and his prospects are not dependent on the superior's judgement.

3. Appointment by free contract, which makes free selection possible, is essential to modern bureaucracy. Where there is a hierarchical organization with impersonal spheres of competence, but occupied by unfree officials – like slaves or dependants, who, however, function in a formally bureaucratic manner – the term 'patrimonial bureaucracy' can be used.

4. The role of technical qualifications in bureaucratic organizations is continually increasing. Even an official in a party or a trade union organization is in need of specialized knowledge, though it is usually of an empirical character, developed by experience, rather than by formal training. In the modern state, the only 'offices' for which no technical qualifications are required are those of ministers and presidents. This only goes to prove that they are 'officials' only in a formal sense, and not substantively, as is true of the managing director or president of a large business corporation. There is no question but

that the 'position' of the capitalistic entrepreneur is as definitely appropriated as is that of a monarch. Thus at the top of a bureaucratic organization, there is necessarily an element which is at least not purely bureaucratic. The category of bureaucracy is one applying only to the exercise of control by means of a particular kind of administrative staff.

5. The bureaucratic official normally receives a fixed salary. By contrast, sources of income which are privately appropriated will be called 'benefices'. Bureaucratic salaries are also normally paid in money. Though this is not essential to the concept of bureaucracy, it is the arrangement which best fits the pure type. Payments in kind are apt to have the character of benefices, and the receipt of a benefice normally implies the appropriation of opportunities for earnings and of positions. There are, however, gradual transitions in this field with many intermediate types. Appropriation by virtue of leasing or sale of offices or the pledge of income from office are phenomena foreign to the pure type of bureaucracy. [. . .]

6. The typical 'bureaucratic' official occupies the office as his principal occupation.

7. With respect to the separation of the official from ownership of the means of administration, the situation is essentially the same in the field of public administration and in private bureaucratic organizations, such as the large-scale capitalistic enterprise.

[. . .]

The monocratic type of bureaucratic administration

Experience tends universally to show that the purely bureaucratic type of administrative organization – that is the monocratic variety of bureaucracy – is, from a purely technical point of view, capable of attaining the highest degree of efficiency and is in this sense formally the most rational known means of carrying out imperative control over human beings. It is superior to any other form in precision, in stability, in the stringency of its discipline, and in its reliability. It thus makes possible a particularly high degree of calculability of results for the heads of the organization and for those acting in relation to it. It is finally superior both in intensive efficiency and in the scope of its operations, and is formally capable of application to all kinds of administrative tasks.

The development of the modern form of the organization of corporate groups in all fields is nothing less than identical with the development and continual spread of bureaucratic administration. This is true of church and state, of armies, political parties, economic enterprises, organizations to promote all kinds of causes, private associations, clubs, and many others. Its development is, to take the most striking case, the most crucial phenomenon of the modern Western state. However many forms there may be which do not appear to fit this pattern, such as collegial representative bodies, parliamentary committees, soviets, honorary officers, lay judges, and what not, and however much people may complain about the 'evils of bureaucracy', it would be sheer illusion to think for a moment that continuous administrative work can be carried out in any field except by means of officials working in offices. The whole pattern of everyday life is cut to fit this framework. For bureaucratic administration is, other things being equal, always, from a formal, technical point of view, the most rational type. For the needs of mass administration today, it is completely indispensable. The choice is only that between bureaucracy and dilettantism in the field of administration.

The primary source of the superiority of bureaucratic administration lies in the role of technical knowledge which, through the development of modern technology and business methods in the production of goods, has become completely indispensable. In this respect, it makes no difference whether the economic system is organized on a capitalistic or a socialistic basis. Indeed, if in the latter case a comparable level of technical efficiency were to be achieved, it would mean a tremendous increase in the importance of specialized bureaucracy.

When those subject to bureaucratic control seek to escape the influence of the existing bureaucratic apparatus, this is normally possible only by creating an organization of their own which is equally subject to the process of bureaucratization. Similarly, the existing bureaucratic apparatus is driven to continue functioning by the most powerful interests which are material and objective, but also ideal in character. Without it, a society like our own – with a separation of officials, employees and workers from ownership of the means of administration, dependent on discipline and on technical training – could no longer function. The only exception would be those groups, such as the peasantry, who are still in possession of their own means of subsistence. Even in the case of revolution by force or of occupation by an enemy, the bureaucratic machinery will normally continue to function just as it has for the previous legal government.

The question is always who controls the existing bureaucratic machinery. And such control is possible only in a very limited degree to persons who are not technical specialists. Generally speaking, the trained permanent official is more likely to get his way in the long run than his nominal superior, the Cabinet minister, who is not a specialist.

Though by no means alone, the capitalistic system has undeniably played a major role in the development of bureaucracy. Indeed, without it capitalistic production could not continue and any rational type of socialism would have simply to take it over and increase its importance. Its development, largely under capitalistic auspices, has created an urgent need for stable, strict, intensive and calculable administration. It is this need which gives bureaucracy a crucial role in our society as the central element in any kind of large-scale administration. Only by reversion in every field – political, religious, economic, and so on – to small-scale organization, would it be possible to any considerable extent to escape its influence. On the one hand, capitalism in its modern stages of development strongly tends to foster the development of bureaucracy, though both capitalism and bureaucracy have arisen from many different historical sources. Conversely, capitalism is the most rational economic basis for bureaucratic administration and enables it to develop in the most rational form, especially because, from a fiscal point of view, it supplies the necessary money resources.

Along with these fiscal conditions of efficient bureaucratic administration, there are certain extremely important conditions in the fields of communication and transportation. The precision of its functioning requires the services of the railway, the telegraph and the telephone, and becomes increasingly dependent on them. A socialistic form of organization would not alter this fact. It would be a question whether in a socialistic system it would be possible to provide conditions for carrying out as stringent bureaucratic organization as has been possible in a capitalistic order. For socialism would, in fact, require a still higher degree of formal bureaucratization than capitalism. If this should prove not to be possible, it would demonstrate the existence of another of those fundamental elements of irrationality in social systems – a conflict between formal and substantive rationality of the sort which sociology so often encounters.

Bureaucratic administration means fundamentally the exercise of control on the basis of knowledge. This is the feature of it which makes it specifically rational. This consists on the one hand in technical knowledge which, by itself, is sufficient to ensure it a position of extraordinary power. But in addition to this, bureaucratic organizations, or the holders of power who make use of them, have the tendency to increase their power still further by the knowledge growing out of experience in the service. For they acquire through the conduct of office a special knowledge of facts and have available a store of documentary material peculiar to themselves. While not peculiar to bureaucratic organizations, the concept of 'official secrets' is certainly typical of them. It stands in relation to technical knowledge in somewhat the same position as commercial secrets do to technological training. It is a product of the striving for power.

Bureaucracy is superior in knowledge, including both technical knowledge and knowledge of the concrete fact within its own sphere of interest, which is usually confined to the interests of a private business – a capitalistic enterprise. The capitalistic entrepreneur is, in our society, the only type who has been able to maintain at least relative immunity from subjection to the control of rational bureaucratic knowledge. All the rest of the population have tended to be organized in large-scale corporate groups which are inevitably subject to bureaucratic control, This is as inevitable as the dominance of precision machinery in the mass production of goods.

The following are the principal more general social consequences of bureaucratic control:

1. The tendency to 'levelling' in the interest of the broadest possible basis of recruitment in terms of technical competence.
2. The tendency to plutocracy growing out of the interest in the greatest possible length of technical training. Today this often lasts up to the age of 30.
3. The dominance of a spirit of formalistic impersonality, *Sine ira et studio*, without hatred or passion, and hence without affection or enthusiasm. The dominant norms are concepts of straightforward duty without regard to personal considerations. Everyone is subject to formal equality of treatment, that is everyone in the same empirical situation. This is the spirit in which the ideal official conducts his office.

The development of bureaucracy greatly favours the levelling of social classes and this can be shown historically to be the normal tendency. Conversely, every process of social levelling creates a favourable situation for the development of bureaucracy; for it tends to eliminate class privileges, which include the appropriation of means of administration and the appropriation of authority as well as the occupation of offices on an honorary basis or as an avocation by virtue of wealth. This combination everywhere inevitably foreshadows the development of mass democracy. [. . .]

The 'spirit' of rational bureaucracy has normally the following general characteristics:

1. Formalism, which is promoted by all the interests which are concerned with the security of their own personal situation, whatever this may consist in. Otherwise the door would be open to arbitrariness and hence formalism is the line of least resistance.
2. There is another tendency, which is apparently in contradiction to the above, a contradiction which is in part genuine. It is the tendency of officials to treat their official function from what is substantively a utilitarian point of view in the interest of the welfare of those under their authority. But this utilitarian tendency is generally expressed in the enactment of corresponding regulatory measures which themselves have a formal character and tend to be treated in a formalistic spirit. This tendency to substantive rationality is supported by all those subject to authority who are not included in the class mentioned above as interested in the security of advantages already controlled. The problems which open up at this point belong in the theory of 'democracy'.

[. . .]

10

Models of bureaucracy

David Beetham

The purpose of this chapter is to explore the models of bureaucracy developed within different academic disciplines. What is a model for? People who talk about 'models' in social science often confuse three quite different purposes which the construction of a model can serve: to provide a *definitional* test; to set a *normative* standard; to develop an *explanatory* framework. A definitional model of bureaucracy will be concerned to specify the criteria which determine what is to count as a bureaucracy, and what is not. It answers the question: how do we recognize a bureaucracy when we see one? A normative model seeks to prescribe what are the necessary conditions for organizational efficiency or effectiveness, and to explore how far bureaucracy (either in general or in particular) is able to satisfy these conditions. It answers the question: how efficient are bureaucracies? An explanatory model aims to provide a framework for explaining the way bureaucracies function in practice, and why they have the consequences they do for the formation and execution of policy. It answers the question: why do bureaucracies function as they do?

Now of course these different questions are interrelated. To answer the question about bureaucratic efficiency, we need to know how bureaucracies actually work; and a typical reason for finding out why bureaucracies function as they do, is to discover how they might be made more efficient, and what are the major limitations or obstacles to making them. But the fact that the three types of question – definitional, normative and explanatory – are interrelated, does not make them the same question, and we need first of all to distinguish them in order to understand their interconnection. Those writers who *define* bureaucracy as organizational efficiency or inefficiency are confusing two different questions that need to be kept apart. And a similar mistake is made by those who assume that a normative model of 'rational' decision-making will suffice to explain how decision-making actually takes place; or, conversely, who believe that what actually occurs somehow sets the standard for what is attainable. In order to avoid this kind of confusion, the first part of the present chapter will concentrate on the question of bureaucratic efficiency, and the later part on explanatory models of bureaucratic functioning; in this way we

Adapted from *Bureaucracy* (Milton Keynes: Open University Press, 1987), pp. 9–47.

shall also come to understand their interconnection more clearly.

But why do we need models at all? The reason is that societies are enormously complex, and present formidable problems to those who seek to understand them. The characteristic method of social science is to construct simplified conceptions or models of social life to help define, evaluate or explain this complexity. Of course the world as it is will not exactly match the models we construct. In practice it may be difficult to say whether a particular organization meets the definitional criteria for a bureaucracy; in some respects it may, in others it may not. It will be a matter of degree. In practice we may find that the general principles of organizational efficiency need modification to take account of actual variations in organizational purpose and context. And an explanatory model may require considerable elaboration in order to accommodate the complexity of social reality. But we can only grasp the complexity at all by starting with simplification, and by representing the complexity as so many variations around, or modifications of, or deviations from, the simplification we have constructed. Naturally, if the deviations become too great, we shall need to revise or even abandon our model. In this way the world of actual practice imposes its own discipline upon the flights of intellectual speculation, and provides the decisive test of more or less useful model building. But to abandon model-building itself is to become bogged down in a morass of descriptive detail, or in interminable lists of principles to meet every possible contingency, such as clog up much of the writing on organization theory.

In this chapter, then, we shall explore the models of bureaucracy developed within the academic disciplines of sociology and political economy. In doing so we shall find that they differ, not only in terms of their particular focus of interest (social, economic or political), but also in terms of their distinctive method of simplification or model construction. The aim will be to clarify these differences, and to assess whether they are mutually conflicting or complementary; whether, that is to say, they embody antithetical approaches between which we have to choose, or whether they can be integrated into a larger and more comprehensive theory of bureaucracy.

Bureaucracy and administrative efficiency

The sociology of organization

What do the Vatican and General Motors, NASA and the British Health Service have in common? Organizational sociology sets itself the task of answering such questions, through an exploration of the most general features common to organizations in all sectors of modern society, and by theorizing about the conditions for organizational efficiency, regardless of whether the institution concerned is public or private, sacred or secular, devoted to profits or to preaching, to saving life or to ending it. In doing so it takes its starting point from the work of Max Weber, who was among the first to develop a generalizable theory of organization applicable across modern society. Weber's answer to the above question would have been simple: they are all bureaucracies.

In his definition of bureaucracy, Weber sought to identify the most basic features common to modern systems of large-scale administration. He distinguished ten or eleven of these, but they can be reduced for convenience to four main features. Bureaucratic administration, according to Weber, is characterized by: hierarchy (each official has a clearly defined competence within a hierarchical division of labour, and is answerable for its performance to a superior); continuity (the office constitutes a full-time salaried occupation, with a career structure that offers the prospect of regular advancement); impersonality (the work is conducted according to prescribed rules, without arbitrariness or favouritism, and a written record is kept of each transaction); expertise (officials are selected according to merit, are trained for their function, and control access to the knowledge stored in the files). Together these features constitute Weber's definitional model of bureaucracy: the criteria that a system of administration has to meet for it to be properly called 'bureaucratic'.

But what exactly is 'administration' or a 'system of administration'? At its simplest, administration can be understood as the coordination and execution of policy, and a system of administration as an arrangement of offices concerned with translating policy into directives to be executed at the front line of an organization (shop floor, coal face, battlefield and so on). That is to say, not everyone who works in a bureaucratic organization is a bureaucrat. As administrators, bureaucrats have to be distinguished from 'chiefs' above, and 'front-line workers' below. Let us consider each of these in turn.

In his discussion of bureaucracy, Weber drew a sharp distinction between an administrative staff and the association or corporate group which employs it. A corporate group is a voluntary or compulsory association of people (anything from a nation down to a trade union, company, political party, university and so on) which either directly or indirectly elects a leadership or governing body to manage its affairs (cabinet, committee, board, council). The governing body in turn employs an administrative staff to carry out its policies. This administrative staff, if constituted according to the criteria listed above, will be called a bureaucracy. It is important, therefore, to distinguish between a bureaucracy and the governing body which employs it. The members of each differ crucially in the nature of their position, function and responsibility. Members of a governing body are typically elected and may work only part-time; their function is the broadest formulation of policy and rules for the association, and the provision of the necessary funds for its administration; their responsibility is outwards to the association as a whole (electorate, shareholders, members). Members of a bureaucracy, in contrast, are always appointed from above, and are responsible to the governing body for the execution of its policy and the administration of its funds. Although this distinction may sometimes be blurred in practice, it is vital in principle.

If at the upper end of an organization the distinction between bureaucrats and 'chiefs' or 'leaders' is relatively clear, drawing a sharp boundary at the lower end is more problematic. According to Weber, the essential characteristic of a bureaucrat is the exercise of authority within a bureau. Production workers neither exercise authority nor work in a bureau. Secretaries or typists are employed in a bureau, and their work is essential to the basic bureaucratic activity of maintaining the files. But they do not exercise authority; they are 'office workers', not 'officials'. On the other hand, many staff working in government offices at the bottom of its employment hierarchy exercise authority over a relevant public if not over other workers (social security officials, customs officers and so on). To exclude such archetypically bureaucratic figures from the ranks of a bureaucracy would be paradoxical indeed. So the boundary line cannot simply be drawn above 'front-line workers', as I suggested initially. It depends on the nature of the organization. In a private industry, bureaucratic authority will be coterminous with management; in a government agency, it may extend right down to those who staff the counter, and who comprise an essential part of the administration of policy and the exercise of authority.

Boundaries constitute a problem for any concept, and insistence on precision in all circumstances can become mere pedantry. Provided we are clear that bureaucrats are by definition both subject to higher authority and involved in exercising authority themselves, then we can call those organizations bureaucratic whose administration is arranged according to the principles of Weber's model, even though not everyone working within them, either at the top or bottom of the hierarchy, is necessarily to be counted a 'bureaucrat'.

So far we have been concerned with Weber's definitional model of bureaucracy, with the criteria a system of administration must meet if it is to count as bureaucratic. Many organizational sociologists have accepted Weber's definition because it is clear, precise and generalizable. But Weber also claimed, much more controversially, that the closer an organization approximated to his model, the more efficient it was likely to be; and that it was the superior efficiency of bureaucratic administration that accounted for its general expansion within modern society. In other words, Weber believed that the defining characteristics of bureaucracy were *also* necessary conditions for administrative or organizational efficiency; in effect, that his definitional model served as a normative model a well. 'Experience tends to show,' he wrote, 'that the purely bureaucratic type of administrative organization is, from a purely technical point of view, capable of attaining the highest degree of efficiency [. . .] it is superior to any other form in precision, in stability, in the stringency of its discipline, and in its reliability.' And in another passage he wrote: 'the fully developed bureaucratic mechanism compares with other organizations exactly as does the machine with the non-mechanical modes of production.'

How did Weber justify this claim? There are two things to note about it at the outset. First, when he insisted on the superiority of bureaucracy, his standard of comparison was not some absolute ideal, but the forms of administration known to past history: by unpaid volunteers, local notables, collegial bodies or kinship networks. To adapt Weber's own analogy, the internal combustion engine may appear wasteful when compared with some ideal of maximum energy utilization, but it is vastly superior to a horse. Secondly, by 'efficiency' Weber meant not one single characteristic, but a complex of values which included quality of performance (for example speed, predictability), expansion of scope and cost-effectiveness of operation. These were in his view the characteristics required of an administrative system which had to meet the complex and large-scale administrative needs of a mass industrial society, rather than those of a localized economy geared to the rhythms of nature and the political requirements of a narrow elite.

If we examine the different elements of Weber's bureaucratic model, we can see how each could contribute to meeting these criteria of efficiency. The central feature of bureaucracy is the systematic division of labour, whereby complex administrative problems are broken down into manageable and repetitive tasks, each the province of a particular 'office', and then coordinated under a centralized hierarchy of command. The mechanical analogy is here quite precise; the subdivision of a complex set of movements into their constituent elements, and their reassembly into a coordinated process, achieves an enormous expansion of scope, precision and cost-effectiveness of operation. Other aspects of bureaucracy contribute to the same end. Its impersonality ensures that there is no favouritism either in the selection of personnel, who are appointed according to merit, or in administrative action, which is kept free from the unpredictability of personal connections. Its rule-governed character enables a bureaucracy to deal with large numbers of cases in a uniform manner, by means of categorization, while systematic procedures for changing the rules free the administration from the inflexibility of tradition ('the way things have always been done'). For Weber, the contrast with traditional forms of administration offered not only an essential point of comparison, but a means of identifying features of bureaucracy that would otherwise be taken for granted. Thus the separation of the official from ownership of the means of administration ensured that the operation as a whole was freed from the financial limitations of the private household, and that the individual was rendered dependent upon the organization for his or her livelihood, and thus amenable to its discipline. Such factors secured an enormous expansion in administrative capacity and predictability in comparison with the non-bureaucratic systems of the past.

Weber's claim that the defining criteria of bureaucracy also constitute a model of administrative efficiency is one that has been widely challenged by subsequent sociologists. Their studies of how organizations actually work in practice suggest that adherence to bureaucratic norms can hamper efficiency as much as promote it. This is because the principles of bureaucratic organization, so they argue, are more ambiguous than Weber realized, producing significant 'dysfunctional' effects, which become more accentuated the more rigorously the principles are applied. Each, that is to say, has its distinctively pathological manifestation. Adherence to rules can become inflexibility and 'red tape'. Impersonality produces bureaucratic indifference and insensitivity. Hierarchy discourages individual responsibility and initiative. Officialdom in general promotes 'officiousness', 'officialese' and similar pathologies. Max Weber, it is argued, failed to recognize the ambivalent character of bureaucracy, partly because studies of organization were in their infancy in the early decades of the century. But it was also because his ideas were unduly influenced by the examples of the Prussian army and the Taylorian system of scientific management. The model of machine-like discipline that they both offered obscured key dimensions of organizations, an understanding of which is necessary to secure their efficient operation.

What are these dimensions? They can best be grasped by counterposing to Weber's essentially mechanistic model alternative conceptions of organization developed by later sociologists. One alternative is the idea of an organization as a social system or network of interpersonal relations. Weber's model of organizational efficiency assumes that all aspects of the individual personality which are not relevant to the strict performance of his or her duties will be cast off as the individual enters the organization, or suppressed through effective socialization. If this were so, then a complete account of an organization could be given by providing a formal definition of the duties of each office, and of the relation between them; efficiency, in turn, would be a matter of securing a rational division of tasks at every level. In practice, however, people's personalities are never so totally subsumed into their roles. They come to the organization as individuals, with personal needs and expectations for which they seek satisfaction: from social intercourse at the workplace; from the exercise of skill and a measure of control over the work process; from being treated 'as people' rather than as the impersonal occupants of a role. And the manner of their social interaction at work can be crucial to the effectiveness of their performance. Any authority which ignores these factors or tries to suppress them is likely to meet with resistance. People can be compelled to work upon command, but not to work efficiently or with commitment. That requires their active cooperation, which is as much a matter of informal negotiation as of authoritative command.

A different perspective on organizations is to see them as communications systems, in which the efficient transmission and processing of information is necessary to effective decision-taking. Arguably, Weber's concept of administration put too much emphasis on the execution of policy, to the exclusion of policy formation and review, both of which require effective mechanisms for collecting and processing information within the organization. There are good reasons for believing that a strictly hierarchical structure is not the most appropriate for these tasks. One is that its direction of emphasis is from the top downwards, whereas the transmission of information also requires effective channels of communication upwards from the 'grass roots' of the organization. Admittedly, it is always possible for those at the top of a hierarchy to construct separate institutional arrangements for monitoring performance outside the normal structures of policy execution. But this produces wasteful duplication, and in any case those know most about the adequacy of a policy who are responsible for actually administering it. A further defect of hierarchies is that they are constructed in a pyramidal fashion, narrowing as they approach the summit. Again, while this may be an effective structure for subdividing tasks and processing instructions downwards, it creates potentially enormous problems of overload or blockage in processing information in the opposite direction. Hierarchical systems suffer from too much information as much as from too little; or, rather, it is information in the wrong place, and it requires sophisticated procedures for sifting as well as transmitting it, if it is to be useful to policy formation and review. This is the argument for decentralized types of organization, in which the responsibility for decision-making is pushed downwards to the point where the information is available to make them.

A similar conclusion can be reached from a different conception of organizations, which emphasizes the role of specialist expertise within them. Such a conception typically draws a contrast between two forms of authority, which, it is argued, Weber did not adequately distinguish. The first is bureaucratic authority, which derives from the occupation of a position or office within a hierarchical structure, and from the powers that reside in the office. The second is the authority which derives from expertise, which resides in the individual as 'an authority', not in the position he or she occupies. Now Weber would no doubt have said that the two tend to coincide, and that the occupants of a bureaucratic office typically develop their own administrative or managerial expertise. However, this overlooks the fact that most administrators are involved in supervising people with expertise which they do not themselves possess: financial technical or professional. For these subordinate experts there can be considerable conflict between obedience to the instructions of a superior or the rules of the organization, and obedience to the requirements or principles of their profession. The one involves an externally imposed discipline, the other one that is internal to the nature of the specialism itself. The conclusion is then drawn that the most effective form of organization for experts is not a bureaucratic hierarchy, but a lateral network, whose discipline is maintained by loyalty to the organization as a whole, rather than to the narrowly defined duties of a specific office.

Each of these three alternative conceptions corresponds to a different historical phase in the study of organizations since Weber's time: to a shift from the 'scientific management' to the 'human relations' school; from mechanical to cybernetic or information models; from organizations as hierarchies to organizations as associations of experts. Each has its corresponding prescriptions for organizational efficiency. It follows from the Weberian conception of bureaucracy as a hierarchy of offices that efficiency is to be attained by a rational division of labour, and a clear definition of competences. For those who see organizations as a system of interpersonal relations, efficiency becomes a matter of motivating subordinates within arrangements involving mutual give and take. For those to whom organizations are a communications system, efficiency is to be achieved by the effective sifting and transmission of information, and by locating decisions where such information is most readily available. For those, finally, to whom organization is a matter of the effective application of expertise to essentially technical problems, efficiency means finding arrangements under which experts are best able to exercise their distinctively professional capacities.

Each of these conceptions has in its time been presented as the final truth. It would be more plausible, however, to see them, not as mutually exclusive alternatives, either to the Weberian model or to one another, but as each emphasizing an essential aspect of organizational reality, all of which need taking into account and which together necessitate a modification in the strictly bureaucratic conception of organizational efficiency, rather than its outright replacement. Common to them all is the recognition that authority cannot be just a matter of the assertion of official powers vested in a formal hierarchy or a particular position. This is because subordinates possess their own powers, which reside in informal social networks, in the control of information, or in their own expertise. If the characteristic power of superiors is to initiate, the power of subordinates can be used to modify, delay or obstruct those initiatives. It is the ability to harness such powers to serve the goals of the organization, rather than merely the convenience of those who possess them, that constitutes the exercise of authority in its widest sense. From a sociological standpoint, success in this is not primarily a matter of individual personality, but of how the organization itself is structured. Too monolithic a hierarchy will produce a mentality of 'work to rule'; too decentralized a structure without corresponding means of monitoring or influencing performance will produce a 'work to convenience'. Each represents a distinctive form of bureaucratic inertia; in extreme circumstances they can occur simultaneously.

The conclusion that organizations are a combination of formal and

informal relations, and that they need to balance the competing requirements of authority and initiative, of command and communication, may
seem merely platitudinous. Indeed, it is precisely because general conclusions about organizational efficiency have the quality of platitude that
many recent sociologists would argue against generalizing about the
matter at all, in abstraction from the particular contexts in which
organizations have to operate. There is no 'one best way', they would
argue, no universally applicable principles of organizational efficiency.
This does not mean that anything goes, or that the question can be
reduced to hunch or intuition; but that the criteria for effective operation
will vary systematically with the purposes, technology and environment of
the organization. On this view, it is the task of theory, not to produce a
list of abstract generalizations that are true everywhere, but to discover
which types of organization are most appropriate to which particular
kinds of context.

[. . .]

Political economy

As its name implies, political economy approaches the study of bureaucracy from an economic point of view. This means not only that it is
concerned with the way organizations are financed, and with the effects
the form of financing has upon the way they function. It is also that, in
its neo-classical form at least, political economy locates bureaucracies on
one side of a fundamental divide between two contrasting methods of
social coordination: markets and hierarchies. Markets are arrangements
which coordinate the actions of large numbers of people automatically,
and on a lateral basis, through the operation of the price mechanism,
without infringing their freedom or requiring inequalities of status.
Hierarchies, by contrast, coordinate action vertically, via a structure of
consciously exercised authority and compulsion, in which people's status
is by definition unequal. We shall consider later some of the implications
of this distinction. For the present we should note that political economy
proceeds to draw a further contrast, between two different types of
hierarchy: those which are situated within a market environment (firms)
and those which are not (bureaucracies). In contrast to the sociology of
organization, political economy embraces an exclusive rather than
inclusive definition of bureaucracy: only those types of hierarchy are
'bureaucratic' which operate outside a market environment.

If political economy's focus of interest is different from that of
sociology, so too is its characteristic method of analysis, or model-
building. Its starting point lies not with the social totality and the way it
is structured, but with the individual, as conceived independently of any
particular context. From this starting point, the method seeks to explain
the different kinds of social institution that exist by demonstrating their
necessity to the individuals so conceived. In other words, it asks the

question: if individuals are as we assume they are, what social arrangements or institutions would they find necessary? We should note that the method does not pretend to offer a historical account of the origins of such institutions, but rather to explain the form they have come to take, and their continued existence, in terms of their ability to satisfy the purposes of individuals. Of all forms of model-building in the social sciences, this makes the most ambitious claims for its ability to construct a complex social world by strict deduction from the simplest of premises. Starting from these premises, we shall follow the model through until we reach bureaucracy. Those impatient to go straight to our subject should appreciate that it is of the essence of any deductive method that the earlier stages of the argument are essential to the later.

The individuals who constitute the subjects of political economy are conceived as purposive agents, who pursue their own individual interest or advantage in a rational, that is calculating, manner. Since such agents are not self-sufficient, they need the assistance of others to achieve their purposes. This assistance is typically sought through relations of exchange. The distinctive characteristic of an exchange relationship, as Adam Smith pointed out, is that one party to it can only obtain what he or she wants through satisfying the wants of another; it is a relationship based upon a mutuality of self-interest. In many spheres of life, such relations are determined personally, on an individual basis, and the precise nature of the bargain struck may never be made explicit (association, friendship, marriage). Where the same exchange is repeated on many occasions by many different people, we can talk of a 'market', in which the terms of the bargain are determined impersonally and explicitly, according to the relative demand and supply of the goods being exchanged. Markets have many well-known (and much-applauded) characteristics, of which only one will concern us for the moment: they carry with them their own system of rewards and penalties, incentives and sanctions, which are imposed automatically. If you possess some commodity that is valued highly on the market, for whatever reason, you will receive a lot in exchange; if you have nothing that is so valued, or insufficiently, you will receive little or nothing in return. In extreme cases you may starve. If so, it is a death penalty that is executed, as it were, automatically and impersonally, not by personal decree or conscious human agency.

Not all social life can be carried on according to relations of exchange, nor all economic activity by means of market relations. In modern economies, the market has to be supplemented by two forms of hierarchy: one that is constituted within the market (firms), the other outside it (government or bureaucracy). The necessity for each can be demonstrated from the same premise as that of the market itself: the pursuit of their self-interest by individuals. Let us start with the theory of the firm. If every single operation in a complex process of production were carried out by separate producers, each exchanging their goods and services with one another on the market, the result would be an enormous waste of resources through the necessity of multiple transactions, with their communication and information costs, and so on. Market selection would itself ensure that the cost of such transactions was reduced, by the coordination of these operations on non-market principles within a single firm. The spontaneous division of labour coordinated externally by the market would come to be replaced by an internal and consciously arranged coordination of the division of labour by administrative means.

But why should this internal coordination be arranged hierarchically, and not by lateral cooperation between equals? A commonsense answer might be that the internal hierarchy of the firm is the product of a preexisting structure of ownership. However, political economy leaves nothing to common sense, and refuses to take ownership for granted. It identifies the explanation for hierarchy in the problems of maintaining cooperation between self-interested individuals within non-market relations. Where an equal share of the product is guaranteed to all, so it is argued, each has an incentive to secure some additional personal benefit through reduced effort or 'shirking'; and the incentive is the greater, the larger the association, and the less difference one person's effort will make to the overall product. After all, 'labour' is by definition something unpleasant, which we all avoid if we can. So everyone comes to have an interest in the creation of a system of supervision, which will monitor the work of each, and devise a framework of rewards and penalties to secure maximum performance overall. Unlike the incentives and sanctions of the market, which operate 'naturally', this is an artificial construction consciously designed to modify the direction of individual self-interest, so that it works to further the interest of all. But what incentive will the supervisors have in their turn to perform their supervision adequately? Only if at the top of the hierarchy there is an individual or group, whose reward is dependent upon the performance of the firm as a whole in the market, and who gains or loses according to the effectiveness of their coordination and supervision. Here is one characteristic justification for the profit-taking entrepreneur.

If the firm is defined as a hierarchy that operates within the market, and subject to its incentives and sanctions, government bureaucracies are hierarchies which operate outside them. The necessity for government can be readily demonstrated from the same premises considered already. People in pursuit of their individual interest will not only engage in relations of exchange, but will be inclined not to keep their bargains, to take what is not their own, and so on. If such behaviour were generalized, exchange could never take place at all. A necessary condition for the market to operate, therefore, is a framework of legal compulsion, to guarantee the security of person and property, the integrity of contracts and the soundness of the monetary system. Such a framework could never itself be supplied on market principles, nor yet by voluntary subscription, and therefore has to be financed through compulsory taxation by government. Beyond the provision of internal order and external defence, governments also have a role in supplying those other public goods which would be provided either insufficiently, or only with great inconvenience, if charged for at the point of provision (such as roads, education or scientific research). Although political economists disagree about how far it is necessary or desirable to extend this list, it is clear that all these functions require an extensive hierarchy to administer. Such forms of administrative hierarchy are called 'bureaucracies', because they are financed outside the market.

[. . .]

Overview

The purpose of this survey of how bureaucracy is treated within the different disciplines has been to clarify the differences in their definition of the concept, and in their respective approaches to the question of administrative efficiency. It has also sought to identify the reasons for these differences, in their differing conceptions of method, and divergent focus of interest. Should we then conclude from such a survey that there can be no agreement on how bureaucracy is to be defined, or on the criteria and conditions for administrative efficiency? Is it all simply a question of our initial standpoint or disciplinary perspective? Before we hasten to draw such a conclusion, we ought first to explore whether there is any common ground between the respective approaches, or any way of integrating them within the framework of a more general theory of bureaucracy. In doing this we shall naturally have to move beyond the confines of any one disciplinary position.

Let us take the definitional question first. As we have seen, the sociology of organization adopts an inclusive concept of bureaucracy, since its interest lies in modern organizations as a whole, and its concern is with their most general features (though it also recognizes differences between them). For political economy, on the other hand, it is the differences that are the most significant, whether in their method of funding or mode of accountability; and they therefore adopt an exclusive definition of bureaucracy which limits it to grant-funded organizations or public administration respectively. If we stand outside the particular disciplines, however, there is no reason why we should give priority either to what organizations have in common, or to what differentiates them. Both are important to a general theory of bureaucracy, and we therefore need a conceptual strategy that will encompass both. The most obvious strategy is to use the term 'bureaucracy' in the wider Weberian sense of those criteria typical of modern large-scale administration in general, and then to identify the most important lines of variation or differentiation within this wider category. We need, that is to say, both a conception of bureaucracy in general, and a typology of bureaucracies; we shall need to talk both of bureaucracy as such, and of particular bureaucratic *types*.

Which, then, are the most significant lines of differentiation that will give us a coherent typology of bureaucracies? According to the sociology of organization, the key variable is organizational structure: this will be more rigid or more flexible, with more or less detailed role definition and control over 'front-line' workers, according to the organization's goal or product, and the environment in which it operates. For political economy, the most important differentiating feature is the method by which an organization is financed: whether from a grant or by the unit sale of its product.

11

Survival inside bureaucracy

Guy Benveniste

To understand the games played within bureaucracy, it is necessary to understand individual career motivations. Individual career paths determine some of the strategies that bureaucrats use to protect themselves. In some cases individuals are attempting to climb a status ladder; in other cases they seek to stay where they are. They are satisfied with their current situations. Without agreeing with the Peter Principle, which states that individuals in organizations climb the ladder until they occupy a position they are unable to perform and, therefore, move no further (Peter and Hull, 1970), it is correct to say that, for one reason or another, many position-holders are where they want to be or have no illusion that they can do better elsewhere. They have reached the top of their salary scale and there is no incentive for them to take any risk. But these individuals also need to protect their positions and so they too play games.

In this chapter I describe how individual needs for protection result in several games. I discuss output measures, and such rules as bureaucratic insurance risk avoidance, excessive coordination, documented histories, and doing nothing.

Organizational careers

Members of organizations occupy successive positions in one or more organizations over time. The succession of positions one occupies forms an organizational career (Glaser, 1968).

Closed sector careers take place either in a single organization or in other organizations that are similar. Knowledge and experience with the organization or the sector are of first importance. Transfers from organizations in other fields of endeavor in different sectors occur only in rare instances. Once an individual initiates a career in such sectors as cinema, education, the military, banking and so on, the experience is most valued in the same area. A person may go from sales to production to assistant director for R&D to general manager. Moreover, in many such closed sectors, career paths are strongly determined by the status of

Reprinted from G. Benveniste, *Bureaucracy* (San Francisco: Boyd and Fraser Publishing Company, 1977), pp. 93–111.

the initial appointment location. If one is first appointed as an assistant professor in an unknown junior college, the probability of ever being appointed in a large university is low; but if one is first appointed at Columbia, there is a higher probability that one may end as a full professor at Harvard.

Open sector careers are skill-oriented. It is not the sector that matters (banking, education), but the kind of work performed. If one is a specialist in control system design or in public relations, the specialization may take one to different kinds of organizations as one acquires renown in the skill or profession: 'This person is very good; she worked with the teachers' unions – got them in order and then went to . . .'

The level one occupies within an organization is related to the nature of the skill: 'She is a top-notch personnel manager – has a background in government service but worked several years with a private utility . . .' Certain skills permit upward mobility within organizations: 'He started as a production troubleshooter for an electric firm, later became a negotiator in international sales and, ultimately, became their lobbyist in Washington, DC . . .'

Location-dominated careers are controlled by desirable locations. It is not the sector or skill that matters. The relevant progression is from less desirable to more desirable locations: 'When I got out of school, I could not find a job. Finally, I started teaching in a small town in a rural area . . . Four years later, we moved to Boston, but we did not like it there. . . . We came west to California, and I run a bookstore. . . .'

'Career movement for the Chicago teacher is, in essence, movement from one school to another, some schools being more and others less satisfactory places to work' (Becker, 1952: 383).

Evaluations and evaluators

Each person in the organization plays the incumbent role according to his or her perception of the way the performance will be judged by significant evaluators. Those seeking advancement desire positive evaluations. Those who want to stay where they are seek to avoid negative evaluations.

Significant evaluators may be located within the same or in another or several other organizations; they can be a single person or they may be a multitude of persons who, in one way or another, are perceived to be important to one's career.

This point is particularly important because much of our current thinking treats organizations as units of analysis. We assume that behavior within organizations is explained in terms of the structure or the reward system of individual organizations. In fact, organizations operate in a larger environment, and that environment may be more important than the organization in explaining individual behavior.

Individual perceptions of evaluations may be vague and indefinite. To be sure, individuals who are pursuing closed-sector career paths often possess precise knowledge about how their performances are evaluated and by whom. But in some large organizations and at the higher levels of responsibility, individuals often do not have a clear perception of their evaluators. This lack of clarity occurs in large government bureaucracies, especially when the general environment is perceived to be threatening, but when the exact source of trouble or potential trouble is vague. Such ill-defined evaluators create fear. 'You never know who might be watching – who might send an anonymous report.' As one worker reported, the supervisor 'can push a button on this special console. Just to see if I'm pleasant enough . . . [or] if I make a personal call. Ma Bell is listening. And you don't know. That's why it's smart to do the right thing most of the time. Keep your nose clean' (in Terkel, 1974: 69).

In many organizations there are no criteria of evaluation because there is no exact knowledge about how the role should be played. For example, this is true of teaching, where it is not possible to know what makes a good teacher. In such organizations, pseudo-evaluations are often used; in education, it is possible to invent criteria of competency, but these are often considered meaningless by teachers. This imprecision tends to exacerbate the uncertainty of evaluations since no one really knows what criteria are used in making decisions.

These fears are shared both by those who strive upward and those without ambition. In fact, fear may be more serious for the latter type. If individuals remain in the same position or the same line of work for many years, they may become obsolete for most other tasks. Such people recognize how vulnerable they are if their organization or department is embroiled in any difficulty and if, as a result, they fall into disgrace. If these people are middle-aged and have acquired responsibilities, they are doubly vulnerable. Even with strong unions or civil service protection, the fear prevails because everyone has heard, or seen at first hand, cases of individuals who were destroyed by events beyond their control. As a business consultant reports:

> Fear is always prevalent in the corporate structure. Even if you're a top man, even if you're hard, even if you do your job – by the slight flick of a finger, your boss can fire you. There's always the insecurity. You bungle a job. You're fearful of losing a big customer. You're fearful so many things will appear on your record, stand against you. You're always fearful of the big mistake. (in Terkel, 1974: 531)

Closed-sector career paths

At the beginning of a career, closed-sector career path evaluations take place within sub-units of the organization. As one starts a career, the relevant evaluator is the immediate hierarchical supervisor. As one's chances improve, and after a few promotions, the alternatives for future mobility become more restricted while the number of significant evaluators increases. To be promoted from sales manager to vice-president for operations in Company X means that six or eight division heads have to agree not to oppose the appointment; the board, the president, and two other vice-presidents have to agree it. The significant evaluators include not only the person who has to make the final decision but all those whose opposition to the promotion might jeopardize it. The more important the position is in terms of the number of individuals affected by it, the larger the number of significant evaluators. Therefore, the more one advances in a closed career path, the more difficult it becomes to make the next progression upward and the more one becomes cautious and avoids risk.

In closed-sector career paths, the possibility of mobility from one organization to another decreases the longer one is identified with a single organization. Individuals who have served four to six years in one organization and who are still young may be able to move to another organization, but these opportunities tend to become scarcer the higher they move and the longer they stay within one organization. Therefore, such individuals are increasingly concerned about their lack of mobility and their excessive dependence on their position.

One result of this concern is that, at the middle level, there is a tendency to maintain friendly relations with members of different organizations in the same sector. Contrary to expectation, there is considerable supportive behavior between members of competing organizations simply because one's competitors are also one's potential employers.

Since the rhetoric prevailing in all organizations is oriented toward innovation, risk-taking and getting results, the cautious game is one that appears to innovate and appears to take risks, but really focuses on preserving the status quo. Perhaps a few errors are permitted, but not many. The strategy consists of looking good and conforming.

A New York management expert says that he would never promote into a top-level job a man who is not making mistakes – and big ones at that. 'Otherwise, he is sure to be mediocre.' (Proxy, 1969: 65)

In politics, as in surgery, a big mistake can be fatal. But in a fast moving, modern corporation, mistakes are inevitable. It's the number and frequency that makes differences on balance sheets. (Horn, 1964: 88)

Can a business maverick survive in today's modern corporate structure? In a large company, the answer is yes but only at the relatively low levels of the management structure. The minute the business maverick reaches middle or top management, his jealous associates cut him down as a trouble-making non-conformist. (Lund, 1973: 109)

1. You decide what it is you want to find out from this meeting and what you want to impart during it.
2. You decide what it is you want to press hard for.
3. You know the impression you want to create.

4. You know the particular problem you want to get solved.
5. You try to anticipate what most of the others in the meeting will do and say and how they will react. (Edgett, 1972: 199–200)

These statements suggest that in closed-sector paths the growth of one's organization is the stimulator of one's career progression. This process is particularly clear in new organizations, in which being at the right place at the right time can lead to greatly expanded role responsibility as the organization expands. Thus the incentive for organizational spread and domination is also related to its resulting impact on the careers of middle and top echelon personnel.

Open-sector career paths

Open-sector career path evaluations are recognized as taking place both in one's organization and in other organizations. To the extent that outside evaluations are important, they include both the individual's performance and the performance of the organization. While in closed-sector career development one is not too concerned with the way one's organization is perceived, such perceptions are important in open-sector career assessment.

The principal strategy consists of 'being seen', of finding a way to do things that capture the imagination and attract attention to one's name. Open-sector career paths mean that individuals are less concerned with overall task performance and more with the way their organization – more specifically, *some aspect* of their organization – is perceived by significant outside evaluators. Inside evaluators, and clients, are of little relevance as long as outside evaluators think that 'something interesting is going on'.

Individuals in open-sector career paths do not disregard inside evaluations. It is not as easy to move from one organization to another if one is forced to move. Successful pursuit from the outside frequently depends on one's ability to wait. Therefore, inside evaluations must at least be positive. For this reason, individuals in this situation tend to be as conservative and cautious as their colleagues pursuing closed-sector career paths, *except* in a single narrow topic area where they pursue the limelight.

If accountability is the fashion, they will support accountability and seek to make accountability 'the thing'. If community participation is fashionable, they will attempt to be known as people who know how to make community participation work. If these individuals are talented, they will invent new approaches; they will be real innovators. If they are mediocre, they will only *seem* to invent.

The advantage of appearing to invent is that little change occurs. Such inertia has a double benefit. For some outsiders, you appear to be an innovator, and this is an advantage. For those in the know, however, you are really conservative, but you know how to appear to be innovative, and this duplicity may be a second advantage. Therefore, this mediocre approach tends to prevail. A copy chief reports:

> There is a kind of cool paradox in advertising. There's a pressure toward the safe, tried and true that has worked in the past. But there's a tremendous need in the agency business for the fresh and the new, to differentiate this one agency from another. Writers are constantly torn between these two goals: selling the product and selling themselves. (In Terkel, 1974: 117)

Open-sector career paths mean one is more concerned with how one is perceived by people in the organizations one wants to move toward than with one's immediate co-workers and clients. A city manager in a small town, aspiring to move to a larger gown, pursues policies and earns a reputation for handling those aspects of small-town problems that are more akin to the problems of the larger towns where he hopes to be in five years' time. He is grooming for his next assignment. He wants his work in his present assignment to look good to those who will hire him later. He does not really care about this present clientele. If the clientele belongs to one class (the poor) and the significant evaluators to another (upper middle class), we can expect him to be more attentive to the class to which the evaluators belong.

Open-sector paths also mean that one is more concerned with public relations than with task performance: even if the clientele is aware that the service is terrible, that the morale of the staff is collapsing, that the place is in disrepair, the public relations of the organization will continue imperturbably as if nothing were amiss. The rosy messages sent out are intended for people other than the clientele, for people who are unlikely to find out what is actually happening . . .

Output measures as evaluation insurance

Output measures serve as evaluation insurance. When evaluators and criteria of evaluation are unknown, output measures are used to demonstrate performance. But different output measures can be used by different evaluators, thus causing confusion for those being evaluated. For example, legislative bodies wanting to control an agency may focus on one kind of performance evaluation while members of the agency may focus on another, thus placing the management of the agency in a conflict between the legislature and the professionals. Such conflicts are common in universities where funding agencies may be concerned with such measures as teacher–student contact hours and output of PhDs per year while the faculty evaluates itself on the basis of the quality and volume of its publications.

Nevertheless, while there may be some dispute about what output measures are relevant and should be used, there is a natural tendency for members of organizations to prefer output measures because they remove some uncertainty from evaluations. If it is not clear who is doing the evaluating or what criteria are used, there will be a preference for output measures that can be easily applied to one's own performance. These measures will be one's own output or, if one holds a middle-level position, the output of one's unit in the organization. This standard greatly limits discretion for cooperation with other parts of the organization and leads to the well-documented practice of non-cooperative bureaucratic empires having little, if any, relation to other parts of their organization.

It also leads to a narrowing of responsibility. Individuals are more concerned with the consequences of their acts during the period when they believe they are evaluated than with longer-term consequences which will not show up in the output measures. In many organizations, cost-cutting is a visible output easily attributable to the unit achieving it. Increasing productivity can be achieved by reducing costs per unit, and increases in productivity are a central concern of all modern organizations.

If there are no known ways to change a process or if change cannot be implemented because internal conditions are not amenable to change, it will not be possible to reduce costs through an increase in productivity. Therefore, one might be evaluated unfavorably even though one had no good way to act differently. A normal strategy in such cases would attempt to reduce costs without altering productivity. This alternative means reducing the quality of the goods or services produced.

The game of using cost reductions to protect one's career leads to mediocre service, particularly when the organization controls supply and clients have no alternative suppliers and so cannot exit. Organizations often produce mediocre products and services, not because clients really prefer mediocrity, but simply because individuals within the organization need to protect themselves, can only look good if they can reduce costs, and therefore reduce costs at the expense of the service as long as consumers do not balk.

Rules as evaluation insurance

When output measures are unavailable or when it is not known how a different course of action might lead to different measures, members of organizations use the rules of the organization to justify and protect their behavior.

Suppose we have a department head in a large bureaucracy – a ministry in Ruritania. This person has no idea about how things are going to work out in the coming three years; there is conflict among the clients of her department; the politics are unclear; great energy is spent by eight different factions attempting to push the department in different directions. The top administration of the ministry is unpredictable; most of the directors and the minister have just been appointed. It is not clear how the president thinks, if he thinks at all, or how the department head perceives her evaluators or their criteria for evaluation.

Obviously, there are no guidelines to follow, and whatever this individual does will result in unknown outcomes. The individual does not have a clear basis for choice. It is not possible to relate actions to desirable evaluation results. What is left? When outcomes cannot be predicted, rules are used as protection: 'When in doubt, be sure to be clear; follow the rules.'

The more the environment is uncertain and the more it is difficult to predict outcomes, the more there is need for process rules to protect individual role performances, and the more rules will be established for this purpose. In addition, the more that rules are used to protect individual behavior, the more need for documented evidence; that is, the more bureaucrats produce forms, reports, accounts and other written (or taped) documents. These are the defensive histories used to legitimize actions. In other words, when the environment is uncertain and the organization needs to be flexible, the members of the organization pursue defensive strategies that have exactly opposite consequences. They establish a barricade of rules which rigidifies performance and guarantees that service will be that much poorer than otherwise.

The game of risk avoidance

Taking risks results in positive evaluation *only* if the outcome is successful – that is, if the risk solves the problem at hand. Any innovation that fails implies bad judgement by the innovator, who is implicitly criticizing what was done previously.

Even if the outcome is successful, evaluators may react negatively. Any innovation that succeeds implies that the innovator exercised bad judgement by pushing herself too much; the innovator also exercised bad judgement in threatening others less successful than herself.

Not taking risks implies that the non-innovator feels that past procedures were correct, that past evaluations were reasonable. The non-innovator presents no threat to anyone. It is safe to evaluate such a person positively. Not taking risks means that the service continues to be mediocre, as it has been in the past, but at least it is predictable. No innovation also means that there is no need to keep trying to innovate, because there is no better way to provide service.

For these reasons, risks are taken only when past procedures are clearly inapplicable. For example, when the organization is in crisis, introducing innovations is not perceived as criticism of the old ways, especially when continuing in the old ways is perceived as too risky.

Risks are taken only when the situation has clearly changed and it is apparent that risks must be taken. But most individuals in organizations are not ready even for these risks. As far as possible, therefore, they attempt to avoid recognizing this condition. By contrast, however, the rhetoric of organizations emphasizes risk-raking. Therefore, there is a tendency for individuals in organizations to *appear* to be taking risks and to invent false risks.

In government, high-level appointments are made for political reasons and are usually of short duration. One is appointed Secretary or Assistant Secretary for an unknown term and is dismissed at discretion. High-level government appointees want and need to 'make a difference' either because it is possible to make a difference (this is exercise of personal power and is most satisfying to the ego), or because their high ambitions in open career paths require them to be highly visible. In these situations, risk-taking is part of the reward system and is an accepted way of life. Since dismissal or forced resignation is always possible, there is little time to act. Risks have to be taken immediately; there is a great hurry to bring about changes and innovations. It is no surprise that large government bureaucracies are continually being reorganized or announcing major new programs.

In contrast, the majority of individuals in the organization are part of the permanent hierarchy. They pursue closed career paths within the civil service and respond to a perceived reward system that deters risk-taking. It makes no sense for low- or middle-level bureaucrats to stick their necks out. Their aim is to remain quiet, to follow instructions, to stick to the rules.

This dichotomy is the basis for conflict. Individuals on the lower levels of the organization clearly perceive these differences. But they have to seek support outside the organization if they are to resist their hierarchical supervisors. To accomplish this goal, the public administration often reveals its conflict outside the organization where other arbitrators are available. Allies are sought in the permanent staffs of other departments or in the legislative bodies charged with the overall control of each agency. When allies are unavailable, the bureaucrats turn to the general public and leak stories to the press. Sooner or later, the ambitious masters realize the power of their minions, and the major reforms become small changes which may not be any reform at all.

Sending risks upstairs

Low- or middle-level bureaucrats prefer to send risky decisions upstairs. The top echelon – in government or private service – wants power, is anxious to intervene where it can be seen, and invites the upward flow of decisions. The top echelon may require the lower levels to channel all controversial decisions upward, particularly if it mistrusts its troops. But the top echelon receives more messages and is forced to deal with more issues than it can possibly handle. It therefore cannot spend as much time as it should on those decisions that are best taken at the top. The top echelon panics and decides to avoid risks. Big reforms become small adjustments, which may not be any change at all.

Inventing false risks

Lower and middle levels respond positively to any suggestions from above that *appear* to be major innovations but do not alter any fundamental aspect of the way things are done. Since upper echelons are anxious to seek the limelight, since the easiest innovations they can introduce – that is, the innovations that the lower and middle levels will readily endorse – are those that are mostly appearance and little reality, it follows that most administrative reforms follow particular fads which provide legitimacy without affecting procedures.

When there is a change in the administration and a new government takes control, many of the new approaches of the previous administration are quickly forgotten; the new administration returns to normal before embarking on another set of innovations. The rapidity of these swings is well documented. For example, a study of the 1965 reform of the administrative unit of the US Department of State showed that as soon as the Undersecretary of State for Administration resigned, his reforms were abolished: 'Hence, within nine months of Crockett's departure, every experimental program in the former Office of Management Planning had been eliminated, eviscerated or totally redirected. MOP (Management by Objectives and Programs) had been mopped' (Warwick, 1975: 55).

Excessive coordination

One function of coordination is to facilitate organizational spread. Another function is to protect members of organizations by providing a formal *sharing* of the responsibility for any decision. Coordination also has the advantage of creating the appearance that the house is in good order, that duplication is avoided and redundancy eliminated. But attempts at coordination do not alter the fact that most large organizations are composed of many independent empires that do not allow effective coordination to take place. Therefore much apparent coordination is not concerned with the rationalization of service but with providing protection for the members of organizations. We call it excessive coordination.

Excessive coordination is achieved through three processes: (1) lateral coordination via clearances; (2) lateral coordination via intra- or inter-committee work; and (3) hierarchical coordination. Two of these processes (committee work and hierarchical coordination) also serve other functions, such as providing visibility and mobility for middle-level staff (open career) and providing opportunities for defensive coalitions against top echelons and for hierarchical visibility (closed career).

Coordination procedures are rules that provide (1) documentation and (2) evidence of shared responsibility. If and when risks are taken, they are not taken by a single position-holder but by a long series of endorsers who agree to a decision and sign a document. This document becomes part of the evidence that is used to legitimize errors.

The more uncertain the environment, the more need there is for risk-sharing. This situation, in turn, reduces the extent of discretion and simultaneously creates a need for an increase in coordination procedures. But coordination takes time. Therefore, the more uncertain the environment, the more the organization is sluggish and slow to respond . . .

We find therefore that when the environment is highly uncertain, organizations invent complex means of sharing responsibility among many members to reduce the possibility that any single individual might be blamed for errors.

Documented histories

Documented histories, as the name implies, are written or otherwise preserved documents that serve to protect individuals. Rules generate forms that confirm performance. Thus, individuals can document that they follow the rules; coordination clearance procedures provide documented histories. Coordinating committees write reports and memos providing proof of past individual behavior.

Documented histories are circulated to improve their defensive usefulness: 'How can you blame us now? You knew all along what we were doing: your office was kept informed of every decision; we sent your office copies of all our internal memoranda and of our correspondence.' Copies of documents are sent out 'for information' or 'for initial clearance'. Instructions are requested in writing. 'We would appreciate if your office would confirm these instructions in writing.'

Documented histories are the assets of a bureaucracy in fear. Files are jealously kept up to date. Even when conversations are not confirmed in writing, it is common practice to immediately dictate a memorandum for the file which can be used later as proof of one's original understanding. Most senior officials use a secretary to transcribe telephone conversations in shorthand, and the practice of taping conversations received much publicity during the administration of President Nixon.

A well-documented history can be used as both a defensive and an offensive weapon when difficulties arise. Therefore, all parties attempt to build histories that justify their actions. Since documented histories are used to share risks, bureaucrats resist becoming implicated in the documented histories of other departments or individuals. Officials who receive copies of decisions made elsewhere which they are supposed to clear or even concur in, defend themselves by suggesting changes, asking for additional information, or sending different points of view. One purpose is to show that the concurring unit never really approved the move. Another is to discourage others from involving one's unit in risk-taking.

Coordination meetings illustrate these processes. If several departments have to agree before a decisions is taken, the originating unit seeks endorsements in order to share the risks with 'others'. But the 'others' seek to avoid responsibility. They lengthen the decision-making process and avoid participating in the discussions in order to protect themselves from future involvement. They insist on the most minute documentation from the originating unit to justify their own participation. 'We asked them to document their arguments, which they did, and we were reasonably satisfied that we could proceed.'

These bureaucratic processes easily become intolerable, and for this reason informal exchanges emerge: 'I'll gladly give you a clearance for this, but give me a clearance for that.' As a result, mutual trust emerges gradually. If and when trouble arises, elegant performances are appreciated. People who stand on their own feet and are not unreasonable in placing blame elsewhere acquire a reputation for 'playing the game fairly'. They become trusted members of the organization and acquire the ability to transact business. Trust is built gradually over the length of bureaucratic careers, and it is central to bureaucratic survival.

But trust is easily lost. When personal careers are at stake – when the issues are highly controversial – it is difficult for anyone to be sure that others will behave elegantly. The card castle collapses as everyone attempts to protect his own interests. Accusations fly into the open; the scandal is leaked outside the organization, and trust evaporates. The organization is in crisis.

Doing nothing

Many persons in large organizations pursue a simple strategy: do nothing. Doing nothing is relatively safe because it is non-controversial.

Doing nothing is not as easy as it sounds, because organizational roles have discretion; there are decisions to make; decisions are opportunities for controversy, and controversy can lead to negative evaluations. Moreover, the ideology of the organization calls for active innovations.

Doing nothing, while appearing to act, is accomplished as follows:

- By greatly complicating the sequences of clearances, review and reporting, so that considerable energy is spent by anyone attempting to do something within the organization. Careful procedures are established to guarantee that every attention is paid to make the new venture succeed. Proposals for new efforts are scrutinized indefinitely until their timeliness is past.

- By starting small pilot projects that dissipate the energy of the innovators without committing anyone. Once the pilot project is completed, other pilot projects are initiated.

- By encouraging competitive proposals for innovations from different portions of the organization and letting the innovators spend their energies competing against each other.

- By introducing outside experts who are asked to assist in redesigning projects. The internal innovators enter into competition with the outside group. They spend their energies against each other.

- By initiating a major review of existing activities and a massive reorganization. During the period of internal insecurity, when reorganization is under way, all new programs are postponed.

References

Becker, H.S. (1952) 'The career of the Chicago public school teacher', *American Journal of Sociology*, 57: 470–7; reprinted in part in Barney G. Glaser (ed.), *Organizational Careers* (1968), pp. 381–7. Chicago: Aldine.

Edgett, J.D. (1972) *How to Manage Your Way to the Top*. West Nyack, NY: Parker.

Glaser, B.G. (ed.) (1968) *Organizational Careers*. Chicago: Aldine.

Horn, J.C. (1964) *How to Become Head of Your Firm Before Forty*, New York: Coleridge Press.

Lund, H.F. (1973) *The Real Official Executive Survival Handbook: How to Stay in Office Politics*. New York: Dial Press.

Peter, L.J. and Hull, R. (1970) *The Peter Principle*. New York: Bantam Books.

Proxy, G. (1969) *How to Get Your Boss's Job: The Secrets of Executive Success*. New York: Funk and Wagnalls.

Terkel, S. (1974) *Working*. New York: Avon Books.

Warwick, D.P. (1975) *A Theory of Public Bureaucracy: Politics, Personality and Organization in the State Department*. Cambridge, MA: Harvard University Press.

12

Market, capitalism, planning and technocracy

Giovanni Sartori

What is planning?

[. . .] To a greater or lesser extent, and varying from place to place, the democratic state has increasingly become a do-everything state. Whether this happens under the pressure of circumstances or by virtue of deliberate choice, our political systems are intervening more and more in hitherto unregulated realms. More and more areas of decision are collectivized, that is, decided authoritatively for all. Much of this expansion is either sought or deemed acceptable. The battle begins, however, where the 'visible hand' of the state enters a course of collision with the 'invisible hand' of the market.

To be sure, states have always intervened in economic matters. Laissez-faire resulted from interventions against trade impediments. Industrialization was sustained in most countries by protective interventions. And states intervene in the free market in order to 'free it' from monopolistic and other ills or evils. What is crucially at stake, then, is not the extent of state intervention or regulation but whether our economic systems should remain, at base, market systems. Market or non-market – that is the question.

I have said: market versus non-market. But much of the discussion has been sidetracked, from the 1930s onward, on to the notion of planning. The question at center stage has been: Are democracy and state economic planning compatible? Since 'planning', especially in English, is a remarkably loose term, one can with equal reason answer yes or no, depending on how the term is defined. For instance, in 1953 Dahl and Lindblom defined planning as 'an attempt at rationally calculated action to achieve a goal'.[1] This is by no means a technical meaning, and it is certainly not the meaning intended by the economists who coined the term (with reference to the Soviet Union). To them planning was 'collectivistic planning' or total planning, that is, a centralized state management that replaced the market; and their view was that planning was highly

Adapted from *The Theory of Democracy Revisited, Part II* (Chatham, NJ: Chatham House Publishers, 1987), pp. 399–449.

irrational.[2] Between these two very different, if not contrasting, meanings, the term came gradually to denote what may be called 'limited planning'. Notice that this minor specimen was seldom called planning by the economists of the 1930s and early 1940s. French authors variously spoke of 'directed' or, more softly, of 'concerted' and 'controlled' economy. Italian authors characteristically said 'programed' or 'dirigiste' economy.[3] It was only from the late 1940s onward that 'planning' (the English word) overcame the other labels, thus acquiring a third signification. Taking stock, our present-day discussions relate to three different referents and meanings, to wit:

- Planning as rational organization
- Limited planning
- Total planning

As already noted, planning conceived as *rational organization* (as in the focus of Dahl and Lindblom) does not represent a technical connotation of the term and is handicapped by excessive looseness. Nevertheless, this meaning cannot be dismissed. First, it does reflect a widespread understanding of 'planning', if for no other reason than that people find it so defined in dictionaries. Second, and more important, expressions such as 'rational organization', rationally calculated action, rational coordination, and the like, do represent the underlying common thread of any and all demands for some kind of planning. Regardless of which planning (limited or total) is preferred, pro-planners find the market system irrational, at least in the sense that the automatisms of the market baffle the rational, deliberate control of our own destiny. Since a market system is a 'spontaneous order' monitored by its feedbacks, it conflicts with a 'rational order' shaped by targets. So, planning may well be conceived as a rational organization; but when planning is so conceived it does not denote a specific type of planning. Reference is not made here to a concrete specimen but to *reasons for* planning and, by implication, to a criterion for evaluating planning policies.

Let us turn to *limited planning*, that is, to one of the two technical meanings of the term. Since there are many degrees and forms of limited planning, there are many names for it. In addition to directed economy and programmed economy (the older labels), we hear of framework planning, indicative planning, planning by inducement, and the like. Whatever the labels, we must determine where the wide spectrum of limited planning begins and where it ends.

Planning begins as something *more* than mere government intervention and regulation. Every present-day government incessantly interferes with the economic process; and, of course, every government makes plans. But this is not yet 'planning' in any technical sense of the word. Limited planning always coexists (by definition) with the market system, but is not yet in existence when a government simply enacts monetary or Keynesian policies and manipulates the automatic stabilizers of the economic process. All this is not yet planning because it does not add up to an organic plan that is both *coordinated* and *future oriented* toward targets – targets that cannot be attained by market mechanisms. By definition, planning does not consist of piecemeal responses to the contingencies of the day. Limited planning always coexists with the market system, but as a corrective of, and an antidote to, a market system. In varying degrees, planning is intended to compensate for the inadequacies or faults of market processes. Under a system of limited planning, the market still provides the 'efficiency pricing' for all calculations and still reveals consumers' preferences. Yet we now have a politico-economic system monitored *in part* by consumer sovereignty but *in part* by a central agency that does not respond to market signals. Rather, the planning agency pursues development goals (industrial or other) or equalization goals.[4] The objection might be that despite efforts to draw one, the border that separates government intervention from limited planning is not clear cut. Since limited planning always coexists, if more or less uneasily, with the market economy, the respective jurisdictions are necessarily porous ones. This does not detract from the fact that at some point important differences and importantly different consequences are involved.

Just as it is unnecessary to determine exactly where limited planning begins, it is equally unnecessary to determine exactly where it ends. A breaking point is reached at which the market is destroyed as an efficient mechanism for determining costs and prices (for the productive economy as a whole).[5] At that point, planning is no longer 'limited'. So, if it is true that, aside from the market, no other mechanism exists for efficiency pricing, enough has been said for tracing the ultimate frontier of limited planning.[6]

We are left with *total planning*, often called, totalitarian planning, collectivistic planning, central authoritative planning, or command economy. These labels all stand for a centrally commanded economy in which a master mind displaces and replaces the market. This is the Communist or Soviet meaning of planning, and it may be reconstructed, by hindsight, as an unintended outcome of Marxian and, even more, Saint-Simonian premisses. Marx concentrated his artillery on the abolition of private property, but this was a fairly common stance around the 1820s and 1830s among socialist groups.[7] The Saint-Simonians went further.[8] It was very clear to them that, along with property, what had to go was the market, replaced by a centrally directed economy; and they did work out detailed schemes of a non-market, centralized economic system. Thus the Saint-Simonians (not Marx) hit on the crucial point. In truth, Marx never envisaged the requirements, let alone the concrete implications, of a command economic system based on state ownership. More often than not, Marx advocated the centralization of all means of production in the hands of the state; but he also advocated (especially, though not only, in his 1871 writings on the Paris Commune) a decentralized self-management of the producers. In the long run it was the latter view that was consistent with his ultimate vision of a stateless, associational, 'transparent' society where all the people continually exercise collective control over their own life.[9] In reality, Soviet planning is Stalin's creature.[10] Since Marx afforded no guidance, planning in the Soviet Union was improvised and imposed by the force of the sword. Soviet planning was, then, an unintended outcome. It was not intended by Marx, and it was intended differently (although Lenin and Stalin never knew it) by the only ancestry it had: the early Saint-Simonian planners of planning.

I said at the beginning that the issue ultimately boils down to the alternative market versus non-market. The standard retort will be that this is dichotomous thinking and that even in this matter differences are largely of degree. But the evidence for this objection is meagre. The critic can only point out that in actual practice even command economies tolerate a black market or indeed encourage a secondary, parallel 'private market'. But in order to prove that black or private markets attest to anything other than failures of total planning, one has to prove that they assist the calculations of the master mind. Do they? How in fact do the Soviet and Soviet-inspired planners decide what is to be done?

Certainly not on the basis of information provided by secondary 'free' markets. Society planners can see by eyesight which consumer goods are scarce and which are in demand – and they tolerate a private market precisely because they are unable to supply them. It is equally certain that consumer preferences, even if known or surmised, are in no way sovereign. Total planning is the planning of an all-owner and all-seller state that is the sole decider of the allocation of resources, of what the wages are, and of what consumers have to accept (or do without). In short, total planning is a planning in the name of the sovereignty of the objectives. But, then, what about costs? Economists have endlessly pondered how a command economy could perform, so to speak, economically. By the middle of the 1930s the central objection was already spelled out in full force: It was theoretically and practically impossible for the collectivistic planner to *calculate costs*.[11] His costs and prices are, and can only be, arbitrary. To be sure, arbitrary not in the sense that they are established at whim but in the sense that they are *baseless*; they cannot be derived from any economically significant base or baseline.

[. . .]

To make a long and complex story short, today the consensus among economists largely is that if the cost (or efficiency pricing) problem of collectivized planning has a solution, it can only be a solution of this sort: In the absence of a real market, the planner must be able to 'simulate a market'.[12] Without a market system, resources cannot be rationally or efficiently allocated, and this because the collectivistic planner goes around in circles – he has no (economic) cost basis from which to go.

Before proceeding further, let us recall that thus far I have merely, or mostly, sought to clarify the meanings and referents of 'planning'. It is argued that since the term planning denotes widely different phenomena, it is best to leave it undefined. On this view, only haziness and much futility have in fact followed. There are people who reject limited planning (definition 2) because they confuse it with total planning (definition 3). There are some, on the other hand, who accept total planning in terms of planning as a rational ideal (definition 1). There are still others who demand planning as a rationalization of economic processes, are presented with forms of state intervention that are neither economic nor rational, and yet are happy all the same because they behold the word and are unable to see into the thing. In parallel and equally confusing fashion the assertion is, on the one hand, that democracy and planning are incompatible, and on the other, that they are perfectly or even necessarily interlinked. Clearly, only if planning is spoken of intelligibly can it be discussed intelligently.

The *anti-planning* thesis applies to total planning; the thesis that planning is *necessary* best applies to 'rationally calculated action' (a criterion, not a real-world specimen); and the *compatibility* between democracy and planning is a thesis that applies to limited planning. As these theses fit into place, we can also appreciate the fact that the 'grand alternatives' are all still with us. They have been dismissed on the ground that governments have in fact a limited range of choice and do not actually make 'great global choices among grand alternatives.'[13] True, but only for Western governments; not true for much of the Third World.

[. . .]

Democratic planning

So far the argument was confined basically to economic problems discussed in economic terms. An economic system is not a political system. Yet the two are interconnected, and I turn now, in order to appreciate the connections, to political problems discussed in political terms.

On economic grounds alone it is fair to say that the pro-market thesis wins. If it does not win, and indeed if it should lose, it will be on political grounds. As pointed out earlier, the market's spontaneous order, or self-ordering, runs against the powerful tide of the egalitarian project and specifically the tide of the 'redistributive project'. It is here that the market system finds its implacable enemies. One may note that this is at base an ethical, not a political, stance. Even so, the redistributive project hinges entirely on *political means*; it is entrusted to the public hand and, if need be, to a strongly coercive hand.

[. . .]

We may speak of the state that manages the economic system as an 'economic state' and of the state that owns industries as an 'industrial state'. Nonetheless, the 'political state' is still there, and it is the political agency that runs the economic one. Up until now I have discussed *plannings*, not *planners*. But plannings are not disembodied entities; they are planned by individuals empowered with the power to plan, to decide for others, who in turn are deprived of the power to decide for themselves. It is only with reference to the market system – that is, to a self-ordering order – that we can avoid asking, Who markets? With reference to planning, Who plans? is not an avoidable question. Up until now the distinction has been between limited and total planning. In political terms, however, the distinction is between democratic planning and non-democratic planning, and the issue thus becomes: To what extent and in what manner is planning compatible with democracy? To be sure, in a first approximation limited planning can be translated into democratic planning, whereas total planning can be said to correspond to non-democratic planning. Nonetheless, as we switch from the economic to the political labels, we correspondingly switch to different problems.

Let us re-enter politics via the question, *Who are the planners?* In a democratic system the main lines of an economic policy must be approved by parliaments and deliberated on by governments, thus falling within the province of politicians recruited through universal suffrage. On this simple consideration it is already no wonder that our democracies have made so little headway, thus far, in terms of either rational planning (the criterion) or limited planning. We can build up a mountain of regulations, counter-regulations, exceptions, and nationalizations; but even an Everest of interventions does not, in and by itself, add up to 'planning' in any meaningful sense of the term. Where is the coordination? Where is the overall project? Much of this, even if called planning, is in fact chaos. In like manner, and reverting to planning as 'rational organization', how much rationality can we expect from legislators and governments? Granted, it is rational for the politician to pay votes with favors; and each single policy measure can be defended on some ground or other of rationality. But here reference is to planning: What is required to be rational is the overall design. And even a far from stringent underpinning of 'rational planning' requires that two conditions must be met: The whole must display some inner congruence (*rationality as coherence*); and the means must be sufficient and in fact conducive to the desired ends (*means-ends rationality*).[14]

If so, the chances that such conditions are fulfilled by democratic governments are slim. The sheer calculus of the means requires a high level of professional expertise, and the coherence of the overall design must be sustained by autonomy of decision, by not having to yield to sectorial and short-range demands. The reality is, instead, that the recruitment of political personnel has little to do with the expertise in question and that politicians generally handle economic policies within a very short time horizon and by yielding to contradictory cross-pressures, by keeping a keen eye on immediate electoral costs and gains. Thus, when we ask rational planning of our politicians, we are asking for the very thing that is hardest to obtain.

The question, Who are the planners? may receive a different answer, namely, that they are *experts*, not politicians. The politicians cover up for the experts, but they are in fact advised by experts (economists and ad hoc bureaucracies) who are also, and this is the crucial point, in charge of the implementation. To the extent that this is so, the chances of rational planning (as defined) become brighter. But as soon as the expert enters the scene, we hear the complaint of the participationist democrat. This, he will say, is another step away, and indeed against, democracy – democracy as demo-power. On my criteria, however, this would be a shift from democracy *in input* (how much the voice of the people counts) to democracy *in output* (how much the people benefit), and I have held that this is not only a legitimate but also a hardly avoidable shift. But I have never held that democracy in output – conceived as demo-distributions – can be entirely disconnected from democracy in input. The moment has come to look attentively into this connection, for a connection must remain.

Putting the case in a nutshell, the more we lean on the demos, the less we are likely to achieve rational planning; conversely, the more we lean on the expert, the less democratic we are in demo-power terms. This reflection compounds the problems of *democratic planning*. As I was saying, democratic planning is not the same as limited planning; it confronts us with a distinctly political set of problems.

Mannheim believed that democratic planning should ultimately presuppose and rest on a 'planning for freedom' understood as a social science manipulation of the environment from which to obtain spontaneously from the individuals the appropriate and desired behavior.[15] I am not prepared in the least to go that far. The point that I intend to pursue is a much simpler one, namely, that if we speak of democratic planning, there must be something democratic about it. I have conceded that the democratic element need not be in input and that, indeed, it will have to be much more in output. Yet I must forcefully say it again: it is democracy (a power vested in the people) that must monitor and enforce demophily and demo-benefits. This means that the political structure of democracy must remain. At the same time it must accommodate experts, for there is no sense in planning by inexperts. We are thus required to assess, in the final analysis, the role and weight of the expert. In order to appreciate the ponderousness of this problem fully, it is well to tackle it where it begins. Actually, two distinct beginnings are involved. One thread starts with the question, What is the democratic solution to the problem of power? The other thread rests on the premiss that democracy does not presuppose, in any sense, competency.

Notes

1. *Politics, Economics and Welfare*, (New York: Harper and Row, 1955) p. 20 (and Chapters 1–3 *passim*). As if to leave no doubt as to the latitude of their definition, Dahl and Lindblom further state: 'The attempt to achieve rational politico-economic action may [. . .] be described as economic planning whether the attempt employs the market or master mind.'

2. The first major analysis was by Ludwig von Mises, *Die Gemeinwirthschaft*, published in 1922, translated and revised under the title *Socialism* (London: Cape, 1936). But see especially F.A. von Hayek *et al.*, *Collectivist Economic Planning* (London: Routledge & Kegan Paul, 1935). This pace-setting symposium includes the initial doubts of N.G. Pierson (1902) and E. Barone (1908), the first attack of Mises (1920), and two original contributions of von Hayek himself in which he expands upon the Mises thesis that the information required by economic calculation requires, in turn, market-determined prices.

3. The first label was devised by Bertrand de Jouvenel, *L'Economie Dirigée* (Paris, 1928). The Italian *dirigismo* was a calque of the French *dirigée*. The debate was a very lively one in Italy. See *La Crisi del Capitalismo* (Firenze: Sansoni, 1933), with contributions by Pirou, Sombart, Durbin, Patterson, Spirito; and especially *L'Economia Programmatica* (Firenze: Sansoni, 1933), with contributions by Brocard, Landauer, J.A. Hobson, Lorwin, Dobbert, Spirito.

4. Under this definition the welfare state, or sheer public ownership of industries, banks, and utilities, is not 'planning'. Despite a deluge of works in Western countries bearing the word planning in the title, the fact remains that welfare policies and programs are just that. Likewise, the sheer addition of one rationalization to another has to do with the expansion of the state sector, not with planning.

5. While I single out the pricing function and specifically the calculation of costs as the *sine qua non* function, it is by no means the sole property of market systems.

6. Limited planning is also limited by democratic constraints. As long as the planners perform within a democratic framework, freedom of consumption and freedom of occupation (the choice of one's occupation) are not easily trampled upon.

7. It was not, however, a demand either of Saint-Simon or of Comte. Both were socialists in the sense that they negated liberalism, individualism, democracy and the market system. Both also advocated a radical restructuring of property. Yet both believed that property had to be retained for 'industrialism' (a term coined by Saint-Simon) to be efficient.

8. Reference is made to the Saint-Simonians rather than to Saint-Simon himself for two reasons. First, the doctrine ascribed to Henri de Saint-Simon found its streamlined formulation in a course of lectures delivered after his death by his pupils: *Doctrine de Saint-Simon: Exposition* (1829–30). Second, there are two differences between Saint-Simon and the doctrine attributed to him in the *Exposition* (compare, e.g., the *Exposition* with Saint-Simon's *Système Industriel* of 1821–2). One is that only the pupils, not Saint-Simon (see n. 7 above) requested the abolition of private property. The second difference is that the school (especially Enfantin) went further than Saint-Simon in outlining a 'planned economy' managed by a 'unitary, directing bank'. Bearing the various paternities in mind, it is appropriate to conclude that the *Exposition* is 'one of the great landmarks in the history of socialism' and that with respect to the organization of a planned economy it carried 'socialist thought further than was done for nearly a hundred years after its publication'. F.A. von Hayek, *The Counter-Revolution of Science: Studies on the Abuse of Reason* (Glencoe: Free Press, 1952), p. 147. The most important history of Saint-Simonianism remains S. Charléty, *Histoire du Saint-Simonisme* (Paris: Hartmann, 1931).

9. The essential point is that Marx's centralization of the means of production was conceived negatively rather than positively, as a taking away, not as an economic command system.

10. Lenin engaged first, until the spring of 1921, in what was subsequently and misleadingly called 'war Communism'. What he had in mind was not 'emergency economics', but some kind of natural economic system. Faced with collapse, Lenin retreated into the 'New Economic Policy' (NEP). Lenin died in 1924, NEP lasted from 1921 to 1927, and the first Five Year Plan, the actual inception of total planning, was decided by Stalin in 1928. As Alec Nove puts it, 'The word "planning" had very different meaning in 1923–26 to that which it later acquired. There was [. . .] no "command economy". [. . .] What emerged from these calculations [of the Gosplan, the state general-planning commission] were not plans in the sense of orders to act, but "control figures", which were partly a forecast and partly a guide [. . .] for discussing and determining priorities' (*An Economic History of the USSR*, rev. edn. Harmondsworth: Penguin Books, 1982), p. 101.

11. This was the central objection of the 1935 symposium on *Collectivist Economic Planning* (see n. 2 above) and came to be known as the Mises-Hayek line of criticism. A good overview of the state of the debate in the late 1930s is T.J.B. Hoff (1938), *Economic Calculation in the Socialist Society* (Indianapolis: Liberty Press, 1981). Von Hayek wrote in 1940 another important article on economic calculation, 'The competitive solution', now in *Individualism and Economic Order* (Chicago: University of Chicago Press, 1948).

12. The single prominent economist who straightforwardly dismissed the Mises-Hayek objection was Maurice Dobb, *Political Economy and Capitalism* (London: Routledge & Kegan Paul, 1937). Another standard exposition is Paul M. Sweezy, *The Theory of Capitalist Development* (New York: Oxford University Press, 1942). As a rule, in the West the principles of Marxist political economy are most persuasively expounded *ex adverso* against the background of capitalism. See also Paul A. Baran, *The Political Economy of Growth* (New York: Marzani & Munsell, 1960); Ernest Mandel, *Marxist Economic Theory*, 2 vols (New York: Monthly Review, 1968); and M. Dobb, *Socialist Planning: Some Problems* (London: Lawrence & Wishart, 1970).

13. R.A. Dahl, in S.K. Bailey *et al.*, *Research Frontiers in Politics and Government* (Washington, DC: Brookings Institution, 1955), p. 46. See also *Politics, Economics and Welfare*, where Dahl and Lindblom speak of 'tyranny of the *isms*' and assert: 'The great issues are no longer the great issues, if ever they were' (p. 5). In *Politics and Markets* Lindblom still abides by the 'anti-isms' minimizing strategy: his leitmotif is that reality smooths out what theory (erroneously, in his view) separates.

14. This was, in essence, Max Weber's understanding of rationality, and specifically of *Zweckrationalität*. Mannheim called the coordination between means and ends 'functional rationality'. See *Man and Society in an Age of Reconstruction* (London: Routledge & Kegan Paul, 1940), pp. 52–60.

15. See 'Planned society and the problem of human personality' in *Essays on Sociology and Social Psychology* (London: Routledge & Kegan Paul, 1953), part 4; and *Freedom, Power and Democratic Planning* (London: Routledge & Kegan Paul, 1950), *passim*. Mannheim himself was aware of the danger of a planning that ultimately addresses the very nature of man. Answering the question, Who plans those who do the planning? he avowed: 'The longer I reflect on this question, the more it haunts me' (*Man and Society in an Age of Reconstruction*, p. 74).

13

New directions for industrial policy in the area of regulatory reform

John Vickers

Deregulation, along with privatization, is one of the most vaunted elements of recent industrial policy in a number of countries. In the USA deregulation began in the 1970s; it has affected telecommunications, energy, financial services, airlines, trucking, and several other sectors. Deregulation in Britain in the 1980s has been a key element in policy towards the utility industries (telecommunications, gas, electricity), transport (airlines, buses), financial services (stockbroking, insurance, building societies), and even the professions (opticians and possibly lawyers). Even countries not predisposed to deregulation are having to consider it, because of the forces of international competition and technological advance.

It is often claimed, in Britain and elsewhere:

- That recent regulatory policy has had a clear direction – towards less regulation;
- That less regulation means more competition, and that deregulation has therefore been a success.

In the following I will critically evaluate these claims, and in doing so suggest some points for future directions in regulatory policy.

Objectives of regulation/deregulation

First we must clarify the objectives of regulation and deregulation. The main criterion should be the economic performance of the industries in question – the productive, allocative and dynamic efficiency with which they meet consumers' demands. Other ends, such as distributional objectives, are usually better promoted by instruments other than those of regulation.

Thus the primary rationale for regulation, as for other elements of industrial policy, is to remedy various kinds of *market failure*. It is important to be clear what the market failures are that regulatory policy is

Reprinted from K. Cowling and H. Tomann (eds) *Industrial Policy After 1992* (Anglo-German Foundation, 1990), pp. 210–21.

trying to remedy in an industry. For example, the reasons for regulating financial services are quite different from the reasons for regulating the gas industry. At least three kinds of market failure can be distinguished.

Externalities

Externalities arise when the well-being of an economic agent (consumer or firm) is directly affected by the actions of another. The classic example is pollution. Pollution, like other externalities, can be dealt with in various ways, including quantitative limits or the price mechanism (via taxes). An idea being discussed in the USA is that of pollution permits – tradeable rights to emit certain amounts of pollution. In Britain, the government is to restrict the proportion of electricity generated by fossil fuel, and to introduce a tax with which to subsidize the cost of nuclear power. (Whether concern for pollution is the motivation for these measures is another matter.) Pollution externalities are, of course, central to the debate on water privatization and EC directives on water quality.

Externalities of another kind arise in financial services. If a large number of depositors simultaneously attempted to withdraw their funds from a bank or building society, there might be a danger that insufficient funds would be available to honour their claims. A large negative externality between depositors – in the limit a zero-sum game – would result. Requirements on capital adequacy, and schemes of deposit insurance, are aimed at minimizing the risk of this happening.

Monopoly and competition

Market power is detrimental to economic efficiency in several ways. Allocative efficiency is undermined by the incentive for dominant firms to raise prices above marginal costs of supply, and the lack of competitive stimulus further blunts incentives for dynamic and productive efficiency. On the other hand, competition is not *always* for the best – in a natural monopoly supply by a single firm minimizes cost – and neither is competition always feasible (at any rate in the absence of government intervention). Figure 1 attempts to clarify these two issues.

The picture suggests that there are three kinds of market failure involving monopoly and competition. First, there is the case where competition is neither feasible nor desirable, which holds under conditions of severe natural monopoly. Anti-monopoly regulation is then the only check on the firm's behaviour. (Those sold on contestability theory might contend that the threat of potential competition could provide sufficient discipline even in these circumstances, but their argument would rely on implausible and non-robust assumptions, for example about move order. That is not to deny the importance of potential entry in other conditions.)

Second, there is the case in which competition is undesirable but feasible. Theoretical examples – involving 'cream-skimming', for instance – can be constructed in whichever efficiency would be greater if competition

Is competition desirable?

	Yes	No
Yes	Typical case	Cream-skimming
No	Dominant incumbent(s) prevents entry	Severe natural monopoly

Is competition feasible?

Figure 1 *Desirability and feasibility of competition*

were limited. However, although the case for regulation to restrict undesirable or destructive competition cannot always be dismissed out of hand, the private interest in it is invariably greater than the public interest. Where competition is undesirable, it will not usually come about anyway. The burden of proof on those arguing for limits to competition would be heavy indeed.

The third case – competition desirable but in danger of being thwarted, for example by anti-competitive behaviour by dominant incumbent firm(s) – is central to the present discussion. If this case were very rare, with competition being the natural order of things, then deregulation would generally go hand in hand with increased competition. If, however, the case is common, with competition being fragile in a number of circumstances where it is desirable, then deregulation and competition are not necessarily associated: laissez-faire and competition can come apart. Modern theories of strategic competition and recent experience in several 'deregulated' industries in Britain (not to mention Adam Smith's remark about what businessmen get up to in coffee houses), suggest that this case should be taken very seriously. It will be considered further below.

To summarize, three kinds of market failure involving monopoly and competition have been distinguished. Correspondingly, there are three types of regulation (and hence types of deregulation) in this area: regulation to contain monopolistic behaviour, regulation to limit competition, and regulation to promote competition.

Information problems

Market failures in this category include asymmetric information about product quality, problems arising from imperfect price information, and failures in markets for information. Perhaps the first of these deserves most attention. Information asymmetries pervade markets for professional services and many financial services. The customer cannot easily tell whether good advice is being offered, whether a stock market transaction is being carried out on the best available terms, or whether a bank or insurance company has adequate solvency margins. There are several ways of attempting to overcome problems of asymmetric information, some of which (such as warranties, guarantees and reputations) require no intervention by external agencies. But *unaided* market mechanisms are not always enough, especially when – as with many professional and financial services – quality cannot even be detected *ex post*. Alternative modes of regulation to combat some of these information problems will be discussed below.

Deregulation?

Is it true that recent regulatory policy in countries such as Britain has had a clear direction – towards less regulation? In a number of areas the answer is certainly positive. Telephone apparatus, spectacles, bus rides (at least in Oxford), and conveyancing are examples of products and services now available from a wider range of competing sources than they used to be. Monopoly rights – enjoyed by firms such as BT and groups such as registered opticians – have been abolished in some activities.

However, the picture is more complex than it may appear at first. As older systems of regulation have been dismantled, new and generally more explicit regulatory structures have been simultaneously erected in place of what went before. For example, financial services is one of the most important sectors to have been 'deregulated' (Big Bang and all that). Yet the Financial Services Act of 1986, the Securities and Investment Board with its rule books, and self-regulatory organizations constitute a major new regulatory system.

In the utility industries there have been measures of deregulation, but at the same time the construction of new regulatory frameworks and institutions. Deregulation in the utilities has had a mixed record: perhaps paradoxically, it has often been ineffective unless accompanied by appropriate measures of regulation. The extent of deregulation in the utilities has, moreover, been limited at certain points in the privatization programme. There is an obvious contrast between the liberalizing intent of the 1981 Telecommunications Act (introduced before the privatization of BT was seriously contemplated) and the limits to competition set by the government once it wanted to sell BT. Thus competition to the BT/ Mercury duopoly, resale of basic capacity, and independent cable competition were all disallowed. Similar events occurred in the cases of British Gas and British Airways.

As noted above, where deregulation has occurred, it has often been accompanied by new forms of regulation – re-regulation, as it were. This suggests that 'deregulation' is not the right label. Rather than *less* regulation, there has been a *change in the mode of regulation* in several industries. (Hence the use of the term 'regulatory reform' in the title of this chapter.) Two questions arise: how are the changes in the modes of regulation to be characterized, and are they to be welcomed? These questions are very broad, and the following remarks are therefore tentative.

Modes of regulation

In the paper referred to in the note at the end of this chapter John Kay and I distinguished between two modes of regulation – *structure regulation* and *conduct regulation* – and suggested that the combination of deregulation and re-regulation could be seen partly as a shift from the former to the latter. In a number of areas the British government has opted for conduct regulation over structure regulation when facing a choice between the two, though the approach to electricity privatization may signal a change in this regard.

'Structure regulation' refers to the determination of which firms (or types thereof) are allowed to engage in which activities. Examples include the decision not to allow others to compete with the BT/Mercury duopoly, the British Gas statutory monopoly over the domestic market, the rule that used to separate brokers and jobbers in the stock market, and the rule that bars solicitors from acting in the higher courts. The break-up of the Central Electricity Generating Board (CEGB), and the American break-up of AT & T are other examples. Restructuring BT, or disallowing its takeover of Mitel, would have been structure regulation.

'Conduct regulation' refers to measures concerned with how firms behave in their chosen activities. Examples include measures to guard against anti-competitive behaviour by dominant firms, the BT/Mercury interconnection ruling, 'best execution' rules in stockbroking, 'Chinese walls' to stop inside information being passed around firms, and rules against advertising by professional firms.

The regulation of structure is designed to reduce or remove the incentive and opportunity for undesired conduct, whereas conduct regulation is designed to stop it occurring. Structure regulation has the advantages of being once and for all and less demanding of regulatory information and effort. Conduct regulation, however, can be better targeted on the market failures in question. Consider a merger, such as BA/BCal or BT/Mitel, which raises concern for competition. The concern is removed if the merger is disallowed, but this might lose synergy benefits (if they exist). The concern remains if the merger goes through, and so does the need for continuing regulation to guard against anti-competitive behaviour, but any synergy benefits are preserved. In the overall balance, much depends on the effectiveness of policy against anti-competitive practices: the weaker it is, the tougher merger policy needs to be.

Matters are more complicated if the issue is the vertical separation of a firm with market power, for example BT, AT & T, or the CEGB. Here, conduct regulation in the form of price control over the natural monopoly activities will continue in any event. Thus, separating the generating and transmission activities of the CEGB does not do away with the need for conduct regulation altogether: part of it – the control of prices charged by the natural monopoly transmission activity – remains, but the need to regulate against anti-competitive behaviour might be diminished.

If the definition of structure regulation is extended to include the structure of ownership, then the most important shift from structure to conduct regulation has been the privatization programme itself. With Herbert Morrison's 'high custodians of the public interest' running industries, what need for conduct regulation (or competition)? Flaws in his vision led, over time, to more and more conduct regulation (for example financial limits), and ultimately to privatization. Obligations to private shareholders mean that Sir Denis Rooke of British Gas, and others like him, can no longer be high custodians of the public interest, even if they want to be. Hence privatization requires the apparatus of conduct regulation that now exists (RPI-x, Oftel and so on). Many of these measures would have been desirable, even under continued public ownership, but the change towards private objectives entailed by privatization makes them all the more important. Indeed, much of the wisdom of privatization depends critically upon the effectiveness of such conduct regulation, in combination with appropriate structural measures to promote competition.

Like all such distinctions, that between structure and conduct regulation is not clear-cut. Nevertheless, it offers a perspective on recent regulatory developments, and recent combinations of deregulation and re-regulation are perhaps less paradoxical if it is remembered that there are the two broad types of regulation. The direction of regulatory policy has not been entirely towards deregulation. Shifts of emphasis, and choices, between structure and conduct regulation are an important part of the story.

Deregulation and competition

Does deregulation mean more competition? It often does, of course, but in recent important cases deregulation has *not* led to more competition.

The 1983 Energy Act sought to deregulate electricity generation. Statutory barriers to entry were removed, but no effective competition – or even effective entry threats – resulted. The Act required the distribution companies to offer to buy power from new entrants at prices reflecting their avoidable costs, reclassified as fixed costs. Moreover, the CEGB owned the transmission grid, which any entrant would need access to. The Act required the CEGB to publish fair carriage charges, but little was done to implement this. In short, major barriers to entry – some of them the direct result of unchecked anti-competitive behaviour by the dominant incumbent firm – faced potential entrants. The removal of legal barriers to entry was far from sufficient to create conditions for effective competition.

The gas industry is a similar story. The Oil and Gas (Enterprise) Act 1982 ended British Gas's monopsony over North Sea gas purchases, and made it theoretically possible for independent suppliers to use the British Gas pipeline network. But the terms on which they could do so were not laid down. Of course British Gas has no desire to provide its rivals with easy access to its network, but without fair access their challenge was rendered ineffective. The 1986 Gas Act, which privatized the company, did nothing to improve matters. Indeed, the privatization of British Gas was a dismal affair from the point of view of consumers and competition. Selective and opaque price cuts in the 'deregulated' industrial market, monopolization of North Sea supplies, and control over the pipeline network gave British Gas an extraordinary degree of private market power. Ofgas, the regulatory body, did not have powers to intervene in the deregulated market, but a reference to the Monopolies Commission led to a damning report in 1988 which seeks to redress the situation. In future, British Gas must have transparent, non-discriminatory prices, open up access to its pipeline network and limit its purchases of North Sea supplies.

These measures will depend for their success on regulatory vigilance, which will in turn require suitable regulatory powers and information. The same is true of the future regime for the electricity supply industry. In telecommunications, competition has been somewhat more successful in places, despite the government's limits to competition referred to above. This has been due in no small part to Oftel's energies in promoting competition, as reflected in its ruling on interconnection between the BT and Mercury networks, for example. A number of areas of difficulty remain, however, and it will be interesting to see the extent and effectiveness of further liberalization in the 1990s.

What is common to the cases of ineffective deregulation is a *failure of regulation*. Conditions for effective competition require:

- The absence of legal barriers to entry, and
- Measures to guard against anti-competitive practices by dominant firms.

While the former is welcome and necessary for competition, it is by no means sufficient. In circumstances where competition is capable of being undermined, deregulation must be complemented by regulation – regulation *for* competition. This is just one example of competition and regulation being complements (others are yardstick competition and franchising), rather than substitutes, as they are often regarded.

Conclusions

It be better to think of the 1980s in Britain as the decade of regulatory reform, rather than the decade of deregulation. First, new frameworks of regulation have often been erected, just as old ones were taken down. Second, deregulation was sometimes deliberately limited in its scope, for example, at sensitive points in the privatization programme. Third, where deregulation in the sense of the removal of legal barriers to entry has occurred, it has often not been complemented by appropriate measures to make competition effective.

Have the frontiers of the state been rolled back in the area of regulation? Should they be? I think that the initial attempts to regulate the privatized telecommunications and gas industries 'with a light touch' were a mistake. A number of the developments referred to above suggest that even the government now thinks so, and its attitude to privatization of the electricity supply industry reflects a rather different approach that does not look much like rolling back the frontiers of the state.

The question whether deregulation should go further is perhaps not the right one. Some regulation is unnecessary, but much is required by the market failures that inevitably exist in some industries. Better targeting of regulatory policy on those market failures is not a simple matter of more or less regulation. There are several kinds of regulation, and those which harness and assist market forces should generally be preferred to those which do not.

Note

This chapter borrows from J. Kay, and J. Vickers, (1988) 'Regulatory reform in Britain', in *Economic Policy*, 7: 286–351. Also see J. Vickers and G. Yarrow, *Privatisation: an Economic Analysis*. Cambridge, MA: MIT Press, 1988.

Networks

Introduction

Grahame Thompson

The chapters in this section deal with the idea of networks as a means of coordination. Examples of the network approach are drawn from a variety of social science and organizational theory sources. The key feature of networks that they all address, however, is the way cooperation and trust are formed and sustained within networks. In contrast to either hierarchy or market, networks coordinate through less formal, more egalitarian and cooperative means. Exactly how these features operate in a range of different environments and contexts is the subject of each chapter.

The chapter by Knoke and Kuklinski draws on the sociological tradition of network analysis to outline the manner in which 'network structures' are formed and operate. They suggest that a range of attributes and relationships underpins network structures, and that they work at different dimensions and levels. On the basis of any particular problem or objective, it is up to the social analyst to decide exactly how the network study is to be set up and the features it will exemplify.

A particular type of network operating in the field of economic organization is discussed in Chapter 15. This reports a study into the French engineering industry situated around Lyons in France. Comprising mainly small to medium-sized firms, Lorenz found a surprisingly dense network of subcontracting and main firms, existing in the form of an industrial district, that were very dynamic and innovative in the introduction of new technology. He analyses how cooperation and trust are formed and sustained amongst the network of firms despite the strong competition existing between them. They forgo short-run profit maximization for the longer-term benefits of mutual cooperation.

One way of characterizing the kind of intra- and inter-firm relationships discussed in Lorenz's case study is as a 'value-adding partnership'. Johnston and Lawrence (Chapter 16) see the typical vertically integrated firm being broken up in the face of the need for flexibility in response to the rapidity of market demand changes. The different, and now increasingly organizationally autonomous, parts of the overall productive chain or network they designate as akin to a partnership rather than as a market or hierarchical organization.

Policy networks are an example of the informal personal ties that develop between professional groups within the public sector and elsewhere. In Chapter 17 Rhodes draws attention to the way these operate within sub-central government in the UK. He looks at the processes of exchange going on within these kinds of network and at the rules and strategies governing resource translations between the participants.

Another example of the way informal relationships can serve to articulate personal networks is demonstrated by Pnina Werbner's analysis of female working and domestic bonds amongst Pakistani immigrant women (Chapter 18). This serves to highlight the strong gender and ethnic character of a good many network structures. It points to the manner in which personal contacts and community values help to reinforce a soldaristic bond so necessary for the operation of local and small-scale network arrangements.

Finally in this section we focus on a more overtly political aspect to networks. What is the political form of a typical government structure? In their analysis of the way private interests are governed in the advanced industrial democracies of the West, Streeck and Schmitter (Chapter 19) argue that as well as the market, the state and the community operating as ordering mechanisms, there exists another equally important co-ordinating arrangement which they term 'associations'. These associations act as a kind of network in which the multifarious interests represented within the private sphere are made manifest and given an expression. They suggest that the network of associations so created provides an important adjunct to the traditional modes of political representation organized around the state. It helps coordinate the political realm by bargaining and negotiating away what might otherwise arise as conflictual and antagonistic social tensions.

14

Network analysis: basic concepts

David Knoke and James H. Kuklinski

[. . .]

To appreciate fully the distinctive theoretical underpinnings of network approaches to social phenomena, a comparison with more traditional, individualistic approaches may be useful. In the atomistic perspectives typically assumed by economics and psychology, individual actors are depicted as making choices and acting without regard to the behavior of other actors. Whether analysed as purposive action based on rational calculations of utility maximization, or as drive-reduction motivation based on causal antecedents, such individualistic explanations generally ignore the social contexts within which the social actor is embedded.

In contrast, network analysis incorporates two significant assumptions about social behavior. Its first essential insight is that any actor typically participates in a social system involving many other actors, who are significant reference points in one another's decisions. The nature of the relationships a given actor has with other system members thus may affect that focal actor's perceptions, beliefs and actions. But network analysis does not stop with an account of the social behavior of individuals. Its second essential insight lies in the importance of elucidating the various levels of structure in a social system, where structure consists of 'regularities in the patterns of relations among concrete entities' (White et al., 1976). In the individualistic approach, social structure is seldom an explicit focus of inquiry, to the extent that it is even considered at all. Network analysis, by emphasizing relations that connect the social positions within a system, offers a powerful brush for painting a systematic picture of global social structures and their components. The organization of social relations thus becomes a central concept in analysing the structural properties of the networks within which individual actors are embedded, and for detecting emergent social phenomena that have no existence at the level of the individual actor. [. . .]

Adapted from D. Knoke and J.H. Kuklinski, *Network Analysis* (Beverly Hills: Sage Publications, 1982), pp. 9–21.

Attributes and relations

Two basic approaches to viewing and classifying the various aspects of the social world – according to their attributes or their relationships – are often treated as antithetical and even irreconcilable. We need to make clear from the outset how these two approaches to measurement differ. We shall also point out that neither perspective by itself yields satisfactory understandings of social phenomena.

Attributes are intrinsic characteristics of people, objects or events. When we think of explaining variance among such units of observation, we almost naturally resort to attribute measures, those qualities that inherently belong to a unit apart from its relations with other units or the specific context within which it is observed. Various types of attribute can be measured: an occupation's average income, a nation's gross national product, a riot's duration, a birth cohort's mean formal schooling, a person's opinion about the president.

Persons, objects and events may also be involved in relationships, that is, actions or qualities that exist only if two or more entities are considered together. A relation is not an intrinsic characteristic of either party taken in isolation, but is an emergent property of the connection or linkage between units of observation. Where attributes persist across the various contexts in which an actor is involved (for example a person's age, sex, intelligence, income, and the like remain unchanged whether at home, at work or at church), relations are context specific and alter or disappear upon an actor's removal from interaction with the relevant other parties (a student/teacher relation does not exist outside a school setting; a marital relation vanishes upon death or divorce of a spouse). A wide variety of relational properties can be measured: the strengths of the friendships among pupils in a classroom, the kinship obligations among family members, the economic exchanges between organizations.

Many aspects of social behavior can be treated from both the attribute and the relational perspectives, with only a slight alteration of conceptualization. For example, the value of goods that a nation imports in foreign trade each year is an attribute of the nation's economy, but the volume of goods exchanged between each pair of nations measures an exchange relationship. Similarly, while a college student's home state is a personal attribute, a structural relationship between colleges and states could be measured by the proportions of enrolled students coming to each college from each state. [. . .] The point we are stressing is that, while attributes and relationships are conceptually distinct approaches to social research, they should be seen as neither polar nor mutually exclusive measurement options. [. . .] Relational measures capture emergent properties of social systems that cannot be measured by simply aggregating the attributes of individual members. Furthermore, such emergent properties may significantly affect both system performance and the behavior of network members. For example, the structure of informal friendships and antagonisms in formal work groups can affect both group and individual productivity rates in ways not predictable from such personal attributes as age, experience, intelligence, and the like (Homans, 1950). As another example, the structure of communication among medical practitioners can shape the rate of diffusion of medical innovations in a local community and can determine which physicians are likely to be early or late adopters (Coleman *et al.*, 1966).

[. . .]

Networks

Relations are the building blocks of network analysis. A *network* is generally defined as a specific type of relation linking a defined set of persons, objects or events (see Mitchell, 1969). Different types of relations identify different networks, even when imposed on the identical set of elements. For example, in a set of employees at a workplace, the advice-giving network is unlikely to be the same as the friendship network or the formal authority network. The set of persons, objects or events on which a network is defined may be called the *actors* or *nodes*. These elements possess some attribute(s) that identify them as members of the same equivalence class for purposes of determining the network of relations among them. For example, we might stipulate that all payroll employees at plant six of the National Widget Corp. comprise the set of actors among whom an advice-giving network is sought. Additional restrictions on the permissible actors could be imposed (for example only males in managerial jobs), indicating that delimiting network boundaries depends to a great extent upon a researcher's purposes.

Our generic definition of a network may imply that only those linkages that actually occur are part of a network. But network analysis must take into account both the relations that occur and those that do not exist among the actors. For example, attending only to the gossip connections in a community and not to the structural 'holes' that occur where links are absent might result in an inaccurate understanding of how rumors spread or evaporate. The configuration of present and absent ties between the network actors reveals a specific *network structure*. Structures vary dramatically in form, from the isolated structure in which no actor is connected to any other actor, to the saturated structure in which every actor is directly linked to every other individual. More typical of real networks are various intermediate structures in which some actors are more extensively connected among themselves than are others. [. . .]

If network analysis were limited just to a conceptual framework for identifying how a set of actors is linked together, it would not have excited much interest and effort among social researchers. But network analysis contains a further explicit premise of great consequence: *The structure of relations among actors and the location of individual actors in the network have important behavioral, perceptual and attitudinal consequences both for the individual units and for the system as a whole.* In Mitchell's (1969) felicitous terms, 'The patterning of linkages can be used to account for some aspects of behavior of those involved.' For example, a formal organization with a centralized structure of authority among its various divisions and departments may be most effective (for example enjoying high growth and profitability) in a relatively placid environment, but in a turbulent, rapidly changing environment an organization with a less centralized structure may be more adaptable.

[. . .]

To illustrate the potential power of a network approach, consider a variety of contemporary social science problems: the sources of homophyly of beliefs within a power-elite, the adoption of technological innovations, the causes of corporate profitability, the income earnings of occupational groups, the recruitment processes of social movement organizations, the development of non-traditional sex roles. In each of these and many other substantive areas, a large research literature can be uncovered that attempts to explain the phenomena as a function of individual or group attributes. Yet in many instances, such characteristics may predict behavior only because of underlying patterns of relations that are often associated with these attributes. [. . .] Network approaches can more faithfully capture the context of social relations within which actors participate and make behavioral decisions.

Research design elements

Network analyses take many forms to suit researchers' diverse theoretical and substantive concerns. Four elements of a research design in particular shape the measurement and analysis strategies available to a researcher: the choice of sampling units, the form of relations, the relational content, and the level of data analysis. Varying combinations of these design elements have created a wide diversity among network studies that is evident in the research literature.

Sampling units

Before collecting data, a network researcher must decide the most relevant type of social organization and the units within that social form that comprise the network nodes. Ordered in a roughly increasing scale of size and complexity are a half-dozen basic units from which samples may be drawn: individuals, groups (both formal and informal), complex formal organizations, classes and strata, communities, and nation-states. A typical design involves some higher-level system whose network is to be investigated with one or more lower-level units as the nodes, for example a corporation with its departments and individual employees as the actors,

or a city with its firms, bureaus and voluntary associations as the nodes.
[. . .]

Form of relations

The relations between actors have both content and form. Content refers to the substantive type of relation represented in the connections (such as supervising, helping, gossiping), and an inventory of content types is presented below. *Relational form* refers to properties of the connections between pairs of actors (dyads) that exist independently of specific contents. Two basic aspects of relational form are (a) the intensity or strength of the link between two actors, and (b) the level of joint involvement in the same activities (Burt, 1982: 22).
[. . .]

Relational content

In conjunction with choosing the appropriate sampling units, a network analyst must decide what specific network linkages to investigate. [. . .]
Because researchers' capacities to conceptualize and operationalize various types of network are almost unlimited, we can only list the more common types of relational content, citing some representative studies:

- *Transaction relations:* Actors exchange control over physical or symbolic media, for example in gift giving or economic sales and purchases (Burt *et al.*, 1980; Laumann *et al.*, 1978).
- *Communication relations:* Linkages between actors are channels by which messages may be transmitted from one actor to another in a system (Marshall, 1971; Lin, 1975; Rogers and Kincaid, 1981).
- *Boundary penetration relations:* The ties between actors consist of constituent subcomponents held in common, for example, corporation boards of directors with overlapping members (Levine, 1972; Allen, 1974; Mariolis, 1975; Sonquist and Koenig, 1975; Burt, 1982: ch. 8).
- *Instrumental relations:* Actors contact one another in efforts to secure valuable goods, services or information, such as a job, an abortion, political advice, recruitment to a social movement (Granovetter, 1974; Boissevain, 1974).
- *Sentiment relations:* Perhaps the most frequently investigated networks are those in which individuals express their feelings of affection, admiration, deference, loathing or hostility toward each other (Hunter, 1979; Hallinan, 1974; Sampson, 1969).
- *Authority/power relations:* These networks, usually occurring in complex formal organizations, indicate the rights and obligations of actors to issue and obey commands (White, 1961; Cook and Emerson, 1978; Williamson, 1970; Lincoln and Miller, 1979).
- *Kinship and descent relations:* A special instance of several preceding generic types of networks, these bonds indicate role relationships among family members (Nadel, 1957; Bott, 1955; White, 1963).

Levels of analysis

After selecting the sampling units and relational content, a network analyst will have several alternative levels at which to analyse the data collected for a project. Here we consider four conceptually distinct levels of analysis at which an investigation can focus.

The simplest level is the *egocentric* network, consisting of each individual node, all others with which it has relations, and the relations among these nodes. If the sample size is N, there are N units of analysis at the ego-centered level. Each actor can be described by the number, the magnitude, and other characteristics of its linkages with the other actors, for example, the proportion of reciprocated linkages or the density of ties between the actors in ego's first 'zone' (that is the set of actors directly connected to ego).

[. . .]

At the next highest level of analysis is the *dyad*, formed by a pair of nodes. If the sample size is N, there are $(N^2 - N)/2$ distinct units of analysis at the dyadic level. The basic question about a dyad is whether or not a direct tie exists between the two actors, or whether indirect connections might exist via other actors in the system to which they are connected. Typical dyadic analyses seek to explain variation in dyadic relations as a function of joint characteristics of the pair, for example the degree of similarity of their attribute profiles. [. . .]

Not surprisingly, the third level of analysis consists of *triads*. If N is the sample size, there are $(\frac{N}{3})$ distinct triads formed by selecting each possible subset of three nodes and their linkages. Research using triads has largely concentrated on the local structure of sentiment ties among individual actors, with a particular concern for determining transitivity relations (that is, if A chooses B and B chooses C, does A tend to choose C?). [. . .]

Beyond the triadic level, the most important level of analysis is that of the *complete network*, or system. In these analyses, a researcher uses the complete information about patterning of ties between all actors to ascertain the existence of distinct positions or roles within the system and to describe the nature of relations among these positions. Although the sample may consist of N nodes and $(N^2 - N)$ possible dyadic ties of a given type, these elements altogether add up to only a single system.

[. . .]

Structure in complete networks

One major use of network analysis in sociology and anthropology has been to uncover the social structure of a total system. Systems may be as small as an elementary school classroom and a native village, or as large as a national industry and the world system of nation-states. But for any system, an important step is a structural analysis to identify the significant positions within a given network of relations that link the system actors. The observable actors – be they pupils, organizations or national governments – are not the social structure. The regular pattern of relations among the positions composed of concrete actors constitutes the social structure of the system. Hence identification of positions is a necessary but incomplete prelude in complete network analysis, which requires the subsequent appraisal of the relations connecting positions one to another.

Positions, or social roles, are subgroups within a network defined by the pattern of relations (which represent real observable behaviors) that connect the empirical actors to each other.

[. . .]

By occupying positions in a network structure, individual actors have certain connections to other actors, who in turn also occupy unique structural positions.

Although empirical actors and their observable linkages provide the data for identifying positions, a network's positions are conceptually distinct from any specific incumbents. For example, in a hospital system the positions defined by patterns of relations between actors – given such conventional labels as doctor, patient, nurse, administrator, paraprofessional, and so forth – persist despite frequent changes in the unique individuals occupying these positions. New positions may be created when an actor(s) establishes a unique set of ties to the pre-existing positions, for example when data-processing specialists are hired to manage the diagnostic and administrative information flow of the hospital. [. . .]

In the process, the complexity of the network is typically simplified, reducing a large number of N actors into a smaller number of M positions, since typically several empirical actors occupy the same position (many doctors, many nurses, many patients, and so on).

In deciding the basis on which to identify the positions in a complete network and to determine which actors jointly occupy each position, the network analyst has two basic alternatives (Burt, 1978). The first criterion is *social cohesion*. Actors are aggregated together into a position to the degree that they are connected directly to each other by cohesive bonds. Positions so identified are called 'cliques' if every actor is directly tied to every other actor in the position (maximal connection), or 'social circles' if the analyst permits a less stringent frequency of direct contact. [. . .]

The second criterion for identifying network positions is *structural equivalence* (Lorrain and White, 1971; White *et al.*, 1976; Sailer, 1978). Actors are aggregated into a jointly occupied position or role to the extent that they have a common set of linkages to the other actors in the system. [. . .]

A simple hypothetical example should make these conceptual distinctions clearer. Figure 1 portrays a fictional medical practice network. The lines connecting the actors represent 'frequent contacts on medical matters' (the figure is an unrealistic representation, but useful for

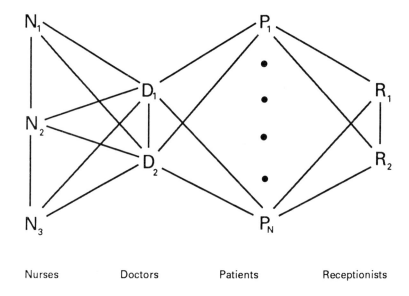

| Nurses | Doctors | Patients | Receptionists |

Figure 1   *A hypothetical medical practice network*

illustrative purposes). A social cohesion criterion identifies two distinct cliques, a small one involving just the two receptionists, and a large one containing all three nurses and both physicians. But using structural equivalence criteria, four distinct positions would emerge, corresponding to the four roles labeled in the figure. Nurses and doctors are no longer aggregated because they differ in their patterns of contacts with the other actors (the doctors are linked to the patients but the nurses are not, undoubtedly untrue in a real system). Three of these structurally equivalent positions are also cliques, but the patient position is not a clique because its occupants do not discuss medical matters among themselves. The point of this exercise is that different criteria for identifying structural positions in networks can, and usually do, yield different results. The choice of methods for locating positions in an empirical network ultimately depends, as in the application of any method, on the substantive and theoretical problem the analyst is addressing. For some purposes a clique approach will be preferred, while in other situations a structural equivalence procedure will be more useful. To state a definitive rule about which one to choose that would cover all situations is impossible.

[. . .]

References

Allen, M.P. (1974) 'The structure of interorganizational elite cooptation: interlocking corporate directors.' *American Sociological Review* 39: 393–406.

Boissevain, J. (1974) *Friends of Friends: Networks, Manipulators, and Coalitions*. New York: St Martin's.

Bott, E. (1955) 'Urban families: conjugal roles and social networks.' *Human Relations* 8: 345–83.

Burt, R.S. (1978) 'Cohesion versus structural equivalence as a basis for network subgroups.' *Sociological Methods & Research* 7: 189–212.

Burt, R.S. (1982) *Toward a Structural Theory of Action: Network Models of Social Structure, Perceptions and Action*. New York: Academic.

Burt, R.S., Christman, K.P. and Kilburn, Jr H.C. (1980) 'Testing a structural theory of corporate cooptation: interorganizational directorate ties as a strategy for avoiding market constraints on profits.' *American Sociological Review* 45: 821–41.

Coleman, J.S. and MacRae, Jr D. (1960) 'Electronic processing of sociometric data for groups up to 1000 in size.' *American Sociological Review* 25: 722–7.

Coleman, J.S., Katz, E. and Menzel, H. (1966) *Medical Innovation: A Diffusion Study*. Indianapolis: Bobbs-Merrill.

Cook, K.S. and Emerson, R.M. (1978) 'Power, equity and commitment in exchange networks.' *American Sociological Review* 43: 721–39.

Granovetter, M. (1974) *Getting a Job: A Study of Contacts and Careers*. Cambridge, MA: Harvard University Press.

Hallinan, M.T. (1974) *The Structure of Positive Sentiment*. Amsterdam: Elsevier.

Homans, G. (1950) *The Human Group*. New York: Harcourt, Brace, Jovanovich.

Hubbell, C.H. (1965) 'An input-output approach to clique identification.' *Sociometry* 28: 377–99.

Hunter, J.E. (1979) 'Toward a general framework for dynamic theories of sentiment in small groups derived from theories of attitude change', pp. 223–38 in Paul W. Holland and Samuel Leinhardt (eds) *Perspectives on Social Network Research*. New York: Academic.

Laumann, E.O., Galaskiewicz, J. and Marsden, P.V. (1978) 'Community structure as interorganizational linkages', pp. 455–84 in A. Inkeles *et al.* (eds) *Annual Review of Sociology*, Vol. 4, Palo Alto, CA: Annual Reviews.

Levine, J. (1972) 'The sphere of influence.' *American Sociological Review* 37: 14–27.

Lin, N. (1975) 'Analysis of communication relations', in Gerhard J. Hannemann and William J. McElwen (eds) *Communication and Behavior*. Reading, MA: Addison-Wesley.

Lin, N. (1976) *Foundations of Social Research*. New York: McGraw-Hill.

Lincoln, J.R. and Miller, J. (1979) 'Work and friendship ties in organizations: A comparative analysis of relational networks.' *Administrative Science Quarterly* 24: 181–99.

Lorrain, F. and White, H.C. (1971) 'Structural equivalence of individuals in social networks.' *Journal of Mathematical Sociology* 1: 49–80.

Mariolis, P. (1975) 'Interlocking directorates and control of corporations.' *Social Science Quarterly* 56: 425–39.

Marshall, J.F. (1971) 'Topics and networks in intra-village communication.' pp. 160–6 in Steven Polgar (ed.) *Culture and Population: A Collection of Current Studies*. Monograph 9. Chapel Hill, NC: Carolina Population Center.

Mitchell, J.C. (1969) 'The concept and use of social networks', pp. 1–50 in J. Clyde Mitchell (ed.) *Social Networks in Urban Situations*. Manchester: Manchester University Press.

Nadel, S.F. (1957) *The Theory of Social Structure*. London: Cohen & West.

Rogers, E.M. and Kincaid, D.I. (1981) *Communication Networks: Toward a New Paradigm for Research*. New York: Macmillan.

Sailer, L.D. (1978) 'Structural equivalence: meaning and definition, computation and application', *Social Networks* 1: 73–90.

Sampson, S.F. (1969) 'Crisis in a cloister.' PhD dissertation, Cornell University, Ithaca, New York.

Sonquist, J. and Koenig, T. (1975) 'Interlocking directorates in the top US corporations: a graph theory approach.' *Insurgent Sociologist* 5: 196–229.

White, H.C. (1961) 'Management conflict and sociometric structure.' *American Journal of Sociology* 67: 185–7.

White, H.C. (1963) *An Anatomy of Kinship.* Englewood Cliffs, NJ: Prentice-Hall.

White, H.C., Boorman, A. and Breiger, R.L. (1976) 'Social structure from multiple networks 1. Blockmodels of roles and positions.' *American Journal of Sociology* 81: 730–80.

Williamson, O.E. (1970) *Corporate Control and Business Behavior.* Englewood Cliffs, NJ: Prentice-Hall.

15

Neither friends nor strangers: informal networks of subcontracting in French industry

Edward H. Lorenz

Economists as a rule have attached little importance to the role of such social ties as trust and friendliness in market exchange. As Albert Hirschman (1982) has observed, this can be explained by the fact that the ideal market upon which claims of allocative efficiency rest involves large numbers of price-taking anonymous buyers and sellers supplied with perfect information. With such markets there is no room for bargaining, negotiation or mutual adjustment, and the operators that contract together need not enter into a recurrent or continuing relationship.

This chapter considers a case which does not conform to the economist's competitive ideal, that of continuing and recurrent relations between French firms and their subcontractors. These are relations involving mutual dependency, where each firm's actions influence the other. The situation by its very nature calls for cooperation, and it is reasonable to ask whether trust plays a role in this process.

In 1985 I began a study of the introduction of new technology in small and medium French engineering firms.[1] This was prompted by a number of intriguing bits of evidence. From 1975 firms in this category had improved their performance relative to large firms in terms of profitability and rates of growth of output and employment. Further, in terms of the latter two criteria, the smaller firms in this category (between 10 and 100 employees) had outperformed the larger (Delattre, 1982). Secondary sources also showed that small and medium firms had been some of the most dynamic investors in advanced computer-based technology, primarily NC and CNC machine tools (Cavestro, 1984).

This picture of comparatively rapid growth and technological sophistication contradicted established views of the role of small firms in the French economy. [. . .]

Preliminary visits to firms with 200 to 500 employees revealed that most had substantially reduced their employment levels since 1980. The value

Adapted from Gambetta, D. (ed.) *Trust: Making and Breaking of Cooperative Relations* (Oxford: Basil Blackwell, 1989), pp. 194–210.

of their sales, however, had in most cases increased after a dip in 1982–3. This could be explained in part by improvements in their productivity, but also by a substantial increase in their use of subcontracting for intermediate component production.

To some extent, of course, the firms had used subcontracting before; few were of sufficient scale in their operations to warrant investing in plant for such specialized tasks as gear grinding or heat treatment. And they all made use of subcontracting to meet temporary capacity constraints. What I was observing, however, was different. It was a shift to subcontracting on a permanent basis for such standard operations as turning, milling and drilling. It allowed the firms to avoid making investments in up-to-date machine tools and was frequently the occasion for a reduction in capacity, with some existing plant being sold off. While the general type of operation subcontracted was not specialized or specific to the particular firm in question, the design and specifications of the components were. Thus it was not a case of substituting in-house production for standardized components available in the market: rather, components were being machined (turned, milled, and so on) by subcontractors according to firm-specific plans produced in the design offices of the client firm.

What appeared to be taking place, then, was a process of industrial disintegration similar to the well-documented Italian *decentramento* (Piore and Sabel, 1984; Sabel and Zeitlin, 1985). The small-firm sector was benefiting from large firms hiving off some of the activities formerly undertaken in-house. When I questioned management about these policies, they generally attributed the decision to increase subcontracting to the 1981–2 depression in engineering together with the tremendous improvements in productivity then being made possible through the introduction of the CNC machine tools. Most argued that given the slow-growing and uncertain markets in which their firms operated, it would be impossible to amortize investments in CNC equipment. They were not in a position to continuously operate the equipment for the 12 to 16 hours a day required to achieve a satisfactory return on the investment. Smaller specialists, on the other hand, were in a position to do this, in part because they aggregated demands from multiple clients, and in part because of their greater internal flexibility in terms of shift work and overtime. In short, subcontractors could do it more cheaply.

Cost considerations, then, dictated the initial switch from in-house production to reliance on the market. Further discussion showed that these evolving market relations were a far cry from those of the standard textbook, where 'faceless buyers and sellers meet for an instant to exchange standardized goods'. By 1984–5 the firms had begun to use a suggestive word to describe their relationship to these new subcontractors: partnership (*partenariat*). In the course of conversations in which I myself participated, other equally emotive terms evoked the nature of interfirm relations: the importance of loyalty (*fidélité*); the existence of a moral contract (*contrat moral*); and the need for mutual trust (*confiance mutuelle*). This language suggests a certain anxiety inherent in subcontracting, and the need for something like trust if the relationship was to work smoothly. Such considerations led me to structure my interviews around the following set of questions:

1. What risks does subcontracting pose, and what safeguards do firms make use of to minimize these risks?
2. What are the mutual obligations implicit in the relation of partnership?
3. What is the role of reputation in ensuring that contractual obligations are met?
4. How does a firm decide if it can trust another, and can this trust be intentionally created?

   [. . .]

I

Trusting behaviour consists in action that (1) increases one's vulnerability to another whose behaviour is not under one's control, and (2) takes place in a situation where the penalty suffered if the trust is abused would lead one to regret the action. [. . .]

It is perhaps worth while to elaborate further on the implications of this definition. Firstly, trust presupposes decision-making in a situation of risk, where the risk is attributable to the strategic behaviour of others or to the possibility that they will behave opportunistically. By opportunistic behaviour I have in mind not only such blatant forms as stealing and lying, but also more subtle techniques such as withholding information in an effort to confuse. If all people are invariably honest, doing their best to fulfil their commitments, then there is no problem of trust as I have defined it.

Secondly, the action and hence the risks are avoidable: one does not have to engage in trade with another firm (although this implies forgoing the potential benefits of trade). Being able to avoid the relation is fundamental. If you could not, you might say something like: 'I have no choice but to trust this person, institution, etc.' Clearly, there being no choice, we need not invoke trust to explain our behaviour. [. . .]

Thirdly, it is useful to distinguish between risk associated with the behaviour of others and the risk of what economists call uncertain or exogenous events, such as acts of Nature or unpredictable changes in consumer demand and prices. Trust in this context is unrelated to our concerns of possible opportunism and the violation of commitment.

II

Hirschman (1982) suggests that recent approaches in economics can address the role of social ties such as trust in market exchange. These approaches are concerned to explain the existence of continuing relations between economic actors by placing stress on such factors as transaction cost, limited information and imperfect maximization.

I would like to suggest that the transaction cost literature (associated notably with Williamson, 1975, 1985) can tell us something about the role of trust in the economy. As the term 'transaction cost' suggests, this literature is concerned with the organizational implications of the costs of making a transaction. This includes not only the cost of reaching an agreement satisfactory to both sides, but also that of adapting the agreement to unanticipated contingencies and of enforcing its terms. Enforcement refers not only to potential litigation, but also to the use of private safeguards to prevent violation. [. . .] If transaction costs are thought of as friction in the economy, then trust can be seen as an extremely effective lubricant. To quote Arrow (1974: 23): 'It saves a lot of trouble to have a fair degree of reliance in other people's word.'

I should emphasize that my use of the legalistic term 'contract' does not imply a comprehensive written agreement. In the subcontracting cases in question, agreements are never written. The only written document is the order form. Certainly there is no effort to engage in comprehensive planning. The initial agreement is a reference point, the gaps in planning being intentional, and it is understood that adaptations will have to be made if the relation is to continue. This incompleteness of contracts is one of the reasons (though not the only one) why, to my knowledge, there is no use of the courts to resolve disputes. It requires both subcontractor and client to engage in an ongoing process of discussion in order to resolve misunderstandings and ambiguities and arrive at acceptable terms.

Given the possibility of opportunistic behaviour, trust is an essential ingredient in intermediate product subcontracting in so far as the two firms are locked into the relation. By lock-in effects I mean not only that the mutual benefits will be achieved only if trade takes place, but that the identity of the partners counts. Switching partners involves a loss for both sides. [. . .]

My concern here is with the possibility of *ex post* opportunism: either reneging on the agreement or using the occasion of unanticipated contingencies to try to shift the distribution of joint profits in one's favour.[2] Suppose the subcontractor and the client agree on a contract price, allowing the subcontractor to break even on the proposed investment. Once the investment is made, however, the subcontractor's vulnerability is increased. The client is in a position to appropriate the subcontractor, demanding a new contract price. [. . .] He may justify this in the name of unexpected financial difficulties, which the subcontractor is generally not able to verify. Conversely, the subcontractor, realizing that the client faces stiff penalties for late delivery of the product to the final customer, may opportunistically use his bargaining power to push up the contract price, similarly claiming unforeseen costs. Verification may again be both difficult and expensive. [. . .]

The implication of this discussion is that the problem of trust in economic exchange is raised by the potential for opportunism inherent in investment in specific assets. [. . .]

In conclusion, then, once firms are locked into a relation, trust is essential. The need for trust can be circumscribed through the efforts of the parties to engage in comprehensive contracting. But the limits to our rationality in a world where surprise is inevitable ensure that such efforts will be imperfect at best. Trust cannot be disposed of entirely. The implications of this for economic exchange are threefold:

1. The right sort of investments may not be made, since actors do not trust each other to refrain from abusing their bargaining power to renege on contract terms or to use a shift in circumstances to shift the division of profits in their favour.
2. A considerable amount of expense may go into fashioning safeguards designed to minimize the risks of being a victim of opportunistic behaviour. These expenses could be avoided if there were mutual trust.
3. More subtly, those in a bilateral monopoly may hesitate to demand legitimate adaptations to changed conditions, fearing such demands may cause conflict owing to a suspicion that they are in fact illegitimate, and intended only to change the agreed distribution of profits.

III

The theoretical discussion implies that given plausible assumptions about the economic world, trust has an important role to play in facilitating efficient contractual relations. Is this born out in practice? I now turn to an interpretation of the empirical results, addressing in turn each of the questions raised in the introductory section. These results are based on interviews conducted with the managerial personnel of ten client firms, all located in the Lyons conurbation. The firms include the following subsectors of mechanical engineering: machine tools, textile machinery, packaging machinery, mining equipment and industrial filters. They are not mass producers: their products are large, complex, customized and expensive. As production is to order they find it difficult to predict their requirements with any accuracy beyond a horizon of six months to a year. [. . .]

The first point to be made is that there is extensive use of safeguards by client firms to minimize the possibility of being the victim of opportunistic behaviour and hence the need to rely on trust. There is an Italian saying which captures much of the sentiment: 'It is good to trust but it

is better not to trust.' First, client firms prefer to solicit tenders from a
minimum of three subcontractors in order to preclude an opportunistic
distortion of production costs. They also prefer to split an order between
a minimum of two subcontractors so that if difficulties develop with one
it is possible to switch to the other. This practice may, of course, entail
a loss of potential scale economies depending on batch size.

Once firms are locked into a relation owing to investment in specific
assets, such policies no longer apply. It is then impossible to refer to the
market to ensure competitive pricing. In the case of physical assets (such
as machine tools) it is extremely rare for subcontractors to invest in
machinery specific to a particular client's requirements. I only came
across one significant example. The problem potentially arises in the case
of tooling, that is specialized dies and moulds for forging and casting, and
specialized fixtures and cutting tools for component machining. But risks
are easily avoided: these physical assets are mobile and the client
purchases them and retains control. If problems develop with one subcontractor the tooling is recovered and transferred to another. The rule is that
subcontractors invest only in general purpose equipment.

[. . .]

Specific investment can take other forms, for example in training and
skills. In the case of component machining this is relatively unimportant.
As one production manager observed, 'nobody has a monopoly position
in turning or milling'. There is a degree of skill specificity in the case of
assembly work, and the general policy is that employees of the subcontracting firm undergo a period of on-the-job training in the assembly
shops of the client firm before undertaking subcontracting on their own
premises. In short, the costs of training in specific skills are borne by the
client. The hazards implicit in such an arrangement no doubt help explain
why so little assembly work is contracted out.

Assembly subcontracting poses a further hazard of the fly-by-night kind
through private information on quality. In the case of individual component production, quality can be readily controlled. The client firm is as
technically knowledgeable as the subcontractor. As a rule individual
components are inspected on delivery and payment is made only after
ascertaining that they meet the stipulated standards. In the case of
subassemblies or entire machine assemblies, however, it is impossible to
check the individual components, and problems due to poor workmanship
may appear some time after the machine has been sold to the final
customer. According to the client firms, it is primarily this problem of
quality assurance which discourages them from resorting to assembly
subcontracting on a regular basis.

[. . .]

One of the most interesting results of the study is that not only do
subcontractors seek to diversify their clients in order to reduce the risks
of dependency, but so too do client firms. The accepted rule among the
engineering employers of Lyons is that orders should be limited to

between 10 and 15 per cent of a subcontractor's sales. The maximum figure is set to avoid the possibility of one's own market difficulties having a crippling effect on the subcontractor. Any figure less than 10 per cent, however, would imply too insignificant a position in the subcontractor's order book to warrant the desired consideration.

Effectively, then, clients put themselves in the position of the subcontractor in determining the optimal level of orders. From the subcontractor's perspective a reliable client is one who maintains a level of work. If a client firm wants a subcontractor to take its interests into account on recurrent contracts regarding quality and delivery, it is simply not acceptable to pull the work back in-house (assuming this were possible) whenever the firm faces a fall in final demand. Quantity adaptations also pose a trust problem. How is a subcontractor to interpret a decline in the level of work from a particular client? Is the client facing legitimate difficulties, or is it opportunistically pulling work back in-house having first encouraged a capacity expansion? In the case of dedicated capacity expansions of a general purpose nature, quantity adaptations can be quite as contentious as price adaptations.

The 10 to 15 per cent figure seems to represent an optimum. It allows the client a degree of flexibility without undermining the viability of the subcontractor, and at the same time ensures the client is considered sufficiently important to make a continuing relation of interest.

This brings us to my second point, the meaning of the term 'partnership' or the expectations implicit in the moral contract. Partnership clearly implies something more than what is stated on the order form. It is not merely a question of not buying more than you know you can pay for. It seems rather to involve the following: in exchange for improved performance by the subcontractor on quality and delivery, the client firm will make every effort to guarantee a level of work; furthermore, any adaptations to price, quantity and delivery are to be made in a non-opportunistic way by both sides, with full disclosure of the relevant information. In particular, this implies that the subcontractor will not be unconditionally dropped if a differential in terms of price or quality emerges with respect to competitors. Rather, clients stated that they operate a system of advance warnings; a reasonable period is allowed to their partner to match the competition. It also implies that clients will not pull back work in-house each time product demand falls. A number of firms observed explicit sharing rules to resolve problems associated with uncontrollable fluctuations in demand. A typical procedure was to guarantee that a constant fraction of work would be produced both in-house and by subcontractors regardless of the absolute level of output.

To sum up, partnership entails a long-term commitment and reflects a condition of mutual dependency where both client and subcontractor are in a position to influence the other by their behaviour. Partnership is a set of normative rules, determining what behaviour is permissible and what constitutes a violation of trust. The rules are designed to facilitate exchange in a situation otherwise open to exploitation.

The third point under consideration is the role of reputation in assuring compliance with the terms of the 'moral contract'. To put this question in another way: do firms rely on reputation alone in determining whether to trust each other? The evidence suggests that reputation is important but no substitute for experience. The client firms are comparatively visible, being prominent members of the Lyons engineering community and in most cases larger than the subcontractors. My interviews suggested that they are acutely aware of their reputation for reliability. When asked how they signalled their trustworthiness to potential subcontractors, they invariably referred to this.

But let us consider the conditions necessary for reputation effects to deter defection, here defined as violating the implicit terms of the partnership relation:

1. Common knowledge: all defections have to be made public. This does not simply mean a public announcement. It has to be possible to distinguish between real and bogus claims, to know who really was the offending party. This is frequently impossible.
2. The defector has to pay the full penalty: the firm cannot simply change its management team and ask for and receive forgiveness from the community.[3]

These are stringent conditions. In general, it is clear that client firms do not rely solely on reputation to determine the trustworthiness of a subcontractor, in the sense of his willingness to uphold the terms of the moral contract. To know whether a subcontractor is trustworthy (and this is my fourth point) they rely additionally on their own experience. One manager said a minimum of a year and a number of contracts was required, though he claimed that after three months he had an intuitive sense of how things would turn out based on personal contact with his opposite number. Another firm gave the figure of two to three years. During this period they operated a conscious testing process. Initially short-term contracts were given, it being understood that renewal would depend on performance. Once satisfied, a one-year contract was offered in which for a fixed price they guaranteed a level of work. At this point, according to the manager, the two firms were partners.

Time and experience were critical elements in deciding whether or not to trust. [. . .]

How are we to interpret this stress on the importance of personal relations? Is this evidence that friendship or caring is involved in efficient economics? Are we to conclude that trust between firms depends on bonds of friendship between the respective employers or managers? From the structure of this chapter you can probably foresee that my answer is negative. It would be difficult to explain how trust could be present as often as it is in subcontracting if it were to depend on sentiments of friendship. [. . .]

I interpret the stress on personal contact in a different way and as primarily to do with a pervasive problem in continuing economic relations: the need to adapt to contingency. Personal contact facilitates this by allowing for an easier exchange of information. You learn about the other person's idiosyncrasies and together you forge a special language which permits more sensitive interpretation. In short, you develop what might be called an understanding. [. . .]

IV

Economists generally assume that the narrow pursuit of interest results in efficient economic exchange. The aim of this chapter has been to dispute this assumption.

The theoretical section addressed two issues: to determine the conditions under which the need for trust develops in relations of economic exchange, and to show that business interests cannot negate that need because human rationality is limited and the environment is uncertain. Trust is crucial when contracting parties invest in specific assets, locking them into a relation. Limited rationality means that efforts to protect ourselves from opportunism through comprehensive contracting will inevitably be deficient. Rational comprehensive contracting is impossible. Trust is expedient.

The empirical investigation of machinery producers and their subcontractors in Lyons illustrates these themes. Firstly, it indicates that promoting trust is costly. In addition to the time it takes to establish a personal rapport between client and subcontractor, it involves a set of policies referred to as partnership. Client firms offer substantial guarantees on the level of orders and prices in exchange for improved performance on quality and delivery. Secondly, it demonstrates that while trust is costly, lack of trust is more costly still. Without the long-term commitment of partnership, the client's use of subcontractors is dictated by the changing demands of his market. This makes the subcontractor's orders volatile. Volatility inhibits quality-improving investment in up-to-date technology. It discourages flexibility in recontracting terms. Competitive success increasingly depends on cooperation as requirements for quality have escalated internationally and markets have become more uncertain. Clients should be called upon to recognize their dependence on subcontractors in this respect. Thirdly, it is apparent that where possible clients and subcontractors limit the dependence that creates the need for trust in the first place. Subcontractors avoid investing in capital equipment or skills specific to the client's needs. For similar reasons, clients avoid subcontracting final assembly operations. These are general rules with few exceptions: the exceptions that occur do so within trust.

[. . .]

Notes

1. The small and medium category (*petites et moyennes enterprises* or PME) refers to enterprises employing between 20 and 499 employees.
2. This is not to preclude the possibility of opportunism at the negotiation stage. Less trust implies that each side will take more costly measures to ensure that the other is truthfully disclosing their costs and revenues.
3. One client firm, close to bankruptcy in 1980 and now supported by the state, was actively trying to improve its reputation for reliability. Management spoke as if the world began in 1983. The success of the publicity campaign was not entirely clear, but there was no evidence that this firm experienced greater problems with subcontracting than others in the region.

References

Arrow, K. (1974) *The Limits of Organization*. New York: Norton.

Cavestro, W. (1984) 'L'automation dans les industries de biens d'équipement'. II.

Collection des Études. Centre d'Études et de Recherches sur les Qualifications.

Delattre, M. (1982) 'Les PME face aux grandes entreprises'. *Economie et statistique* 148, 3–19.

Hirschman, A.O. (1982) 'Rival interpretations of market society: civilizing, destructive, or feeble?', *Journal of Economic Literature* 20, 1463–84.

Piore, S. and Sable, C. (1984) *The Second Industrial Divide*. New York: Basic Books.

Sabel, C. and Zeitlin, J. (1985) 'Historical alternatives to mass production: politics, markets and technology in nineteenth-century industrialization'. *Past and Present* 108, 133–76.

Williamson, O.E. (1975) *Market and Hierarchies: analysis and antitrust implications*. New York: Free Press.

Williamson, O.E. (1985) *The Economic Institutions of Capitalism*. New York: Free Press.

16

Beyond vertical integration – the rise of the value-adding partnership

Russell Johnston and Paul R. Lawrence

For decades large, vertically integrated companies have reaped the benefits of their size, growing stronger with every competitor they eliminated or engulfed. But the elephants aren't grazing so freely anymore. Another beast has been nibbling at the herbage, and its presence is beginning to be felt.

That beast is the 'value-adding partnership' (VAP) – a set of independent companies that work closely together to manage the flow of goods and services along the entire value-added chain.

Most historians agree that the development of cheap, centralized power and efficient but costly production machinery tipped the competitive advantage toward large companies that could achieve economies of scale. Today, low-cost computing and communication seem to be tipping the competitive advantage back toward partnerships of smaller companies, each of which performs one part of the value-added chain and coordinates its activities with the rest of the chain.

VAPs are not, however, necessarily technology driven. They may emerge as the result of computerized links between companies or they may exist before the technical links have been made. In all cases they depend largely on the attitudes and practices of the participating managers. Computers simply make it easier to communicate, share information, and respond quickly to shifts in demand. They facilitate VAPs but alone don't create them.

To better understand what a value-adding partnership is and how it works, let's look at some that are doing especially well.[1]

McKesson Corporation, the $6.67 billion distributor of drugs, health care products, and other consumer goods, is among the most successful. The business press has often cited McKesson for its innovative use of information technology to improve customer service and cut order-entry costs. But McKesson's story is much richer than most people know. Once a conventional wholesale distributor squeezed by vertically integrated chain stores McKesson has transformed itself into the hub of a large value-adding partnership that can more than hold its own against the chains.

Adapted from *Harvard Business Review*, July–August 1988: 94–101.

McKesson's evolution to a VAP was triggered by fierce competition from large drugstore chains, which were eating into the business of the independent stores McKesson serviced. McKesson realized that if the independents died, it would soon follow suit. To protect their business, McKesson's managers began to look for ways to help customers.

Their search focused on a rudimentary order-entry system at one of McKesson's warehouses. In the early stages, the system included data-collection devices, powered by car batteries, that were wheeled around customers' stores in shopping carts. The system dramatically cut the costs of processing orders by expediting the steps of checking inventory, calling in an order, manually recording the order, and eventually packing and shipping it. McKesson soon discovered that the system could also specify how to pack orders so that they coincided with the arrangement of customers' shelves. Doing so made restocking more efficient.

These successful uses of information technology spurred the search for others. McKesson managers soon realized they could use the computer to manipulate data to help customers set prices and design store layouts to maximize the profits of each particular store. They also began using it to perform accounting services, such as producing balance sheets and income statements. And they discovered that the system could be used to warn customers of potentially harmful drug combinations by tracking prescriptions histories.

McKesson thus offered the independent drugstores many advantages of computerized systems that no one store could afford by itself. The drugstores were able to offer their customers better prices, a more targeted product mix, and better services, all of which helped them stand up against the chains. Still, the drugstores maintained their autonomy, so they could be responsive to the needs of the local area and form lasting ties with the community. This actually gave them an advantage over the chain stores, whose managers had to answer to headquarters and could be transferred from one location to another.

[. . .]

The close and productive link with customers wasn't good enough, however, to satisfy McKesson's imagination. The company recognized that the up-to-date information on sales had immense value to product managers of consumer goods manufacturers and proceeded to sell it to its own suppliers. Suppliers used it to make more timely shipments to McKesson in much the same way as McKesson had done with the drugstores. Computer-to-computer ordering from suppliers permitted McKesson to cut its staff of buyers from 140 to 12. Meanwhile, suppliers could schedule production more efficiently and streamline their inventories.

Another McKesson innovation was to use the computer system to help process insurance claim applications for prescription reimbursement. This strengthened the ties among insurance companies, consumers and drugstores by speeding payments and smoothing administrative hassles.

What's a Value-Added Chain?

The term *value-added chain* comes from the field of microeconomics, where it is used to describe the various steps a good or service goes through from raw material to final consumption. Economics has traditionally conceived of transactions between steps in the chain as being arm's-length relationships or hierarchies of common ownership. Value-adding partnerships are an alternative to those two types of relationship. Usually, the partnerships first develop between organizations that perform adjacent steps in the chain. A value-added chain for packaged foods might look like this:

farmer → broker → basic → packaged → distributor → retailer → consumer
processor   goods
producer

McKesson's total network thus includes manufacturer, distributor, retailer, consumer and third-party insurance supplier.

What makes McKesson so powerful – and what makes it a VAP – is the understanding that each player in the value-added chain has a stake in the other's success. McKesson managers see the entire VAP – not just one part of it – as one competitive unit. It was this awareness that allowed McKessons's managers to look for opportunities beyond their own corporate boundaries. They looked for ways the resources at one part of the value-added chain could be used in another. And their efforts to be competitive went beyond cost cutting. Many companies focus on trimming costs to increase profits, and they consider opportunities only within the unit defined by ownership. McKesson also looks for ways to add value by creating new services.

This ability to see beyond the corporate boundaries has another important advantage. It permits recognition of serious threats that lie elsewhere along the value-added chain. Because McKesson knows its own fate depends on that of its suppliers and customers, the company monitors competitive dynamics throughout the chain and tries to fix weaknesses wherever they occur. When all the partners are strong, the entire value-added chain can stand up to the toughest of competitors, integrated or not.

It is easy to make the mistake of thinking that McKesson's network is nothing more than a computer system with terminals in someone else's building. The wires and processors are not what make McKesson successful. True, the McKesson VAP grew out of the company's computer system, but information technology did not create the VAP. Rather, it was the managers who understood the relationships along the entire value-added chain and the need for each link in the chain to be as strong as possible. Information technology is not even a necessary ingredient in a VAP, as the next example demonstrates.

The textile industry of central Italy comprises many successful VAPs, which have evolved very differently from McKesson.[2] Over the past 20 years, 15,000 to 20,000 smaller companies have replaced all but one of the large, vertically integrated textile mills of the Prato area. By 1982, these companies were employing 70,000 people and exporting about $1.5 billion worth of products. The industry's disintegration may have begun partly to avoid labor legislation, but the new structure has allowed the industry to thrive for more basic reasons.

The Italian story really begins in the early 1970s, when Massimo Menichetti took over a large, integrated textile mill from his father.[3] At that time the company's future – indeed that of the whole Italian textile industry – looked bleak. Labor costs were soaring throughout Italy, and foreign competition was intensifying. Furthermore, a trend toward greater product variety meant that companies had to be able to create new designs quickly and efficiently, shifting production from one product to another without wasting time or materials. Innovation and flexibility had become critical to survival. Increasingly squeezed between rising production costs and falling market prices, Menichetti's mill had been losing money for several years.

Menichetti believed that the company had become too big and bureaucratic to adapt to the new competitive demands, so he proceeded to break the company into eight independent organizations. [. . .] The ownership transfer was to be gradual, over the course of three years. By the end of that period, the new enterprises would have to make half their sales to outside companies – to avoid a slip into complacency.

Within three years the dismantling of the Menichetti mill was complete and business was being conducted very differently. Since then, other integrated mills have patterned themselves after the Menichetti VAP. Small companies with cooperative relationships are now spread through the entire Prato area of central Italy.

Formerly, in each large mill, one group of managers oversaw the entire process, from assessing the market to designing fabric to supervising every detail of production. Now, small groups – sometimes a family – take total responsibility for their part in the process. Each shop has certain special skills. One may be particularly good at producing high-quality knits for dresses; another may be expert at mixing colors. Work is contracted out to whichever shop can meet the market's needs at the time. Each, therefore, has great incentive to stay in touch with fashion trends and environmental changes and to be ready to react quickly. Otherwise, it would lose business to other producers and might even go out of business.

At the center of each set of small companies is an independent master broker, or *impannatore*. In the Menichetti VAP, Massimo Menichetti himself plays this role. The *impannatore* manage the relationships among the various shops. They are facilitators and problem solvers who carry information from one place among the value-added chain to wherever it will be most useful. They get involved in all aspects of the textile business: raw materials purchases, fabric design, production contracts, transportation and sales. They look at the weaver's samples for next year and if they think they will sell, take them to customers all over the world. If the market objects to the weaver's price, the *impannatore* may help the weaver find ways to trim costs. They also negotiate with raw materials suppliers and transportation providers.

Being close to the customer, the *impannatore* were the first to realize that market changes required increased innovation and flexibility. They took the lesson to heart and, more importantly, carried the word back to the small manufacturers. To avoid losing business because of an inability to react fast enough, the production shops have adopted the latest textile machinery, including numerically controlled looms. Whole chains, not just individual players, adapted quickly to the market information, and all have benefitted.

Realizing that their partners must also be financially sound, efficient and marketwise if they themselves are to be competitive, the players in the Italian textile VAPs are eager to share information and cooperate. In recent years they have developed computer systems that rush information from partner to partner. The technology enhances coordination and boosts the speed and quality of responses to the market. The computer systems enhance the VAPs, but again, do not create them.

Of course, sharing information is very different from sharing rewards. In a VAP, as in any other industrial or organizational structure, innovation and adaptation must be rewarded if they are to be encouraged. In the Prato area, the *impannatore* can ensure that the rewards are shared appropriately by influencing prices and channeling work only to cooperative members. They can, for instance, withhold work from a shop that is trying to drive out otherwise successful competitors through predatory pricing.

The Prato mammoths gave way quietly and gracefully to the extraordinarily successful VAPs. Systematic, close coordination is now the rule, not the exception. In fact, the ties exist not only vertically, with suppliers and customers, but also horizontally, with what would usually be considered direct competitors. A weaver that guesses wrong one season might well receive overflow orders from a competitor that guessed right. They both understand that next year their roles may be reversed. And they know that if they help each other through tough times, they can avoid building overcapacity that could eventually hurt them all. Computer networks have been extended to interconnect the Italian VAPs, so when one VAP cannot deliver, another can be called on right away.

After only five years, all Menichetti's productive units had over 90 per cent utilization of their machines. Both labor and machine productivity had increased. New machines had been added, increasing capacity by 25 per cent. Product variety was increased in each of the eight units from an average of 600 to 6,000 different yarns. Average in-process and finished-goods inventory dropped from four months to 15 days. What works for Menichetti works for the Italian textile industry as a whole. From 1970 to 1982, Prato production of textile more than doubled, while that in the rest of Europe declined steeply.

Other VAPs are alive and well and show that Prato and McKesson are not flukes. The construction industry is a third example. It has operated like a value-adding partnership since the time of the Roman Empire. General contractors subcontract almost all the work on a construction job, soliciting bids from a selected set of subcontractors they trust and making contracts with 'partners' who offer reasonable prices – not always the lowest bid.

Japanese trading companies are venerable VAPs that are even more extensive than those in the construction industry. They arrange for the buying and selling of goods at every step of the value-added chain, from mines to household consumers, across several continents. They never get involved in operations. Although some Japanese companies are now choosing to develop their own brand images and find their own way to foreign markets, trading companies remain central to Japan's economic success.

Japanese auto companies also operate as VAPs. Toyota, for example, directly produces only 20 per cent or so of the value of its cars, while GM and Ford produce 70 per cent and 50 per cent respectively. [. . .]

In the past 30 years, book publishing has evolved toward a VAP. The leading competitors have taken turns divesting various operations that were formerly vertically integrated. The printing function was one of the first to be farmed out, followed by graphics and artwork. Now the usual core function of publishing is brokerage and marketing.

The movie industry has been moving in a somewhat parallel way. Full-blown movie studios that hold exclusive long-term contracts with actors and directors, have a staff of full-time composers and scriptwriters, and own and operate fully equipped production lots are a thing of the past. Now the studios act like brokers who negotiate a set of contracts for a single film production. Old-fashioned studios have been unable to compete.

At least in theory, whenever a non-integrated company deals with another company that performs the next phase of the value-added chain, both stand to benefit from the other's success. But usually such companies hold each other at arm's length and struggle to keep any economic gains to themselves. In fact, organizations often try to weaken a supplier or customer to ensure their own control of profits. This is understandable, given that the widely followed competitive model suggests that companies will lose bargaining power – and therefore the ability to control profits – as suppliers or customers gain strength.

The relationship between companies connected only by free-market business transactions and guided by such a model of competitiveness is often guarded, if not antagonistic, and rooted in fear that the other will become a competitor or engage in some other opportunistic behavior. Naturally, such companies tend to share as little information as possible, and consequently managers often lack knowledge of the activities elsewhere along the value-added chain. If a company perceives a trading partner as an adversary, it may ship shoddy material, squeeze margins, delay payment, pirate employees, steal ideas, start price wars, or corner a critical resource – all practices that reveal a lack of concern for the supplier's or customer's well-being.

The conventional solution for ending such destructive games and for controlling resources is vertical integration. When organizations along the value chain are under one management, it is presumed that they can coordinate their activities and work toward a common purpose. And, of course, they can often realize economies of scale.

But vertical integration has its weaknesses. In the process of exploiting their distinctive competences, many large, integrated companies emphasize one competitive dimension. In an integrated company, such focus can actually be a liability, because the strong culture that supports that focus makes it hard to perform tasks that require distinctly different orientations and values. A business that emphasizes low cost, for instance, may run its factories well, but its R&D, design or marketing functions may have trouble innovating. In a chemical company dominated by commodity production, the culture may inhibit specialty operations. The packaging division of a large paper manufacturer that emphasizes mass production may have trouble responding to the market as an independent competitor.

Perhaps the best example of this problem is in manufacturing. Many manufacturing companies that have invested heavily in flexible manufacturing systems in recent years have had trouble making the new technology achieve its potential. The culture and practices that support long production runs of standardized parts don't fit the new emphasis on wide product variety.

The problem of focus applies to horizontally integrated companies as well. A manufacturer of automobile parts is unlikely to be equally successful at making other products. Although the similarities may be many, whatever differences exist are likely to keep one or the other line from doing as well as it could if it were the company's sole product. And in many companies, large size itself creates a certain complexity that inhibits communication, innovation and flexibility.

In a VAP, each small operating company focuses on doing just one step of the value-added chain. Therefore each unit can tailor all aspects of the organization to this single task. Personnel, plant and equipment, compensation schemes, career tracks, accounting systems, and management styles – all vary depending on the work to be done. The drugstores in the McKesson VAP can attend to their customers' needs and let someone else concentrate on getting the products on the shelf at the right time. In the Prato area, the small companies that produce fabric strive for low cost, coupled with flexibility; those who design the fabric emphasize innovation and creativity.

This sense of focus translates into low overhead, lean staff and few middle managers. Decisions are made and executed quickly, so response time is short. Creative ideas are less likely to be suppressed, and more employees are exposed to the demands of the market. The fact that each company in a VAP is free to be different from the others creates a diversity that can be the seedbed of innovation. And marketing orientation becomes not an edict or a difficult task. It follows naturally from the free flow of information throughout the value-added chain to so many of the people who actually do the work.

At the same time, value-adding partnerships have some of the advantages of vertically integrated companies. Managers in a VAP take an interest in the success of other companies in the value-added chain. Their partnership orientation means they work toward the common goal of making the whole VAP competitive. They have command of facts about the market and empathy for the other organizations they deal with. Because information is shared throughout the chain, they know a lot about the competition. And they coordinate their activities with those of their trading partners.

VAPs can also secure the benefits of economies of scale by sharing such things as purchasing services, warehouses, research and development centers and, of course, information. McKesson's partners share access to the computer system. Partners in the Menichetti VAP are so congenial that they are housed under one roof; lines on the floor mark where one ends and the other begins. And that VAP has a cooperative transport system.

The power of the VAP is undeniable. To a great extent, VAPs have the best of both worlds: the coordination and scale associated with large companies and the flexibility, creativity and low overhead usually found in small companies. VAPs share knowledge and insight but aren't burdened with guidelines from a distant headquarters. They don't have long forms to fill out and weekly reports to render. They can act promptly, without having to consult a thick manual of standard operating procedures. In an increasing number of industries, they are proving to be fiercely competitive against both large companies and small independents.

Indeed, the spate of failed mergers and subsequent divestitures and spin-offs, what some people call downsizing, demonstrates that conglomerates and vertically integrated corporations are not always the most competitive organizational forms. [. . .]

Small size alone is not the answer. Many small companies that have open-market relationships with other businesses survive only at the whim of a larger competitor, customer or supplier that could readily drive it out of business or acquire it if margins become attractive enough. Always constrained by fierce competitiveness and trading partners that know no loyalty, they have little freedom to make financial and operating decisions that are best in the long run.

The delicate issue of control raises questions about the viability of a VAP over time. Let's not forget how creative business people can be. They can invent dozens of ways to take advantage of each other. What prevents them from playing destructive games with their VAP partners, who are, after all, potential competitors? What prevents hostile takeovers? In short, what is to stop a VAP from devolving into anarchy or back to a vertically integrated giant?

For a VAP to exist, its partners must adopt and adhere to a set of ground rules that generates trustworthy transactions. The sense of partnership must become an enforceable reality, despite the many uncertainties and opportunities for playing games. Advice on the best way to do this comes not only, from the examples of successful VAPs but also from economists and political scientists who have experimented with the 'prisoner's dilemma'. The prisoner's dilemma is a game in which two 'prisoners' are separated. Each has the option of either squealing on the other, thereby getting more lenient treatment for himself, or remaining silent, thereby saving both himself and his partner in crime. Of course, if one prisoner remains silent but the partner squeals, the silent person will suffer.

When the games are repeated over and over again, the strategy proving most beneficial is 'tit for tat'. That is, those players who cooperate on the first round and thereafter do whatever the other player did on the previous move are more successful. Those who don't catch on get eliminated. Robert Axelrod has summarized the extensive studies of the prisoner's dilemma in his 1984 book, *The Evolution of Cooperation*. His advice is particularly relevant to business people in a VAP: (1) don't be the first to play games, (2) reciprocate with both cooperation and lack of it, (3) don't be too greedy, and (4) don't be too clever and try to outsmart your partner.

Studies of existing VAPs are far from conclusive, but early indications are that VAPs follow Axelrod's advice intuitively. They are thus very different from the theoretically perfect markets of economic theory, in which bidders balance supply and demand around price and *caveat emptor* is the guiding principle. Each company in a VAP cultivates relationships with only a few (from two to six) suppliers of critical items and customers. Having too many partners means few repeat transactions and no time for close relationships to develop. At the same time, partners avoid becoming overdependent on one relationship. A company can keep potential partners 'on reserve' through occasional transactions so its welfare won't be harmed if a regular player fails to cooperate.

If partners are to help one another, VAPs must have ways of sharing information. If a partner's costs are creeping out of line, others must know so they can explore ways of helping with cost controls. Technological developments are making it easier for companies to exchange information. But, also important, successful VAPs must be able to punish partners for acts of opportunism and gaming.

In the Prato textile area, late delivery sometimes calls for withholding of new orders until the problem is rectified. And the construction industry has invented many ways to cope with changes in job specifications and raw materials costs as well as strikes and bad weather. The ultimate sanction, of course, is to terminate the partnership. In the Prato area, this could happen if, for instance, an *impannatore* failed to pass orders back to the weaver who had supplied the fabric design that was being sold.

It seems clear that, for at least some value-added chains, a value-adding partnership is a viable and advantageous means of achieving the benefits of vertical integration. By observing the characteristics of and the processes followed by successful partnerships, executives can determine whether VAPs might pay off for their organizations. Business relationships premised on the need to achieve bargaining power may be more aggressively competitive than is in their best interest. Remember that the examples cited earlier – US automobiles, Italian textiles, and drug distribution – all evolved from competitive, sometimes acrimonious relationships.

Notes

1. For other discussions of the new organizational forms, see Raymond Miles and Charles Snow, 'Network organizations: new concepts for new forms', *California Management Review*, Spring 1987, p. 62; Robert G. Eccles, 'The quasifirm in the construction industry', *Journal of Economic Behavior and Organization*, December 1981, p. 335; Calvin Pava, 'Managing the new information technology: design or default?', in *HRM Trends and Challenges*, ed. Richard E. Walton and Paul R. Lawrence (Boston: Harvard Business School Press, 1985); and Andrea Larson, 'Networks as organizations', unpublished manuscript, 1987.
2. This description draws heavily on Michael J. Piore and Charles F. Sabel, *The Second Industrial Divide* (New York: Basic Books, 1984) and on Gianni Lorenzoni, *Una Politica Innovative* (Milan: Etas Libri, 1979).
3. The facts about Massimo Menichetti are excerpted from the HBS case, Massimo Menichetti (B) 686–135, revised October 1986, prepared by Ramchandran Jaikumar.

17

Policy networks and sub-central government

R.A.W. Rhodes

[. . .]

Varieties of network

Following Benson (1982: 148), a policy network can be defined as a 'complex of organizations connected to each other by resource dependencies and distinguished from other [. . .] complexes by breaks in the structure of resource dependencies'.

Rhodes (1981: ch. 5, 1985, and 1986: ch. 2) elaborates this definition, arguing that networks have different structures of dependencies, structures which vary along five key dimensions:

- *Constellation of interests* – the interests of participants in a network vary by service/economic function, territory, client group and common expertise (and most commonly some combination of the foregoing).
- *Membership* – membership differs in terms of the balance between public and private sector; and between political-administrative elites, professions, trade unions and clients.
- *Vertical interdependence* – intra-network relationships vary in their degree of interdependence, especially of central or sub-central actors for the implementation of policies from which, none the less, they have service delivery responsibilities.
- *Horizontal interdependence* – relationships *between* the networks vary in their degree of horizontal articulation: that is, in the extent to which a network is insulated from, or in conflict with, other networks.
- *The distribution of resources* – actors control different types and amounts of resources, and such variations in the distribution of resources affect the patterns of vertical and horizontal interdependence.

Although the available research on British policy networks is limited, none

Adapted from R.A.W. Rhodes, *Beyond Westminster and Whitehall: The Sub-central Governments of Britain* (London: Unwin Hyman, 1988), pp. 77–85.

the less it is possible to identify some of the main varieties in sub-central government (SCG).[1] Thus it is possible to distinguish, at a minimum, between policy and territorial *communities* on the one hand and issue, professionalized, intergovernmental and producer *networks* on the other.

Policy communities are networks characterized by stability of relationships, continuity of a highly restrictive membership, vertical interdependence based on shared service delivery responsibilities and insulation from other networks and invariably from the general public (including Parliament). They have a high degree of vertical interdependence and limited horizontal articulation. They are highly integrated. The distinction between policy and *territorial communities* refers, rather obviously, to differences in their constellation of interests. Policy communities are based on the major functional interests in and of government – for example education, fire (Richardson and Jordan, 1979; Rhodes, 1986: ch. 8) – whereas territorial communities encompass the major territorial interests – for example in Scotland, Wales and Northern Ireland (Keating and Midwinter, 1983; Rhodes, 1986: ch. 7).

Other networks differ in that they are less integrated. The least integrated form is the *issue network*. The distinctive features of this kind of network are its large number of participants and their limited degree of interdependence. Stability and continuity are at a premium, and the structure tends to be atomistic (Heclo, 1978). Commonly, there is no single focal point at the centre with which other actors need to bargain for resources. The prime example in British government seems to be the field of leisure and recreation. Seven central departments have responsibilities in this area, and at the sub-central level there are many non-departmental and intermediate organizations as well as all the tiers of local government (see Travis *et al.*, 1978, esp. p. 27a).

Professionalized networks are characterized by the pre-eminence of one class of participant in policy-making: the profession. The most cited example of a professionalized policy network is the National Health Service, wherein the power of the medical profession is substantial. The water service provides a further example wherein the constraints on water engineers seem particularly weak (Keating and Rhodes, 1981; Gray 1982; Saunders, 1983: 34–7)[2]. In short, professionalized networks express the interests of a particular profession and manifest a substantial degree of vertical independence whilst insulating themselves from other networks.

The analysis of the influence of professions cannot be confined to the distribution of resources but must also cover ideology. Dunleavy (1981a: 10) suggests that professions with operational control in peripheral agencies will develop a national-level ideological system. Consequently, trends in national professional opinion constrain or influence the centre, and the national professional association will both periodically formalize professional opinion and continuously disseminate information on best professional practice. Peripheral agencies see the national-level system as a source of ideas; it sets the parameters to their decision-making. Finally, the rotation of professions between peripheral agencies coupled with the usual traits of a profession, such as training and qualifications, serve to reinforce the national-level ideology: to present a unified 'view of the world' based on common ideas, values and knowledge. And Dunleavy's (1981b) case study of high-rise housing illustrates the operation of one such national-level ideological structure. Professional influence is exercised in traditional interest group activities (for example lobbying) it is institutionalized in policy networks; and it sets the parameters to decision-making through national-level ideological structures.

Intergovernmental networks or, in the case of England, the 'national community of local government' (Rhodes, 1986: 11–16 and ch. 3) are the networks based on the representative organizations of local authorities. Their distinctive characteristics are topocratic membership (and the explicit exclusion of all public sector unions); an extensive constellation of interests encompassing all the services (and associated expertise and clients) of local authorities; limited vertical interdependence because they have no service delivery responsibilities but extensive horizontal articulation or ability to penetrate a range of other networks. The intergovernmental networks differ between the four nations. In England, there are a large number of organizations acting on behalf of local authorities in some capacity. This set of organizations speaks for disparate interests but manifests a high degree of interdependence, hence the appellation 'national community'. However, their links with individual local authorities – their members – are sporadic. In Scotland, Wales and Northern Ireland there is no equivalent to the English national community. Local authorities in each nation have their representative organizations, and only in Wales is there more than one such body. Moreover, the reduced scale of the networks means that they operate informally with far less reliance on explicit consultative mechanisms and far greater exchange with their members (James, 1982; Connolly, 1983; Rhodes, 1986, 256–67).

Given its topocratic membership, it might be anticipated that the national community of local government would conflict with the technocratic policy communities. However, national-level ideological structures are not limited to the service-specific policy communities and their associated professions. There is a 'national local government system' – which incorporates not only the national community and the policy communities for local government services but also the territorial intergovernmental networks – and this set of organizations defines the national role and state of opinion in local government as a whole (Dunleavy, 1981b: 105; Dunleavy and Rhodes, 1983: 121–2; Rhodes, 1986: 31–2, 36, 416). It is a key means by which local government can convey a wide variety of different views to Whitehall and it also provides a framework within which any individual local authority can situate its problems, concerns and strategies. Local authority actors do not decide policies for their area in isolation; they look to the national local government system for guidance about what standard of service to provide, for ideas to imitate or avoid, for ways of tackling common problems and for justifications or philosophies of particular strategies. Some councils are innovators across a wide field of policy, but they are rather exceptional. Most councils of the time follow national trends in the local government world, or national trends in their kind of authority facing their kind of general problem under their kind of political control. Each of them will innovate from time to time in one issue area or another, adding their own small contribution to the national picture. But most of the time local decisions are made within nationally defined parameters of what counts as good policy, rather than helping to redefine those parameters. If policy networks represent the all-pervasive functionalism in the organization of British government, then the national local government system is a mechanism of ideological integration.

Producer networks are distinguished by the prominent role of economic interests (both the public and the private sector), in policy-making; their fluctuating membership; the dependence of the centre on industrial organizations for delivering the desired goods and for expertise; and the limited interdependence of the economic interests. Thus Tivey (1982) describes the development of the Nationalized Industries Chairmen's Group, its links with the Treasury and how it uses its knowledge of its industries to compete with the private sector for government resources. However, the effectiveness of the Group is constrained by competition between its members: competition which extends beyond the distribution of public money between the industries to the market-place and the sale of their respective products. Similarly, Dunleavy (1982: 191 and 192 fig. 11.2) suggests that private industry has been a major influence on the development of policy in the nuclear network – a network in which, for example, GEC is firmly embedded.

Of late, the analysis of economic producer groups has been dominated by corporatist theory. Apart from the conceptual inadequacies of this theory, it has not fared well when applied to policy-making in British government. Leaving aside the bi-partite 'Social Contract' – the archetypical case which has been over-cited and remains a bad example – the case of industrial policy offers little solace. Thus, Hogwood (1979) and Grant (1982) argue that an industrial policy community exists but its boundaries are imprecise and, in spite of a degree of informal contact, it remains loosely integrated. Clarity is served if this network is distinguished from the highly integrated policy communities, but it is clear that producer networks have few if any corporatist characteristics. It is possible that the concept of corporatism could retain some utility but only if limited to government-imposed integration/regulation: 'state corporatism' in Schmitter's (1979: 20) formulation. When so restricted, it does at least refer to a specific type of network relationship.

The distinction between the public and private sector does not refer solely to industry; it is also relevant in the analysis of professions.

Dunleavy (1982: 193–5) argues that, when a profession is split between the public and the private sector, the latter tends to have a higher status within a unified profession. When the public and private sectors work together, for example in research and development, the flow of influence will be from the professionals in the private sector to those in the public sector. A profession can be a key channel of influence for the private sector. Thus:

> the concentration of nuclear engineers in these governmental bodies (i.e. UK Atomic Energy Authority, Atomic Energy Commission of America) working very closely with nuclear power plant manufacturers, has distorted their conceptions of the public interest on nuclear power. (Dunleavy, 1982: 197)

In yet another form, professional influence emerges as a key element in policy networks.

The variety of networks is potentially much greater than the examples discussed above. However, the most important conclusion to be drawn from the examples concerns the need to compare networks. There is no one pattern of relationships for all policy areas. The definition of networks and the discussion of characteristics and types have suggested a basis for such comparison and illustrated the known variety. Two topics remain to be explored: the relationship between networks and the national government environment and relationships within and between networks. To this point, the analysis of networks has been static, an exercise in definition and typology. It is also necessary to explain changes in the context and in the relationships of policy networks.

Policy networks and the national government environment

Within a unitary institutional structure, the centre is the fulcrum of policy networks. Allied to the tradition of executive authority, central government cannot be treated as one more group; its role is constitutive. It can specify unilaterally, substantive policies, control access to the networks, set the agenda of issues, specify the rules of the game surrounding consultation, determine the timing and scope of consultation, even call a network into being. Whilst it may prefer, and on occasion be constrained, 'to create a nexus of interests so that co-operation flows from a sense of mutual advantage' (Richardson and Jordan, 1979: 105), it retains the option of coercion. Through the substantial resources it controls, the centre has the luxury of choice between the many available strategies. Policy networks are not necessarily a constraint on government but can be manipulated by government in its own interest; the relationship is asymmetric.

This general point to one side, it is necessary to recognize that the centre has a multiplicity of interests. Policy networks may be based on a department or even a section of a department, each of which can have a distinct style. Relationships within a network are shaped by the 'departmental philosophy' or the 'store of knowledge and experience in the subjects handled, something which eventually takes shape as a practical philosophy' (Bridges, 1971: 50). This observation is unremarkable, but it is difficult to explain variations in style if the central department is treated as a unitary. If the era of the 'giant department' (Clarke, 1971) has passed, none the less large, multi-functional departments persist. Thus, the Department of the Environment (DoE) is composed of major divisions including (at various times during the 1970s) water, transport, local government, housing, planning and construction. By no means all of these divisions are at the heart of a function-specific network, but equally there is no single DoE policy network. It is inadequate, therefore, to search for *a* departmental philosophy. It is also necessary to search for variations within departments to determine whether or not a single department has several distinct styles: a possibility rendered all the more probable when it has been created from several previously separate departments. The separate organizational arrangements devised for transport and construction during the 1970s attest to their distinctiveness. The terms 'central government' and 'the centre' have to be understood, therefore, as shorthand for a diverse collection of departments *and* divisions.

It is only to be expected that this diversity is matched by the range of interests within central government. At its simplest, it is possible to distinguish between the 'guardians', or the Treasury, concerned to restrain public expenditure and 'advocates' or the service spending departments (Wildavsky, 1975: 7). However, a further two distinctions are necessary. The 'advocates' comprise those departments (and policy networks) which have a direct involvement with the services of SCG and those which have no such involvement. The latter will be at least neutral in, for example, any argument with the Treasury involving local expenditure, and more probably they will have a healthy interest in local authorities bearing the brunt of any reductions in expenditure. Last but by no means least is the DoE, which, as the areal department responsible for local government, acts both as guardian in the negotiations about government grant and as 'advocate' for spending on those services for which it has responsibility. And this characterization of the interests within central government is general, omitting the particular interests associated with, for example, a specific policy initiative. To the range of policy networks, therefore, it is necessary to add a parallel and profuse range of interests.

Second, the analysis of policy networks presupposes that they have a key impact on policy content. However, as Lowi (1972) has argued, the 'politics determines policy' axiom can be turned on its head; 'policies determine politics'. It is no mere coincidence that the Home Office, responsible for policies on police, fire and prisons, should be repeatedly characterized as authoritarian, secretive and directive. Lowi's reversal of conventional axioms has the virtue of pungent argument but the problem of overstatement; policy is both a dependent and an independent variable. But leaving such complexities to one side, it is clear that the analysis of policy networks cannot be limited to an analysis of process; it must encompass policy content.

The second feature of the British political tradition which conditions the operation of policy networks is the two-party system. Ministers face in two directions. They are the heads of the bureaucracies at the heart of the policy networks but they are also the leaders of the majority party. Policy networks have not supplanted party political channels of communication and influence. Party is at times a complementary and at other times a rival channel of influence. The effects of party are pervasive. It spans levels of government and communicates a range of interests. Most important, it spans the policy network. If policy networks are closed, then party is one of the means for prising them open. Rhodes (1986: 387–9) concluded from his study of the national community of local government that party was the grit in the molluscs of Whitehall-based policy networks, capable of stimulating change. Of course, British government cannot be reduced to the simplistic duality of party versus bureaucracy. But the fluctuating relationship between the two is central to understanding the sources of inertia and innovation in the policy process.

[. . .]

The emphasis throughout the post-war period has fallen on the extension of functional politics at the expense of territorial representation. The dual polity was created, local elites were marginalized, and uniform service provision prevailed over regional/national differences. These developments are only half the story. Paradoxically, the extension of functional politics also served to politicize SCG. Policy networks may reflect many features of the national government environment but they also changed that environment.

The most obvious reactions to the extension of functional politics were the re-emergence of nationalism and the emergence of the topocratic professions and the intergovernmental lobby to counter the influence of the technocrats and the function-specific policy networks. An intermediate tier of representation supplanted direct contact with local political elites but functional politics also led to the modernization of SCG and the attendant spread of party politics. It generated sectoral cleavages and contributed to class de-alignment. SCG became the locus of conflicts rooted in multiple social cleavages, and the politicization of local government began to pervade central – local relations with the onset of economic decline. SCG politics became the politics of Westminster and Whitehall. The extension of functional politics was an important factor in the erosion of the dual polity and the politicization of SCG.

A number of features of this trend warrant further comment. First local government witnessed the revival of municipal socialism in new clothes.[3] The 'new urban Left' (Gyford, 1983a, 1983b, 1984, 1985) rejected the legacy of a centralized, reformist socialism. As Beer (1982: 167) notes, the

Labour Party was 'wholeheartedly democratic, but the democracy to which it adhered in theory and practice was not participatory, but deferential, representative, indirect and centralized. Populism was as foreign to it as localism and individualism.' The romantic radicalism of the new urban Left rejected the responsibility ethic as but deference in a different guise. Rather local government was to be the means for resisting the 'cuts' but also an example of what socialism could achieve. The bases of support for this programme of radical activism were diverse, encompassing party and community activists, radical elements in the local government professions and socialist councillors. The 'new alliance' embraced the women's movement, black organizations, environmentalists and CND: indeed, the spectrum of social movements with their origins in the 1960s (Boddy and Fudge, 1984a: 7–9). And local government's 'responsibility ethic' was anathema to the new urban Left. The politics of confrontation saw new stars in the firmament with Ken Livingstone and David Blunkett becoming national figures. Conflict over the GLC's 'fare's fair' policy and the Liverpool budget were not isolated incidents but illustrations of the new style in SCG.

Furthermore, the landscape of local politics changed markedly with the rise of the SDP/Liberal Alliance. After the 1985 shire county council elections, twenty-five out of forty-six English and Welsh parties had no overall control. The Alliance was the largest single party on two councils and formed the minority administration on five councils. As yet this change has had its most marked effects on council procedures; but, with the onset of the budgetary process:

> The newly hung counties can certainly expect a new period of uncertainty, with protracted negotiations, an increasingly delicate officer role in terms of confidential briefings and information distribution, and committee and council meetings of quite unprecedented length. (Leach and Stewart, 1986: 15)

The rise of the Alliance in local government not only fosters its parliamentary aspirations but destabilizes local politics at a time of unprecedented instability and holds out the prospect of complex coalition politics.

Third, politicization was not a feature of local government alone. Public sector unions, disillusioned by fifteen years of pay policy, reacted angrily to the 'cuts' in public expenditure, privatization and a government which sought to limit drastically union power. The ever-present threat of unemployment may have exercised a restraining influence on some unions, but militancy was the order of the day in the NHS, the nationalized industries and the civil service.

The government confronted, therefore, an increasingly turbulent sub-central system, but the policy networks, as part of the national government environment, now constrained the ability of the centre to respond to the changes in SCG. The very existence of the networks caused certain policy-making processes and outcomes. A product of the welfare state,

Table 1   *Growth of public expenditure by programme in cost terms*

	% changes 1980–81 to 1983–84
Defence	14.2
Overseas aid and services	4.4
Net payments to EEC	83.9
Agriculture	23.9
Industry, etc.	– 3.8
Arts	6.0
Transport	– 5.1
Housing	– 49.3
Other environmental services	0.6
Law and order	19.0
Education	0.0
Health	5.8
Social security	25.5
Other public services	– 16.1
Common services	29.9
Scotland	3.3
Wales	0.0
N. Ireland	7.9
Asset sales	– 63.5
Planning total	7.0
Planning total, excl. asset sales	7.7
Planning total, excl. asset sales and net sales of land and buildings	8.4
Net interest	26.7
Total expenditure, incl. interest	9.2

Note: Figures are adjusted for reduction in National Insurance surcharge and changes in treatment of housing and sickness benefits and of Property Services Agency.
Source: Ward, 1984, table 7, p. 6.

they had a vested interest in, and helped to fuel, its continued expansion. In an era of economic decline, they resisted political pressure for cuts: a bulwark of inertia. As the centre sought to control SCG, its bureaucratic strategies foundered on the disaggregation of policy systems, politicization and the multiplicity of interests in and of the centre. Thus, local government current expenditure rose in real terms between 1979 and 1983 (see HMSO, 1983). Nor was this pattern exceptional. Total public expenditure continued to rise and in spite of repeated cries of anguish, NHS expenditure rose by 14 per cent in real terms in the same period (*Social Trends*, 1985: 122). Indeed, as Ward (1984: 26) demonstrates, only housing of the major welfare services experienced a 'cut' in expenditure in real terms (see Table 1), although a focus on resources is unable to demonstrate whether or not there has been marked deterioration in service levels. Thus, although the NHS had a 17 per cent increase in volume expenditure (1979-84), this figure reduced to 7.2 per cent (4 per cent for hospitals, etc.) when the relative price effect (or higher costs of the NHS) was taken into account. It was further estimated by the Department of Health and Social Security that demographic and technological pressures required an increase in expenditure of approximately 6 per cent. Consequently, the hospital and community health sector experienced problems in meeting demands (Social Services Committee, 1984: x–xi). As the committee commented, the NHS needs to live at the same rates of pay and price inflation as the rest of us. None the less the alleged dismantling of the welfare state remains some way off.

Policy networks have become as central a feature of the national government environment as some of the hoary old chestnuts of constitution, less prominent and debated but a more determinant influence. They lie at the heart of one of the major problems of British government: policy messes, or the non-correspondence of policy systems and policy problems. The failure to appreciate that service delivery systems are complex, disaggregated and indeterminate has led to the failure of policies. The process of differentiation in government requires not only policies on substantive problems but also policies on the procedures for managing differentiation (or institutionalizing indeterminacy). Moreover, these comments are a critique not of functional differentiation in itself but of the failure to recognize that it is a central feature of the policy process; substance and procedure have to be endlessly traded off in the internally differentiated or pluralized system of SCG.

Policy networks in all their variety are a defining characteristic of SCG. Exploring this variety requires an examination of relationships within networks, of the process of exchange and the rules and strategies governing resource transactions.

[. . .]

Notes

1. This classification is an empirical one, restricted to SCG. Benson, 1982, pp. 154–8, distinguishes between all governmental networks in terms of their 'types of structural interests': i.e. demand (or client) groups; support groups (which provide needed resources for the public sector organizations); administrative groups (or those occupying positions of administrative control); provider groups (which deliver services); and co-ordinating groups (or those responsible for rationalization within and between programmes). Networks will vary, therefore, as the configuration of interest varies. There are a number of problems with this approach. First, the constellation of interests is only one relevant dimension of network structure. Second, in the context of British SCG, it is difficult to distinguish demand from support groups and administrative groups from provider groups. Third, economic functional groups are omitted as such, forming part of (presumably) support or provider groups. Equating manufacturing industry with either environmental groups on the one hand or the medical profession on the other seems unhelpful. However, given the current state of research on networks any classification must be treated with caution. The listing employed here is tentative.
2. Since this was written the regional water authorities have been privatized and are now run as private companies. [eds]
3. Although space precludes a detailed discussion, my survey of the available theories omits

a large but diffuse socialist literature. A useful preliminary survey is provided by Sancton, 1976, and some more recent contributions are summarized and evaluated in Gyford, 1985. Not only is there a need for a historical account of socialist thinking on decentralization, the areal division of powers and local government, but there are also a number of more specific gaps – for example, Herbert Morrison and Harold Laski's democratic centralism and its implications for local government. The liberal theory of local government has been, better served by commentators than the socialist theory, and it is time that the inequity was redressed. My thanks to Peter Richards (Southampton) for prompting these reflections.

References

Barker, A. (1982) *Quangos in Britain*. London: Macmillan

Beer, S.H. (1982) *Britain Against Itself*. London: Faber & Faber.

Benson, J.K. (1982) 'A framework for policy analysis', in Rogers *et al.* 137–76.

Boddy, M. and Fudge, C. (1984a) 'Labour councils and the new left alternative', in Boddy and Fudge: 1–21.

Boddy, M. and Fudge, C. (eds) (1984b) *Local Socialism?* London: Macmillan.

Bridges, Sir Edward (1971) 'Portrait of a profession', in Chapman and Dunsire: 44–60.

Chapman, R.A. and Dunsire, A. (eds) (1971) *Style in Administration*. London: Allen & Unwin.

Clarke, Sir Richard (1971) *New Trends in Government*. London: HMSO.

Connolly, M. (1983) *Central-Local Relations in Northern Ireland*. (Final Report to Social Science Research Council).

Drucker, H., Dunleavy, P., Gamble, A. and Peele, G. (eds) (1983) *Developments in British Politics*. London: Macmillan.

Dunleavy, P. (1981a) 'Professions and policy change: notes towards a model of ideological corporatism', *Public Administration Bulletin*, 36: 3–16.

Dunleavy, P. (1981b) *The Politics of Mass Housing in Britain, 1945-75*. Oxford: Clarendon Press.

Dunleavy, P. (1982) 'Quasi-governmental sector professionalism: some implications for public policy-making in Britain', in Barker: 181–205.

Dunleavy, P. and Rhodes, R.A.W. (1983) 'Beyond Whitehall', in Drucker *et al.* (eds): 106–33.

Grant, W.P. (1982) *The Political Economy of Industrial Policy*. London: Butterworths.

Gray, C. (1982) 'The regional water authorities', in Hogwood and Keating: 143–67.

Gyford, J. (1983a) 'The implications of local socialism', *Local Government Studies*, 9(1): 13–17.

Gyford, J. (1983b) 'The new urban Left: a local road to socialism?', *New Society*, 21 April: 91–3.

Gyford, J. (1984) 'From community action to local socialism', *Local Government Studies*, 10(4): 5–10.

Gyford, J. (1985) *The Politics of Local Socialism*. London: Allen & Unwin.

Heclo, H. (1978) 'Issue networks and the executive establishment', in King: 87–124.

HMSO (1983) *Rates*. London: HMSO.

Hogwood, B. (1979) 'Analysing industrial policy: a multi-perspective approach', *Public Administration Bulletin*, 29: 18–42.

Hogwood, B. and Keating, M. (1982) *Regional Government in England*. Oxford: Clarendon Press.

James, M. (1982) 'The Welsh local authority associations', paper presented to the Conference of the Political Studies Association, Queen's University, Belfast, September.

Keating, M. and Midwinter, A. (1983) *The Government of Scotland*. Edinburgh: Mainstream.

Keating, M. and Rhodes, R.A.W. (1981) 'Politics or technocracy? The regional water authorities', *Political Quarterly*, 55: 78–84.

King, A. (ed.) (1978) *The New American Political System*. Washington, DC: American Enterprise.

Leach, S. and Stewart, J.D. (1986) *The Hung Counties*. Luton: Local Government Training Board (mimeo).

Lowi, T.J. (1972) 'Four systems of policy, politics and choice', *Public Administration Review*, 32: 298–310.

Rhodes, R.A.W. (1981) *Control and Power in Central–Local Government Relations*. Aldershot: Gower.

Rhodes, R.A.W. (1985) 'Corporatism, pay negotiations and local government', *Public Administration*, 63: 287–307.

Rhodes, R.A.W. (1986) *The National World of Local Government*, London: Allen & Unwin.

Richardson, J.J. and Jordan, G. (1979) *Governing under Pressure*. Oxford: Martin Robertson.

Rogers, D., Whitten, D. and Associates (eds) (1982) *Interorganizational Coordination*. Ames, Iowa: Iowa State University Press.

Sancton, A. (1976) 'British socialist theory of the division of power by area', *Political Studies*, 24: 158–70.

Saunders, P. (1983) 'The "regional state": a review of literature and agenda for research', Paper presented at the Social Science Research Council conference on Political Theory and Intergovernmental Relations, Nuffield College, Oxford, September.

Schmitter, P.C. (1979) 'Still the century of corporatism?', in Schmitter and Lehmbruch: 7–52.

Schmitter, P.C. and Lehmbruch, G. (eds) (1979) *Trends towards Corporatist Intermediation*. London: Sage.

Social Services Committee (1984) *Public Expenditure on the Social Services, Fourth Report, Session 1983–4*. HC395. London: HMSO.

Tivey, L. (1982) 'Nationalized industries as organized interests', *Public Administration*, 60: 42–55.

Travis, A.S., Veal, A.J., Duesbury, K. and White, J. (1978) *The Role of Central Government in Relation to the Provision of Leisure Services in England and Wales*. Birmingham University, Centre for Urban and Regional Studies, Research Memorandum 86.

Treasury and Civil Service Committee (1984) *Third Report. The Government's Expenditure Plans 1984–85 to 1986–87*. Session 1983–4, HC285, London: HMSO.

Ward, T. (1984) Memorandum by Mr. Terry Ward, specialist adviser to the committee, in Treasury and Civil Service Committee: Appendix 1.

Wildavsky, A. (1975) *Budgeting: A Comparative Theory of the Budgetary Process*. Boston: Little Brown.

18

Taking and giving: working women and female bonds in a Pakistani immigrant neighbourhood[1]

Pnina Werbner

Women-centred networks

The focus on practices of female seclusion and veiling in Islamic societies has sometimes obscured the importance of extra-domestic networks sustained by women within their 'separate world'. Yet such extra-domestic, women-centred networks have important bearings on gender relations, conjugal roles and the external support women can draw upon. Purdah, as Papanek points out in a seminal paper (Papanek, 1973), is both a system of task allocations and an expression of male and family status. In the latter sense, purdah is non-complementary. It rests on the conception of an active male, an achiever in the public domain, and a passive female, secluded within the domestic domain, the object of male protection. [. . .]

Once we examine the 'world of women' not simply as a world of domestic chores or idle gossip, but as the complex world of extra-domestic female relationships, we are able to shift from the presentation of purdah as a cultural logic to a sociological analysis of variations in conjugal relations as these obtain in purdah societies. As Rosaldo hypothesized at the outset of the current debate on gender relations:

> Women's status will be the lowest in those societies where there is a firm differentiation between domestic and public spheres of activity and where women are isolated from one another and placed under a single man's authority, in the home. Their position is raised when they can challenge those claims to authority, either by taking on men's roles or by establishing social ties, by creating a sense of rank, order and value in a world of their own. (Rosaldo, 1974: 36)

In Manchester, Pakistani migrant women living in the central residential enclave initiate and sustain widely ramifying women-centred networks. Through the contacts they forge with other women, they extend the family

Adapted from S. Westwood and P. Bhachu (eds) *Enterprising Women: Ethnicity, Economy and Gender Relations* (London: Routledge, 1988), pp. 177–202.

network, incorporating their husbands into the networks they form.

The nature of participation in extra-domestic networks and the 'shape' of these networks is important to define clearly. Anwar (1979: 50–95) stresses the primacy of kinship ties in the formation of extra-domestic networks amongst Pakistani migrants. Friends, he argues, are assimilated into kin-category networks (1979: 62). Theoretical discussions of inter-household female-centred networks have also so far focused on the 'matri-lateral bias' characterizing kin networks in urban industrial societies (Yanagisako, 1977). The bias expresses itself in the closer ties maintained by female kinswomen (primarily mothers, daughters and sisters). Yanagisako labels this tendency 'women-centred *kin* networks' in preference to terms stressing the primacy of the maternal role. The debate thus surrounds the economic and normative basis of kinship in urban industrial societies which gives rise to this affective solidarity among female kin.

Although there is some evidence of a matrilateral bias developing among second-generation female kin, my discussion here is somewhat differently focused: it concerns the formation and implications of women-centred *friendship* networks. In these networks female kinswomen and affines are crucial pivotal points; friendship networks aggregate around the 'solidary core' of female affines or relatives (Yanagisako, 1977: 212). This conjunc-tion of friendship and kinship is, I will show, a basis for the achievement of status and reputation within a neighbourhood locality, as well as in the wider community. Moreover, such networks crucially affect the conjugal status and influence of women in the domestic household unit.

It is important to stress the central role of friendship, as *distinct* from kinship, in these networks. Friendship ties, which may be conceived of as 'weak' ties, constitute crucial 'bridging' ties (Granovetter, 1973). As such, they facilitate communication between different kin groups and across different strata. They are thus potential points of mobilization and change. New friendships and acquaintances forged by Pakistani migrants extend their horizons and support processes of mobility and social transforma-tion.

A further feature of these friendship-cum-kinship networks needs to be stressed. It relates to the exclusivity of networks and the fundamental idea of purdah as a symbolic shelter. Network exclusivity is clearly related to status considerations. Elite families in Manchester sustain exclusive networks (Werbner, 1981). While women, *qua* women, may share certain predicaments, they rarely form a solidary group. Instead, they tend to 'organize themselves to protect class privileges in activities which comple-ment their husbands' objective positions in the class hierarchy' (Bujra, 1974: 16). The 'open' networks of women in the central Pakistani residen-tial enclave are a feature of their low-income status. This openness is the basis for a form of female solidarity uniting women in common predica-ments and painful experiences or in the sharing of joyful occasions. Although the establishment of this 'women's world' is not a basis for a feminist consciousness (Bujra, 1974), it supports women's status and self-confidence in the domestic sphere. It thus protects women from the more iniquitous consequences of strict purdah, interpreted as physical seclusion and isolation.

Labour migration and changes in female status

To appreciate the full significance of Pakistani women's 'networking' activity, it must be seen from a broader perspective of labour migration and its differing impact on the perceived status of migrant men and women.

Saifullah Khan, commenting on the migration of Mirpuri women to Bradford, presents a picture of radical dislocation. She notes that in Pakistan 'women invariably spend their day in the company of other women' and goes on to argue that 'it is this "women's world" and the incumbent emotional and physical support which is abruptly ended when Asian women move to Britain' (1975: 179). In Bradford Mirpuri women were, she found, 'alone and restricted to the house' and such isolation, she argues may generate considerable anxieties and tension (1976: 104). Moreover, migrant men's work outside the home 'causes Mirpuri women to be subject to a stricter form of purdah than they experienced in the home village . . . [they] contribute less to, and have less control over, the household income in Britain' (1979: 53). This stricter system of purdah is sustained by male networks based on prior village and kinship connections.

This picture appears to confirm the conception of purdah as a protection from the 'real dangers of a segregated world' (Papanek, 1973: 316). Britain as an unknown and alien environment might well be expected in these terms to generate a more extreme form of purdah. The physical isolation of migrant women in their homes does, indeed, occur in Manchester under some conditions, and I discuss this phenomenon below. For many Pakistani women the move to Britain has meant, however, a move towards greater independence. They have escaped the proverbial domination of older female relatives, the constraints of extreme purdah as symbolized by the *burqa* and the restriction on movement,[2] and the deprivations of extreme financial hardships. Many are able to work and their earnings, unlike those of women in rural Punjab (see Sharma, 1980: 107) are their own to do with as they choose. Secluded nevertheless in the domestic world of the neighbourhood, women come into little status-threatening contact with the host society. Non-immigrant women they encounter in the neighbourhood are primarily, like themselves, housewives and mothers.
[. . .]

Clearly, extreme female seclusion precludes [. . .] active 'networking' on the part of women. It is significant, perhaps, that most migrant men in Manchester look upon such extreme purdah with disapproving amusement.[3]

For Pakistani women the formation of extra-domestic networks is not a novel phenomenon, unique to the urban industrial context. What is novel is the extension of ties with prior strangers. Facilitating this interaction is the flow of customary ceremonial gifting which has been adapted and extended to the Manchester context.

Taking and giving: ceremonial gifting

Women are central to the Punjabi Muslim system of ceremonial exchange. The system, according to Eglar (1960), is anchored in the pivotal role of the daughter as the constant recipient of gifts from her patrikin (p. 107). By extension it is a system of reciprocal exchange between households. Amongst Pakistani migrants in Manchester such inter-household gifting is known, variably, as *lena dena* (*len den* in Urdu), that is 'take give', or as *vartan* (the exchange of goods, barter). The basic rule of *lena dena* is that a gift returned should always exceed the initial gift in value (p. 125), thus perpetuating the relationship. The gifts of *vartan* – cloth, sweets, gold, or money – are known locally as *bhanji* (thus Eglar refers to the system as *vartan bhanji*, 'dealing sweets', although this conjunction of terms was, according to my inquiries, not used by local migrants). Ceremonial gifting and hospitality takes place primarily on festive and life crisis occasions. In Manchester, trips to Pakistan are a major occasion for hosting departing and returning travellers who receive gifts on their departure, and bring gifts from Pakistan on their return to Britain. Weddings, in particular, are central occasions for *lena dena* transactions.

In Pakistan as in Manchester, *lena dena* is primarily the prerogative of women. They are 'the guardians of *vartan bhanji*, who know to whom and when and how much a family is to give as well as from whom and when and how much it should receive' (Eglar, 1960: 138). As in Pakistan, so too in Manchester, *vartan* signals a relationship of mutual help, one in which 'two parties . . . feel free to ask favours of each other' (p. 106). That such a crucial and delicate relationship should be handled by women pinpoints their key role in Punjabi Muslim society.

Although the most valuable gifts and costly hospitality are reserved primarily for close kinsmen, the system extends to include friends, caste members, neighbours and fellow villagers (p 117). It is this potential for extension beyond the kin group which makes the system so crucial for the formation of inter-household networks in Manchester.

The proper conduct of *vartan* is a source of honour and prestige, *izzel*, for a woman and her family. Thus Eglar comments that:

> The number and quality of the gifts given and received are indicators of the family's knowledge and ability in dealing with people and provide an index of its status, influence and power and of the breadth of its social circle – all of which mean *izzel*. On all such occasions daughters are crucial to the exchange and hence to the acquisition of *izzel*. (1960: 111)

In Manchester, migrant women who work use some of their earnings to initiate and extend *lena dena* with neighbours and acquaintances. Their independent incomes have facilitated the building up of locally based friendship networks. Families who remain highly oriented to a return to Pakistan try to avoid extensive ceremonial gifting with local acquaintances: they regard such gifting as wasteful (Werbner, 1981). The more 'rooted' Pakistanis are locally and the more involved in the local competition stakes for status and prestige, the more likely they are to engage in *lena dena* with friends made locally.

It would be a mistake to attribute the style of neighbourliness which has evolved locally solely to women's independent incomes. Neighbourly relations bear a striking similarity to those obtaining in the North Indian urban neighbourhood studied by Vatuk (1972: 149–89). There too *lena dena* and 'open' networks predominated. Yet the women studied by Vatuk did not have independent incomes (1972: 164). It must be stressed, however, that overseas labour migration is an expensive enterprise allowing for little surplus. Women's independent earnings are probably more crucial in this context for the building up of local friendship networks since the highest priority in resource allocation remains, for most migrants, the maintenance of relations with family at home, in Pakistan.[4]

The pivotal role fulfilled by women in the formation of inter-household networks raises the question whether these networks may be regarded as part of the 'domestic' or 'public' domains (cf. Rosaldo, 1974; Yanagisako, 1977: 222; Bujra, 1974). I prefer to regard them as constituting the nexus of the public and domestic, mediating between the more formal context of public activity and the privacy and affectivity of domestic household life. As in other 'honour and shame' societies, for Pakistanis a man's status remains crucially anchored in this inter-domestic realm, in large measure controlled by his wife.

[. . .]

Kinship and friendship

Although most Pakistanis in Manchester live as nuclear families in separate houses, a set of brothers in the central cluster often regard themselves as members of a single *ghar*, 'house' (or extended family), and expect to make certain decisions jointly. These pertain mainly to the marriage of children, to investment in Pakistan where they often own a house or land jointly, and to the fortunes of ageing parents. More distant kin, both patrilateral and matrilateral, are regarded as belonging to separate *ghars*, but are of the same *biraderi*. They are *rishtedar* (relations). Cast members from the same home town or village locality are also *biraderi*, and even caste members from other parts of Pakistan are sometimes regarded as *biraderi*.

People of one's own caste and others from the same town or village in Pakistan are talked of and addressed as 'sister' or 'brother', although if they are of different castes they will not, of course, intermarry. Very generally, friends and neighbours in the central residential cluster address each other in honorary kinship terms: *baji* (older sister) between women, or women and men of the same age; *khala ji* (mother's sister) to older women or mothers of friends, and *khalo ji* to their husbands, or *chacha ji* (father's younger brother) to father's close friends. Men are more often addressed by their names with the honorary suffix *ji*.

Friendships in the central cluster, especially between women, may be formed very rapidly. There are few overt pretensions of superiority, and people are outgoing and interested in their neighbours. Women meet in English classes, in factories, in the market, even in the street. They make friends with the mothers of their daughters' school friends, the friendship thus spanning two generations. They make friends with women living elsewhere in the central cluster who are friendly neighbours of their close kinswomen. As a result of this pattern of friendship the extended family – the *ghar* – becomes the focus of a shared social network. At weddings this is demonstrated dramatically, for the guests include friends of all members of the *ghar*, not merely of the parents of the bride and groom. Furthermore, it is whole *ghars* that are invited – a set of brothers, their children and even grandchildren. A family invited may thus comprise 20 or 30 people, including children.

[. . .]

Although friends are easily made and frequently seen, relations with them are not confused with those between kinsmen or between 'home' people. The 'folk model' of friendship preferences which migrants in the central cluster expressed is that people closest to them are either kinsmen or come from the same area of origin. My own plotting of their circle of friends and their participation in indexical occasions indicates that reliance on kinsmen is very high, with the most exclusive or demanding occasions reserved for them, or for close friends, usually known from Pakistan. Beyond the extended family and people actually known from Pakistan, however, the circle widens to include friends from various areas of Pakistan. Networks are not exclusive and tend to be very large; so much so that it was virtually impossible to construct a full network matrix of migrants' social networks.

Because of the great amount of time they spend socializing, women in the central cluster tend to dominate in the choice of family friends. They share a joint network with their spouses, but it is they who maintain the viability of many of the friendships. An associated feature of this is the fact that the conjugal role relations are often relatively unsegregated, while at the same time women control the domestic sphere. They are extremely influential in decision-making, and are consulted on all domestic matters. Men and boys help with the housework and shopping. They are often expected to manage on their own as women go on prolonged visits back home to Pakistan. In their behaviour women are vocal and assertive, vigorous and affectionate. They move within the city freely, without asking permission. They shop as they wish. Indeed, they often seem to rule their families. Networks may therefore be said to be 'women centred' without thereby denying the standing of men, who remain the legal guardians and deal with all 'external' matters to do with the authorities. Men are active in associational activities, take an interest in politics, and often attend Friday meetings at the mosque, jobs permitting. Otherwise their time is spent with their families, caught up in their wives' social affairs.

Working, saving, and the domestic economy

The influential position of women in the family and in wider social contexts is related to a number of other factors. The fact that they earn an income gives them a right to decide on its expenditure. It also gives them a measure of independence. Usually, the husband's income – the regular income – covers the mortgage, and expenditure on food and fuel. The woman's income is allocated to incidental and non-recurrent expenses such as house decoration, consumer goods, trips to Pakistan, weddings, gifts, and so on. Women control the Pakistani ceremonial exchange system and much of a woman's earnings are devoted to it. In particular, women accumulate vast quantities of cloth which is either given away on trips to Pakistan or at weddings in Manchester. If a woman has daughters she must also collect material for their dowries.

Residents in the central cluster are on the whole not particularly wealthy, and some of the least prosperous Pakistanis live in the neighbourhood. This is also an area where migrants from artisan and other low caste backgrounds may be found in substantial numbers. However, their poor background does not directly affect their income in Manchester for most men have jobs, either unskilled or semi-skilled, and earn somewhat similar incomes. Only the recent rise in unemployment has affected this situation, as migrants who are unskilled or illiterate have difficulty in finding jobs if their factories close down. But most men are semi-skilled workers and there are even a few professionals. The neighbourhood also includes some quite prosperous businessmen, while an increasing number of men, especially of the younger generation, are turning away from wage employment to self-employment. Usually they start off as market traders, but there are also a number of manufacturers and other retailers among them. The garment trade – discussed elsewhere (Werbner, 1984) – provides both women and teenage boys with work. For young schoolboys it provides part-time work on weekends and holidays, for women it provides opportunities mainly for home machining [. . .]

Many of the women save in rotating credit associations, together with men with more lucrative incomes. This type of forced saving is found by most migrants to be the only effective way of accumulating substantial sums of money, since families tend to be under constant pressure to spend. There are so many attractive things to buy, weddings to attend, trips to make, and gifts to give that people are always short of cash. By joining rotating credit associations they force themselves, they say, to cut their standard of living. The associations, or *kommitti* as they are known, are often run by focal people in the neighbourhood. [. . .] Women are primarily 'target workers', saving for specific projects: a wedding, a trip to Pakistan, a tractor to be sent back home, a dowry, as well as current gifting and hospitality. In other words, a woman supports those events which bring joy and 'happiness' to the family and are essential for participation in life cycle and religious events focused on the home. These events encourage the formation of close-knit networks within the neighbourhood.

The focal role of domestic rituals

One reason why the position of women in the central cluster is so powerful relates to the consequences of residence in close proximity to other Pakistani families. This, and the large amounts of spare time they have, enables women in the neighbourhood to develop close-knit networks. These are less costly in time to maintain, and are also more persistent than loose-knit networks. Friends are able to keep up with each other indirectly, through mutual friends, even if they do not manage to see each other for some time.

Religious feeling in Manchester is expressed not so much through the maintenance of strict purdah, but through an emphasis on prayer and through the convening of domestic religious gatherings such as communal Koran readings. In the central cluster *Khatam Koran* rituals, as they are known, are usually held by women, as are many of the weddings rites. Women are involved in matters of birth, marriage and death to a far greater extent than their husbands. They also organize birthday parties for younger children. It is usual to invite friendly neighbours to all these events. Some *Khatme Korans*, for example, are conceived to be mainly neighbourhood affairs and outsiders are not called in. In other *Khatme Korans* the opposite occurs: close friends living outside the neighbourhood are invited – in addition to kinsmen – and neighbours are excluded. This is because the size of the congregation would be too unmanageable and the food costs too high if neighbours were invited as well. Neighbours are perceived as a single category, so that to invite one neighbour would mean having to invite all of them. To weddings, however, neighbours are invariably invited, and they also take an active part in the *mhendi* rite before the wedding itself. At funeral wakes and at the *Khatam* rituals following them neighbours play a major role, as they do in all cases of serious illness, helping especially with children.

Ceremonial exchanges in the neighbourhood, while frequent, are not as costly as they are among the more affluent migrants who live outside it. People in the central cluster monitor their resources very carefully, and the meals given at *Khatam* rituals and weddings are scaled to their income. Usually only two wedding ceremonies are held: *mhendi* (which includes the *thel*) and the reception (which includes the *nikah*). People attending the *mhendi* do not receive a full meal, which is given only at the reception. Most people hold the reception in a hired hall, but some hold it in their homes. In this case people come and go during an extended period of the day, as houses are too small to accommodate everyone at the same time. However, in relation to their incomes, which are much lower than those of the Pakistani elite, such expenditures as residents of the central cluster make can be regarded as equally 'excessive', in neighbourhood terms. [. . .]

While ceremonial gifting is not usually as costly as it is for more wealthy Pakistanis, its value is augmented for the exchange partners by a constant stream of minor acts of reciprocity between neighbours, and by a great deal of mutual aid. Such mutual aid involves giving lifts if one has a car, taking messages if one has a telephone, caring for neighbours' children, putting up neighbours' wedding guests from other towns, taking gifts to Pakistan for neighbours, watching over their houses while they are away, and so on. In these circumstances, ceremonial exchanges can be regarded as indicators of a far more complex exchange relationship, and their value cannot be assessed independently of these other exchanges.

[. . .]

Although close neighbours often become friends and are then invited to attend ritual and ceremonial events (as well as engaging in mutual aid) neighbourliness does not of itself determine the choice of friends and hence also of guests at events such as *Khatam Koran* rituals. The congregations at *Khatam Koran* gathering are not entirely drawn on a territorial basis, as *slametans* are in Java (where, according to Jay, dyadic friendship as we, or indeed as Pakistanis, conceive of it is not a recognized type of relationship – see Jay, 1969: 201–6). Only some neighbours from among those living nearby become friends, and of course, many friends are not neighbours at all. Some family friends are past neighbours who have moved away, others are former acquaintances from work or from Pakistan. The residential turnover in the central clusters is quite high (see Werbner, 1979), and people do not simply discard friends because they have moved away, although they see them less frequently. Moreover, kinsmen seldom live on the same streets, although they often live nearby; nevertheless they are regularly invited to ritual and ceremonial events.

[. . .]

Male and female, public and domestic

A radical opposition between the cultural images of male and female, and the prescribed roles of men and women, may be true only of a specific phase in the domestic life cycle (La Fontaine, 1981). Quite often, as La Fontaine argues, it is married women with young children who epitomize the female image. This image is contrasted with the male image achieved by mature men who gain prominence in the world of public affairs.

For Pakistanis, the complementarity of the two worlds, the world of women and the world of men, seen in terms of a strictly defined division of labour between the sexes, has been modified for many by the migration process. It is, nevertheless, still anchored in key phases of the domestic life cycle. It is also crucially related to certain phases of migration.

Thus, recently arrived pubescent brides or women with young children are most likely to be secluded, sometimes isolated, in their homes. This isolation is particularly extreme if they live outside the central enclave (Werbner, 1979). Husbands are most likely to favour the seclusion of their wives if they are factory workers who work alongside other Pakistani men. This 'bundle' of features fits the Mirpuri women studied by Saifullah Khan.

Extreme female seclusion is, however, in most instances only a phase. Several women with extensive networks told me that when they first arrived in Manchester 'there were no women here'. As women settle down and their children reach school age this isolating tendency is, in most cases, gradually displaced by increasing sociability. Men's control over their wives' movements and circle of acquaintances decreases correspondingly, with significant social implications. As the residential enclave moves outwards, peripherally resident women are joined by Pakistani neighbours. Religious feeling in this context takes a new form. Veiling and physical seclusion become matters of respect and sacred activity, reserved for honoured guests, strangers, prayer and religious observance. The expression of religious feeling through religious gatherings increases as women become more 'rooted' locally.

Purdah has undergone an even more radical change for second-generation migrants. Although young Mancunian Pakistani girls are often chaperoned and watched, they enjoy a kind of freedom unusual in the Pakistan their mothers left. If their brothers are market traders, they often accompany them on trips to distant markets, and assist in selling on the stalls. Many have driving licences. Within the residential enclave they move around freely, visiting school friends. The abandonment of the *burqa* has transformed chaperoned trips with brothers into enjoyable outings. For young married Mancunian women the inevitable long hours of housework and babycare are relieved by visits and telephone calls to sisters or school friends. A girl's mother usually lives nearby and is a constant source of comfort and support.

As their children reach school age, the time women have for work and sociability increases quite suddenly and dramatically. They then move into a phase of network building and consolidation. Their impact and influence on the family's affairs and reputation increase accordingly. As mediators, they not only support or confirm their husbands' status. They also share with their husbands the task of negotiating affairs back home, in Pakistan. Whereas in Islamic societies women rarely have the exclusive mediatory role assigned to women in exogamous patrilineal groups (Strathern, 1972),

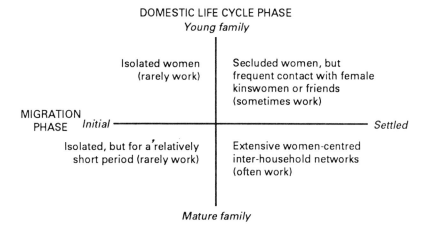

Figure 1   *Variations in purdah*

labour migration has here created a new mediatory role for women. On trips to Pakistan they arrange marriages, property investments, and other affairs on behalf of their family in Britain. They alternate with their husbands in mediating with kinsmen in Pakistan.

Migrant women's 'careers' in purdah may be summed up in Figure 1.

Conclusion

The image of a shy, modest, retiring young woman is still idealized amongst Pakistanis. It is part of a cultural lore of gender-related 'natural' stereotypes (La Fontaine, 1981): the seductive or promiscuous woman, the domineering mother-in-law, the ever-giving mother, or the woman of fortitude. In contrast is a repertoire of male images: the man of honour, the protector of his family and its reputation, the man of violence, of enterprise, or of social responsibility.

As I have shown, the actual roles fulfilled by a woman, and her domestic influence, vary over her lifetime, and the domestic household division of labour is pragmatically negotiated (see Yanagisako, 1979). Stereotypes, enduring values and actual roles remain in some tension (Strathern, 1972). But on formal and sacred occasions the strict separation between the worlds of men and women is upheld. Thus the image of a dual, segregated world persists, anchored in enduring cultural notions regarding the 'natural' attributes and proper roles of men and women.

Notes

1. I conducted fieldwork amongst Pakistanis in Manchester between 1975 and 1978. I am grateful to the ESRC (then SSRC) UK for its generous support.

2. The *burqa* is not commonly worn in Britain, but local Pakistani women continue to cover their heads with chiffon scarves (*dupatta*) in the presence of – Pakistani – male strangers.
3. Purdah is most marked amongst the lower middle class in urban Pakistan. Work for women of this class background outside the home is predominantly menial and degrading (Papanek, 1973).
4. This contrasts with client-based female networks in urban Morocco (Maher, 1976). In Manchester, most households are economically independent, if not wealthy.

References

Anwar, M. (1979) *The Myth of Return: Pakistanis in Britain*. London: Heinemann.

Bujra, J. (1974) 'Introductory: female/solidarity and the sexual division of labour', in P. Caplan and J.M. Bujra (eds) *Women United, Women Divided*. London: Tavistock Publications.

Eglar, Z. (1960) *A Punjabi Village in Pakistan*. New York: Columbia University Press.

Granovetter, M.S. (1973) 'The strength of weak ties', *American Journal of Sociology*, 78 (6): 1360–80.

Jay, R.R. (1969) *Javanese Villagers: Social Relations in Rural Modjukoto*. Cambridge, MA: MIT Press.

Jeffrey, P. (1979) *Frogs in a Well: Indian Women in Purdah*. London: Zed Books.

La Fontaine, J.S. (1981) 'The domestication of the savage male', *Man*, n.s. 16: 333–49.

Maher, V. (1976) 'Kin, clients and accomplices: relationships among women in Morocco', in D.L. Barker and S. Allen (eds) *Sexual Divisions and Society: Process and Change*. London: Tavistock Publications.

Papanek, H. (1973) 'Purdah: separate worlds and symbolic shelter', *Comparative Studies in Society and History*, 15: 289–325.

Rosaldo, M. (1974) 'Women, culture and society: a theoretical overview', in M. Rosaldo and L. Lamphere (eds) *Women, Culture, and Society*. Stanford: Stanford University Press.

Saifullah Khan, V. (1975) 'Asian women in Britain: strategies of adjustment of Indian and Pakistani migrants', in A. de Souza (ed.) *Women in Contemporary India*. New Delhi: Manohar.

Saifullah Khan, V. (1976) 'Purdah in the British situation', in D.L. Barker and S. Allen (eds) *Dependence and Exploitation in Work and Marriage*. London: Longman.

Saifullah Khan, V. (1976) 'Mirpuris and social stress: Mirpuris in Bradford', in Saifullah Khan (ed.) *Minority Families in Britain: Support and Stress*. London: Macmillan.

Sharma, U. (1980) *Women, Work and Property in North-West India*. London: Tavistock Publications.

Strathern, M. (1972) *Women in Between*. London: Seminar Press.

Vatuk, S. (1972) *Kinship and Urbanization: White Collar Migrants in North India*. Berkeley: University of California Press.

Werbner, R.P. (1975) 'Land, movement and status among Kalanga in Botswana', in M. Fortes and S. Pattersons (eds) *Studies in African Social Anthropology*. London: Academic Press, pp. 95–120.

Werbner, P. (1979) 'Avoiding the ghetto: Pakistani migrants and settlement shifts in Manchester', *New Community*, 7: 376–89.

Werbner, P. (1981) 'Manchester Pakistanis: lifestyle, ritual, and the making of social distinctions', *New Community*, 9: 216–29. Reprinted in E. Butterworth and D. Weir (eds) (1984) *The New Sociology of Modern Britain*. London: Fontana.

Werbner, P. (1984) 'Business on trust: Pakistani entrepreneurship in the Manchester garment trade', in R. Ward and R. Jenkins (eds) *Ethnic Communities in Business: Strategies for Economic Survival*. Cambridge: Cambridge University Press.

Yanagisako, S. (1977) 'Women-centred kin networks in urban bilateral kinship', *American Ethnologist*, 4 (2): 207–26.

Yanagisako, S. (1979) 'Family and household: the analysis of domestic groupings', *Annual Review of Anthropology*, 8: 161–205.

19

Community, market, state – and associations? The prospective contribution of interest governance to social order

Wolfgang Streeck and Philippe C. Schmitter

Three models of social order – or four?

Ask a contemporary social scientist the question 'How is social order possible?' and she or he will likely answer – if at all – with a model. No one can possibly observe directly or comprehend totally how such an enormous multitude of independent actors with diverse motives can interact in so many different and changing ways, and yet somehow manage to produce (or better, reproduce) something approaching 'order'. Even to begin to grasp how something so incredibly complex works requires a feat of great intellectual pretension and radical analytical simplification. [. . .] These abstractions reduce the variety of actors to a few ideal types, assign to them a restricted menu of passions or interests, allow them to cooperate and conflict with each other according to certain patterns or rules, and postulate that all this interaction will result in something called an 'equilibrium' – a state in which the actual behaviour of persons and collectivities is both mutually adjusted and predictably variable. [. . .]

Given the magnitude of the intellectual task involved, it is not surprising that there are few such general models available. Three of them seem to have virtually dominated philosophical speculation and social science thought. They tend to be identified by the central institution which embodies (and enforces) their respective and distinctive guiding principles: the *community*, the *market*, and the *state* (or the *bureaucracy*) – although it might be more accurate to label them according to the principles themselves: *spontaneous solidarity*, *dispersed competition* and *hierarchical control*. Clearly, however dominant any one of these three may have been at a given moment and/or for a given set of actors, almost everyone would concede that modern societies/polities/economies can only be analysed in

Adapted from W. Streeck and P.C. Schmitter (eds) *Private Interest Government* (London: Sage, 1985), pp. 1–29.

terms of some mix of them. [. . .]

This chapter will not explore further the relationships, the linkages and the proper balance between community, market and state. While we agree that it is essentially in different mixes of institutions and in the interaction of different modes of coordination that the answer to the question of social order is to be found, we suggest that there exists, in advanced industrial/ capitalist societies, a distinctive fourth institutional basis of order which is more than a transient and expedient amalgam of the three others and, hence, capable of making a lasting and autonomous contribution to rendering the behaviour of social actors reciprocally adjustive and predictable. If we labelled this additional source of social order after its embodying institution, we would call it 'the association'[1] – in contrast to 'the community', 'the market' and 'the state'. If we were to identify it by its guiding principle of interaction and allocation, we would call it 'organizational concertation' – in contrast to 'spontaneous solidarity', 'dispersed competition' and 'hierarchical control'.

Why assign to associations such an elevated theoretical status equal to community, market and state? The background of our argument is the emergence in Western societies of systems of bargained interest accommodation and policy concertation in the 1960s and 1970s (Berger, 1981; Crouch and Pizzorno, 1978; Goldthorpe, 1985; Lehmbruch and Schmitter, 1982; Schmitter and Lehmbruch, 1979). [. . .] One purpose of this chapter is to explore this 'fourth' logic more systematically and to show in what sense it is different from the others. We believe that it is only through an explicit recognition of the specific contribution of associations and organized concertation to social order that we can arrive at a better understanding of today's 'bargained' economies and societies. We also believe that an improved understanding of the actual and potential role of associations may significantly increase the range of strategic alternatives for the solution of public policy problems. We are aware of the fact that, empirically, associations are of different importance in different countries, sectors and policy areas, but as the same applies no less to the three other ordering principles, we do not think that this, by itself, speaks against our argument.

[. . .] Usually the history of democratic/industrialized societies is presented as consisting of two main periods: the expansion of *markets* into pre-existing *communities* in the nineteenth century, and the expansion of the interventionist *state* into the new *market economy* in the twentieth century. Associations were in both periods regarded with suspicion: in the first one, they were seen as impediments to the development of a free market; in the second one, they were viewed as obstacles to the growth of the (democratic) state – a perception which was reinforced by the authoritarian corporatist experiences of some countries in the inter-war years. In spite of historical evidence to the contrary and occasional theoretical dissent, this tendency to discuss associations mainly in terms of their actual or potential dysfunctions for the three other, more established, bases of order has continued to dominate the scene.

In part, this may be explained by the fact that community, market and state all have their specialized professional advocates within the social sciences, while associations typically had to put up with individual dissidents from a variety of disciplines. [. . .] Economists – as far as we know, without exception – have treated associations as cartels, and associative action as a major cause of inefficient, suboptimal resource allocation. Finally, political scientists and public lawyers have, in their great majority, regarded associations as a threat to liberal democracy, parliamentary rule and state sovereignty, pointing to phenomena such as industrial action in defiance of legislation, 'colonization' of state regulatory agencies, or the undermining of parliamentary sovereignty by 'social pacts' negotiated between the government and strong interest groups.

Our point is not that these observations are entirely mistaken. What we are saying, however, is that they are one-sided. The fact that associative action may be dysfunctional for the three (other) institutional bases of social order – a fact which we by no means wish to contest – does not by itself rule out the possibility that it may also contribute to order. As we have seen, community, market and state have dysfunctions for each other as well. What is important is that at the same time they require one another for their respective functioning; and that there are specific problems of order that each of them is better equipped to resolve than the others. The same, we submit, can be said of associations.

[. . .]

An associative model of social order

The *idea* of a distinctive associative order is not new to modern social and political thought. Hegel, for example, had an elaborate, if not particularly accessible, conception of how *Korporationen* emerged from civil society as its highest organized expression and laid the basis (the second *sittliche Wurzel*, alongside the family) for 'the universal, substantial state'. [. . .] With *Rerum Novarum* (1891) and *Quadragesimo Anno* (1931), this became an integral part of Roman Catholic doctrine. On a more secular note, Saint-Simon was promoting the idea of *associationnisme*, as early as the 1830s, as an alternative to capitalism. Even more important, perhaps, was Durkheim with his concept of professional corporations as the main institutional basis of 'organic solidarity' in modern societies characterized by a highly developed division of labour. Indirectly, these models inspired contemporary institutions such as *Mitbestimmung*, *Autogestion* and so on, and have prepared an ideological basis, often via social democracy, for the growing importance of associations and organizational concertation.

Of course, the *fact* of a distinctive associative order has always been on historical display, so to speak, in the experience of the late medieval cities of Italy, France, Catalonia, the Rhineland and Northern Europe whose social and political system was based on a guild structure. Hence, when

Table 1 *The properties of an associative model of social order*

1. Guiding PRINCIPLE of coordination and allocation	Inter- and intra-organizational concertation
2. Predominant, modal, COLLECTIVE ACTOR	Functionally defined interest associations
Other ACTORS	Members (firms, consortia, individuals, social groupings), interlocutors (state agencies, parties, movements)
3. Enabling CONDITIONS for actor entry and inclusion	Capacity for mutual disruption Attainment of monopoly status, willingness and capacity to compromise, symmetry of organizational capacity
4. Principal MEDIUM OF EXCHANGE	Mutual recognition of status and entitlements, compliance of members
5. Principal PRODUCT OF EXCHANGE	Pacts
6. Predominant RESOURCE(S)	Guaranteed access, compulsory contribution and membership, institutionalized forums of representation, centralization, comprehensive scope, jurisdiction and control over member behaviou-, delegated tasks, inter-organizational trust
7. Principal MOTIVE(S) of superordinate actors	Expansion of organizational role, organizational development, career advancement
Principal MOTIVE(S) of subordinate actors	Lessened uncertainty, proportional shares
Common MOTIVE/CALCULUS	'Satisficing (mini-maxing) interests'
8. Principal DECISION RULE(S)	Parity representation, proportional adjustment, concurrent consent
9. Modal TYPE OF GOODS produced and distributed	Categoric goods
10. Principal LINES OF CLEAVAGE	Members vs. associational leaders vs. (state) interlocutors Included vs. excluded (social movements)
Other CLEAVAGES	Well organized vs. less well organized Established vs. rival associations Over- vs. under-represented Majority vs. minority segments National vs. regional vs. local interests (parties, maverick enterprises, community representatives, local notables)
11. Predominant NORMATIVE-LEGAL FOUNDATION	*Pacta sunt servanda*, freedom of association
12. Principal PAY-OFF(S)	Less class exploitation; more symmetric distribution of benefits; greater predictability and stability of socio-economic outcomes (social peace)

John Maynard Keynes reflected on the consequences of 'The end of laissez-faire' and searched for a new order 'somewhere between the individual and the modern state', he naturally looked backward to those experiences and proposed 'a return, it may be said, towards medieval conceptions of separate autonomies'. Let us follow Lord Keynes' suggestion and see what such a neo-medieval order might look like if it were to emerge in the contemporary world.

At its core is a distinctive principle of interaction and allocation among a privileged set of actors. The key actors are (Table 1) organizations defined by their common purpose of defending and promoting functionally defined interests, that is, class, sectoral and professional associations. The central principle is that of concertation, or negotiation within and among a limited and fixed set of interest organizations that recognize each other's status and entitlements and are capable of reaching and implementing relatively stable compromises (*pacts*) in the pursuit of their interests. A corporative-associative order is, therefore, based primarily on interaction within and between interdependent complex organizations. Secondary interactions involve the relations between these associations and their members (including non-members directly affected by the agreements reached) and their interlocutors – outside actors whose resources or support are necessary for the concerted compromise to take effect (often state agencies), and/or whose interests are indirectly affected by the externalities generated by such agreements (for example political parties and social movements).

It is when we turn to 'enabling conditions' that the distinctiveness of corporative–associative action becomes most manifest, especially in contrast to pluralist theories of pressure politics.

[. . .]

In a community order, actor preferences and choices are *interdependent* based on shared norms and jointly produced satisfaction. In a market order, the actions of competitors are supposed to be *independent* since no one singular action can have a determinant and predictable effect upon the eventual allocation of satisfactions. In a state order, the actors are *dependent* upon hierarchical coordination which makes their choices heteronomously determined and asymmetrically predictable according to the structure of legitimate authority and coercive capability. In a corporative–associative order, actors are *contingently* or *strategically interdependent* in the sense that actions of organized collectivities can have a predictable and determinant effect (positive or negative) on the satisfaction of other collectivities' interests, and this induces them to search for relatively stable pacts. To reach this stage, the contracting interest associations have to have attained some degree of symmetry in their respective resources, especially in their capability for representing the interests and controlling the behaviour of their members (and where necessary outside mavericks), and an effective monopoly in their status as intermediaries for a given class, sector of profession. As long as interest associations are fragmented into rival communities, organized into overlapping, competing markets for members and/or resources, completely dependent upon voluntary member support, or manipulated from above by state authority, the enabling conditions for corporative–associative order do not exist.

The medium or 'currency' of the associative model consists predominantly of mutual recognition of status and entitlements. Of course, concerted groups may bring to bear on a given issue customary solidarities, monetary resources, bloc votes and even threats of coercion should the negotiative process break down, but, fundamentally, they are making demands on each other – informing each other about the magnitude and intensity of their preferences and their likely courses of action if agreement is not reached – and offering in return for the satisfaction of these interests to deliver the compliance of their members. [. . .]

Many of those listed under this rubric in Table 1: guaranteed access, compulsory membership and/or contributions institutionalized forums of representation, centralized coordination, comprehensive scope, jurisdiction and control over member behaviour and delegated tasks of policy implementation; depend crucially on the response of one key interlocutor, namely the state, which must be willing *and able* to use its key resource: legitimate control over coercion and authoritative distribution of positions, to promote and/or protect such developments. The 'motivational structure' of corporative associability is, perhaps, not as distinctive as many of its other attributes, at least for superordinate actors. Like their *confrères* in state agencies, their motives should be largely determined by the imperatives of the formal organizational context within which they operate and from which they draw their resources. [. . .]

The motives of subordinate actors (that is members) are more difficult to discern since they are obviously being forced to give up what may often be opportunistically attractive possibilities for acting individually or through less formal groups, in exchange for accepting to be bound by compromised, longer-term and more general obligations negotiated for them by their respective class, sectoral or professional associations. This may be less of a problem for categories of interest where individual actors are very weak and dispersed (for example, farmers, workers, *petit bourgeois*) but could pose a serious challenge in those categories where 'going-it-alone' through market power or state influence is a promising alternative (for example, capitalists and some privileged professions). Presumably, what motivates a subordinate to conform to associationally negotiated pacts is lesser uncertainty about aggregate outcomes and higher assurance of receiving a proportionally more 'equitable' share of whatever is disputed. If one adds to these the probability that certain conditions of macro-societal performance (for example, in terms of inflation, unemployment and strike rates) will be superior in societies whose markets have been tamed by associative action, then we have an even greater reason for understanding member conformity. Basically what seems to happen is a shift in the rationality of social choice. In communities, the calculus rests on satisfying identity, in markets, economic or political, on maximizing advantage/building minimum winning coalitions, in states, on minimizing risk and maximizing predict-ability. What associations in a corporative order strive for is something more prosaic, but quite rational given the structural complexity and infor-mational overload of modern society, namely *satisficing interests*. By deliberate mutual adjustment and repeated interaction, these comprehen-sive, monopolistically privileged actors avoid the temptation to exploit momentary advantages to the maximum and the pitfall of landing in the worst possible situation. In short, they avoid the prisoner's dilemma through inter-organizational trust backed by what we shall call below 'private interest government'. The price for this is a lengthy deliberation process and a series of second-best compromised solutions which are often difficult to justify on aesthetic or normative grounds.

Communities decide by unanimous consent, markets by consumer or majority preference, states by authoritative adjudication and imperative certification. Corporative associations decide by highly complicated formulae which start with parity representation (regardless of members or functional clout), work through a process of sequential proportional adjustments based either on 'splitting the difference' or 'package dealing' arrangements, and then ratify the final pact by concurrent consent. All this takes time and is vulnerable to substantive and normative assaults coming from communitarian, market and state sources. Usually, deliberations are kept informal and secretive in an effort to insulate them as much as possible from outside pressures or from dissidents within the associational ranks.

[. . .]

The final structural element we need to discuss in this exploratory description of an ideal–typical associative order is its lines of cleavage. Here, the principal configuration is tripolar rather than bipolar as in the three other orders. Associational leaders find themselves, Janus-like, in conflict with their members on one side and their (state) interlocutors on the other. While the behaviour and the interests of the members are strongly conditioned by competitive market forces, state officials are primarily concerned with upholding and advancing the hierarchical coordinative capacities and the bureaucratic jurisdiction of the state. This does not necessarily leave those in the middle with much room for manoeuvre. Either economic market forces may prove too strong to be contained by associa-tional compromise; or electoral competition may bring to power parties representing 'true' citizen interests which will dismantle associational rule; or state officials, wary of excessive devolution of 'their' authority to associations they cannot fully control, will simply outlaw them (not to mention the fact that, in some countries, courts may declare associational pacts illegal under the constitution or antitrust laws). It may only be a ques-tion of which of these gets sufficiently aroused first: opportunistic capitalists, radically mobilized workers, outraged voters, offended civil servants (or strict constructionist judges). In addition, the corporative–associative order also has a number of secondary cleavages to cope with, not the least of which is that between those interests which are organized into it and those, less organized or less functionally specifiable, which are excluded from it.

Public policy and the associative model of social order. The concept of 'private interest government'

There is a large and growing body of research on the contribution of associational structures to social order, often but by no means exclusively guided by theories of neo-corporatism (Schmitter, 1974, 1977).[2] The lively interest which this concept has stimulated among social scientists may in itself be an indication that the associative mode of social order has gained, or is gaining, in importance. Moreover, it seems that many of the present political controversies in Western industrialized countries can be described, and better understood, in terms of a search for a new balance, not just between community, market and state, but also between these three and a growing realm of associative action.

In the past four decades the politics of many Western countries seems to have been bound up in a continuous oscillation between state interventionism on the one hand and market liberalism on the other. Today, after the 'long wave' of increasing state interventionism in the late 1960s and early 1970s, the limits and dysfunctions of public bureaucratic regulation have again become a major issue for both the political right and the political left. Catchwords such as 'deregulation', 'de-bureaucratization', '*Entstaat-lichung*', '*Staatsentlastung*', and so on have come to figure prominently in political discourse. Most of the current proposals for retrenchment of the role of the state centre on a return to either the *market* or the *community* as sources of social order. While it is the reinstatement of the market which is at the core of the demands of the powerful neo-liberal movement, off-loading the welfare state to voluntary community action is by no means incompatible with neo-liberal values. Greater reliance on 'community' is also advocated by a wide range of other groups – from adherents to the Catholic doctrine of 'subsidiarity', to various 'autonomous' and 'alter-native' social movements which otherwise have little in common with neo-liberalism and which in particular would not want to ally themselves with its call for 'more market'.

However, for all its powerful influence on the public mind, the widely accepted antimony of *state vs. market/community* appears to be insuffi-ciently complex for both analytical and practical purposes. For one thing, the swing of the pendulum of public policy seems to be different in different countries, with some countries being much less torn between the two extremes than others. As it happens, these countries tend to be those that have relatively strong institutions, often described as 'neo-corporatist', of associational and inter-associational conflict – for example Austria, Norway, Sweden, Switzerland, West Germany. Institutions of this kind, in addition to mediating between the state and the market, seem to limit the extent to which the two can invade each other and enlarge their domain at each other's expense. In this way, they seem to inject an element of stability in their respective polities which makes them less subject to changing political fashions. Also, an elaborate intermediary associational structure seems to enlarge a country's repertoire of policy alternatives – its 'requisite variety' – and this may enable such countries to respond to new problems without having to undergo dramatic internal realignments.

From the viewpoint of public policy, neo-corporatism amounts to an attempt to assign to interest associations a distinct role between the state and 'civil society' (market and community) so as to put to public purposes the type of social order that associations can generate and embody. As an alternative to direct state intervention and regulation, the public use of private organized interests takes the form of the establishment, under state licence and assistance, of 'private interest governments' with devolved public responsibilities – of agencies of 'regulated self-regulation' of social groups with special interests which are made subservient to general interests by appropriately designed institutions. The specificity of this strategy lies, above all, in the kind of interest on which it is based, and in the way in which they are treated. This becomes clearer when one compares it to the two alternative strategies of *Staatsentlastung*. The neo-liberal restoration of the *market* aims essentially at the liberation of *individual self-interests* from bureaucratic-regulatory constraints. It is based on the assumption that individuals act most rationally if they are free to pursue their interests as they see fit, and that in the end, this will benefit everybody. Devolving state functions to the *community* amounts to an attempt to marshal *collective other-regarding interests* for social purposes; its underlying premises are that people hold solidaristic values and communitarian identities that, just as their self-interests, can contribute to social order directly and without state coordination. Both premises may or may not be correct. What they have in common is that they draw on widely accepted assumptions about the motivation and behaviour of *individuals*. By contrast, the corporative–associative delegation of public policy functions to private interest governments represents an attempt to utilize the *collective self-interest* of social *groups* to create and maintain a generally acceptable social order, and it is based on assumptions about the behaviour of *organizations* as transforming agents of individual interests. This makes the idea of responsible associative governance inevitably more abstract and remote from everyday experience than both the neo-liberal appeal to individual self-interest and the neo-communitarian appeal to group altruism, and here – in the intellectual complexity and, indeed, counter-intuitiveness of the idea that organized special interests could be turned into promoters of the public interest – seems to lie one explanation for the lack of public attention which it has so far received.

'Private government' is a concept which has had some currency in the social sciences, and a short definitional excursus may be appropriate. [. . .] In this chapter, we speak of 'private *interest* government' to emphasize that we are exclusively concerned with the self-'government' of *categories of social actors* defined by a *collective self-regarding interest*. Secondly, the concept of 'private government' is often associated with the notion of an illegitimate use of power (Lowi, 1979), for example when Bauer and Cohen (1983) define 'private governments' by their capacity to pre-empt and frustrate public (industrial) policy. For our part, we prefer to reserve the concept for arrangements under which an attempt is made to make associative, self-interested collective action contribute to the achievement of public policy objectives. In generic terms, this is the case where it is in the interest of an organized group to strive for a 'categoric good' which is partially compatible or identical with a 'collective good' for the society as a whole. We maintain that such compatibility or identity may be more frequent than is commonly believed.[3] We also maintain that the extent to which categoric and collective goods overlap depends, within limits, on two factors: on the way in which group interests are organized into associative structures and processes, and on a complex bargaining process between organized group interests and the state – that is, between the governments of private and public interests.

[. . .]

The functional advantages of private interest government

'Regulated self-regulation' by organized interests seems to be capable of solving a number of problems that have been found to be associated with either state intervention, market competition or voluntary community action. As far as the *state* is concerned, two specific deficiencies stand out as of particular importance. One is the *limits of legal regulation*, especially in terms of the *implementation* of regulatory programmes (Luhmann, 1981; Teubner, 1983; Voigt, 1983; Willke, 1983). Private interest government provides for a peculiar amalgamation of policy formation on the one hand and policy implementation on the other, within one and the same organizational structure (Lehmbruch, 1977). The same associations that negotiate the terms of regulation of their members' behaviour, are charged as private governments with responsibility to enforce them. As a result, not only do considerations of enforceability enter directly into the process of policy formation (on the importance of this, see Mayntz, 1983), but the agents of implementation – the professional staff and the officials of the association – are closer to the target group (their members) than state bureaucracies, and they have more intimate knowledge of its situation and concerns. It is likely that this enables them to apply rules less formalistically and to take the specific conditions of individual cases better into account – which, in turn, tends to increase the acceptance of regulation by those affected by it (Streeck, 1983).

Another problem with state hierarchic coordination is that it has always been associated with specific difficulties of *legitimation* (Offe, 1975). These are basically of two kinds: one involves winning the support and the cooperation of groups that are asked to sacrifice some of their interests in favour of general interests; the other involves presenting a consistent image of the societal role and the jurisdiction of legitimate state intervention as such – in other words, a normative definition of the boundaries of the modern state. Private interest government, by providing for a close institutionalized interface between public authorities and specific groups in civil society, can make a significant contribution to the solution of both kinds of problem. By turning behavioural regulation into a matter of the organized self-interest of affected groups, it leaves the legitimation of regulatory interference to group representatives who, instead of having to call upon general, society-wide values and obligations, can have recourse to more tangible group-specific norms and interest perceptions. The most well-known, but by no means the only, example is that of the leaders of a trade union and a business association who defend an industrial agreement as viable and equitable to their respective constituents, with each side using very different arguments and appealing to very different common values. This differentiation of legitimation by conflicting social interests relieves the public government of the need to develop a generally acceptable political formula to defend allocational decisions. It amounts to the utilization, for the purpose of creating public order, of divergent interest perceptions whose ideological integration is difficult or impossible.

Secondly, the notion of collective responsibility of interest organizations for controlling their members in the public interest can serve as a general principle demarcating the limits of direct state responsibility. Here, one comes close to traditional ideas of the state being only subsidiary to society – in the sense that it should content itself with assisting smaller collectivities to help themselves, and intervene directly only if such self-help has turned out to be impossible. [. . .]

Concerning *markets*, their obvious and often analysed problem is that the unregulated interaction of self-interested parties may fail to produce certain collective or categoric goods which are a necessary precondition for an effective functioning of the market ('market failure'). In such cases, the rational behaviour of market participants needs to be subjected to some form of authoritative control – exercised either by the state or by some other agent – to prevent it from becoming self-destructive. Furthermore, free competition may result in social cleavages and inequalities which in turn give rise to 'pluralist' collective action aimed at 'distorting' the market. 'Factionalism' of this kind is not easy to suppress in a democratic society; a state which would try to do so would have to be so autonomous that it would in effect cease to be democratic.[4] In this sense, economic liberalism and political democracy are indeed ultimately incompatible, as has been argued by observers from both the right (von Hayek, 1976–8) and the left (Goldthorpe, 1985). The neo-corporatist transformation of pluralist interest groups into publicly responsible self-regulating bodies can be seen, from this perspective, as an attempt not only to provide for the production of categoric/collective goods by other, and more effective, means than state regulation; it is also an attempt to impose discipline on the inevitable factions which arise in a democratic polity combined with a market economy, and, thereby, to make organized interest politics more compatible with the requirements of the market.

Finally, the Achilles heel of *community* action is that it lacks authoritative means to mobilize resources above and beyond what can be obtained on a voluntary basis. This is a problem which is particularly relevant the less normatively integrated communities are, and there is reason to believe that with increasing mobility of individuals and cultural identities, the sense of altruistic obligation – of 'other-regardingness' – has tended to become weaker in most social groups. In fact, this is precisely the rationale behind the modern transfer of traditional community welfare functions to a growing 'welfare state'. Moreover, communities can be parochial in that their values and accepted mutual obligations may be at odds with the values and requirements of society at large. The backing by public authority of strong intermediary organizations representing specific social groups may offer a way of increasing the latter's self-regulating capacity beyond the limits of voluntarism, and of guiding their collective behaviour in accordance with general rather than exclusively group-specific values and interests.

Interest associations which have been transformed into private interest governments compensate for a number of specific state, market and community failures. By relieving the three other orders of problems they are less well equipped to solve, they not only do not pre-empt them but in fact contribute to their respective functioning. A state that withdraws, in selected areas, from direct to procedural control does not become a weak state; in terms of the effectiveness of its policies, it may in fact gain in strength. Similarly, in order to be efficient mechanisms of allocation markets need to be protected from distortion by pluralist interest politics, and they require regulatory constraints on competitive behaviour as a precondition of stable, long-term exchange and competition (for example, in areas such as technical standardization or vocational training). Finally, communities in a society with a strong state and a free market can better preserve their cultural identities and bring them to bear on the political process if they are effectively organized so as to command more and other resources than those that modern communities can generate on their own.

Private interest government as a 'mixed mode' of policy-making

It is important to emphasize that the state is not absent in the associational mode of social order; nor is the market or the community. Corporative–associative order emerges in thoroughly 'mixed' polities. Typically, institutions of private interest governance are geared to selected sectors, industries and policy areas – with other collectivities and issues being directly governed by the state, left to the forces of the market, or taken care of by community action. Moreover, community, market and state constitute important limiting and facilitating conditions for and inside any given associative arrangement, and without them such arrangements could not exist and function. [. . .]

Conclusion

Private interest government is not about to replace community, market and state. Even where a large share of public policy is made by and implemented through intermediary associations, these are always to some important extent dependent on community values and cohesion, kept in check by economic and political market forces, and subject to hierarchical control, political design and the pressure of possible direct state intervention. Moreover, not all social groups and political issues lend themselves equally well to associational self-regulation, and there undoubtedly are social order problems in modern societies for which the three competing institutions offer more appropriate solutions. The idea of a comprehensive corporative–associative social or political 'system' is therefore fundamentally misleading. At the same time, there is growing evidence that there is a certain range of policy areas for which institutions of group self-regulation may produce more socially adjusted and normatively acceptable results than either communal self-help, free trade, or *étatisme*. Empirical research and theoretical reflection on the preconditions of successful utilization, in a 'mixed polity', of corporative associability for public policy purposes has only begun. Increased efforts in this direction may make it possible to employ more consciously an additional mode of ordering social relationships that compensates for important dysfunctions of community, market and state, and may thus significantly enrich the policy repertory of modern societies.

Notes

1. Actually, it would be more accurate to call it 'the corporative association' since it differs significantly from 'the voluntary association' which preceded it in social and political theory. If the concept 'corporation' had not already been appropriated for use to describe a particular type of market institution, we would have preferred to use that term. We were tempted to invent a new noun, 'the corporative', to replace 'the association', but declined to do so on the grounds that there were already too many neologisms in this kind of field and that it would, in any case, probably be confused with 'the corporation' or 'the cooperative'.
2. Part of the relevant literature has been reviewed by Olsen (1981), under the label of 'integrated organizational participation in government'. Related concepts – of which each stands for another unending list of publications – are 'para-state government', 'public-private interface', 'quangoes', and so on. It is impossible to cite all or most of the studies that have in one way or another influenced the ideas presented in this chapter.

3. That it is *possible* is admitted even by such a formidable critic of 'distributional coalitions' as Mancur Olson: 'Occasionally there are [. . .] situations in which the constituents of special-interest organizations seek to increase social efficiency because they would get a lion's share of the gain in output; this occurs when the special-interest organization provides a collective good to its members that increases their production efficiency and also when it gets the government to provide some public good that generates more income than costs, yet mainly benefits those in the special-interest group' (Olson 1982: 46).

4. This seems to be the central 'policy' problem in Mancur Olson's book, *The Rise and Decline of Nations* (1982). While Olson demonstrates convincingly the allocational superiority of free competition, his sophisticated knowledge of interest politics prevents him from siding with economists like Milton Friedman in their call for a laissez-faire liberal state. Olson is well aware of the fact that a free market in order to remain free, requires continuous, vigorous state intervention. He even goes as far as to say that, 'the absence of government intervention (even if it were invariably desirable) may not be possible anyway, because of the lobbying of special-interest groups, unless we fly to the still greater evil of continuous instability' (1982: 178). But Olson still stops short of explaining what kind of interventionist policy he recommends to governments in relation to group interests, and how a state would have to look in order to provide politically for 'freer trade and fewer impediments to the free movement of factors of production and of firms' (p. 141). Olson does not, at least not explicitly, argue in favour of state support and facilitation of 'comprehensive organization' which for him is no more than a second-best solution. Nor does he advocate the abolishment through government repression of the democratic freedom of association. But he does quote Thomas Jefferson's remark that 'the tree of liberty must be refreshed from time to time with the blood of patriots and tyrants' (p. 141) – the latter clearly being, in the context of Olson's argument, the 'private tyrants' that govern a society's 'distributional coalitions'.

References

Bauer, M. and Cohen E. (1983) *Qui governe les Groupes Industriels?* Paris: Seuil.

Berger, S. (ed.) (1981) *Organizing Interests in Western Europe: Pluralism, Corporatism and the Transformation of Politics*. Cambridge: Cambridge University Press.

Crouch, C. and Pizzorno, A. (eds) (1978) *The Resurgence of Class Conflict in Western Europe since 1968*, 2 vols. London: Macmillan.

Goldthorpe, J.H. (1985) 'The end of convergence: corporatist and dualist tendencies in modern Western societies', in J.H. Goldthorpe (ed.), *Order and Conflict in Contemporary Capitalism*. Oxford: Clarendon Press.

Lehmbruch, G. (1977) 'Liberal corporatism and party government', *Comparative Political Studies*, 10: 91–126. Also in Schmitter and Lehmbruch (eds) (1979).

Lehmbruch, G. and Schmitter, P.C. (eds) (1982) *Patterns of Corporatist Policy-Making*. Beverly Hills and London: Sage Publications.

Lowi, T. (1979) *The End of Liberalism*. New York: W.W. Norton (first publication 1969).

Luhmann, N. (1981) *Politische Theorie im Wohlfahrtsstaat*. Munich: Piper.

Mayntz, R. (1983) 'The conditions of effective public policy: a new challenge for policy analysis', *Policy and Politics*, 11: 123–43.

Offe, C. (1975) 'Überlegungen und Hypothesen zum Problem politischer Legitimation', Beitrag zum Duisburger Kongreß der DVPW (1975). Mimeo.

Olsen, J.P. (1981) 'Integrated organizational participation in government', pp. 492–516 in P.C. Nystrom and W.H. Starbuck (eds), *Handbook of Organizational Design*, vol. 2. Oxford: Oxford University Press.

Olson, M. (1982) *The Rise and Decline of Nations. Economic Growth, Stagflation and Social Rigidities*. New Haven and London: Yale University Press.

Schmitter, P.C. (1974) 'Still the century of corporatism?', *The Review of Politics*, 36: 85–131. Also in Schmitter and Lehmbruch (eds) (1979).

Schmitter, P.C. (1977) 'Modes of interest intermediation and models of societal change in Western Europe', *Comparative Political Studies*, 10: 7–38. Also in Schmitter and Lehmbruch (eds) (1979).

Schmitter, P.C. and Lehmbruch, G. (eds) (1979) *Trends Towards Corporatist Intermediation.* Beverly Hills and London: Sage Publications.

Streeck, W. (1983) 'Zwischen Markt und Staat. Interessenverbaende als Träger öffentlicher Politik', pp. 179–97 in F.W. Scharpf and M. Brockmann (eds), *Institutionelle Bedingungen der Arbeitsmarkt-und Beschäftigungspolitik.* Frankfurt am Main: Campus.

Teubner, G. (1983) 'Substantive and reflective elements in modern law', *Law and Society Review*, 17: 239–85.

Voigt, R. (ed.) (1983) *Gegentendenzen zur Verrechtlichung.* Opladen: Westdeutscher Verlag.

Von Hayek, F.A. (1976–8) *Law, Legislation and Liberty. A New Statement of the Liberal Principles of Justice and Political Economy*, 3 vols. London: Routledge & Kegan Paul.

Willke, H. (1983) *Entzauberung des Staates: Ueberlegungen zu einer sozietalen Steuerungstheorie.* Koenigstein: Athenaeum.

Comparison between models

Introduction

Grahame Thompson

In a number of the chapters in the previous three sections comparison of the models of coordination have been initiated and even developed at length in some cases. In this section we concentrate explicitly upon this issue. The five chapters included here draw on the analysis and comparative aspects of the previous chapters. In their various ways they attempt an explicit comparison of the differences between the three models considered in this book and their operational strengths and weaknesses. Furthermore, these chapters serve to raise a number of additional issues associated with the models that were either neglected or not pursued in the previous sections.

The first four chapters all engage with the idea of transactions costs. Ouchi, in Chapter 20, develops a comparison between the market and hierarchy in which he splits the idea of hierarchy into two types; 'bureaucracies' and 'clans'. Bureaucracies in his terms do not completely eliminate transactions costs; the acts of necessary supervision associated with the 'non-congruence of goals' in the company implies a continuation of transactions costs. With clans on the other hand, where the goals of the organization are agreed and contracts non-specific and long term, transactions costs can be more easily eliminated. It is 'norms' that provide the motivational guide for the operation of clan-type relations.

If we were to introduce networks into Ouchi's framework (which he does not do explicitly), we might end up with something like Figure 1. There are two possible approaches to relationships – competitive and cooperative – which are arrayed along the horizontal axis. There are two unit organizational forms – hierarchical and independent – which are arrayed along the vertical axis. Into the matrix so constructed we can place Ouchi's bureaucracy and clan as hierarchical-competitive systems and hierarchical-cooperative ones respectively. In addition, the classic market form is defined as an independent-competitive combination, while the network structure occupies the independent-cooperative position.

It is with networks that the next chapter is concerned. Johanson and

APPROACH TO RELATIONSHIPS

		Competitive	Cooperative
	Independent	Classic market	Network structure
UNIT ORGANIZATIONAL FORM			
	Hierarchical	Bureaucracy	Clan

Figure 1

Mattsson compare a networks approach with a transaction costs approach, focusing upon industrial networks in particular. The two authors define their idea of network as encompassing certain types of market relations but it also involves the usual network-type relationships that are *in addition to* a traditional price mechanism type market model. Johanson and Mattsson stress the cumulative process of establishing network position by various means, exchanges and adaptations, not just by price competition.

The critique offered of the Williamson-type transaction approach in this chapter is that, in contrast to the network approach, it relies upon the intellectual paraphernalia of neo-classical economics with its emphasis on frequent selfishly motivated and opportunistically driven calculations focusing only on the conditions for a stable equilibrium. But, it is argued, this ignores the 'investments' and 'assets' locked up in a wider set of long-term relationships between firms, located within the system of inter-dependence in which they exist.

A more thoroughgoing comparison between all the models is contained in Powell's defence of the network model as against market and hierarchy in Chapter 22. This serves the function of giving a clear and concise exposition of the intellectual and operational comparative features of the three models, assessing their similarities and differences. In this the comparative table on p. 269 should prove particularly useful.

Bradach and Eccles, in Chapter 23, point to the way the models are not so much mutually exclusive but rather interdependent forms of exchange. Concentrating upon the categories of price, authority and trust, they argue that there is a wide range of organizational forms combining these relation-ships and hence producing hybrid coordinative mechanisms which cannot be simply reduced to the pure market, hierarchy or network forms. They stress the *plurality* of actual organizational forms where elements of the three models coexist and reinforce one another at times.

Finally we round off the book with a rather different comparative chapter. The basic issue posed by von Hayek in Chapter 24 is whether social coordination is achieved 'spontaneously', so to speak, or whether it requires conscious 'planning'. A spontaneous social order – exemplified for von Hayek in the way the market functions – arises out of the unplanned but purposeful activity of humans, coordinating their diverse and often conflicting plans without any single body having to organize this. On the other hand a 'designed order', in von Hayek's terms, imposes a conscious, planned attempt to produce social cohesion and agreed coordination. For him this latter is a much less efficient and freedom-respecting arrangement.

20

Markets, bureaucracies and clans

William G. Ouchi

The nature of organizations

What is an organization, and why do organizations exist? Many of us would answer this question by referring to Barnard's (1968) technological imperative, which argues that a formal organization will arise when technological conditions demand physical power, speed, endurance, mechanical adaptation, or continuity beyond the capacity of a single individual (1968: 27–8). Yet when the stone is too large or the production facility too complex for a single person, what is called for is cooperation, and cooperation need not take the form of a formal organization. Indeed, grain farmers who need a large grain elevator do not form corporations which take over the farms and make the farmers into employees; instead, they form a cooperative to own and operate the elevator.

Others would refer to March and Simon's (1958) argument that an organization will exist so long as it can offer its members inducements which exceed the contributions it asks of them. While this position explains the conditions under which an organization may continue to exist, it does not explain how an organization can create a whole which is so much greater than the sum of its parts that it can give them more than they contribute.

Most of us, however, would refer to Blau and Scott's (1962) definition of a formal organization as a purposive aggregation of individuals who exert concentrated effort toward a common and explicitly recognized goal. Yet we can hardly accept this definition whole, suspecting as Simon (1945: 257–78) has that individuals within organizations rarely have a common understanding of goals.

Another point of view on the question of why organizations exist began with an enquiry by Coase (1937) and has recently been developed by Williamson (1975). In this view, an organization such as a corporation exists because it can mediate economic transactions between its members at lower costs than a market mechanism can. Under certain conditions, markets are more efficient because they can mediate without paying the costs of managers, accountants or personnel departments. Under other conditions, however, a market mechanism becomes so cumbersome that it

Adapted from *Administrative Science Quarterly*, Vol. 25 (1980), pp. 129–41.

is less efficient then a bureaucracy. This transactions cost approach explicitly regards efficiency as the fundamental element in determining the nature of organizations.

Markets, bureaucracies and clans

Transactions costs are a solution to the problem of cooperation in the realm of economic activity. From the perspective of Mayo (1945) and Barnard (1968), the fundamental problem of cooperation stems from the fact that individuals have only partially overlapping goals. Left to their own devices, they pursue incongruent objectives and their efforts are uncoordinated. Any collectivity which has an economic goal must then find a means to control diverse individuals efficiently.

[. . .]

Cooperative action necessarily involves interdependence of individuals. This interdependence calls for a transaction or exchange in which each individual gives something of value (for example, labor) and receives something of value (for example, money) in return. In a market relationship, the transaction takes place between the two parties and is mediated by a price mechanism in which the existence of a competitive market reassures both parties that the terms of exchange are equitable. In a bureaucratic relationship, each party contributes labor to a corporate body which mediates the relationship by placing a value on each contribution and then compensating it fairly. The perception of equity in this case depends upon a social agreement that the bureaucratic hierarchy has the legitimate authority to provide this mediation. In either case, individuals must regard the transaction as equitable: it must meet the standards of reciprocity which Gouldner (1961) has described as a universal requirement for collective life.

It is this demand for equity which brings on transactions costs. A transactions cost is any activity which is engaged in to satisfy each party to an exchange that the value given and received is in accord with his or her expectations.

Transactions costs arise principally when it is difficult to determine the value of the goods or service. Such difficulties can arise from the underlying nature of the goods or service or from a lack of trust between the parties. When a company is being sold by one corporation to another corporation, for example, it may not be unambiguously clear what the true value of that company is. If firms similar to the company are frequently bought and sold, and if those transactions occur under competitive conditions, then the market process will be accepted as a legitimate estimator of the true value. But if the company is unique, and there is only one potential buyer, then market forces are absent. How will the buyer and seller determine a fair price? They may call upon a third party to estimate the value of the company. Each party may in addition call upon other experts who will assist them in evaluating both the value of the company and the adequacy of the judgement of the third party. Each side may also require an extensive and complete contract which will describe exactly what is being bought and sold. Each of these activities is costly, and all of them are regarded here as transactions costs: they are necessary to create a perception of equity among all parties to the transaction.

[. . .]

We have identified two principal mechanisms for mediating these transactions: a market and a bureaucracy. [. . .] However, the paradigm also suggests a third mechanism: if the objectives of individuals are congruent (not mutually exclusive), then the conditions of reciprocity and equity can be met quite differently.

Both Barnard and Mayo pointed out that organizations are difficult to operate because their members do not share a selfless devotion to the same objectives. Mayo (1945) argued that organizations operated more efficiently in preindustrial times, when members typically served an apprenticeship during which they were socialized into accepting the objectives of the craft or organization. Barnard (1968: 42–3) posed the problem thus:

> A formal system of cooperation requires an objective, a purpose, an aim. [. . .] It is important to note the complete distinction between the aim of a cooperative effort and that of an individual. Even in the case where a man enlists the aid of other men to do something which he cannot do alone, such as moving a stone, the objective ceases to be personal.

[. . .]

If the socialization of individuals into an organization is complete, then the basis of reciprocity can be changed. For example, Japanese firms rely to a great extent upon hiring inexperienced workers, socializing them to accept the company's goals as their own, and compensating them according to length of service, number of dependants, and other non-performance criteria (see Abeeglen, 1958; Dore, 1973; Nakane, 1973). It is not necessary for these organizations to measure performance to control or direct their employees, since the employees' natural (socialized) inclination is to do what is best for the firm. It is also unnecessary to derive explicit, verifiable measures of value added, since rewards are distributed according to non-performance-related criteria which are relatively inexpensive to determine (length of service and number of dependants can be ascertained at relatively low costs). Thus, industrial organizations can, in some instances, rely to a great extent on socialization as the principal mechanism of mediation or control, and this 'clan' form ('clan' conforms to Durkheim's meaning of an organic association which resembles a kin network but may not include blood relations, 1933: 175) can be very efficient in mediating transactions between interdependent individuals.

Markets, bureaucracies, and clans are therefore three distinct mechanisms which may be present in differing degrees, in any real organization.[1] Our next objective is to specify the conditions under which the requirements of each form are most efficiently satisfied.

The market failures framework

We can approach this question most effectively by examining the markets and hierarchies approach provided by Williamson (1975), which builds upon earlier statements of the problem by Coase (1937) and others (for a more detailed description of the functioning of each mechanism, see Ouchi, 1979).

Market transactions, or exchanges, consist of contractual relationships. Each exchange is governed by one of three types of contractual relations, all of which can be specified completely. That is, because each party is bound only to deliver that which is specified, the contract must specify who must deliver what under every possible state of nature.

[. . .]

A common device for dealing with the future is the 'contingent claims contract', a document that specifies all the obligations of each party to an exchange, contingent upon all possible future states of nature. However, given a future that is either complex or uncertain, the bounded rationality of individuals makes it impossible to specify such a contract completely. Leaving such a contract incompletely specified is an alternative, but one that will succeed only if each party can trust the other to interpret the uncertain future in a manner that is acceptable to him. Thus, given uncertainty, bounded rationality and opportunism, contingent claims contracting will fail.

Instead of trying to anticipate the future in a giant, once-and-for-all contract, why not employ a series of contracts, each one written for a short period within which future events can confidently be foreseen? The problem with such 'sequential spot contracting' is that in many exchange relationships, the goods or services exchanged are unique, and the supplier requires specialized knowledge of how to supply the customer best and most efficiently. The supplier acquires this knowledge over time and in doing so gains a 'first mover advantage', which enables him to bid more effectively on subsequent contracts than any potential competitor can. Knowing this, potential competitors will not waste their time bidding, thus producing a situation of 'small numbers bargaining' or bilateral monopoly, in which there is only one buyer and seller. Under this condition, competitive pressures are absent, and each party will opportunistically claim higher costs or poor quality, whichever is in his or her interest. [. . .]

Thus, under some conditions no completely contractual market relationship is feasible. Table 1 summarizes the conditions which lead to market failure. According to the paradigm, no one of the four conditions can produce market failure, but almost any pairing of them will do so.

The idea of market failure is an analytical device. Economists do not agree on a specific set of conditions that constitute the failure of a market; indeed one point of view argues that even monopolistic conditions may be competitive. However, the idea of market failure as expressed by Williamson (1975) is useful as a conceptual framework within which to compare the strengths of markets as opposed to bureaucracies. The technique is to

Table 1   *The market failures framework*

Human factors		Environmental factors
Bounded rationality	←————————→	Uncertainty/complexity
Opportunism	←————————→	Small numbers

Source: Adapted from Williamson (1975: 40).

contend that all transactions can be mediated entirely by market relations, and then ask what conditions will cause some of these market mechanisms to fail and be replaced by bureaucratic mechanisms. In this sense, every bureaucratic organization constitutes an example of market failure.

The bureaucratic organization has two principal advantages over the market relationship. First, it uses the employment relation, which is an incomplete contract. In accepting an employment relation, a worker agrees to receive wages in exchange for submitting to the legitimate right of the organization to appoint superior officers who can (1) direct the work activities of the employee from day to day (within some domain or zone of indifference), thus overcoming the problem of dealing with the future all at once and (2) closely monitor the employee's performance, thus minimizing the problem of opportunism.

Second, the bureaucratic organization can create an atmosphere of trust between employees much more readily than a market can between the parties to an exchange. Because members of an organization assume some commonality of purpose, because they learn that long-term relationships will reward good performance and punish poor performance, they develop some goal congruence. This reduces their opportunistic tendencies and thus the need to monitor their performance.

Bureaucracies are also characterized by an emphasis on technical expertise which provides some skill training and some socialization into craft or professional standards. Professionals within a bureaucratic setting thus combine a primary affiliation to a professional body with a career orientation, which increases the sense of affiliation or solidarity with the employer and further reduces goal incongruence.[2]

[. . .]

Extending the market failures framework: clans

Bureaucracies can fail when the ambiguity of performance evaluation becomes significantly greater than that which brings about market failure. A bureaucratic organization operates fundamentally according to a system of hierarchical surveillance, evaluation and direction. In such a system, each superior must have a set of standards to which he can compare behavior or output in order to provide control. These standards only indicate the value of an output approximately, and are subject to idiosyncratic interpretation. People perceive them as equitable only as long as they believe that they contain a reasonable amount of performance information. When tasks become highly unique, completely integrated, or ambiguous for other reasons, then even bureaucratic mechanisms fail. Under these conditions, it becomes impossible to evaluate externally the value added by any individual. Any standard which is applied will be by definition arbitrary and therefore inequitable.

[. . .]

The employment relation is relatively efficient when the measurement of performance is ambiguous but the employer's goals are not. In an employment relation, each employee depends on the employer to distribute rewards equitably; if employees do not trust the employer to do so, they will demand contractual protections such as union representation and the transactions cost will rise.

Thus, the critical element in the efficiency of market versus employment relations has to do with (1) the ambiguity of the measurement of individual performance, and (2) the congruence of the employees' and employer's goals. We can now reformulate the transactions cost problem as follows: in order to mediate transactions efficiently, any organizational form must reduce either the ambiguity of performance evaluation or the goal incongruence between parties. Put this way, market relations are efficient when there is little ambiguity over performance, so the parties can tolerate relatively high levels of opportunism or goal incongruence. And bureaucratic relations are efficient when both performance ambiguity and goal incongruence are moderately high.

What form of mediation succeeds by minimizing goal incongruence and tolerating high levels of ambiguity in performance evaluation? [. . .] The answer is what we have referred to as the clan, which is the obverse of the market relation since it achieves efficiency under the opposite conditions: high performance ambiguity and low opportunism.

Perhaps the clearest exposition of the clan form appears in what Durkheim (1933: 365) refers to as the case of organic solidarity and its contrast with contractual relations:

> For organic solidarity to exist, it is not enough that there be a system of organs necessary to one another, which in a general way feel solidarity, but it is also necessary that the way in which they should come together, if not in every kind of meeting, at least in circumstances which most frequently occur, be predetermined. . . . Otherwise, at every moment new conflicts would have to be equilibrated. . . . It will be said that there are contracts. But, first of all, social relations are not capable of assuming this juridical form. . . . A contract is not self-sufficient, but supposes a regulation which is as extensive and complicated as contractual life itself. . . . A contract is only a truce, and very precarious, it suspends hostilities only for a time.

The solidarity to which Durkheim refers contemplates the union of objectives between individuals which stems from their necessary dependence upon one another. In this sense, any occupational group which has organic solidarity may be considered a clan. Thus, a profession, a labor union or a corporation may be a clan, and the professionalized bureaucracy may be understood as a response to the joint need for efficient transactions within professions (clan) and between professions (bureaucracy). [. . .] A clan, as Durkheim points out, provides great regularity of relations and may in fact be more directive than the other, more explicit mechanisms. That clans display a high degree of discipline is emphasized by Kanter (1972) in her study of utopian communities, some of which were successful businesses such as Oneida and Amana. According to Kanter, this discipline was not achieved through contractualism or surveillance but through an extreme form of the belief that individual interests are best served by a complete immersion of each individual in the interests of the whole (1972: 41).

More recently, Ouchi and Jaeger (1978) and Ouchi and Johnson (1978) have reported on modern industrial organizations which closely resemble the clan form. In these organizations, a variety of social mechanisms reduces differences between individual and organizational goals and produces a strong sense of community (see also Van Maanen, 1975; Katz, 1978). Where individual and organizational interests overlap to this extent, opportunism is unlikely and equity in rewards can be achieved at a relatively low transactions cost. Moreover, these organizations are typically in technologically advanced or closely integrated industries, where teamwork is common, technologies change often, and therefore individual performance is highly ambiguous.

When a bureaucracy fails, then, due to excessively ambiguous performance evaluation, the sole form of mediation remaining is the clan, which relies upon creating goal congruence. Although clans may employ a system of legitimate authority (often the traditional rather than the rational-legal form), they differ fundamentally from bureaucracies in that they do not require explicit auditing and evaluation. Performance evaluation takes place instead through the kind of subtle reading of signals that is possible among intimate co-workers but which cannot be translated into explicit, verifiable measures. This means that there is sufficient information in a clan to promote learning and effective production, but that information cannot withstand the scrutiny of contractual relations. Thus any tendency toward opportunism will be destructive, because the close auditing and hard contracting necessary to combat it are not possible in a clan.
[. . .]

Markets, bureaucracies and clans: an overview

Having distinguished three mechanisms of intermediation, we can now summarize them and attempt to set out the general conditions under which each form will mediate transactions between individuals most efficiently. Table 2 discriminates markets, bureaucracies and clans along two dimensions: their underlying normative and informational requirements.

Normative requirements refer to the basic social agreements that all

Table 2 *An organizational failures framework*

Mode of control	Normative requirements	Informational requirements
Market	Reciprocity	Prices
Bureaucracy	Reciprocity Legitimate authority	Rules
Clan	Reciprocity Legitimate authority Common values and beliefs	Traditions

members of the transactional network must share if the network is to function efficiently, without undue costs of performance auditing or monitoring. A norm of reciprocity, according to Gouldner (1961), is one of only two social agreements that have been found to be universal among societies across time and cultures (the other is the incest taboo). If no such norm were widely shared, then a potential trader would have to consume so much energy in setting the contractural terms of exchange in advance and in auditing the performance of the other party afterwards that the potential transaction would cost too much. Under such conditions, a division of labor is unthinkable and social existence impossible. Therefore, a norm of reciprocity underlies all exchange mechanisms.

A norm of legitimate authority is critical for two reasons. As discussed above, it permits the assignment of organizational superiors who can, on an ad hoc basis, specify the work assignments of subordinates, thus obviating the need for a contingent claims employment contract which would be either so complex as to be infeasible or so simple as to be too confining or else incomplete. Legitimate authority also permits organizational superiors to audit the performance of subordinates more closely than is possible within a market relationship. In a bureaucracy, legitimate authority will commonly take the 'rational/legal' form, whereas in a clan it may take the 'traditional' form (see Blau and Scott, 1962: 27–38). Legitimate authority is not ordinarily created within the organization but is maintained by other institutions such as the church or the educational system (Weber, 1947; Blau and Scott, 1962; Barnard, 1968: 161–84). While the legitimacy of a particular organization may be greater or smaller as a result of its managerial practices, it is fundamentally maintained within a society generally.

[. . .]

A norm of reciprocity is universal, legitimate authority is accepted, though in varying degree, in most formal organizations, and common values and beliefs are relatively rare in formal organizations. Etzioni (1965) has described this last form of control as being common only to 'total organizations' such as the military and mental hospitals, and Light (1972) describes its role in ethnically bound exchange relationships. However, we have also noted that a partially complete form of socialization, accompanied by market or bureaucratic mechanisms, may be effective across a wider range of organizations. Mayo (1945) contended that instability of employment, which upsets the long socialization period necessary, is the chief enemy of the development of this form of control.

The informational prerequisites of each form of control are prices, rules and traditions. Prices are a highly sophisticated form of information for decision-making. However, correct prices are difficult to arrive at, particularly when technological interdependence, novelty, or other forms of ambiguity obscure the boundary between tasks or individuals. Rules, by comparison, are relatively crude informational devices. A rule is specific to a problem, and therefore it takes a large number of rules to control organizational responses. A decision-maker must know the structure of the rules in order to apply the correct one in any given situation. Moreover, an organization can never specify a set of rules that will cover all possible contingencies. Instead, it specifies a smaller set of rules which cover routine decisions, and refers exceptions up the hierarchy where policy-makers can invent rules as needed. As Galbraith (1973) has pointed out, under conditions of uncertainty or complexity the number of exceptions becomes so great that the hierarchy becomes overloaded and the quality of decision-making suffers.

Traditions are implicit rather than explicit rules that govern behavior. Because traditions are not specified, they are not easily accessible, and a new member will not be able to function effectively until he or she has spent a number of years learning them (Van Maanen and Schein, 1978). In terms of the precision of the performance evaluation they permit, traditions may be the crudest informational prerequisite, since they are ordinarily stated in a general way which must be interpreted in a particular situation. On the other hand, the set of traditions in a formal organization may produce a unified, although implicit, philosophy or point of view, functionally equivalent to a theory about how that organization should work. A member who grasps such an essential theory can deduce from it an appropriate rule to govern any possible decision, thus producing a very elegant and complete form of control. Alternatively, a disruption of the socialization process will inhibit the passing on of traditions and bring about organizational inefficiency.

[. . .]

Notes

1. In the broader language necessary to encompass both economics and organization theory, an organization may be thought of as any stable pattern of transactions. In this definition, a market is as much an organization as is a bureaucracy or a clan. The only requirement is that, for the purposes of this discussion, we maintain a clear distinction between the idea of 'bureaucracy' and the idea of 'organization'. Bureaucracy as used here refers specifically to the Weberian model, while organization refers to any stable pattern of transactions between individuals or aggregations of individuals.

2. Despite these desirable properties, the bureaucratic type has continually been under attack and revision. As Williamson points out, the move from U-form (functional) to M-form (divisional) organization among many large firms has been motivated by a desire to simulate a capital market within a bureaucratic frame work because of its superior efficiency. By regrouping the parts of the organization, it is possible to create subentities that are sufficiently autonomous to permit precise measurement and the determination of an effective price mechanism. Although each division may still operate internally as a bureaucracy, the economies which accrue from this partial market solution are often large, offsetting the dis-economies of functional redundancy which often accompany the separation of the organization into divisions.

References

Abegglen, James C. (1958) *The Japanese Factory: Aspects of its Social Organization*. Glencoe: Free Press.

Barnard, Chester I. (1968) *The Functions of the Executive*. 30th anniversary edn. Cambridge, MA: Harvard.

Blau, Peter M. and Scott, W. Richard (1962) *Formal Organizations*. San Francisco: Scott, Foreman.

Coase, R.H. (1937) 'The nature of the firm', *Economica*, n.s. 4: 386–405.

Dore, Ronald (1973) *British Factory–Japanese Factory*. Berkeley: University of California Press.

Durkheim, Emile (1933) *The Division of Labor in Society*. G. Simpson, trans. New York: Free Press.

Etzioni, Amitai (1965) 'Organizational control structure', in James G. March (ed.) *Handbook of Organizations*: 650–77. Chicago: Rand McNally.

Galbraith, Jay (1973) *Designing Complex Organizations*. Reading, MA: Addison-Wesley.

Gouldner, Alvin W. (1961) 'The norm of reciprocity', *American Sociological Review*, 25: 161–79.

Kanter, Rosabeth Moss (1972) *Commitment and Community*. Cambridge, MA: Harvard.

Katz, Ralph (1978) 'Job longevity as a situational factor in job satisfaction', *Administrative Science Quarterly*, 23: 204–23.

Light, Ivan H. (1972) *Ethnic Enterprise in America*. Berkeley: University of California Press.

March, James G. and Simon, Herbert A. (1958) *Organizations*. New York: Wiley.

Mayo, Elton (1945) *The Social Problems of an Industrial Civilization*. Boston: Division of Research, Graduate School of Business Administration, Harvard University.

Nakane, Chie (1973) *Japanese Society*, rev. edn. Harmondsworth, Middlesex: Penguin.

Ouchi, William G. (1979) 'A conceptual framework for the design of organizational control mechanisms', *Management Science*, 25: 833–48.

Ouchi, William G. and Jaeger, Alfred M. (1978) 'Type Z organization: Stability in the midst of mobility', *Academy of Management Review*, 3: 305–14.

Ouchi, William G. and Johnson, Jerry B. (1978) 'Types of organizational control and their relationship to emotional well-being', *Administrative Science Quarterly*, 23: 293–317.

Simon, Herbert A. (1945) *Administrative Behavior*. New York: Free Press.

Van Maanen, John (1975) 'Police socialization: A longitudinal examination of job attitudes in an urban police department', *Administrative Science Quarterly*, 20: 207–28.

Van Maanen, John and Schein, Edgar H. (1978) 'Toward a theory of organizational socialization', Manuscript, Sloan School of Industrial Administration, Massachusetts Institute of Technology.

Weber, Max (1947) *The Theory of Social and Economic Organization* (orig. edn, 1925) A.M. Henderson and T. Parsons, trans. New York: Free Press.

Williamson, O.E. (1975) *Markets and Hierarchies: Analysis and Antitrust Implications*. New York: Free Press.

21

Interorganizational relations in industrial systems: a network approach compared with the transactions-cost approach

Jan Johanson and Lars-Gunnar Mattsson

We shall here consider some aspects of relations among firms engaged in industrial production as those relations are postulated or described in two theoretical approaches to analysing industrial systems. A *network* approach, is compared with the *transactions-cost* approach associated with Oliver Williamson (1975: 5) [. . .]

Industrial networks

In industrial systems, firms are engaged in production, distribution, and use of goods and services. We describe such systems as networks of relationship among firms. There is a division of work in a network that means that firms are dependent on each other. Therefore, their activities need to be coordinated. Coordination is not achieved through a central plan or an organizational hierarchy, nor does it take place through the price mechanism, as in the traditional market model. Instead, coordination takes place through interaction among firms in the network, in which price is just one of several influencing conditions. The firms are free to choose counterparts, and thus 'market forces' are at play. To gain access to external resources, however, and to make it possible to sell products, exchange *relationships* have to be established with other firms. Such relationships take time and effort to establish and develop, which constrains the firms' possibilities to change counterparts. The need for adjustments among the interdependent firms concerning quantity and quality of goods and services exchanged, and the timing of such exchange, call for more or less explicit coordination through joint planning, or through power exercised by one party over the other. Each firm in the network has relationships with customers, distributors, suppliers and so on (and sometimes also directly

Adapted from *International Studies of Management and Organization*, 17(1), 1987, pp. 34–48.

with competitors), plus indirect relations, via those firms, with the suppliers' suppliers, the customers' customers, competitors, and others.
[. . .]

As an aspect of those relationships, *bonds* of various kinds are developed between firms. We distinguish technical, planning, knowledge, socioeconomic and legal bonds. These bonds can be exemplified by, respectively, product and process adjustments, logistical coordination, knowledge about the counterpart, personal confidence and liking, special credit agreements, and long-term contracts.

We stress complementarity in the network. There are also, of course, important competitive relations. Other firms want to get access to specific exchange possibilities, either as sellers or as buyers, and cooperating firms also have partly conflicting objectives.

The relationships imply that there are *specific interfirm dependence* relations that are different in nature from the general dependence relationship to the market in the traditional market model. A firm has direct and specific dependence relations with firms with which it has exchange relations. It has indirect and specific dependence relations with firms with which its counterparts have exchange relationships, that is, the other firms operating in the network in which it is engaged.

To get established in a new market, that is, in a network new to it, the firm has to build relationships that are new to it and to its counterparts. Sometimes this is done by breaking old, existing relationships, and sometimes by adding a relationship to already existing ones. Initiatives can be taken by both the seller and the buyer. A supplier firm can become established in a network that is new to it because a buying firm takes an initiative.

This model of industrial markets implies that a firm's activities in industrial markets are *cumulative processes* in the sense that relationships are constantly being established, maintained, developed and broken in order to give satisfactory, short-term economic returns and to create positions in the network that will ensure the long-term survival and development of the firm. Through its activities in the network the firm develops the relationships that secure its *access to important resources* and the sale of its products and services.

Because of the cumulative nature of the market activities, network *position* is an important concept. At each point in time, the firm has certain positions in the network. They characterize its relations to other firms; are a result of earlier activities in the network, both by the firm and by other firms; and constitute the base that provides the development possibilities and constraints of the firm in the network.
[. . .]

A basic assumption in the network model is that the individual firm is dependent on resources controlled by other firms. The firm gets access to these external resources through its network positions. Since the development of positions takes time and effort, and since the present positions define opportunities and constraints for the future strategic development of the firm, we look at the firm's positions in the network as partially controlled, intangible, *market assets*. Market assets generate revenues for the firm and serve to give the firm access to other firms' internal assets. Because of the interdependencies of firms, the use of an asset in one firm is dependent on the use of other firms' assets. Thus, investment processes and their consequences are also interdependent in the network.

Relationships in industrial networks

In industrial networks, suppliers and customers establish, develop and maintain lasting relationships with each other. Such relationships may be significant to the participants. They may reduce costs of exchange and production; they may promote development of knowledge of the respective parties; they may give the parties some control over each other; they may be used as bridges to other firms; and they may be used when mobilizing partners against third parties.

Basically, an interfirm relationship is a *mutual orientation* of two firms toward each other. This implies that the firms are prepared to interact with each other and expect each other to do so. [. . .]

The relationships arise through *exchange processes* between the parties. The positive inducements they offer each other is the primary feature of those exchange processes. Mutuality, in which the parties demonstrate that they respect each other's interests, is an important aspect of the exchange process. A lasting relationship may emerge if the parties perceive a certain complexity or heterogeneity in the exchange. [. . .]

Single exchanges are integral parts of a process in which the parties gradually build up a mutual trust in each other. In supplier–customer relationships, business exchange is an important aspect of this social exchange process, and the gradual build-up is very familiar to business people.

The social exchange process implies that the relationships have an important social element; but they have important technical, logistical, knowledge, administrative and time elements as well. The exchange process implies that the parties test how well they fit each other. The process is, however, not only a learning process but also an *adaptation process*. In the course of the process, a number of problems usually emerge, the parties do not fit, and a number of activities can be carried out to eliminate the misfits. The parties adapt to each other and influence each other toward adaptation. This is a vital characteristic of the relationships.

Adaptations are made in a number of different dimensions. Firms can adapt to each other technically by modifying products or production processes. They may adapt logistically by adjusting stock levels or developing common delivery systems. Some adapt administratively by modifying planning or scheduling systems. They may also adapt financially by handling payments in special ways. Finally, some firms adapt to each other in terms of knowledge by acting together in some technical development matters.

[. . .]

Adaptations are important for at least three reasons.

First, they strengthen the bonds between firms. Through adaptations the firms become increasingly dependent on each other. The supplier whose products or processes are modified to fit a specific customer's needs becomes dependent on that customer, and a customer who has adjusted production processes and scheduling systems to fit a supplier's capabilities is dependent on that supplier. The dependencies may be mutual, but are not necessarily so; in general, it may be assumed that they are more or less asymmetrical in the sense that one party is more dependent on the relationship than the other.

Second, reinforcement of relationships through adaptations makes them more endurable, which in turn means that disagreements, as a rule, have to be handled within the framework of the relationships. A situation evolves in which 'voice' is better as a conflict-resolution mechanism than 'exit', since exit is not easy or attractive (see Hirschman, 1970: 83). This implies that the existence of relationships need not make firms passive, but they do have to learn conflict-resolution methods other than just switching to new customers or suppliers, methods that are of a more problem-solving nature than the exit method.

Third, adaptations are important because they indicate that there is some space for change in the relationship: everything is not given once and for all; rather, the two parties can adapt to fit each other better. Nevertheless, there are limits to those adaptations, as all adaptations are a kind of investment. The investment has to give some return, which limits the total space for change. Furthermore, adaptations to specific counterparts must be limited to prevent losing one's own independence and identity.

Finally, interaction processes create adaptations in attitudes and knowledge of the parties, that is, a mutual orientation develops. This is manifested in a common language regarding technical matters, contracting rules and standardization of processes, products and routines. [. . .] A most important aspect of the mutual orientation is mutual knowledge, knowledge which the parties assume each has about the other and upon which they draw in communicating with each other. This mutual knowledge may refer to resources, strategies, needs and capabilities of the parties and, in particular, to their relationships with other firms. It is a subtle knowledge based on personal experience, and takes time to develop.

[. . .]

We have discussed interfirm relationships without explicitly referring to individual actors. However, the mutual orientation among firms is principally a mutual orientation among individual actors in those firms. In some cases, the mutuality is primarily a matter of interpersonal relationships between salesmen and purchasers; in other cases, a number of persons on different levels and with different specializations may be mutually oriented toward each other. Correspondingly, the interaction processes are carried out by individuals, though we have discussed them as taking place among firms.

[. . .]

The transactions-cost approach

In a perfect market, transactions are carried out without transaction costs. Information is freely available, decision-making is rational, there are always alternative suppliers and buyers, and there are no carry-over effects from one period to the other of a specific transaction between two parties in the market. When these conditions do not prevail, transactions costs emerge because there is a need to devote efforts to organizing, carrying out and controlling transactions among interdependent actors. The transactions-cost approach tries to explain the institutional form, that is the 'governance structure' (market, hierarchy, or intermediate forms) of these transactions.

Two behavioral characteristics are postulated: decisions and actions are characterized by *bounded rationality* and *opportunistic behavior*. Under conditions of certainty, it is possible, *ex ante*, to gather information and to specify contracts between supplier and buyer, to take care of various future contingencies, and also, *ex post*, to control the fulfillment of the agreement between the parties. However, when *uncertainty* prevails, contracts will be very complex and costly both to construct and to enforce, especially in the case of *small-numbers bargaining*. 'Small numbers' means that there are few, if any, alternatives open for a buyer or for a seller to replace each other in a transaction. The major reason for this is that the *asset specificity* is high. Personal knowledge or skills, type of machinery or products, geographic location and so on are not homogeneous across the population of buyers or sellers. The higher the asset specificity, the more dependent the parties will be on each other, and the higher the costs of switching to another party will become.

Frequency of transactions also enters as a major concept in the analysis. If there are only occasional transactions and the asset specificity is very high, there is no opportunity for vertical integration, and the market transaction must be developed with the aid of some arbitrating agency. If the frequency is high and the asset specificity is high, the transactions-cost approach expects vertical integration to take place. Bilateral market relations are expected to be the most transactions-cost efficient if asset specificity is in the intermediate range (see Williamson, 1981: Fig. 1). Some empirical studies, with somewhat mixed results, have been carried out to test these hypotheses (for example, by Walker and Weber, 1984).

The transactions-cost approach offers an explanation of why industries are characterized by large-scale organizations. Under the label 'theory of internalization', it has become one of the recently most discussed theoretical explanations for the existence of multinational corporations (Rugman, 1982).

The transactions-cost approach has also recently been rather extensively debated and criticized by economists and sociologists. 'Neo-institutionalists' (to be distinguished from the 'new institutionalists') criticize Williamson, for accepting the neo-classical assumption that the most efficient institutional form will 'survive' (Dugger, 1983).

This approach can be used as an argument for vertical or horizontal integration, since the use of hierarchies rather than markets for coordination of interdependent activities may economize on transaction costs. The critics say that the transactions-cost concept is vague, even ill defined, and that there is little, if any, empirical evidence that economizing on transaction costs is a good explanation of, or even a dominating motive for, vertical integration (see, for example, Perrow, 1986 and Kogut, 1985).

Another major objection is that Williamson makes unrealistic assumptions about the differences between markets and hierarchies. Opportunism also exists *within* firms; organizations are not necessarily able to economize on bounded rationality; markets can also be characterized by asymmetrical power relations (controlled by 'fiat'), and so on. Another important issue in the application of transactions-cost analysis is delimitation of the systems to be compared. The transaction is a dyadic relationship, but the industrial system is made up of many such relations that are more or less interdependent. If we pick just one of those dyads and change the institutional form, for example through vertical integration, the other dyads may also be affected. The efficiency of the wider system may very well move in the opposite direction from the efficiency achieved in the original dyad that was changed. It has also been argued that the basically neo-classical approach assumes that there is a unique and stable equilibrium, indicating a single institutional form in specific circumstances; but even casual observation reveals that integrated and non-integrated arrangements coexist.

Among the assumptions and major variables in the transactions-cost model, the postulate that mankind is basically 'opportunistic, with guile and deceit', has been questioned, from both an empirical and a 'moral' point of view. Sociologists, in particular, point out that economic relationships also contain elements of mutual trust and exchange of a social and cultural kind (Perrow, 1986).

A comparison of the transactions-cost approach and the network approach

There are some fundamental differences between the transactions-cost approach and the network approach relative to their theoretical foundations, problem orientation, basic concepts, system delimitation, and nature of the relationships among firms.

Theoretical foundations

Williamson's approach lies firmly within the neo-classical framework focusing on conditions for stable equilibrium. Ours does not. In the network approach, the benchmark models of markets and organizations are not used: the 'markets' are characterized by interaction in systems of connected relationships, between suppliers, customers and other actors, in which the parties have some control over each other and the organizations are not 'pure' hierarchies. For us, the legal frameworks of the transactions are less important, and the boundaries of the individual organizations are unclear. Instead, the network approach views firms as social units and is closer to social exchange theory. In terms of control assumptions, it is based on resource-dependence theory (Pfeffer and Salancik, 1978).

Problem orientation

The transactions-cost approach aims to explain institutional governance structures. Why and when are activities coordinated within, rather than among, firms? Our basic interest lies in describing and analysing dynamic aspects of industrial systems and strategies pursued by firms in such systems. [. . .]

Basic concepts

Williamson's basic concepts, with the exception of opportunism, can also be used to describe important characteristics of networks.

We do not regard *opportunism* as a basic characteristic of the actors. As in social exchange theory, its correlate *trust* is an important concept in the network approach.

Bounded rationality is for us an implicit assumption, in the sense that actors need to handle information, learn by experience and so on. More interesting than boundaries is the formation of new knowledge concerning the handling of resources. An important source of knowledge in the firm is the interaction with other firms within the network relationships.

Uncertainty is, in our model, also linked to the relationships in the network. The nature of the bonds and the extent of structuring of the network influence the degree and type of uncertainty. It is possible to influence the uncertainty both in Williamson's and in our approach; but within Williamson's framework this influence seems to be more related to the legal form of the transaction than is the case in ours.

Asset specificity is very closely related to our stress on *heterogeneity* (Hägg and Johanson, 1982), *mutual adaptation* and *market assets*. However, we basically disagree with Williamson when he argues that a high degree of asset specificity leads to vertical integration. Asset specificity can be the result of internal activities in a firm, but we believe that it is mostly the result of interaction with interorganizational relations. Thus, firms are using each other's assets in a mutual adaptation process.

Asset specificity is one reason why firms are dependent on external resources and devote important resources to investment in relationships. If all these resources are 'internalized', however, a company will find itself in an impossible 'growth' situation. To us, a high degree of asset specificity is the rule rather than the exception, and that variable in itself can hardly explain integration. Furthermore, unless the production and demand capacities of supplier and user, respectively, match each other, surplus supply or surplus demand must be sold/bought in the 'market'.

Small-numbers bargaining is also, for us, a characteristic of the market, as is a relatively high *frequency of transactions* between parties. Since we are dealing with industrial systems, buyers seldom have only occasional need for a specific type of product or service. Even capital goods transactions are often part of long-term relationships, including transfer of service for the maintenance of the function performed by the capital good.

System delimitation

The transactions-cost approach bases its conclusions about governance structures on characteristics of aggregates of specific types of transaction relations. We look at relationships in networks within the context of other network relationships. The network approach bases its analyses on characteristics of systems of interdependent dyadic relations. Thus, if A first buys from B, but then merges with B, not only is the relationship between A and B changed (in our framework, perhaps not very much) but also A's relation to B's other customers, suppliers, competitors and so on. What might be gained in the A–B relationship might very well be lost through the changes in the other relationships that B had before the merger.

Another consequence of our system delimitation is that it is not possible to characterize the system as a typical market or a typical hierarchy. Different governance structures coexist (complementary or competitive) within this wider system.

It can be argued that whereas the function of the dyadic relation in the transactions-cost approach is to analyse the boundaries of organizations and markets, its function in the network approach is to open the systems under study.

Nature of relationships

The most important difference between the two approaches is in the nature of the relationships. For us, industrial markets are characterized by lasting relationships among firms because such relationships can reduce costs of exchange and production and can promote knowledge development and change. Through lasting relationships, firms do get some control over each other, plus indirect access to assets in firms with which they do not have direct relationships. The exchange and adaptation processes are looked upon as investment processes (of course, not always successful ones!). 'Mutual orientation' is developed.

For Williamson, such relationships barely exist in markets, only within hierarchies. 'Bilateral governance', which is his counterpart of our 'relationship', is not considered a stable institutional form. We think the relationships among firms in networks are stable and can basically play the same coordinating and development function as intra-organizational relations. Through relationships with customers, distributors and suppliers a firm can reach out to quite an extensive network. Such indirect relationships may be very important. They are not handled within the transactions-cost approach.

[. . .]

Conclusion

It should be evident from our discussion that the network approach is quite different from the transactions-cost approach. Since the theoretical bases and the problem orientations are different, this is hardly astonishing. These differences indicate the relative usefulness of the two approaches for different purposes. The merits of the transactions-cost approach are related to its ability to explain the existence of different governance structures or institutional forms in different situations. It seems to have a quite wide area of applicability. With its focus on conditions for stable equilibrium, it tends, however, to be deterministic, making it less suitable for strategy analysis. In contrast, the network approach stresses the action possibilities of the firm. In particular, it is a useful tool in analysing approaches to, and strategies in, different markets.

References

Dugger, W.M. (1983) 'The transaction cost analysis of Oliver E. Williamson: a new synthesis?', *Journal of Economic Issues*, 17 (1): 95–114.

Hägg, I. and Johanson, J. (eds) (1982) *Företag i nätverk* [Firms in networks]. Stockholm: SNS.

Hirschman, A.O. (1970) *Exit, Voice and Loyalty*. Cambridge, MA: Harvard University Press.

Kogut, B. (1985) 'A critique of transaction cost economics as a theory of organizational behavior', working paper (WP 84–05) of the Reginald H. Jones Center, Philadelphia, PA, USA.

Perrow, C. (1986) *Complex Organizations. A Critical Essay*, 3rd edn. Glenway, IL: Scott-Foresman.

Pfeffer, J. and Salancik, G.R. (1978) *External Control of Organizations*. New York: Harper & Row.

Rugman, A.M. (ed.) (1982) *New Theories of the Multinational Enterprise*. London: Croom Helm.

Walker, G. and Weber, D. (1984) 'A transaction cost approach to make or buy decisions', *Administrative Science Quarterly*, 29: 373–91.

Williamson, O.E. (1975) *Markets and Hierarchies: Analysis and Antitrust Implications*. New York: Free Press.

Williamson, O.E. (1979) 'Transaction cost economics: the governance of contractural relations', *Journal of Law and Economics*, 22: 233–61.

Williamson, O.E. (1981) 'The economics of organizations: the transaction cost approach', *American Journal of Sociology*, 87: 548–77.

22

Neither market nor hierarchy: network forms of organization

Walter W. Powell

In recent years, there has been a considerable amount of research on organizational practices and arrangements that are network-like in form. This diverse literature shares a common focus on lateral or horizontal patterns of exchange, interdependent flows of resources, and reciprocal lines of communication.

[. . .]

I begin by discussing why the familiar market-hierarchy continuum does not do justice to the notion of network forms of organization. I then contrast three modes of organization – market, hierarchy and network – and stress the salient features of each.

[. . .]

Markets and firms

In his classic article on the nature of the firm, the economist Ronald Coase (1937) conceived of the firm as a governance structure, breaking with orthodox accounts of the firm as a 'black box' production function. Coase's key insight was that firms and markets were alternative means for organizing similar kinds of transaction. This provocative paper, however, lay fallow, so to speak, for nearly four decades, until it was picked up by Williamson and other proponents of transaction costs economics in the 1970s. This work took seriously the notion that organizational form matters a great deal, and in so doing moved the economics of organization much closer to the fields of law, organization theory and business history.

The core of Williamson's (1975, 1985) argument is that transactions that involve uncertainty about their outcome, that recur frequently and require substantial 'transaction-specific investments' – of money, time or energy that cannot be easily transferred – are more likely to take place within hierarchically organized firms. Exchanges that are straightforward, non-repetitive and require no transaction-specific investments will take place across a market interface. Hence, transactions are moved out of markets

Adapted from *Research in Organizational Behaviour* 12 (1990), pp. 295–336.

into hierarchies as knowledge specific to the transaction (asset specificity) builds up. When this occurs, the inefficiencies of bureaucratic organization will be preferred to the relatively greater costs of market transactions. There are two reasons for this: (1) bounded rationality – the inability of economic actors to write contracts that cover all possible contingencies; when transactions are internalized, there is little need to anticipate such contingencies since they can be handled within the firm's 'governance structure'; and (2) 'opportunism' – the rational pursuit by economic actors of their own advantage, with every means at their disposal, including guile and deceit; opportunism is mitigated by authority relations and by the stronger identification that parties presumably have when they are joined under a common roof.

This dichotomous view of markets and hierarchies (Williamson, 1975) sees firms as separate from markets or more broadly, the larger societal context. Outside boundaries of firms are competitors, while inside managers exercise authority and curb opportunistic behavior. This notion of sharp firm boundaries was not just an academic view. A good deal of management practice as well as antitrust law shared the belief that, in Richardson's (1972) colorful language, firms are 'islands of planned co-ordination in a sea of market relations'.

But just as many economists have come to view firms as governance structures, and are providing new insights into the organization of the employment relationship and the multi-divisional firm (to cite only two examples), firms appear to be changing in significant ways and forms of relational contracting appear to have assumed much greater importance. Firms are blurring their established boundaries and engaging in forms of collaboration that resemble neither the familiar alternative of arm's length market contracting nor the formal ideal of vertical integration.

Some scholars respond to these changes by arguing that economic changes can be arrayed in a continuum-like fashion with discrete market transactions located at one end and the highly centralized firm at the other. In between these poles, we find various intermediate or hybrid forms of organization.[1] Moving from the market pole, where prices capture all the relevant information necessary for exchange, we find putting-out systems, various kinds of repeated trading, quasi-firms and subcontracting arrangements; toward the hierarchy pole, franchising, joint ventures, decentralized profit centers and matrix management are located.

Is this continuum view satisfactory? Can transaction costs logic meet the task of explaining this rich array of alternative forms? [. . .]

The view that transactions are distributed at points along a continuum implies that markets are the starting point, the elemental form of exchange out of which other methods evolve. Such a view is, obviously, a distortion of historical and anthropological evidence. As Moses Finley (1973) tells us so well, there was no market in the modern sense of the term in the classical world, only money in the nature of free booty and treasure trove. Nor did markets spring full blown with the Industrial Revolution.

Economic units emerged from the dense webs of political, religious and social affiliations that had enveloped economic activity for centuries. Agnew (1986) documents that the word market first enters the English language during the twelfth century to refer to specific locations where provisions and livestock were sold. The markets of medieval England had a highly personal, symbolic and hierarchical flavor. E.P. Thompson (1971) used the term 'the moral economy' to characterize the intricate pattern of symbolic and statutory expectations that surrounded the eighteenth-century marketplace. It was not until the latter part of the eighteenth century that among the British educated classes the term market became separated from a physical and social space and came to imply a boundless and timeless phenomenon of buying and selling (Agnew, 1986).[2]

By the same token, hierarchies do not represent an evolutionary end-point of economic development. A long view of business history would suggest that firms with strictly defined boundaries and highly centralized operations are quite atypical.[3] The history of modern commerce, whether told by Braudel, Polanyi, Pollard or Wallerstein, is a story of family businesses, guilds, cartels and extended trading companies – all enterprises with loose and highly permeable boundaries.

Recent work on the growth of small firms also casts doubt on the utility of a continuum view of economic exchange. Larson (1988) and Lorenzoni and Ornati (1988) draw similar portraits from very different settings – high-tech start-ups in the United States and craft-based firms in Northern Italy – which do not follow the standard model of small firms developing internally through an incremental and linear process. Instead, they suggest an entirely different model of externally driven growth in which pre-existing networks of relationships enable small firms to gain an established foothold almost overnight. These networks serve as conduits to provide small firms with the capacity to meet resource and functional needs.[4]

The idea that economic exchanges can be usefully arrayed along a continuum is thus too quiescent and mechanical. It fails to capture the complex realities of exchange.[5] The continuum view also misconstrues patterns of economic development and blinds us to the role played by reciprocity and collaboration as alternative governance mechanisms. By sticking to the twin pillars of markets and hierarchies, our attention is deflected from a diversity of organizational designs that are neither fish nor fowl, nor some mongrel hybrid, but a distinctly different form.

To be sure, there are a number of social scientists who question whether the distinction between market and hierarchy is particularly useful in the first place.[6] They contend that no sharp demarcation exists and that the argument is more a matter of academic pigeon-holing than of substantive operational differences. These analysts are united, however, more by their dislike of stylized models of economic exchange than by any shared alternative perspective.

One group of critics emphasizes the embeddedness of economics in social and cultural forces. Markets, in this view, are structured by a complex of local, ethnic and trading cultures, and by varying regimes of state regulation (Gordon, 1985). [. . .] Others maintain that markets cannot be insulated from social structure because differential social access results in information asymmetries, as well as bottlenecks, thus providing some parties with considerable benefits and leaving others disadvantaged (Granovetter, 1985; White, 1981).

Another chorus of skeptics point to the intermingling of various forms of exchange. (See Bradach and Eccles, 1989, for a good review of this literature.) Stinchcombe (1985) shows that there are strong elements of hierarchy and domination in written contracts. Goldberg (1980: 338) notes that many market exchanges have been replaced by interorganizational collaborations. He contends that much economic activity 'takes place within long-term, complex, multiparty contractual (or contract-like) relationships; behavior is in various degrees sheltered from market forces'. Similarly, much of the observed behavior in hierarchical firms seems unrelated to either top management directives or the logic of vertical integration. For example, a firm's relationships with its law, consulting, accounting and banking firms may be much more enduring and personal than its employment relationship with even its most senior employees.[7] The introduction of market processes into the firm also appears to be widespread. Eccles (1985) observes that large firms commonly rely on such market-like methods as transfer pricing and performance-based compensation schemes, while Eccles and Crane (1987) report that dual reporting relationships, internal competition, and compensation based on services provided to clients are the current norm in investment banking.

Markets, hierarchies and networks

I have a good deal of sympathy regarding the view that economic exchange is embedded in a particular social structural context. Yet it is also the case that certain forms of exchange are more social – that is, more dependent on relationships, mutual interests and reputations – as well as less guided by a formal structure of authority. My aim is to identify a coherent set of factors that make it meaningful to talk about networks as a distinctive form of coordinating economic activity. We can then employ these ideas to generate arguments about the frequency, durability and limitations of networks.

When the items exchanged between buyers and sellers possess qualities that are not easily measured, and the relations are so long-term and recurrent that it is difficult to speak of the parties as separate entities, can we still regard this as a market exchange? When the entangling of obligation and reputation reaches a point that the actions of the parties are interdependent, but there is no common ownership or legal framework, do we not need a new conceptual tool kit to describe and analyse this relationship?

Table 1 *Stylized comparison of forms of economic organization*

Key features	Forms		
	Market	Hierarchy	Network
Normative basis	Contract – Property rights	Employment relationship	Complementary strengths
Means of communication	Prices	Routines	Relational
Methods of conflict resolution	Haggling – resort to courts for enforcement	Administrative fiat – supervision	Norm of reciprocity – reputational concerns
Degree of flexibility	High	Low	Medium
Amount of commitment among the parties	Low	Medium to high	Medium to high
Tone or climate	Precision and/or Suspicion	Formal, bureaucratic	Open-ended, mutual benefits
Actor preferences or choices	Independent	Dependent	Interdependent
Mixing of forms	Repeat transactions (Geertz, 1978)	Informal organization (Dalton, 1957)	Status hierarchies
	Contracts as hierarchical documents (Stinchcombe, 1985)	Market-like features: profit centers, transfer pricing (Eccles, 1985)	Multiple partners

Formal rules |

Surely this patterned exchange looks more like a marriage than a one-night stand, but there is no marriage license, no common household, no pooling of assets. In the language I employ below, such an arrangement is neither a market transaction nor a hierarchical governance structure, but a separate, different mode of exchange, one with its own logic, a network.

Many firms are no longer structured like medieval kingdoms, walled off and protected from hostile forces. Instead, we find companies involved in an intricate latticework of collaborative ventures with other firms, most of whom are ostensibly competitors. The dense ties that bind the auto and biotechnology industries cannot be easily explained by saying that these firms are engaged in market transactions for some factors of production, or by suggesting that the biotechnology business is embedded in the international community of science. At what point is it more accurate to characterize these alliances as networks rather than as joint ventures among hierarchical firms?

We need fresh insights into these kinds of arrangement. Whether they are new forms of exchange that have recently emerged or aged-old practices that have gained new prominence they are not satisfactorily explained by existing approaches. Markets, hierarchies and networks are pieces of a larger puzzle that is the economy. The properties of the parts of this system are defined by the kinds of interaction that take place among them. The behavior and interests of individual actors are shaped by these patterns of interaction. Stylized models of markets, hierarchies and networks are not perfectly descriptive of economic reality, but they enable us to make progress in understanding the extraordinary diversity of economic arrangements found in the industrial world today.

Table 1 represents a first cut at summarizing some of the key differences between markets, hierarchies and networks. In market transactions the benefits to be exchanged are clearly specified, no trust is required, and agreements are bolstered by the power of legal sanction. Network forms of exchange, however, entail indefinite, sequential transactions within the context of a general pattern of interaction. Sanctions are typically normative rather than legal. The value of the goods to be exchanged in markets is much more important than the relationship itself; when relations do matter, they are frequently defined as if they were commodities. In hierarchies, communication occurs in the context of the employment contract. Relationships matter and previous interactions shape current ones, but the patterns and context of intra-organizational exchange are most strongly shaped by one's position within the formal hierarchical structure of authority.

The philosophy that undergirds exchange also contrasts sharply across forms. In markets the standard strategy is to drive the hardest possible bargain in the immediate exchange. In networks, the preferred option is often one of creating indebtedness and reliance over the long haul. Each approach thus devalues the other: prosperous market traders would be viewed as petty and untrustworthy shysters in networks, while successful participants in networks who carried those practices into competitive markets would be viewed as naive and foolish. Within hierarchies, communication and exchange is shaped by concerns with career mobility – in this sense, exchange is bound up with considerations of personal advancement. At the same time, intra-organizational communication takes place among parties who generally know one another, have a history of previous interactions, and possess a good deal of firm-specific knowledge, so there is considerable interdependence among the parties. In a market context it is clear to everyone concerned when a debt has been discharged, but such matters are not nearly as obvious in networks or hierarchies.

Markets, as described by economic theory, are a spontaneous coordination mechanism that imparts rationality and consistency to the self-interested actions of individuals and firms. [. . .]

The market is open to all comers, but while it brings people together, it does not establish strong bonds of altruistic attachments. The participants in a market transaction are free of any future commitments. The stereotypical competitive market is the paradigm of individually self-interested, non-cooperative, unconstrained social interaction. As such, markets have powerful incentive effects for they are the arena in which each party can fulfill its own internally defined needs and goals.

Markets offer choice, flexibility and opportunity. They are a remarkable device for fast, simple communication. No one need rely on someone else for direction, prices alone determine production and exchange. Because individual behavior is not dictated by a supervising agent, no organ of systemwide governance or control is necessary. Markets are a form of non-coercive organization, they have coordinating but not integrative effects. As Hayek (1945) suggested, market coordination is the result of human actions but not of human design.

Prices are a simplifying mechanism, consequently they are unsuccessful at capturing the intricacies of idiosyncratic, complex and dynamic exchange. As a result, markets are a poor device for learning and the transfer of technological know-how. In a stylized perfect market, information is freely available, alternative buyers or sellers are easy to come by, and there are no carry-over effects from one transaction to another. But as exchanges become more frequent and complex, the costs of conducting and monitoring them increase, giving rise to the need for other methods of structuring exchange.

Organization, or hierarchy, arises when the boundaries of a firm expand to internalize transactions and resource flows that were previously conducted in the marketplace. The visible hand of management supplants the invisible hand of the market in coordinating supply and demand. Within a hierarchy, individual employees operate under a regime of administrative procedures and work roles defined by higher-level supervisors. Management divides up tasks and positions and establishes an authoritative system of order. Because tasks are often quite specialized, work activities are highly interdependent. The large vertically integrated firm is thus an eminently social institution, with its own routines, expectations and detailed knowledge.

A hierarchical structure – clear departmental boundaries, clean lines of authority, detailed reporting mechanisms, and formal decision-making procedures – is particularly well-suited for mass production and distribution. The requirements of high volume, high-speed operations demand the constant attention of a managerial team. The strength of hierarchical organization, then, is its reliability – its capacity for producing large numbers of goods or services of a given quality repeatedly – and its accountability – its ability to document how resources have been used (DiMaggio and Powell, 1983; Hannan and Freeman, 1984). But when hierarchical forms are confronted by sharp fluctuations in demand and unanticipated changes, their liabilities are exposed.

Networks are 'lighter on their feet' than hierarchies. In networks modes of resource allocation, transactions occur neither through discrete exchanges nor by administrative fiat, but through networks of individuals engaged in reciprocal, preferential, mutually supportive actions. Networks can be complex: they involve neither the explicit criteria of the market, nor the familiar paternalism of the hierarchy. A basic assumption of network relationships is that one party is dependent on resources controlled by another, and that there are gains to be had by the pooling of resources.[8] In essence, the parties to a network agree to forgo the right to pursue their own interests at the expense of others.

In network forms of resource allocation, individuals units exist not by themselves, but in relation to other units. These relationships take considerable effort to establish and sustain, thus they constrain both partners' ability to adapt to changing circumstances. As networks evolve, it becomes more economically sensible to exercise voice rather than exit. Benefits and burdens come to be shared. Expectations are not frozen, but change as circumstances dictate. A mutual orientation – knowledge which the parties assume each has about the other and upon which they draw in communication and problem solving – is established. In short, complementarity and accommodation are the cornerstones of successful production networks. As Macneil (1985) has suggested, the 'entangling strings' of reputation, friendship, interdependence and altruism become integral parts of the relationship.

Networks are particularly apt for circumstances in which there is need for efficient, reliable information. The most useful information is rarely that which flows down the formal chain of command in an organization, or that which can be inferred from shifting price signals. Rather, it is that which is obtained from someone whom you have dealt with in the past and found to be reliable. You trust best information that comes from someone you know well. Kaneko and Imai (1987) suggest that information passed through networks is 'thicker' than information obtained in the market, and 'freer' than that communicated in a hierarchy. Networks, then, are especially useful for the exchange of commodities whose value is not easily measured. Such qualitative matters as know-how, technological capability, a particular approach or style of production, a spirit of innovation or experimentation, or a philosophy of zero defects are very hard to place a price tag on. They are not easily traded in markets nor communicated through a corporate hierarchy. The open-ended, relational features of networks, with their relative absence of explicit *quid pro quo* behavior, greatly enhance the ability to transmit and learn new knowledge and skills.

Reciprocity is central to discussions of network forms of organization. Unfortunately it is a rather ambiguous concept, used in different ways by various social science disciplines. One key point of contention concerns whether reciprocity entails exchanges of roughly equivalent value in a strictly delimited sequence or whether it involves a much less precise definition of equivalence, one that emphasizes indebtedness and obligation. Game theoretic treatments of reciprocity by scholars in political science and economics tend to emphasize equivalence. Axelrod (1984) stresses that reciprocal action implies returning ill for ill as well as good for good. As Keohane (1986) notes, the literature in international relations 'emphatically' associates reciprocity with equivalence of benefits.[9] As a result, these scholars take a view of reciprocity that is entirely consistent with the pursuit of self-interest.

Sociological and anthropological analyses of reciprocity are commonly couched in the language of indebtedness. In this view, a measure of imbalance sustains the partnership, compelling another meeting (Sahlins, 1972). Obligation is a means through which parties remain connected to one another. Calling attention to the need for equivalence might well undermine and devalue the relationship.[10] To be sure, sociologists have long emphasized that reciprocity implies conditional action (Gouldner, 1960). The question is whether there is a relatively immediate assessment or whether 'the books are kept open', in the interests of continuing satisfactory results. This perspective also takes a different tack on the issue of self-interest. In his classic work *The Gift*, Marcel Mauss (1967), attempted to show that the obligations to give, to receive, and to return were not to be understood simply with respect to rational calculations, but fundamentally in terms of underlying cultural tenets that provide objects with their meaning significance, and provide a basis for understanding the implications of their passage from one person to another. Anthropological and sociological approaches, then, tend to focus more on the normative standards that sustain exchange; game theoretic treatments emphasize how individual interests are enhanced through cooperation.

Social scientists do agree, however, that reciprocity is enhanced by taking a long-term perspective. Security and stability encourage the search for new ways of accomplishing tasks, promote learning and the exchange of information, and engender trust. Axelrod's (1984) notion of 'the shadow of the future' – the more the immediate payoff facing players is shaped by future expectations – points to a broadened conception of self-interest. Cooperation thus emerges out of mutual interests and behavior based on standards that no one individual can determine alone. Trust is thereby generated. Trust is, as Arrow (1974) has noted, a remarkably efficient lubricant to economic exchange. In trusting another party, one treats as certain those aspects of life which modernity rendered uncertain (Luhmann, 1979). Trust reduces complex realities far more quickly and economically than prediction, authority or bargaining.

It is inaccurate, however, to characterize networks solely in terms of collaboration and concord. Each point of contact in a network can be a source of conflict as well as harmony. Recall that the term alliance comes from the literature of international relations where it describes relations among nation states in an anarchic world. Keohane (1986) has stressed that processes of reciprocity or cooperation in no way 'insulate practitioners from considerations of power'. Networks also commonly involve aspects of dependency and particularism.[11] By establishing enduring patterns of repeat trading, networks restrict access. Opportunities are thus foreclosed to newcomers, either intentionally or more subtly through such barriers as unwritten rules or informal codes of conduct. In practice, subcontracting networks and research partnerships influence who competes with whom, thereby dictating the adoption of a particular technology and making it much harder for unaffiliated parties to join the fray. As a result of these inherent complications, most potential partners approach the idea of participating in a network with trepidation. All of the parties to network forms of exchange have lost some of their ability to dictate their own future and are increasingly dependent on the activities of others.

[. . .]

Notes

1. See Koenig and Thietart (1988) on intermediate forms in the aerospace industry, Thorelli (1986) on industrial marketing networks, Eccles and White (1986) on transfer pricing, and Powell (1987) on hybrid forms in craft and high technology industries.
2. This does not mean that market forces were of little consequence before the eighteenth century. Braudel (1982) argues that economic history is the story of slowly evolving mixtures of institutional forms. He suggests that we can speak of a market economy when the prices in a given area appear to fluctuate in unison, a phenomenon that has occurred since ancient times. But this does not imply that transactions between individuals were of a discrete, impersonal nature.
3. I owe this observation to comments made by Jim Robins.
4. What is remarkable about the firms in these two studies is how explicitly the entrepreneurs follow a 'network' strategy, intentionally eschewing internalization for such crucial and recurrent activities as manufacturing, sales, and research and development.
5. On this point, Macneil (1985: 496) suggests that 'the transaction costs approach is far too unrelational a starting point in analyzing' relational forms of exchange. Richardson (1972: 884) provides an apt example of these densely connected forms of exchange: 'Firm A . . . is a joint subsidiary of firms B and C, has technical agreements with D and E, subcontracts work to F, is in marketing association with G – and so on. So complex and ramified are these arrangements, indeed, that the skills of a genealogist rather than an economist might often seem appropriate for their disentanglement.'
6. Bob Eccles and Mark Granovetter have repeatedly made this point to me in personal communications, insisting that all forms of exchange contain elements of networks, markets and hierarchies. Since they are smarter than I, I should listen to them. Nevertheless, I hope to show that there is merit in thinking of networks as an empirically identifiable governance structure.
7. Some economists (Alchian and Demsetz, 1972; Klein, 1983) go so far as to regard the firm as merely a set of explicit and implicit contracts among owners of different factors of production.
8. Many other scholars have their own definitions. Jarillo (1988: 32) defines strategic networks as 'long-term, purposeful arrangements among distinct but related for-profit organizations that allow those firms in them to gain or sustain competitive advantage vis-à-vis their competitors outside the network'. Kaneko and Imai (1987) conceive of networks as a particular form of multi-faceted, inter-organizational relationships through which new information is generated. Johanson and Mattsson (1987) regard networks as a method of dividing labor such that firms are highly dependent upon one another. Coordination is not achieved through hierarchy or markets, but through the interaction and mutual obligation of the firms in the network. Gerlach (1990) suggests that alliances among Japanese firms are an important institutional alternative that links Japanese firms to one another in ways that are fundamentally different from US business practices. Alliances, in his view, are coherent networks of rule-ordered exchange, based on the mutual return of obligations among parties bound in durable relationships.

    I find these various definitions very helpful, but also limited. They all describe networks as a form of dense interorganizational relationships. But networks can also evolve out of personal ties, or market relationships among various parties. Many of the arrangements discussed below, commonly found in the publishing, fashion, computer software, construction and entertainment businesses are among individuals, independent production teams, or very small business units. Thus, my conception of networks is closer to Macneil's (1978, 1985) ideas about relational contracts than to the above views.

9. In an illuminating essay, Keohane (1986: 8) defines reciprocity as exchanges of roughly equivalent values in which the actions of each party are contingent on the prior actions of the others in such a way that good is returned for good, and bad for bad.

10. For example, successful reciprocal ties in scholarly book publishing – between authors and editors or between editors in competing houses – were highly implicit, of long-standing duration, and not strictly balanced (Powell, 1985). It was widely believed that the open-ended quality of the relationship meant that the goods being exchanged – advice, recommendations, or manuscripts – were more valuable and reliable.

11. Parties are, of course, free to exit from a network. But the difficulty of abandoning a relationship around which a unit or a company has structured its operations and expectations can keep a party locked into a relationship that it experiences as unsatisfactory. This problem of domination in networks obviously lends itself to transaction costs discussions of credible commitments.

References

Agnew, J. (1986) *Worlds Apart: The Market and the Theater in Anglo-American Thought, 1550–1750*. New York: Cambridge University Press.

Alchian, A. and Demsetz, H. (1972) 'Production, information costs, and economic organization', *American Economic Review*, 62 (5): 777–95.

Arrow, K. (1974) *The Limits of Organization*. New York: Norton.

Axelrod, R. (1984) *The Evolution of Cooperation*. New York: Basic Books.

Bradach, J.L. and Eccles, R.G. (1989) 'Markets versus hierarchies: From ideal types to plural forms', *Annual Review of Sociology*, 15: 97–118. [Chapter 23 of this Reader.]

Braudel, F. (1982) *The Wheels of Commerce*. New York: Harper & Row.

Coase, R. (1937) 'The nature of the firm', *Economica*, 4: 386–405.

Dalton, M. (1957) *Men Who Manage*. New York: Wiley.

DiMaggio, P. and Powell, W.W. (1983) 'The iron cage revisited: Institutional isomorphism and collective rationality in organizational fields', *American Sociological Review*, 48: 147–60.

Eccles, R. (1985) *The Transfer Pricing Problem: A Theory for Practice*. Lexington, MA: Lexington Books.

Eccles, R.G. and Crane, D. (1987) 'Managing through networks in investment banking', *California Management Review*, 30 (1): 176–95.

Eccles, Robert G. and White, Harrison C. (1986) 'Firm and market interfaces of profit center control', pp. 203–20 in *Approaches in Social Theory*, ed. S. Lindenberg, J.S. Coleman and S. Novak. New York: Russell Sage.

Finley, M. (1973) *The Ancient Economy*. Berkeley: University of California Press.

Geertz, C. (1978) 'The bazaar economy: Information and search in peasant marketing', *American Economic Review*, 68 (2): 28–32.

Gerlach, M.L. (1990) *Alliances and the Social Organization of Japanese Business*. Berkeley: University of California Press.

Goldberg, V.P. (1980) 'Relational exchange: Economics and complex contracts', *American Behavioral Scientist*, 23 (3): 337–52.

Gordon, R.W. (1985) 'Macaulay, Macneil, and the discovery of solidarity and power in contract law', *Wisconsin Law Review*, 3: 565–80.

Gouldner, A. (1960) 'The norm of reciprocity: A preliminary statement', *American Sociological Review*, 25: 161–78.

Graham, M. (1985) 'Corporate research and development: The latest transformation', *Technology in Society*, 7 (2/3): 179–96.

Granovetter, M. (1985) 'Economic action and social structure: A theory of embeddedness', *American Journal of Sociology*, 91 (3): 481–510.

Hannan, M. and Freeman, J.H. (1984) 'Structural inertia and organizational change', *American Sociological Review*, 49: 149–64.

Hayek, F. (1945) 'The use of knowledge in society', *American Economic Review*, 35: 519–30.

Jarillo, J.-C. (1988) 'On strategic networks', *Strategic Management Journal*, 9: 31–41.

Johanson, J. and Mattsson, L.-G. (1987) 'Interorganizational relations in industrial systems: A network approach compared with the transactions-cost approach', *International Studies of Management and Organization*, 18 (1): 34–48 (Chapter 21 of the present book).

Kaneko, I. and Imai, K. (1987) 'A network view of the firm', Paper presented at 1st Hitotsubashi-Stanford conference.

Keohane, R. (1986) 'Reciprocity in international relations', *International Organization*, 40 (1): 1–27.

Klein, B. (1983) 'Contracting costs and residual claims: The separation of ownership and control', *Journal of Law and Economics*, 26: 367–74.

Koenig, C. and Thietart, R.A. (1988) 'Manager, engineers and government', *Technology in Society*, 10: 45–69.

Larson, A. (1988) 'Cooperative alliances: A study of entrepreneurship', PhD. dissertation, Harvard Business School.

Lorenzoni, G. and Ornati, O. (1988) 'Constellations of firms and new ventures', *Journal of Business Venturing*, 3: 41–57.

Loveman, G., Piore, M. and Sengenberger, W. (1987) 'The evolving role of small business in industrial economies', Paper presented at conference on New Developments in Labor Market and Human Resource Policies, Sloan School, MIT.

Luhmann, N. (1979) *Trust and Power*. New York: Wiley.

Macneil, I. (1978) 'Contracts: Adjustment of long-term economic relations under classical, neoclassical, and relational contract law', *Northwestern University Law Review*, 72 (6): 854–905.

Macneil, I. (1985) 'Relational contract: What we do and do not know', *Wisconsin Law Review*, 3: 483–526.

Mauss, M. (1967) *The Gift*. New York: Norton. (First published 1925).

Powell, W.W. (1985) *Getting into Print: The decision making process in scholarly publishing*. Chicago: University of Chicago Press.

Powell, W.W. (1987) 'Hybrid organizational arrangements: New form or transitional development?' *California Management Review*, 30 (1): 67–87.

Richardson, G.B. (1972) 'The organization of industry', *Economic Journal*, 82: 883–96.

Sahlins, M. (1972) *Stone Age Economics*. Chicago: Aldine.

Stinchcombe, A. (1985) 'Contracts as hierarchical documents', pp. 121–71 in A. Stinchombe and C. Heimer, *Organization Theory and Project Management*. Oslo: Norwegian University Press.

Thompson, E.P. (1971) 'The moral economy of the English crowd in the eighteenth century', *Past and Present*, 50: 78–98.

Thorelli, H.B. (1986) 'Networks: Between markets and hierarchies', *Strategic Management Journal*, 7: 37–51.

White, H.C. (1981) 'Where do markets come from?', *American Journal of Sociology*, 87: 517–47.

Williamson, O.E. (1975) *Markets and Hierarchies: Analysis and Antitrust Implications*. New York: Free Press.

Williamson, O.E. (1985) *The Economic Institutions of Capitalism*. New York: Free Press.

23

Price, authority and trust: from ideal types to plural forms

Jeffrey L. Bradach and Robert G. Eccles

A growing body of recent research has documented the variety of ways industry is organized. The sharp delineation of markets and hierarchies offered by Coase (1937) has gradually given way to the widely accepted recognition that myriad organizational forms exist along with markets and hierarchies. In particular, much research has pointed out the existence of stable long-term relationships between independent exchange partners. Cooperative arrangements (Richardson, 1972), relational contracting (Macneil, 1978; Goldberg, 1980), joint ventures (Mariti and Smiley, 1983), quasifirms (Eccles, 1981), global coalitions (Porter and Fuller, 1986), and dynamic networks (Miles and Snow, 1986) are but a few of the names these complex forms go by.

Explaining the existence of these assorted forms usually involves cataloging the deficiencies (or failures) of fully integrated hierarchies and/or competitive markets and then arguing that the new forms solve, or at least mitigate, those problems. A thread weaving its way through the discussions of these complex organizational forms is that they fall *between* markets and hierarchies, defined as ideal types. However, the presumption that a continuum runs from market to hierarchy – with relationships between technologically separable units arraying themselves along it – is misleading, as are the three-fold typologies which simply add a category to the market and hierarchy dichotomy (Ouchi, 1980; Williamson, 1985). These approaches rest on the premiss that market and hierarchy are mutually exclusive means to govern transactions.

There are two major problems with this premiss. First, elements of the ideal types (or the poles of the continuum) are often found mixed together empirically: for instance, features of markets and hierarchies are often combined (Eccles, 1985; Stinchcombe, 1985). Second, markets and hierarchies and 'combinations' are often embedded in or lead to the formation of collateral social structures (Macauley, 1963; Macneil, 1978; Granovetter, 1985). The trust produced by these social structures does not simply replace market and hierarchy: frequently it complements the two forms. While transactions are rarely governed *solely* by market, hierarchy or trust,

---

Adapted from *Annual Review of Sociology* (1989): 97–118.

these mechanisms do serve as the building blocks for the complex social structures so common in organizational life.

This chapter is organized around the three control mechanisms that govern economic transactions between actors: price, authority and trust. In contrast to more conventional approaches to the organization of industry, however, this chapter emphasizes how these control mechanisms are *combined* in empirical situations. The next section reviews the transaction cost economic approach, which represents the most ambitious attempt to explain to what extent companies may choose to integrate their operations. Although it is wedded to the view that markets and hierarchies are at opposite ends of a continuum, transaction cost economics raises many of the central issues that face actors and observers of organizations. The following section explores the relationship between price and authority. Both inside and outside the firm we find the concurrent operation of these two mechanisms. The section on Trust considers trust as a control mechanism. We argue that trust often emanates from social norms and personal relationships, and we examine how these factors affect economic exchanges. Trust can also be found combined with price and authority to govern the economic relations between actors, and those cases are considered in the section on Trust, Price and Authority.

The final section steps back from the explanation of the control mechanisms impinging on single transactions and argues that in some cases the overall *structure of transactions* can affect the management of each transaction. Specifically, we examine *Plural Forms*, where distinct and different control mechanisms in the same organizational structure are operated simultaneously by a company to perform the same function. The dynamics at work in plural forms, such as organizations with both franchises and company-owned units, cannot be fully understood on the basis of analysing single transactions.

Markets and hierarchies

Markets and hierarchies have long been viewed as alternative mechanisms for allocating resources. Coase's (1937) classic article about the origins of markets and hierarchies stands at the center of a research tradition that continues to flourish. [. . .]

Coase's insight has been extended and refined by many scholars, but the basic argument remains the same: transactions will be governed by the institutional arrangement that is most efficient. Williamson (1975, 1985) has led the development of this stream of thought – which has come to be known as the 'transaction cost economics approach' – and his work most fully elaborates on Coase's idea. Williamson (1985) identifies three dimensions of transactions which he and other scholars contend dictate whether markets or hierarchies are most efficient: uncertainty, asset specificity and frequency. These dimensions affect the costs associated with writing, executing and enforcing contracts; when such costs are high, markets fail and hierarchies emerge in their place.

[. . .]

The make-or-buy studies (hierarchy or market) exemplify a core assumption of the transaction cost approach: that markets and hierarchies are mutually exclusive means of allocating resources. That is not to say markets and hierarchies are the only ways to transact business. A growing body of work documents the existence of non-market and non-hierarchical organizational forms – forms typically said to reside between markets and hierarchies (Richardson, 1972; Eccles, 1981; Monteverde and Teece, 1982; Mariti and Smiley, 1983; Williamson, 1985; Powell, 1987). This stream of work highlights the fact that relations between independent exchange partners can be stabilized through formal (e.g. written contracts, 'hostage exchanges') and informal mechanisms (e.g. trust). These arrangements are said to enable firms to: gain access to know-how unavailable in-house; spread the risks associated with uncertain ventures; benefit from economies of scale; enter new product and geographic markets rapidly; manage interorganizational dependencies; and respond quickly and flexibly to changing circumstances (Pfeffer and Nowak, 1976; Porter and Fuller, 1986; Miles and Snow, 1986; Powell, 1987; Johnston and Lawrence, 1988; Ouchi and Bolton, 1988).

Williamson (1981, 1985) attempts to integrate these empirical observations and explanations into the transaction cost approach by arguing that these organizational arrangements are a response to efficiency considerations. He operationalizes this argument by dimensionalizing the transaction cost variables: intermediate levels of uncertainty or asset specificity lead to intermediate forms such as quasi-vertical integration (Monteverde and Teece, 1982). Williamson (1985) tags the middle ground with the name 'relational contracting', representing cases where a contractual market relationship is stable and enduring. [. . .]

Williamson's amendment to the transaction cost framework is a stopgap measure which does little to contain a growing number of empirical anomalies.[1] It is becoming clear that market, hierarchy, and relational contracting are not mutually exclusive control mechanisms. For instance, relational contracts are frequently laced with elements of hierarchy (Corey, 1978; Stinchcombe, 1985). Moreover, markets exhibit traits of hierarchies, and hierarchies display properties of markets (Eccles, 1985; Stinchcombe, 1985; Eccles and White, 1988). These studies and others reviewed in the next three sections suggest that the control mechanisms, price, authority, and trust – which map roughly on to market, hierarchy, and relational contracting – are useful concepts provided we recognize that they are *independent and can be combined with each other in a variety of ways.*

Price and authority

Price and authority in the firm

Nowhere is the explicit mixing of price and authority more visible than in the modern multi-divisional firm. With its profit centers and transfer-pricing schemes, the modern firm is widely recognized as introducing features of markets into hierarchies (Chandler, 1962; Vancil, 1978; Anthony and Dearden, 1980). But a firm's transfer-pricing policies represent more than a simple attempt to create a market in the firm. Eccles (1985) found that transfer-pricing policies ranged from mandating internal exchange on a cost basis to allowing profit centers full exchange autonomy with either inside or outside suppliers. In the former case, authority reigns; in the latter instance, price predominates. Even at the extremes, however, the shadow of the other control mechanism is visible. Eccles and White (1988) dissect the exchange autonomy policy and find that managers have a bias against using internal suppliers. They argue that this bias emanates from the risks associated with transacting with someone in the same hierarchy of authority. In a transaction between two profit centers, if a delivery is late or quality is poor, what had been a market relation can, and managers fear will, move through hierarchical channels to a higher authority.

[. . .]

Mandated internal transfers display the same tension between price and authority. Mandated transactions are usually made at cost or at the prevailing market price. Eccles and White provide several examples of the acrimony between division managers precipitated by disagreements over what the full costs of a product are and what a true market price is. The conflict is exacerbated by managerial reward systems that hinge on divisional performance; one manager's victory is another manager's loss. Nevertheless, mandated transfers are common despite the widely held perception among managers that the transaction costs associated with internal transactions *exceed* those of external transactions. This paradox can be understood if one recognizes how the conflicts over prices and costs play out under the watchful eyes of hierarchical authorities: 'Conflict makes information available to top management that otherwise might not be known or would be difficult or expensive to obtain' (Eccles and White, 1988: S30).

Transfer-pricing policies provide a crystal clear example of how price and authority can be intertwined. [. . .]

Price and authority in the market

Similar forces are often at work in the market. Stinchcombe (1985), Ouchi and Bolton (1988), Pfeffer and Nowak (1976) and Abolafia (1984) offer insights into how price and authority are combined in markets. Their work responds to the occasional admonishment by social scientists that we must not let the theory (and myth) of the self-governing, price-controlled market obscure our understanding of how markets actually function as concrete social structures (Barber, 1977; Coleman, 1984; Baker, 1984; Hirschman, 1986; Leifer and White, 1987).

Stinchcombe (1985) offers a variety of examples – from weapons procurement to North Sea oil refining to franchise relationships in the automobile industry – which illustrate the simultaneous use of authority and price in market transactions. He documents several cases where market exchanges are plagued with many of the transactional liabilities highlighted in the section on Markets and Hierarchies: *ex ante* product specifications do not exist; design and production costs are uncertain; and performance measurement is difficult. Yet he finds contracts between independent agents under these conditio...s.

> A structure with legitimate authority, with a manipulable incentive system, with a method for adjusting costs, quantities, and prices, with a structure for dispute resolution, and with a set of standard operating procedures, looks very much like a hierarchy, very little like a competitive market. Yet all these features of hierarchy are routinely obtained by contracts between firms in some sector of the economy. (1985: 126).

Authority mechanisms are written into contracts and also exist implicitly by virtue of industry practice. Quality control systems, inspection arrangements, and agreements about who has the authority to modify contractual provisions are just a few ways authority impinges on the market. Corey (1978) finds the same forces at work in his detailed study of the procurement process in industrial firms.

Ouchi and Bolton (1988) report that similar mechanisms govern joint research and development efforts in the field of high technology. In this area, the task is often uncertain and complex, and hence contracts are difficult to write and monitor. Nonetheless, interorganizational agreements are a common way to develop new technologies (Mariti and Smiley, 1983; Friar and Horwitch, 1985). Ouchi and Bolton's case studies indicate that the problems associated with the inherent uncertainty and complexity of technological research and development are remedied by 'the close and intimate supervision of a commonly agreed upon hierarchy' (Ouchi and Bolton, 1988: 14). The creation of an independent entity controlled by a separate hierarchy establishes an authority structure (board of directors, specified rules for participation, and so on) which binds together the independent exchange partners. At the same time, the price mechanism is involved, since the independent entity often owns the property produced by the joint effort, and price may be used to allocate that property to the participants.

Pfeffer and Nowak (1976) argue that the use of joint ventures is not confined to organizations attempting to develop new technologies or to undertake new activities. Joint ventures are also used to manage interorganizational interdependence. Pfeffer and Nowak studied 166 joint ventures among manufacturing organizations and participants in the oil and gas extraction industry. They found that firms in interdependent businesses were significantly more likely to form joint ventures than were firms in independent businesses. The authors argue that by introducing elements of authority into the market – by creating a joint venture – companies can ensure continuity with their sources of supply or their customers (symbiotic interdependence), reduce the vigor of price competition (competitive interdependence), or both. Joint ventures are just one of several strategies which can be used by companies to manage their dependence on uncertain environments. [. . .]

Trust

Price and authority are specialized control mechanisms created for and attached to each transaction. There exists, however, a class of more general control mechanisms to which we assign the label *trust*. Gambetta, the editor of a recent collection of essays exploring the concept of trust, delineates what is meant when we say we trust someone: '[W]e implicitly mean that the probability that he will perform an action that is beneficial or at least not detrimental to us is high enough for us to consider engaging in some form of cooperation with him' (Gambetta, 1988: 217). Trust is a type of expectation that alleviates the fear that one's exchange partner will act opportunistically. Of course, the risk of opportunism must be present for trust to operate. [. . .]

Arrow (1974: 23) summarizes the obvious advantages of trust as a control mechanism: 'Trust is an important lubricant of a social system. It is extremely efficient; it saves people a lot of trouble to have a fair degree of reliance on other people's word.' Obtaining the advantages offered by trust, however, is not available to everyone. In a provocative discussion of how modes of trust were transformed around the beginning of this century, Zucker (1986) outlines three different ways trust – 'a set of expectations shared by all those in an exchange' (Zucker, 1986: 54) – is produced. Process-based trust emerges from recurrent transactions; characteristic-based trust rests on social similarity; and institution-based trust is tied to formal social structures. Zucker argues that immigration, internal migration and business instability disrupted the first two modes of trust and led to institutions that produced trust, such as professions, bureaucracies and financial intermediaries. [. . .]

Norms of obligation and cooperation

Experiments on social psychology open the door to questions about the assumption of opportunistic actors. Kahneman *et al.* (1986, 1987) report on experiments and survey research that illustrate the power effect norms of fairness have on economic exchanges. The perceived fairness of price and wage adjustments, for example, was found to be contingent on what respondents understood to be the cause of the adjustments. For instance, raising prices in response to increased demand was perceived to be unfair; in contrast, maintaining prices when costs declined was viewed as being fair. In the next section we discuss one way perceptions of fairness might affect exchange relationships. [. . .]

Macauley's classic article (1963) on how and when contracts are used in business affairs stands at the center of this line of argument. Macauley found that 'businessmen often prefer to rely on "a man's word" in a brief letter, a handshake, or "common honesty and decency" – even where the transaction involves exposure to serious risks' (1963: 58). And even when contracts were used, disputes were rarely litigated. As one businessman said, 'You can settle any dispute if you keep the lawyers and accountants out of it' (1963: 61). The norms Macauley illuminated – keeping commitments and standing behind one's products – impose obligations on parties to transactions, and those obligations are ignored at the peril of damaging one's business reputation or personal friendships, or both.

In line with Macauley's findings, Macneil (1978) outlines a theory of relational contracting predicated on the idea that the maintenance of the relation is paramount. Macneil agrees with transaction cost economists that idiosyncratic investment may lead to a relationship, but he differs with them when he explicates how such relations are governed. He argues that two norms are particularly applicable to relational contracts: '(1) harmonizing conflict within the internal matrix of the relation . . . and (2) preservation of the relation' (1978: 895). The first norm implies that the relation as it has developed – with its shared and often implicit understandings – serves as the reference point for resolving disputes. At the same time, internal resolution of the conflict takes place against a backdrop of broader social norms and the desire of the parties to continue the relationship for both economic and social reasons.

Dore (1983) and Sabel and Zeitlin (1985) report on powerful norms of obligation which stabilize economic relationships in two other settings. Dore describes how the weaving segment of the textile industry in Japan changed from an order dominated by large, vertically integrated mills to a system where the production process is fragmented and coordinated among several independent family businesses. He attributes the success of this system to the presence of 'goodwill' in Japanese trading relationships. Goodwill is defined as the 'sentiments of friendship and the sense of diffuse personal obligation which accrue between individuals engaged in a recurring contractual economic exchange' (1983: 460).

In Japan, trust is engendered by the social norm which insists that business relations are personal relations, *not* by overlapping personal and business ties (the topic of the next section.) Dore identifies a collection of characteristics that work to maintain this norm: the treatment of trading relationships as personal relationships; a recognized personal obligation to maintain the association; a disdain for adversarial relationships; and a long-term outlook. The social norm is further bolstered by extensive financial cross-holdings among firms (Gerlach, 1987). Gerlach (1987: 133) contends that these cross-holdings serve to 'create a structure of stable, mutual relationships among trading partners'.

In Sabel and Zeitlin's detailed argument (1985) about the alternatives to modern mass production, they also place a heavy emphasis on the ethos of the industrial community. They report that around the turn of the century (primarily in Europe) a variety of industries – among them silks, specialty steels, ribbons, and textiles – were either 'confederations of small shops, each specializing in a phase of production' (1985: 148) or 'groupings of artisans' shops under one roof' (1985: 150). The vitality of these industries depended on a constant reshuffling of resources to meet ever-changing consumer demand. Sabel and Zeitlin point to the crucial role political institutions played in this process, but they also emphasize that 'the process of socialization created a community across and within generations that protected the economy as a whole against the consequences of short-term calculations of advantage' (1985: 154).

[. . .]

The norms of obligation and cooperation highlighted in these studies all imply the existence of some sort of community of shared values, whether they reside in a network of business relations (Macauley, 1963), a country (Dore, 1983), a geographically bounded industrial district (Sable and Zeitlin, 1985), or a firm (Ouchi, 1980). Zucker's discussion of characteristic-based trust (1986) rests on this notion explicitly, with social similarity serving as an indicator of trust in her scheme. Determining exactly how trust is produced by such communities is elusive, particularly since trust possesses a self-fulfilling quality: the existence of trust gives one reason to trust (for both social and transaction cost reasons), just as distrust begets distrust. The form of trust illustrated above is often tied to formal structures (for example financial cross-holdings and political institutions) and informal sanctioning mechanisms. Still, regardless of the institutional scaffolding, the studies discussed above demonstrate the ways norms serve as a control mechanism for transactions.

Before moving on to the role of personal relationships in economic life, we will briefly mention an argument for the evolution of cooperation which avoids norms and is based on an assumption of rational egoists. Many writers comment on the role that repeated exchanges play in the emergence of stable cooperative relationships. Axelrod's (1984) imaginative experiment captures the essence of the argument employed by many writers. Axelrod found that in repeated trials of the prisoner's dilemma game, the 'Tit for Tat' strategy – cooperate on the first move and then copy your opponent's previous move – outperformed all other strategies. Axelrod argues that the efficacy of this strategy hinges on the existence of *future* transactions. 'The future can [. . .] cast a shadow back upon the present and thereby affect the current strategic situation' (1984: 12). Rational egoists will cooperate, the argument goes, if future transactions offer benefits that outweigh those available by short-run opportunistic acts.

[. . .]

Personal relationships in economic life

The social norms discussed above are not the only source of trust in economic life. Concrete personal relationships also produce trust. Granovetter (1985: 491) observes that 'networks of social relations penetrate irregularly and in differing degrees in different sectors of economic life'. Where economic transactions are embedded in personal relationships the hazards of opportunism are diminished and the need for elaborate formal governance structures is rendered unnecessary. Ben-Porath (1980) pursues a similar argument and proposes that a continuum exists which places the family (high trust) at one pole and the impersonal market (low trust) at the other pole. Friends, business associates, employers, and employees reside in between the two extremes, and require to varying extents the existence of institutional structures to protect against malfeasance.

[. . .]

Macauley was also aware of the force of personal relationships in economic transactions. The norms he identified (and the informal agreements they enabled) were at least partially attributable to the cross-cutting relationships exchange partners had in other contexts. Macauley enumerated a variety of ways executives in two organizations might know each other: 'They might sit together on government or trade committees. They may know each other socially and even belong to the same country club' (1963: 63). In an interesting twist related to personal ties, Macauley found that some business people objected to elaborate contracts because such planning 'indicates a lack of trust and blunts the demands of friendship, turning a cooperative venture into an antagonistic horsetrade' (1963: 64).

The relationship between sales agents and their customers is a classic example of personal relationships overlapping with business ties. Because salespeople are at the boundary of their organization, they sometimes come to identify more closely with their customers than they do their own company. This fact often leads to the distrust of the salesperson by his or her own organization (Webster, 1984: 53). On top of the ambiguity surrounding organizational identification, salespeople may also develop personal relationships with members of the buying organization. These personal ties solidify the relationship between the buying and selling organizations, because they (presumably) reduce transaction costs as well as enable individuals to maintain valued personal relationships (Webster and Wind, 1972: 15). It is worth noting, however, that the companies employing salespeople frequently view such personal relationships as a threat to their business.[2]

Identifying the existence of trust and specifying how it is produced is a complicated task. Multiple subtle, mutually reinforcing mechanisms provide the basis for trust; norms of obligation, recurrent transactions, and personal relationships often overlap. [. . .] While more questions than answers exist on this topic, it should be clear that the social context as manifested in trust serves as a powerful control mechanism, just as price and authority do.

Trust, price and authority

The previous section focused on the role trust plays in controlling exchanges. Often, though, trust does not work alone; it is intertwined with authority and price. This section begins with an examination of how trust and price play off each other. In an inversion of Granovetter's (1985) embeddedness argument, the research reviewed here indicates that trust is sometimes embedded in the market. The section concludes with a few comments on the relationship between trust and hierarchy.

In Eccles' (1981: 340) study of 26 residential homebuilders, he found that relationships between general contractors and subcontractors were 'stable and continuous over fairly long periods of time and only infrequently established through competitive bidding'. Eccles called this bilateral arrangement the 'quasifirm'. General contractors do not rely on trust alone, however: they periodically test the market and solicit bids from other subcontractors. The fact that relatively low levels of asset specificity characterize these transactions makes switching subcontractors fairly easy. At the same time, the presence of market prices also *facilitates* the development of trust and enables the creation of stable exchange relationships.
    [. . .]
The trust–price control mechanism has recently received increased attention. Several contemporary observers of organizational life have noted (and advocated) the use of loose collections of independent firms, tied together by mutual understandings, to produce and market products (Miles and Snow, 1986; Johnston and Lawrence, 1988). These confederations are sometimes born out of the disaggregation of fully integrated firms (Dore, 1983; Mariotti and Cainarca, 1986), and sometimes they emerge out of the reconfiguration of former market relationships (Powell, 1987; Johnston and Lawrence, 1988). In almost all of these studies, mutual dependence between exchange partners is said to promote trust. This contrasts sharply with the argument central to transaction cost economics that bilateral monopoly (i.e. dependence) fosters opportunistic behavior (Williamson, 1985). Mutual dependence, however, is rarely complete in these situations: two or three suppliers may replace ten or fifteen, for example. Options remain. Trust and price are joined.
    [. . .]
While this section has emphasized price-trust mechanisms, authority and trust also are mixed in the empirical world. One of the greatest contributions

sociology has made to our understanding of organizations is its illumination of informal groups. These trust-bound groups are sometimes provoked by authority and serve to impede production (Roethlisberger and Dickson, 1939; Burawoy, 1979), while at other times they may work with authority to govern transactions (Walton and Hackman, 1986). Although it is beyond the scope of this chapter to delve into the mammoth literature on informal groups, it is important to note that trust and authority are also mixed.

Plural forms

The previous sections show how viewing price, authority, and trust as separate but often intertwined control mechanisms enhances our understanding of inter- and intra-organizational control. For the most part, this perspective emphasizes the ways individual transactions and individual relationships are controlled. Such a micro focus, though, misses subtle and important features of the macro structure which affect individual transactions.

This final section examines how transactions are embedded in a context of *other transactions*, as well as in a social context. Specifically, we consider 'plural forms' – an arrangement where distinct organizational control mechanisms are operated simultaneously for *the same function* by *the same firm*. For example, companies often make and buy the same part; companies frequently franch e units and own units in the same restaurant or hotel chain; and companies sometimes use a direct sales force and third party distributors. As these examples indicate, plural forms are comprised of two distinct control mechanisms. In the case of making and buying parts, authority and price are juxtaposed; with franchise units and company-owned units, a hybrid price-authority mechanism (franchise) is coupled with an authority mechanism. While most investigations of these mechanisms have focused on explaining how transactions are assigned to one mechanism or the other (typically by establishing which mechanism is more efficient), this section emphasizes how transactions controlled by one mechanism are profoundly affected by the simultaneous use of an alternative control mechanism.

The forces at work in plural forms are alluded to in Walker and Weber's thorough study (1984) of make-or-buy decisions in the automobile industry.

[. . .] They suggest that: 'a cyclical pattern for complex components may be found in which components are brought into the firm so it can gain production experience and reduce uncertainty and then are shifted back to the market when contracting hazards can be managed' (1984: 389).

The same benefits can be obtained by operating the two forms *simultaneously* and playing them off one another. When a company makes as well as buys, it not only possesses information it can use to manage the subcontractor (or franchisee), but the ideas and innovations of the subcontractor can be brought to bear on the company's business. Harrigan (1984: 643) applies the term 'taper integration' to a similar organizational form: 'when firms are backward or forward integrated but rely on outsiders for a portion of their supplies or distribution'. She emphasizes the role such arrangements play in balancing economies of scale in the value chain and in reducing a company's vulnerability to strikes and shortages; she also recognizes that such forms open up a new avenue of information about competitors' activities.

A hidden dimension of the plural form, however, and one we believe is crucial, is the control it affords to the managers of companies. They can use it to employ a racheting strategy where management and technical innovations generated by one mechanism can be borrowed and utilized by participants controlled by the other mechanism. Relying solely on an arm's-length contractual arrangement *or* on an authority structure presents obvious difficulties. As Walker and Weber (1984) point out, contracting is problematic without in-house experience, and the maladies associated with hierarchy are widely recognized. The remedy for these difficulties may be the simultaneous use of the two mechanisms, creating in essence competition between them. [. . .]

Franchising is an excellent example of the plural form. Almost all franchise systems are composed of company-owned units and franchise units. The company-owned units are managed in a hierarchical authority structure. Within this authority structure, profit centers and management incentive programs introduce some elements of a price control mechanism. In contrast, the franchise-owned units are managed by independent business people who have signed long-term contracts with the company. The franchisee usually pays a flat fee up front and then pays a fixed percentage of revenue generated by the unit to the company: in the language of agency theory, the franchisee is the residual claimant of the revenue (and profit) stream. It is important to note that franchisees are not fully independent entrepreneurs; hierarchical authority governs many of their activities. The contracts franchisees sign typically specify in great detail the manner in which the franchise is to be run in order to protect the value of the trademark.

These two distinct control mechanisms are used by most companies engaged in franchising. For example, McDonald's own 2280 of its units and franchises 7274 units; Pizza Hut owns 2660 and franchises 2603; Sheraton Inns owns 148 hotels and franchises 335; Holiday Inns owns 204 hotels and franchises 1420 ('Ninth Annual Franchise 500'. *Entrepreneur*, January 1988). Soft drink bottlers, food stores, and a variety of service businesses, among others, follow this same plural form structure.

Explanations for the plural form in franchising have focused on the differing abilities of company-owned and franchised units to inhibit opportunism and to operate efficiently (Caves and Murphy, 1976; Rubin, 1978; Brickly and Dark, 1987). The assumptions guiding this work are that company-owned units provide to the company the entire profit stream, but such units suffer the liability that managers will shirk unless monitored. In contrast, franchisees, it is argued, operate efficiently because they have a piece of the pie, although they too must be monitored to ensure they do not degrade the trademark, or they must be located in places with repeat customers so that they internalize the costs of their opportunistic actions. While these explanations certainly have some merit, they are able to explain only a modest amount of the variance in these forms. The other commonsense explanation – that the need for capital early in a company's life leads to franchising – is belied by the large number of financially vigorous firms that continue to franchise, as well as by the fact that acquiring capital from the relatively undiversified portfolios of prospective franchisees may be an expensive way to generate funds (Rubin, 1978).

[. . .]

We hypothesize that in many cases *either* mechanism will work and the choice of mechanism is primarily a function of the vagaries of circumstance – who comes up with the idea for a new site, who has cash, whether qualified managers are available, and so forth. Accordingly, interpreting the choice of a control mechanism for a specific site as a rational response to efficiency or control considerations may reveal little about the dynamics at work in these structures. While much more research needs to be done on these structures, we suspect that the contours of these systems (for example the number of franchise and company-owned units) are a product of microlevel decisions (which may be fairly idiosyncratic) and macrolevel strategic objectives which are at least in part driven by senior management's recognition of the indirect control afforded by plural forms.

[. . .]

Make-or-buy decisions and franchises are only the most obvious examples of the plural form. Along similar lines, many companies simultaneously employ a direct salesforce and utilize third-party distributors (Anderson and Schmittlein, 1984). There is anecdotal evidence that state and local governments are finding arrangements that mix public and private services more effective than those that rely fully on privatized services (Uchitelle, 1988). These examples beg for an analysis of the dynamics that accompany the transactional architecture taken as a whole. In many cases, microanalytic approaches miss important features of these structures.

Conclusion

The ideal types of market and hierarchy serve as a useful starting point for studying the organization of industry. The assumption that these mechanisms are mutually exclusive, however, obscures rather than clarifies our understanding. As this review has shown, price, authority and trust are combined with each other in assorted ways in the empirical world.

The combinations of control mechanisms discussed in this chapter have been characterized as overlapping, embedded, intertwined, juxtaposed and nested. These descriptions were not intended as strict categories, but instead suggest that researchers need to embrace the subtlety and complexity of economic and social control mechanisms. Much of the complexity results because only occasionally are control mechanisms created on 'greenfield' sites. Typically, control mechanisms are grafted on to and leveraged off existing social structures. The installation of price mechanisms in hierarchies (Eccles, 1985) and the functioning of business relationships in industrial communities (Sabel and Zeitlin, 1985) are examples of this.

The most sophisticated mixture of control mechanisms can be seen in the plural form. Here, two distinct control mechanisms are operated simultaneously by the same company. To understand the plural form, the analytic focus must be moved away from exclusive attention to individual transactions; instead, the dynamics of whole structures must be examined since the transactional context affects the control that can be brought to bear on individual transactions. It is worth noting that matrix structures are a close cousin to the plural form. They are similar in that both are built on distinct control mechanisms, with matrix structures based on dual authority mechanisms; they differ because in matrix structures the mechanisms intersect while in plural forms the mechanisms run in parallel. In both cases, individual transactions are inextricably tied to the larger architecture of control mechanisms.

[. . .]

Notes

1. For more extensive critiques of the transaction cost approach, see Perrow (1986) and Oberschall and Leifer (1986).
2. Granovetter (1985: 492) makes the important point that 'Both enormous trust and enormous malfeasance . . . may follow from personal relations.' Malfeasance is tied to personal relations in two main ways. First, trusting a person may leave you more vulnerable to their opportunistic behavior (although the opportunistic actor probably has only one chance to benefit from this situation). Second, malfeasance is often dependent on the efforts of a group, which is bound together by trust.

References

Abolafia, M. (1984) 'Structured anarchy: formal organization in the commodities futures market.' In *The Social Dynamics of Financial Markets*, ed. P. Adler, Greenwich, Conn: JAI.

Anderson, E. Schmittlein, D. (1984) 'Integration of the sales force: an empirical examination.' *Rand J. Econ.* 15: 385–95.

Anthony, R., Dearden, J. (1980) *Management Control Systems*. Homewood. Ill: Irwin. 4th edn.

Arrow, K. (1974) *The Limits of Organization*. New York: Norton.

Axelrod, R. (1984) *The Evolution of Cooperation*. New York: Basic.

Baker, W. (1984) 'The social structure of a national securities market.' *Am. J. Sociol.* 89: 775–811.

Barber, B. (1977) 'Absolutization of the market.' In *Markets and Morals*, ed. G. Dworkin, G. Bermant, P. Brown. New York: Wiley.

Ben-Porath, Y. (1980) 'The f-connection: families, friends, and firms and the organization of exchange.' *Popul. Dev. Rev.* 6: 1–30.

Brickley, J., Dark, F. (1987) 'The choice of organizational form: the case of franchising.' *J. Financ. Econ.* 18: 401–20.

Burawoy, M. (1979) *Manufacturing Consent*. Chicago: Univ. Chicago Press.

Caves, R., Murphy, W. (1976) 'Franchising: firms, markets, and intangible assets.' *S. Econ. J.* 42: 572–86.

Chandler, A.D. (1962) *Strategy and Structure: Chapters in the History of the American Industrial Enterprise*. Cambridge. Mass: MIT Press.

Coase, R. (1937) 'The nature of the firm.' *Economica* 4: 386–405.

Coleman, J. (1984) 'Introducing social structure into economic analysis.' *Am. Econ. Rev.* 74: 84–8.

Corey, R. (1978) *Procurement Management: Strategy, Organization, and Decision-Making*. Boston: CBI.

Dore, R. (1983) 'Goodwill and the spirit of market capitalism.' *Br. J. Sociol.* 34: 459–82.

Eccles, R. (1981) 'The quasifirm in the construction industry.' *J. Econ. Behav. Organ.* 2: 335–57.

Eccles, R. (1985) *The Transfer Pricing Problem: A Theory for Practice*. Lexington, Mass: Lexington.

Eccles, R., White, H. (1988) 'Price and authority in inter-profit center transactions.' *Am. J. Sociol. Suppl.* 94: S17–S51.

Friar, J., Horwitch, M. (1985) 'The emergence of technology strategy.' *Technol. Soc.* 7: 143–178.

Gambetta, D. (1988) 'Can we trust trust?' In *Trust: Making and Breaking Cooperative Relations*, ed. D. Gambetta. New York: Blackwell.

Gerlach, M. (1987) 'Business alliances and the strategy of the Japanese firm.' *Calif. Mgmt. Rev.* 30.

Goldberg, V. (1980) 'Relational exchange: economics and complex contracts.' *Am. Behav. Sci.* 23: 337–52.

Granovetter, M. (1985) 'Economic action and social structure: the problem of embeddedness.' *Am. J. Sociol.* 91: 481–510.

Harrigan, K. (1984) 'Formulating vertical integration strategies.' *Acad. Mgmt. Rev.* 9: 638–52.

Hirschman, A. (1986) *Rival Views of Market Society*. New York: Viking Penguin.

Johnston, R., Lawrence, P. (1988) 'Beyond vertical integration – the rise of the value-adding partnership.' *Harvard Bus. Rev.* 88: 94–104.

Kahneman, D., Knetsch, J., Thaler, R. (1986) 'Fairness as a constraint on profit-seeking: entitlements in the market.' *Am. Econ. Rev.* 76: 728–41.

Kahneman, D., Knetsch, J., Thaler, R. (1987), 'Fairness and the assumptions of economics.' In *Rational Choice*. ed. R. Hogarth, M. Reder. Chicago: Univ. Chicago Press.

Leifer, E., White, H. (1987) 'A structural approach to markets.' In *The Structural Analysis of Business*, ed., M. Mizruchi, M. Schwartz. Cambridge: Cambridge Univ. Press.

Macauley, S. (1963) 'Non-contractual relations in business: a preliminary study.' *Am. Sociol. Rev.* 28: 55–67.

Macneil, I. (1978) 'Contracts: adjustment of long-term economic relations under classical, neo-classical, and relational contract law.' *Northwestern Law Rev.* 72: 854–906.

Mariotti, S., Cainarca, G. (1986) 'The evolution of transaction governance in the textile clothing industry.' *J. Econ. Behav. Organ.* 7: 351–74.

Mariti, P., Smiley, R. (1983) 'Co-operative agreements and the organization of industry.'

J. Ind. Econ. 31: 437–51.

Miles, R., Snow, C. (1986) 'Organizations: new concepts for new forms.' *Calif. Mgmt. Rev.* 28: 62–73.

Monteverde, K., Teece, D. (1982) 'Appropriable rents and quasi-vertical integration.' *J. Law Econ.* 25: 321–28.

Oberschall, A., Leifer, E. (1986) 'Efficiency and social institutions: uses and misuses of economic reasoning in sociology.' *Ann. Rev. Sociol.* 12: 233–53.

Ouchi, W. (1980) 'Markets, bureaucracies, and clans.' *Admin. Sci. Q.* 25: 129–41.

Ouchi, W., Bolton, M. (1988) 'The logic of joint research and development.' *Calif. Mgmt. Rev.* 30: 9–33.

Perrow, C. (1986) *Complex Organizations: A Critical Essay.* New York: Random House. 3rd edn.

Pfeffer, J., Nowak, P. (1976) 'Joint ventures and interorganizational interdependence.' *Admin. Sci. Q.* 21: 398–418.

Porter, M., Fuller, M. (1986) 'Coalitions and global strategy.' In *Competition in Global Industries*, ed., M. Porter. Boston: Harvard Bus. School Press.

Powell, W. (1987) 'Hybrid organizational arrangements: new forms or transitional development.' *Calif. Mgmt. Rev.* 30.

Richardson, G. (1972) 'The organization of industry.' *Econ. J.* 82: 883–96.

Roethlisberger, F., Dickson, W. (1939) *Management and the Worker.* Cambridge, Mass: Harvard Univ. Press.

Rubin, P. (1978) 'The theory of the firm and the structure of the franchise contract.' *J. Law Econ.* 21: 223–33.

Sabel, C., Zeitlin, J. (1985) 'Historical alternatives to mass production: politics, markets and technology in nineteenth-century industrialization.' *Past & Present* 108: 133–76.

Stinchcombe, A. (1985) 'Contracts as hierarchical documents.' In *Organization Theory and Project Management*, ed. A. Stinchcombe, C. Heimer. Bergen, Norway: Norwegian Univ. Press.

Uchitelle, L. (1988) 'Public services found better if private agencies compete.' *New York Times*, April 26, p. 1.

US Department of Commerce (1987) *Franchising in the Economy 1985–1987.* United States General Post Office.

Vancil, R. (1978) *Decentralization: Managerial Ambiguity by Design.* Homewood, Ill: Irwin.

Walker, G., Weber, D. (1984) 'A transaction cost approach to make-or-buy decisions.' *Admin. Sci. Q.* 29: 373–91.

Walton, R., Hackman, R. (1986) 'Groups under contrasting management strategies.' In *Designing Effective Work Groups*, ed. P. Goodman. San Francisco: Jossey-Bass.

Webster, F. (1984) *Industrial Marketing Strategy.* New York: Wiley, 2nd edn.

Webster, F., Wind, Y. (1972) *Organizational Buying Behavior.* Englewood Cliffs, NJ: Prentice-Hall.

Williamson, O. (1975) *Markets and Hierarchies: Analysis and Anti-Trust Implications.* New York: Free Press.

Williamson, O. (1981) 'The economics of organization: the transaction cost approach.' *Am. J. Sociol.* 87: 548–77.

Williamson, O. (1985) *The Economic Institutions of Capitalism.* New York: Free Press.

Zucker, L. (1986) 'Production of trust: institutional sources of economic structure, 1840–1920.' In *Res. Organ. Behav.* 8: 53–111.

24

Spontaneous ('grown') order and organized ('made') order

Frederick von Hayek

By *'order'* we shall throughout describe *a state of affairs in which a multiplicity of elements of various kinds are so related to each other that we may learn from our acquaintance with some spatial or temporal part of the whole to form correct expectations concerning the rest, or at least expectations which have a good chance of proving correct*. It is clear that every society must in this sense possess an order and that such an order will often exist without having been deliberately created.

[. . .]

Living as members of society and dependent for the satisfaction of most of our needs on various forms of cooperation with others, we depend for the effective pursuit of our aims clearly on the correspondence of the expectations concerning the actions of others on which our plans are based with what they will really do. This matching of the intentions and expectations that determine the actions of different individuals is the form in which order manifests itself in social life; and it will be the question of how such an order does come about that will be our immediate concern. The first answer to which our anthropomorphic habits of thought almost inevitably lead us is that it must be due to the design of some thinking mind. And because order has been generally interpreted as such a deliberate *arrangement* by somebody, the concept has become unpopular among most friends of liberty and has been favoured mainly by authoritarians. According to this interpretation order in society must rest on a relation of command and obedience, or a hierarchical structure of the whole of society in which the will of superiors, and ultimately of some single supreme authority, determines what each individual must do.

This authoritarian connotation of the concept of order derives, however, entirely from the belief that order can be treated only by forces outside the system (or 'exogenously'). It does not apply to an equilibrium set up from within (or 'endogenously') such as that which the general theory of the market endeavours to explain. A spontaneous order of this kind has in many respects properties different from those of a made order.

Adapted from N. Modlovsky (ed.) *Order – With or Without Design?* (London: Centre for Research into Communist Economies, 1989), pp. 101–23.

Two sources of order

The study of spontaneous orders has long been the peculiar task of economic theory, although, of course, biology has from its beginning been concerned with that special kind of spontaneous order which we call an organism. Only recently has there arisen within the physical sciences under the name of cybernetics a special discipline which is also concerned with what are called self-organizing or self-generating systems.

The distinction of this kind of order from one which has been made by somebody putting the elements of a set in their places or directing their movements is indispensable for any understanding of the processes of society as well as for all social policy. There are several terms available for describing each kind of order. The made order which we have already referred to as an exogenous order or an arrangement may again be described as a construction, an artificial order or, especially where we have to deal with a directed social order, as an *organization*. The grown order, on the other hand, which we have referred to as a self-generating or endogenous order, is in English most conveniently described as a *spontaneous order*. Classical Greek was more fortunate in possessing distinct single words for the two kinds of order, namely *taxis* for a made order, such as, for example, an order of battle, and *kosmos* for a grown order, meaning originally 'a right order in a state or a community'. We shall occasionally avail ourselves of these Greek words as technical terms to describe the two kinds of order.

It would be no exaggeration to say that social theory begins with – and has an object only because of – the discovery that there exist orderly structures which are the product of the action of many men but are not the result of human design. In some fields this is now universally accepted. Although there was a time when men believed that even language and morals had been 'invented' by some genius of the past, everybody recognizes now that they are the outcome of a process of evolution whose results nobody foresaw or designed. But in other fields many people still treat with suspicion the claim that the patterns of interaction of many men can show an order that is of nobody's deliberate making; in the economic sphere, in particular, critics still pour uncomprehending ridicule on Adam Smith's expression of the 'invisible hand' by which, in the language of his time, he described how man is led 'to promote an end which was no part of his intentions'. If indignant reformers still complain of the chaos of economic affairs, insinuating a complete absence of order, this is partly because they cannot conceive of an order which is not deliberately made, and partly because to them an order means something aiming at concrete purposes which is, as we shall see, what a spontaneous order cannot do.
[. . .]

In any group of men of more than the smallest size, collaboration will always rest both on spontaneous order as well as on deliberate organization. There is no doubt that for many limited tasks organization is the most powerful method of effective coordination because it enables us to adapt the resulting order much more fully to our wishes, while where, because of the complexity of the circumstances to be taken into account, we must rely on the forces making for a spontaneous order, our power over the particular contents of this order is necessarily restricted.

That the two kinds of order will regularly coexist in every society of any degree of complexity does not mean, however, that we can combine them in any manner we like. What in fact we find in all free societies is that, although groups of men will join in organizations for the achievement of some particular ends, the coordination of the activities of all these separate organizations, as well as of the separate individuals, is brought about by the forces making for a spontaneous order. The family, the farm, the plant, the firm, the corporation and the various associations, and all the public institutions including government, are organizations which in turn are integrated into a more comprehensive spontaneous order. It is advisable to reserve the term 'society' for this spontaneous overall order so that we may distinguish it from all the organized smaller groups which will exist within it, as well as from such smaller and more or less isolated groups as the horde, the tribe, or the clan, whose members will at least in some respects act under a central direction for common purposes. [. . .]

Of the organizations existing within the Great Society one which regularly occupies a very special position will be that which we call government. Although it is conceivable that the spontaneous order which we call society may exist without government, if the minimum of rules required for the formation of such an order is observed without an organized apparatus for their enforcement, in most circumstances the organization which we call government becomes indispensable in order to ensure that those rules are obeyed.

This particular function of government is somewhat like that of a maintenance squad of a factory, its object being not to produce any particular services or products to be consumed by the citizens, but rather to see that the mechanism which regulates the production of those goods and services is kept in working order. The purposes for which this machinery is currently being used will be determined by those who operate its parts and in the last resort by those who buy its products.

The same organization that is charged with keeping in order an operating structure which the individuals will use for their own purposes, will, however, in addition to the task of enforcing the rules on which that order rests, usually be expected also to render other services which the spontaneous order cannot produce adequately. These two distinct functions of government are usually not clearly separated; yet, as we shall see, the distinction between the coercive functions in which government enforces rules of conduct, and its service functions in which it need merely administer resources placed at its disposal, is of fundamental importance. In the second it is one organization among many and like the others part of a spontaneous overall order, while in the first it provides an essential condition for the preservation of that overall order.

The rules of spontaneous order and the rules of organization

One of our chief contentions will be that, though spontaneous order and organization will always coexist, it is still not possible to mix these two principles of order in any manner we like. If this is not more generally understood it is due to the fact that for the determination of both kinds of order we have to rely on rules, and the important differences between the kinds of rules which the two different kinds of order require are generally not recognized.

To some extent every organization must rely also on rules and not only on specific commands. The reason here is the same as that which makes it necessary for a spontaneous order to rely solely on rules: namely that by guiding the actions of individuals by rules rather than specific commands it is possible to make use of knowledge which nobody possesses as a whole. Every organization in which the members are not mere tools of the organizer will determine by commands only the function to be performed by each member, the purposes to be achieved, and certain general aspects of the methods to be employed, and will leave the detail to be decided by the individuals on the basis of their respective knowledge and skills.

Organization encounters here the problem which any attempt to bring order into complex human activities meets: the organizer must wish the individuals who are to cooperate to make use of knowledge that he himself does not possess. In none but the most simple kind of organization is it conceivable that all the details of all activities are governed by a single mind. Certainly nobody has yet succeeded in deliberately arranging all the activities that go on in a complex society. If anyone did ever succeed in fully organizing such a society, it would no longer make use of many minds but would be altogether dependent on one mind; it would certainly not be very complex but extremely primitive – and so would soon be the mind whose knowledge and will determined everything. [. . .]

What distinguishes the rules which will govern action within an organization is that they must be rules for the performance of assigned tasks. They presuppose that the place of each individual in fixed structure is determined by command and that the rules each individual must obey depend on the place which he has been assigned and on the particular ends which have been indicated for him by the commanding authority. The rules will thus regulate merely the detail of the action of appointed functionaries or agencies of government.

Rules of organization are thus necessarily subsidiary to commands, filling in the gaps left by the commands. Such rules will be different for the different members of the organization according to the different roles which have been assigned to them, and they will have to be interpreted in the light of the purposes determined by the commands. Without the assignment of a function and the determination of the ends to be pursued by particular commands, the bare abstract rule would not be sufficient to tell each individual what he must do.

By contrast, the rules governing a spontaneous order must be independent of purpose and be the same, if not necessarily for all members, at least for whole classes of members not individually designated by name. They must, as we shall see, be rules applicable to an unknown and indeterminable number of persons and instances. They will have to be applied by the individuals in the light of their respective knowledge and purposes; and their application will be independent of any common purpose, which the individual need not even know.

[. . .] In the most complex types of organizations, indeed, little more than the assignment of particular functions and the general aim will be determined by command of the supreme authority, while the performance of these functions will be regulated only by rules – yet by rules which at least to some degree are specific to the functions assigned to particular persons. Only when we pass from the biggest kind of organization, government, which as organization must still be dedicated to a circumscribed and determined set of specific purposes, to the overall order of the whole of society, do we find an order which relies solely on rules and is entirely spontaneous in character.

It is because it was not dependent on organization but grew up as a spontaneous order that the structure of modern society has attained that degree of complexity which it possesses and which far exceeds any that could have been achieved by deliberate organization. In fact, of course, the rules which made the growth of this complex order possible were initially not designed in expectation of that result; but those people who happened to adopt suitable rules developed a complex civilization which then often spread to others. To maintain that we must deliberately plan modern society because it has become so complex is therefore paradoxical, and the result of a complete misunderstanding of these circumstances. The fact is, rather, that we can preserve an order of such complexity not by the method of directing the members, but only indirectly by enforcing and improving the rules conducive to the formation of a spontaneous order.

We shall see that it is impossible, not only to replace the spontaneous order by organization and at the same time to utilize as much of the dispersed knowledge of all its members as possible, but also to improve or correct this order by interfering in it by direct commands. Such a combination of spontaneous order and organization it can never be rational to adopt. While it is sensible to supplement the commands determining an organization by subsidiary rules, and to use organizations as elements of a spontaneous order, it can never be advantageous to supplement the rules governing a spontaneous order by isolated and subsidiary commands concerning those activities where the actions are guided by the general rules of conduct. This is the gist of the argument against 'interference' or 'intervention' in the market order. The reason why such isolated commands requiring specific actions by members of the spontaneous order can never improve but must disrupt that order is that they will refer to a part of a system of interdependent actions determined by information and guided by purposes known only to the several acting persons but not to the directing authority. The spontaneous order arises from each element balancing all the various factors operating on it and by adjusting all its various actions to each other, a balance which will be destroyed if some of the actions are determined by another agency on the basis of different knowledge and in the service of different ends.

What the general argument against 'interference' thus amounts to is that, although we can endeavour to improve a spontaneous order by revising the general rules on which it rests, and can supplement its results by the efforts of various organizations, we cannot improve the results by specific commands that deprive its members of the possibility of using their knowledge for their purposes.

[. . .]

The market order or catallaxy

[. . .] It is necessary now to examine more fully the special attributes possessed by the order of the market and the nature of the benefits we owe to it. This order serves our ends not merely, as all order does, by guiding us in our actions and bringing about a certain correspondence between the expectations of the different persons, but also, in a sense which we must now make more precise, by increasing the prospects or chances of every one of a greater command over the various goods (that is, commodities and services) than we are able to secure in any other way. We shall see, however, that this manner oᶠ coordinating individual actions will secure a high degree of coincidence of expectations and an effective utilization of the knowledge and skills of the several members only at the price of a constant disappointment of some expectations. [. . .] Since the name 'catallactics' has long ago been suggested for the science which deals with the market order and has more recently been revived, it would seem appropriate to adopt a corresponding term for the market order itself. The term 'catallactics' was derived from the Greek verb *katallattein* (or *katallassein*) which meant, significantly, not only 'to exchange' but also 'to admit into the community' and 'to change from enemy into friend'. From it the adjective 'catallactic' has been derived to serve in the place of 'economic' to describe the kind of phenomena with which the science of catallactics deals. The ancient Greeks knew neither this term nor had a corresponding noun; if they had formed one it would probably have been *katallaxia*. From this we can form an English term *catallaxy* which we shall use to describe the order brought about by the mutual adjustment of many individual economies in a market. A catallaxy is thus the special kind of spontaneous order produced by the market through people acting within the rules of the law of property, tort and contract.

[. . .]

The suggestion that in this wide sense the only ties which hold the whole of a Great Society together are purely 'economic' (more precisely 'catallactic') arouses great emotional resistance. Yet the fact can hardly be denied; nor the fact that, in a society of the dimensions and complexity of a modern country or of the world, it can hardly be otherwise. Most people are still reluctant to accept the fact that it should be the disdained 'cash-nexus' which holds the Great Society together, that the great ideal of the unity of mankind should in the last resort depend on the relations between the parts being governed by the striving for the better satisfaction of their material needs.

It is of course true that within the overall framework of the Great Society there exist numerous networks of other relations that are in no sense economic. But this does not alter the fact that it is the market order which makes peaceful reconciliation of the divergent purposes possible – and possible by a process which rebounds to the benefit of all. That interdependence of all men, which is now in everybody's mouth and which tends to make all mankind One World, not only is the effect of the market order but could not have been brought about by any other means. What today connects the life of any European or American with what happens in Australia, Japan or Zaire are repercussions transmitted by the network of market relations. This is clearly seen when we reflect how little, for instance, all the technological possibilities of transportation and communication would matter if the conditions of production were the same in all the different parts of the world.

The benefits from the knowledge which others possess, including all the advances of science, reach us through channels provided and directed by the market mechanism. Even the degree to which we can participate in the aesthetic or moral strivings of men in other parts of the world we owe to the economic nexus. [. . .] The truth is that catallactics is the science which describes the only overall order that comprehends nearly all mankind, and that the economist is therefore entitled to insist that conduciveness to that order be accepted as a standard by which all particular institutions are judged.

It is, however, a misunderstanding to represent this as an effort to make 'economic ends' prevail over others. There are, in the last resort, no economic ends. The economic efforts of the individuals as well as the services which the market order renders to them, consist in an allocation of means for the competing ultimate purposes which are always non-economic. The task of all economic activity is to reconcile the competing ends by deciding for which of them the limited means are to be used. The market order reconciles the claims of the different non-economic ends by the only known process that benefits all – without, however, assuring that the more important comes before the less important, for the simple reason that there can exist in such a system no single ordering of needs. What it tends to bring about is merely a state of affairs in which no need is served at the cost of withdrawing a greater amount of means from the use for other needs than is necessary to satisfy it. The market is the only known method by which this can be achieved without an agreement on the relative importance of the different ultimate ends, and solely on the basis of a principle of reciprocity through which the opportunities of any person are likely to be greater than they would otherwise be.

[. . .]

The game of catallaxy

The best way to understand how the operation of the market system leads not only to the creation of an order, but also to a great increase of the return which men receive from their efforts, is to think of it as a game which we may now call the game of catallaxy. It is a wealth-creating game (and not what game theory calls a zero-sum game), that is, one that leads to an increase of the stream of goods and of the prospects of all participants to satisfy their needs, but which retains the character of a game in the sense in which the term is defined by the *Oxford English Dictionary*: 'a contest played according to rules and decided by superior skill, strength or good fortune'. The outcome of this game for each will, because of its very character, necessarily be determined by a mixture of skill and chance.

The chief cause of the wealth-creating character of the game is that the returns of the efforts of each player act as the signs which enable him to contribute to the satisfaction of needs of which he does not know, and to do so by taking advantage of conditions of which he also learns only indirectly through their being reflected in the prices of the factors of production which they use. It is thus a wealth-producing game because it supplies to each player information which enables him to provide for needs of which he has no direct knowledge and by the use of means of the existence of which without it he would have no cognizance, thus bringing about the satisfaction of a greater range of needs than would otherwise be possible.

[. . .]

There is no need morally to justify specific distributions (of income or wealth) which have not been brought about deliberately but are the outcome of a game that is played because it improves the chances of all. In such a game nobody 'treats' people differently and it is entirely consistent with respecting all people equally that the outcome of the game for different people is very different. It would also be as much a gamble what the effects of any one man's efforts would be worth if they were directed by a planning authority, only that not his knowledge but that of the authority would be used in determining the success or failure of his efforts.

The sum of information reflected or precipitated in the prices is wholly the product of competition, or at least of the openness of the market to anyone who has relevant information about some source of demand or supply for the good in question. Competition operates as a discovery procedure not only by giving anyone who has the opportunity to exploit special circumstances the possibility to do so profitably, but also by conveying to the other parties the information that there is some such opportunity. It is by this conveying of information in coded form that the competitive efforts of the market game secure the utilization of widely dispersed knowledge.

[. . .]

The effect of all this is thus that, while the share of each factor of production in the total output is determined by the instrumental necessities of the only known process by which we can secure a steady approach to that horizon, the material equivalent of any given individual share will be as large as it can possibly be made. In other words, while the share of each player in the game of catallaxy will be determined partly by skill and partly by chance, the content of the share which is allocated to him by that mixed game of chance and skill will be a true maximum.

It would, of course, be unreasonable to demand more from the operation of a system in which the several actors do not serve a common hierarchy of ends but cooperate with each other only because they can thereby mutually assist each other in their respective pursuit of their individual ends. Nothing else is indeed possible in an order in which the participants are free in the sense of being allowed to use their own knowledge for their own purposes. So long as the game is played by which alone all this knowledge can be utilized and all these ends taken into account it would be inconsistent and unjust to divert some part of the stream of goods to some group of players whom some authority thinks deserves it. On the other hand, in a centrally directed system, it would be impossible to reward people in accordance with the value which their voluntary contributions have to their fellows, because, without an effective market, the individuals could neither know, nor be allowed to decide, where to apply their efforts. The responsibility for the use of his gifts and the usefulness of the results would rest entirely with the directing authority.

Men can be allowed to act on their own knowledge and for their own purposes only if the reward they obtain is dependent in part on circumstances which they can neither control nor foresee. And if they are allowed to be guided in their actions by their own moral beliefs, it cannot also be morally required that the aggregate effects of their respective actions on the different people should correspond to some ideal of distributive justice. In this sense freedom is inseparable from rewards which often have no connection with merit and are therefore felt to be unjust.

[. . .]

Index

Abegglan, J.C., 248
Abolafia, M., 280
accountability: group, 110–11; of managers, 112–13
adaptation processes in industrial networks, 258-9, 262
admininstration, defined, 130
administrative efficiency: and bureaucracy, 129-40
Agnew, J., 267, 268
air passenger transport and the SEM, 88-9
Akerlof, G., 68
Alchian, A.A., 67
Allen, M.P., 177
allocation of resources, 21-2, 35-6; and bureaucratic self-interest, 46-7; government and, 37, 40-1, 42-3, 45-7; and political interests, 47
Anderson, E., 289
Anthony, R., 280
Anwar, M., 216
Arrow, K., 186, 273, 282
asset specificity, 69, 260, 262-3, 266, 278
associations, 16, 172, 227-39
attribute measures and network analysis, 174
authority: legal/legitimate, 119-27, 252, 253; and price, 280-2, 286; and trust, 286-7
Axelrod, R., 201, 272, 273, 284

Baker, W., 281
banking services and the SEM, 87-8, 90, 93
Barber, B., 281
Barnard, C.I., 246, 247, 248, 253
Bauer, M., 236
Becker, H.S., 142
Beer, S.H., 209
Ben-Ner, A., 75
Ben-Porath, Y., 285
benefices, 124
Berger, S., 240
Bevan, G., 103
Blau, P.M., 246, 253
Boddy, M., 210
Boissevain, J., 177
Bolton, M., 279, 280, 281
bonds: among Pakistani working women, 215-25; in industrial networks, 257
Bott, E., 177
bounded rationality, 67-8, 260, 261, 262, 266; and managerial hierarchies, 76, 77
Bradach, J.L., 268
Brazier, J.E., 99
Brickly, J., 288
Bridges, Sir Edward, 208
British Gas, 167, 169
British Telecom, 166, 167, 169
Brown, C., 97
Bujra, J., 216, 217, 219
Burawoy, M., 287
bureaucracy, 9-10, 11, 105-6, 141-53, 243, 250; and administrative efficiency, 129-40; capitalism and the development of, 125-6; career paths within, 141-2, 143-6; and employment relations, 250, 251; legal authority in, 119-27, 253; models of, 128-40; monocratic type of, 124-7; political economy approach to, 136, 138-9, 140; social consequences of, 127; and the sociology of organization, 129-36, 139, 140; and transactions costs, 247, 251
bureaucratic self-interest, 46-7
Burt, R.S., 177, 179
business cooperation and the SEM, 89

Cable, J., 78

Cainarca, G., 286
capital movements and the SEM, 87
capitalism: and the development of bureaucracy, 125-6; and markets, 49-50
careers, organizational, 141-2, 143-6
Carvel, J., 96
catallaxy, 298-301
Caves, R., 288
Cavestro, W., 183
Cecchini, P., 90
central economic planning, 11-12, 51-2; see also total planning
Central Electricity Generating Board (CEGB), 167, 168
ceremonial gifting, 218-19, 223
Chandler, A.D., 10, 75, 280
church, bureaucratic organization in, 123
clans, 243, 248, 251-2, 253
Clarke, Sir Richard, 208
cliques, 179, 180
closed-sector careers, 141-2, 143-5
Coase, R., 67, 72, 246, 249, 265, 277, 278
Cockfield Report, 84
Cohen, E., 236
Coleman, J., 281
Coleman, J.S., 175
collective goods, 37-41
collective responsibility of interest organizations, 237
collective self-interest, 235, 236
collectivistic planning see total planning
collegiate organizations, 14
command economy see total planning
common goods, 38, 40
communities, industrial, 284
community action, 234, 238
company law and the SEM, 89
competition, 54-5, 56-7, 61, 63-4, 65, 301; degree of, 41; and deregulation, 168-9; entrepreneurial, 58, 59, 62, 63, 65; imperfect see imperfect competition; monopolistic, 7; oligopolistic, 7; perfect, 6, 7, 22, 54-5
competition policy, 42-3
competitive process approach to markets, 6-7, 8
complete network analysis, 178
computer systems and networks, 193-4, 195, 197
conduct regulation, 167, 168
Connolly, M., 205
construction industry, value-added partnerships in, 198
consumer sovereignty, 8-9
consumption: excludability/non-excludability in, 38, 39; rivalry/non-rivalry in, 38, 39
contingent claims contract, 249
contracting out, 15-16; in the public sector, 23
contractual relationships, 249, 251, 279, 281, 283
Cook, K.S., 177
cooperative relationships, 243, 244, 246, 247, 248, 282-5
coordination: defined, 3; excessive, 150-1; limits to, 4-5; models of, 3-4, 5-6, 16-19
Corey, R., 279, 281
corporate groups, 130
corporatism 206; see also neo-corporatism
corporative-associative order, 231-4
corruption, 14
Crane, D., 268
Crouch, C., 228
Culyer, A.J., 99, 101, 103
currency, single European, 91-2

Dahl, R.A., 154
Dark, F., 288
Dearden, J., 280

decision-making and hierarchical systems, 74-5
dedicated asset specificity, 69
Delattre, M., 183
Delors, J., 92, 93
demand and supply, 21, 24-34
demand management, 12, 13
democratic planning, 158-60
Demsetz, H., 67
dependence relations, 286; in industrial networks, 257, 263, 272, 273-4
deregulation, 163, 165, 166-7, 170; and competition, 168-9
Diagnostic Related Groups (DRGs), 99
Dickson, W., 287
dignity, concept of, 68
DiMaggio, P., 271
directed economy *see* limited planning
directorates, interlocking, 16
documented histories, 151-2
Dore, R., 248, 283, 284
Dugger, W.M., 261
Dunleavy, P., 204, 205, 206, 207
Durkheim, E., 29, 248, 251, 252
dyadic network analysis, 178

Eccles, R.G., 268, 277, 279, 280, 286, 290
economic integration in Europe, 23, 82; *see also* Single European Market
economic planning *see* planning
economizing, 70-1
Edgett, J.D., 145
efficiency: and analysis of organizations, 71; and hierarchical systems, 73-5; *see also under* bureaucracy
Eglar, Z., 218
egocentric network analysis, 178
electricity supply industry: deregulation of, 167, 168, 170
elite groups, 14
Emerson, R.M., 177
employment relations, 250, 251
endogenous order 293, 294; *see also* spontaneous order
Energy Act (1983), 168
Enthoven, A.C., 96
entrepreneurship, 55, 57-9, 60, 61, 62, 63-5
equality and equity in health care provision, 102-3
equilibrium economics, 64-5
equilibrium-amount of a commodity, 30
Etzioni, A., 253
European Community (EC), 23, 82, 83; and Japan, 93; and the legislative process, 93-4; and the UK, 84, 91, 92; *see also* Single European Market
European Company Statute, 89
European Economic Community (EEC) *see* European Community
European Economic Interest Grouping, 89
European Monetary System, 92
European Parliament (EP), 84, 93-4
European Political Cooperation Procedure, 82
evaluation and evaluators: organizational, 142-3, 144, 145, 146-8, 250-1, 252, 254
excludability in consumption, 38, 39
exogenous order, 293, 294; *see also* organized order
expenses of production, 27
external benefits, 36
external costs, 36
externalities and market failure, 22, 36-41, 164

factors of production, 27; free movement of, in the EC, 83, 87
film industry, value-added partnerships in, 198
financial services: deregulation of, 166; externalities in, 164; *see also* banking
Finley, M., 266
firms: and the competitive process, 8; and governmental agencies, 8; horizontal integration of, 10, 11, 199, 261; investment strategies, 8; network view of, 256-60, 262, 263, 264; price and authority in, 280; and price theory, 64-5; theory of, 66-80, 137-8, 265-6, 267, 268; vertical integration of, 10-11, 199, 261
France, subcontracting networks in industry in, 183-5, 187-91
franchising, 288-9
free-rider problem of public goods, 39
Freeman, J.H., 271
Friar, J., 281

friendship networks, 216, 219-21, 222, 223
frontier controls and the SEM, 85, 92
Fudge, C., 210
Fuller, M., 277, 279
futures, dealing in, 26

Galbraith, J., 254
Gambetta, D., 282
Gas Act (1986), 169
gas supply industry: deregulation of, 167, 169, 170
Gerlach, M., 284
Glaser, B.G., 141
Goldberg, V., 268, 277
Goldthorpe, J.H., 228, 237
goods: collective, 37-41; standards relating to, 85-6
goodwill, 283
Gordon, R.W., 268
Gouldner, A., 247, 253, 273
government(s): bureaucracies, 138-9, 149; and efficiency of resource allocation, 37, 40-1, 42-3, 45-7; failure, 45-7; and imperfect competition, 45-6; investment by, 44-5; and policy networks, 207-12; private interest, 234-9; purchasing by, and the SEM, 86-7; and social order, 295-6
Granovetter, M., 177, 216, 268, 277, 285
Grant, W.P., 206
Gray, C., 204
Gyford, J., 209

Hackman, R., 287
Hägg, I., 262
Hallinan, M.T., 177
Hannan, M., 271
Harrigan, K., 288
Hayek, F.A. von, 237, 271
health care and internal market systems, 96-104
Health Maintenance Organizations, 98, 100
Heclo, H., 204
Hegel, G.W.F., 229
Hencke, D., 96
hierarchical decomposition, 75-8
hierarchical layering, 114-17
hierarchies, 3, 9-14, 18, 105-18, 154-70, 266, 267, 269, 277, 278-9; communication and exchange in, 270, 272; managerial, 73-5, 108-18, 271; *see also* bureaucracy
Hirschman, A., 183, 186, 259, 281
Hogwood, B., 206
Homans, G., 175
horizontal integration of firms, 10, 11, 199, 261
Horn, J.C., 144
Horwitch, M., 281
Hull, R., 141
Hunter, J.E., 177

Imai, K., 272
imperfect competition, 55; and government, 45-6; and market failure, 22, 41-3, 164-5
indicative planning, 12; *see also* limited planning
industrial communities, 284
industrial cooperation and the SEM, 89
industrial policy and regulatory reform, 163-70
industrial systems: interorganizational relations in, 256-64
information technology and networks, 193-4, 195, 197
informational inadequacy and market failure, 22, 43-5, 165-6
insurance-based health care systems, 98-100
interest associations, 16, 172, 227-39
intergovernmental networks, 205
interlocking directorates, 16
internal forms of organization, 72-8
internal market(s): in Europe *see* Single European Market; and the National Health Service, 96-104; in the private sector, 23; in the public sector, 8-9, 23
internalization of transactions, 72-3, 260-1, 271, 280
investment, 44-5; by government, 44-5; strategies, 8
issue networks, 204
Italy, value-added partnerships in, 195-7

Jaeger, A.M., 252
James, M., 205
Japan: business relationships in, 283-4; and the EC, 93; value-added partnerships in, 198
Jay, R.R., 223
Johanson, J., 262

Johnson, J.B., 252
Johnston, R., 279, 286
joint ventures, 281-2
Jordan, G., 204, 207

Kahneman, D., 282
Kaneko, I., 272
Kanter, R.M., 252
Katz, R., 252
Keating, N., 204
Keohane, R., 272, 273
Keynes, J.M., 231
Khatam rituals, 222-3
Kincaid, D.I., 177
kinship networks, 216, 219-21
knowledge, bureaucratic, 126
Koenig, T., 177
Kogut, B., 261
kosmos, 294

labour, market power of, 42, 43
labour market, failure of, 44
La Fontaine, J.S., 223, 225
Larson, A., 267
Laumann, E.O., 177
Lawrence, P., 279, 286
layering in managerial hierarchies, 114-17
Leach, S., 210
legal/legitimate authority: in a bureaucracy, 119-27; norm of, 252, 253
legislative processes in the EC, 93-4
Lehmbruch, G., 228, 236
Leifer, E., 281
Levine, J., 177
liberalization, 106, 107
Light, I.H., 253
limited planning 155-6, 158, 159; *see also* indicative planning
Lin, N., 177
Lincoln, J.R., 177
local government, 205-6; politicization of, 209-10; location-dominated careers, 142
Lorenzoni, G., 267
Lorrain, F., 179
Lowi, T., 208, 236
Luhmann, N., 236, 273
Lund, H.F., 144

M-form business organizational units, 10, 75, 77-8
Macauley, S., 277, 283, 284, 285
McKesson Corporation, 193-5
Macneil, I., 272, 277, 283
Mafia, 14
make-or-buy decisions, 287-8
Malcomson, J., 79
managerial hierarchies, 73-5, 108-18, 271
managers, role of, 112-13
mandated internal transfers, 280
March, J.G., 246
Marglin, S., 79
Mariolis, P., 177
Mariotti, S., 286
Mariti, P., 277, 279, 281
market disequilibrium, 6
market equilibrium, 6, 21, 53-4, 56, 64, 65
market failure, 22, 163-6, 170, 237, 249-50; due to externalities, 22, 36-41, 164; due to imperfect competition, 22, 41-3, 164-5; due to inadequate information, 22, 43-5, 165-6
market order, 298-301
market power, 41-2
market process, 55-63
markets, 6-9, 18, 21-104, 136, 137, 265-72 *passim*, 277, 278-9; and capitalism, 49-50; internal *see* internal markets; labour, 42, 43; neo-Austrian conception of 6-7, 22; *see also* competitive process approach; neo-classical conception of, 6, 21-2; price and authority in, 280-2; quasi-, 8-9; as social/cultural constructions, 267-8, 274n; and socialism, 49-52; and transactions costs, 247
Marshall, J.F., 177
Marx, K., 156, 157
Mauss, M., 273
Mayntz, R., 236

Mayo, E., 247, 248, 254
Menichetti, M., 196
mergers and takeovers, 8
Midwinter, A., 204
Miles, R., 277, 279, 286
Miller, J., 177
Mitchell, J.C., 176
models, 2-3; of coordination, 3-4, 5-6, 16-19
monetary union in Europe, 91-2
monopolistic competition, 7
monopoly 6-7, 55, 61-4, 107, 164-5; *see also* natural monopolies
Monteverde, K., 279
Morrison, H., 168
movie industry, value-added partnerships in, 198
Murphy, W., 288

Nadel, S.F., 177
Nakane, C., 248
National Association of Health Authorities, 97-8, 103
National Health Service: expenditure levels, 211-12; and internal market systems, 96-104
nationalization, 12, 42
Nationalized Industries Chairman's Group, 206
natural monopolies, 42, 164, 167-8
neo-corporatism, 234-5
network analysis, 171, 173-80
network positions, 179-80, 257-8
network structures, 175-6, 178-80
networks, 3-4, 14-16, 18, 171-239; friendship, 216, 219-21, 222, 223; industrial 256-60, 262, 263, 264, 268-9, 270, 271-4, 274-5n; kinship, 216, 219-21; women-centred, 215-25
new urban left, 209-10
1992 *see* Single European Market
non-excludable goods, 38, 39
non-rivalry in consumption, 38, 39
Nowak, P., 279, 280, 281-2

obligation, norms of, 282-4
Offe, C., 237
Office of Fair Trading, 43
Oil and Gas (Enterprise) Act (1982), 169
oligopolistic competition, 7
Olson, M., 240n
open-sector careers, 142, 145-6
opportunism, 68, 186-7, 252, 260, 261, 262, 266; and implementation of decisions, 74-5; and managerial hierarchies, 76-7
opportunity costs, 41
order: concepts of, 293-301; market, 298-301
organizational careers, 141-2, 143-6
organizational concertation, 228, 231
organization(s): nature of, 246-7; rules and traditions in, 254, 296-8; sociology of, 129-36, 139, 140
organized ('made') order, 293-301
Ornati, O., 267
Ouchi, W., 71, 249, 252, 277, 279, 280, 281, 284
output measures and organizational performance evaluation, 146-7

Pakistani migrants, women-centred networks among, 215-25
Papanek, H., 215, 217
Pareto equilibrium, 6
partnership, 14, 189-90, 191; value-adding, 171-2, 193-202
party system and policy networks, 209
patrimonial bureaucracy, 123
peer groups and decision-making, 74
perfect competition, 6, 7, 22, 54-5
performance evaluation: organizational, 142-3, 144, 145, 146-8, 250-1, 252, 254
Perrow, C., 261
personal relationships in economic life, 285-6
Peter, L.J., 141
Pfeffer, J., 262, 279, 280, 281-2
Piore, S., 184
Pizzorno, A., 228
planning, economic 11-13, 51-2, 106, 154-60; central or total, 11-12, 51-2, 154, 156-7, 158, 159; democratic, 158-60; indicative or limited, 12, 155-6, 158, 159; as rational organization, 155, 159
planning, health care, 101-2

plural forms, 287–9, 290
policy communities, 204
policy networks, 172, 203–12
political economy, 136–9; and study of bureaucracy, 136, 138–9, 140
political interests and efficient resource allocation, 47
political party system and policy networks, 209
political union in Europe, 82, 91
pollution externalities, 164
Porter, M., 277, 279
Powell, W.W., 271, 279, 286
power and the analysis of organizations, 71
price(s), 271, 279; -authority control mechanisms, 280–2; demand, 28, 30; equilibrium, 6, 22, 25, 26, 30, 53–4; fairness of, 282–3; market, 7, 9, 25–31, 254; neo-Austrian theory of, 53–4; neo-classical theory of, 53; supply, 26, 27, 29–30; theory of, 53–4, 64; -trust control mechanisms, 286
private costs and benefits, 36–7
private goods, 38, 39
private interest government, 234–9
private sector: internal markets in, 23; investment by, 44
privatization, 106–7, 166, 168, 170
producer networks, 206
producers and the market process, 59–61
production: expenses of, 27; factors of, 27; monopolistic, 62, 63; real cost of, 27
professional groups, 14
professionalized networks, 204–5, 206–7
programmed economy *see* limited planning
property rights, 37, 40
Proxy, H., 144
public goods, 38, 39–40
public policy and associative model of social order, 234–6
public procurement and the SEM, 86–7
public sector: bureaucratic self-interest in, 46–7; contracting out in, 23; internal markets in, 8–9, 23
purdah, 215, 217, 224
pure public goods, 38, 39
Putterman, L., 79

quasi-markets, 8–9

Radner, R., 68
rationality, bounded *see* bounded rationality
real cost of production, 27
reciprocity, norm of, 247, 253, 272–3, 275n
Reddy, W.M., 268
regulation, economic, 12–13, 163–70; of natural monopolies, 42
relational contracting, 249, 251, 279, 281, 283
relational measures and network analysis, 174–5, 177
resource allocation *see* allocation of resources
responsibility time spans, 113–15, 117
restrictive practices, 43, 45–6
Rhodes, R.A.W., 204, 205, 209
Richardson, G., 266, 277, 279
Richardson, J.J., 204, 207
risk avoidance, organizational, 148–50
risk(s), 185; inventing false, 150
ritual, Pakistani, 222–3
rivalry in consumption, 38, 39
Roethlisberger, F., 287
Rogers, E.M., 177
Rosaldo, M., 215, 219
Rubin, P., 288, 289
Rugman, A.M., 261
rules: of organization, 254, 296–8; and organizational performance evaluation, 147–8; of spontaneous order, 296–8

Sabel, C., 184, 283, 284, 290
Sahlins, M., 273
Saifullah Khan, V., 217
Sailer, L.D., 179
Saint-Simon, H. de, 229
Saint-Simonianism, 156
Salancik, G.R., 262
salaries, bureaucratic, 122, 124
Sampson, S.F., 177
Saunders, P., 204
Schein, E.H., 254
Schmitter, P.C., 206, 228, 234
Schmittlein, D., 289

Scott, W.R., 246, 253
self-generating order, 294 *see also* spontaneous order
self-interest: bureaucratic, 46–7; collective, 235, 236; mutuality of, 138–9
self-regulation: associational, 236–8
sequential spot contracting, 249
Sharma, U., 217
Simon, H., 67, 76, 246
Single European Act (1986), 82, 84, 90, 92
Single European Market, 23; air passenger transport services in, 88–9; banking services in, 87–8, 90, 93; business cooperation in, 89; capital movements in, 87; creation of, 9, 82–95; frontier controls and, 85, 92; government purchasing and, 86–7; harmonization of standards in, 85–6; indirect tax harmonization in, 89, 90
small-numbers bargaining, 260, 263
Smiley, R., 277, 279, 281
Smith, A., 294
Snow, C., 277, 279, 286
social agents and agencies: and limits to coordination, 4–5
social classes and development of bureaucracy, 127
social cohesion and network analysis, 179, 180
social costs and benefits, 36–7, 45
social efficiency of resource allocation *see* allocation of resources
socialism: and bureaucratic organization, 126; and markets, 49–52; models of, 48–9
socialization: organizational, 248, 253–4
sociology of organization: 129–36, 139, 140
Sonquist, J., 177
spontaneous ('grown') order, 293–301
Staatsentlastung, 234, 235
standards, harmonization of, in Europe, 85–6
'stationary state', 31–2
Steer, P., 78
Stewart, J.D., 210
Stinchcombe, A., 268, 277, 279, 280, 281
Strathern, M., 224, 225
Streeck, W., 236
structural equivalence and network analysis, 179, 180
structure regulation, 167, 168
sub-central government and policy networks, 208–12
subcontracting networks, 15–16, 183–91
subsidization, 13
substitution, principle of, 28
supply and demand, 21, 24–34

takeovers and mergers, 8
taxes, indirect, 89; *see also* Value Added Tax
taxis, 294
technical knowledge and bureaucratic organizations, 123, 125, 126
Teece, D., 279
telecommunications industry: deregulation of, 166, 167, 169, 170
Terkel, S., 143, 146
territorial communities, 204
Teubner, G., 236
textile industry, value-added partnerships in, 195–7
Thatcher, M., 91, 92
Thompson, E.P., 267
Tivey, L., 206
toll goods, 38, 40
total planning 154, 156–7, 158, 159; *see also* central economic planning
trade unions, 42, 43
traditions, organizational, 254
transactions: frequency of, 70, 260, 263, 278; internalization of, 72–3, 260–1, 271, 280; nature of, 68–70; uncertainty of, 70, 260, 262, 278
transactions costs, 247–8, 251; and industrial systems, 260–1, 262, 263, 264; theory of, 13–14, 186, 243, 278–9
transfer-pricing policies, 280
Travis, A.S., 204
triadic network analysis, 178
trust, 15, 23, 185, 186, 187, 190–1, 262, 273, 277, 278, 279, 282–7

U-form business organizational units, 10, 75–7
Uchitelle, L., 289
unemployment, 44
United Kingdom and the EC, 84, 91, 92
utility industries: deregulation in, 166, 167, 168–9

Value Added Tax (VAT), 89, 90, 94
value-added chain, 195
value-adding partnership (VAP), 171-2, 193-202
Vancil, R., 280
Van Maanen, J., 252, 254
Vatuk, S., 219
vertical integration of firms, 10-11, 199, 261
Voigt, R., 236
Von Hayek, F.A., 237, 271

Walker, G., 260, 287, 288
Walton, R., 287
Ward, T., 211
Warwick, D.P., 150
Weber, D., 260, 287, 288
Weber, M., 130, 131-2, 133, 253
Webster, F., 285

Werbner, P., 216, 219, 221, 223, 224
White, H., 279, 280, 281
White, H.C., 173, 177, 179, 268
Wildavsky, A., 208
Williamson, O., 66-80 *passim*, 177, 186, 246, 249, 260,
    262, 265, 266, 277, 279
Willke, H., 236
Wind, Y., 285
women-centred networks among Pakistani migrants,
    215-25
Wood, N., 97

Yanagisako, S., 216, 219, 225

Zeitlin, J., 184, 283, 284, 290
Zelizer, V., 268
Zucker, L., 282, 284